THE RAINBOW'S GRAVITY

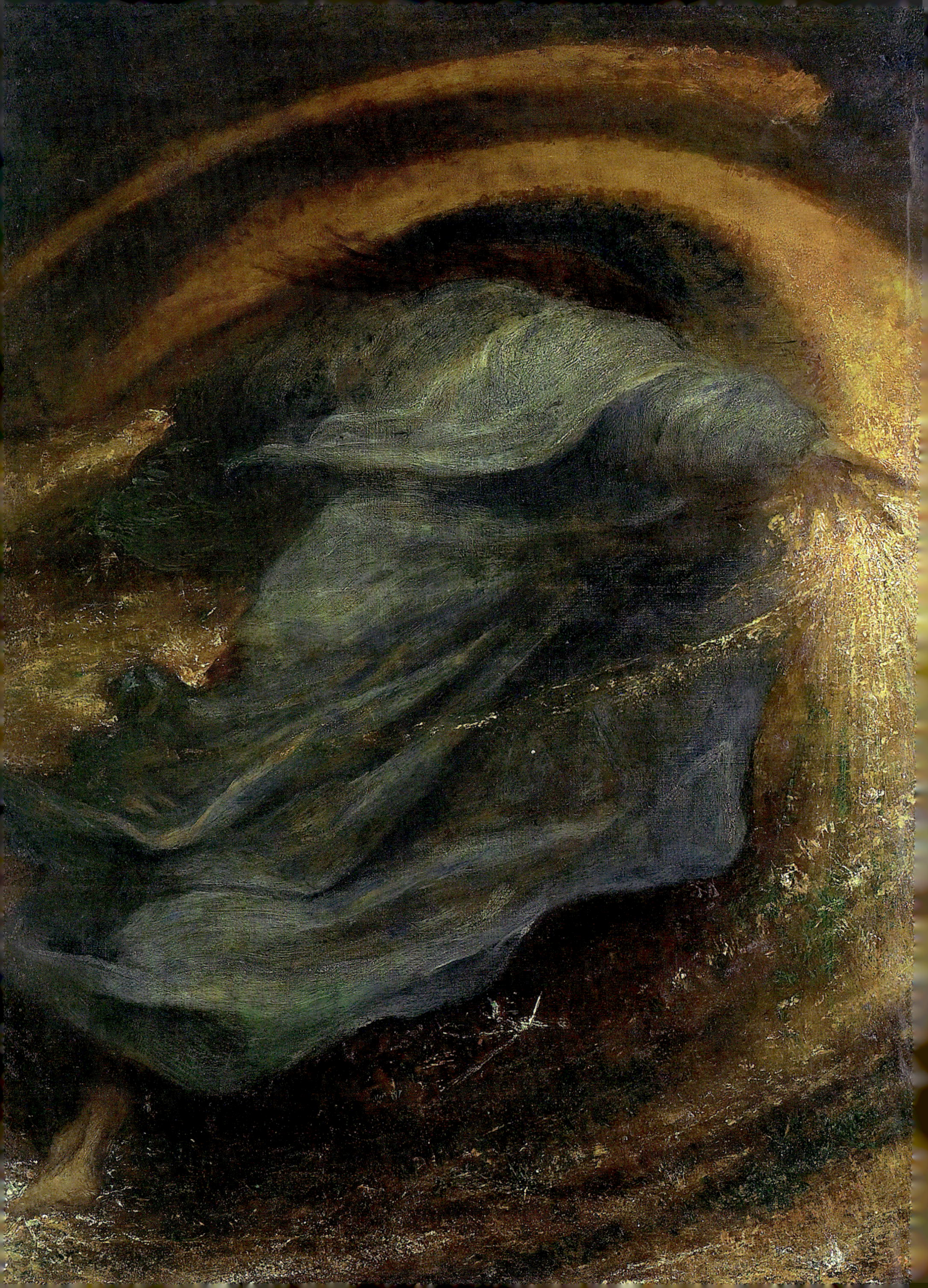

Kirsty Sinclair Dootson

THE RAINBOW'S GRAVITY

Colour, Materiality and British Modernity

Paul Mellon Centre
for Studies in British Art

Distributed by Yale University Press
New Haven and London

FOR MOIRA

First published in 2023 by the Paul Mellon Centre for Studies in British Art
16 Bedford Square, London, WC1B 3JA
paul-mellon-centre.ac.uk

ISBN 978-1-913107-36-9 HB
Library of Congress Control Number: 2022949510

British Library Cataloguing-in-Publication Data
A catalogue record for this book is available from the British Library

Designed by Emily Lees
Origination by DL Imaging
Printed in China through World Print Ltd

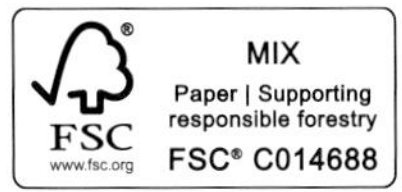

Frontispiece: George Frederic Watts, *The Sower of the Systems*, c.1902. Collection of the Art Gallery of Ontario, Toronto (see fig. 16).

Contents

Acknowledgements

This book began as my PhD project at Yale and the first acknowledgements must therefore go to its first readers and champions – the unbeatable triumvirate of Tim Barringer, Katie Trumpener and J. D. Connor. For helping me think about Britain expansively, about art allegorically, and for encouraging me to keep 'Dootsonian levity' in the text, I am massively grateful. Jennifer Roberts also very generously acted as the outside reader for my PhD, and I am indebted to her for the invaluable feedback she offered, which became the roadmap for transforming my dissertation into this book. During my time at Yale I was lucky to receive a number of fellowships that enabled the archival research presented here. I must acknowledge the Yale Center for British Art, the Paul Mellon Centre and the Huntington Library for financing my many trips back to the UK, as well as the Yale / UCL exchange, which meant the project benefited from a semester of supervision from Lee Grieveson and his ever-astute questions. I was fortunate to be at Yale at the same time as a number of brilliant human beings and scholars whose intellectual camaraderie made my years there a complete treat. Thanks above all to Caitlin Woolsey, Michelle Oing, Viktoria Paranyuk, and my academic brother, Nicholas Forster. (A special acknowledgement must also go to Audrey Sands for asking me the crucial question: 'have you heard of this photographer called Madame Yevonde?')

The majority of this book was written during my tenure as a Junior Research Fellow at Cambridge University's Newnham College (a.k.a. heaven). Thank you to all the fellows and college staff who made my time there so delightful. At Cambridge J. D. Rhodes warmly welcomed me into the Centre for Film and Screen, while Katherine Reinhardt and Jessica Maratsos welcomed me with equal warmth into another venerated Cambridge institution: Art History Pub Night. I hope this book reflects the generative conversations held across both these esteemed establishments.

This book was completed at the University of St Andrews, where the tremendous advice offered by my outstanding colleagues in both Film Studies and Art History (often during blustery walks across Fife's beaches) helped get this project over the finish line. I am particularly indebted to those colleagues who kindly offered to read parts of the book. Thank you Tom Rice, Philippa Lovatt, Sam Rose and Natalie Adamson, for your crucial feedback on the writing, and thank you Stephanie O'Rourke, Marika Takanishi Knowles and Lucy Fife Donaldson for that and a whole Nebuchadnezzar more. Thanks too to Steve Drasco, who kindly assisted with the modicum of maths contained within these pages, and to Scott Donaldson, who cooked every good meal I've ever eaten in St Andrews.

Other very kind folks – who weren't even forced by the conventions of collegiality at St Andrews – also read chapters of this book while it was in-progress. Huge thanks are therefore due to the enormously generous Priya Jaikumar, Jennifer Y. Chuong, Susan Murray and Esther Chadwick for helping improve this book no end through their constructive criticism and penetrating questions. While I'm grateful for all the opportunities I've had to present my work through talks and conference papers, I wanted to specially thank Richard Taws for the invitation to present my research on chromolithography at UCL's History of Art department. Feedback from the faculty and graduate students there completely transformed Chapter Two for the better.

Over the course of researching and writing this book my ideas about colour have taken shape through vivid conversations with Sarah Street, Joshua Yumibe, Laura Kalba, Lynda Nead, Nicholas Gaskill, Natasha Eaton, Zhaoyu Zhu, Keith M. Johnston, Elizabeth Savage, Sarah Gould, Helen Wheatley and Charlotte Ribeyrol. Thanks to them for sharing their ideas (as well as many glasses of wine) with me at colour conferences through the years. For their technical expertise on all the juiciest material in the book (from inks, oils and lipstick to dyes and dope) thanks must also go to the material historians, archivists, conservators and other wizards whose techno-material answers to all my nerdiest questions were vital to the completion of this book. Thank you Alice Lovejoy, Pansy Duncan, Kieron Webb, Jessica David, James Bennett, Mark Aronson, Sally Marriott, Theresa Fairbanks-Harris, Ad Stijnman, Josephine Diecke, Bob Richardson, Clare Freestone, Michael Twyman and Sophia Lorent.

The Paul Mellon Centre have long been supporters of this project, and I am grateful to Mark Hallett and Sarah Turner for their early investments in my work. I cannot thank my editor, Emily Lees, and the rest of the publications team at the PMC enough for all their patience throughout the process of putting this book together (not least my long-suffering copy editor, Hazel Bird). I am also thankful to the anonymous peer reviewers of the manuscript whose comments vastly improved this book. Much of Chapter One has already been published as 'The Texture of Capitalism: Industrial Oil Colours and the Politics of Paint in the Work of G. F. Watts', *British Art Studies*, Issue 14, and I am grateful to the journal's editors for allowing this material to be reprinted here. The many illustrations in this book were made possbile by the Historians of British Art Publication Grant and the Association of Print Scholars Publication Grant.

Institutional support comes in many forms, of course, and this book would not have been completed without a legal outlet for all my most violent urges. So, thank you to every single one of the inspirational skaters I've had the privilege to play roller derby with. Special thanks to my beloved teams and leagues: the Connecticut Cutthroats (WALK THE PLANK!), Cambridge Rollerbillies (LEOPARD LOVE!) and Dundee Roller Derby (WEARETHEDRD!).

The biggest of all the thanks goes to my mum, Moira. Thanks for proofreading *almost* everything I've ever written (bet you're glad you didn't have to proof this!), for the endless love you provided through the worst parts of writing this book, and the champagne you provided during the best bits as well.

Finally, thanks to David for being … 'kinda great'.

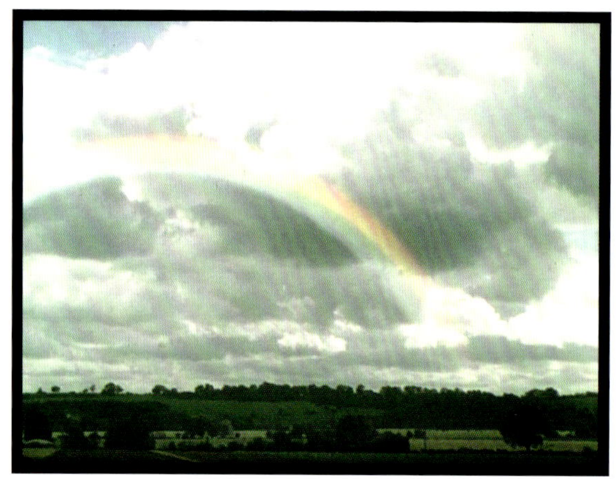

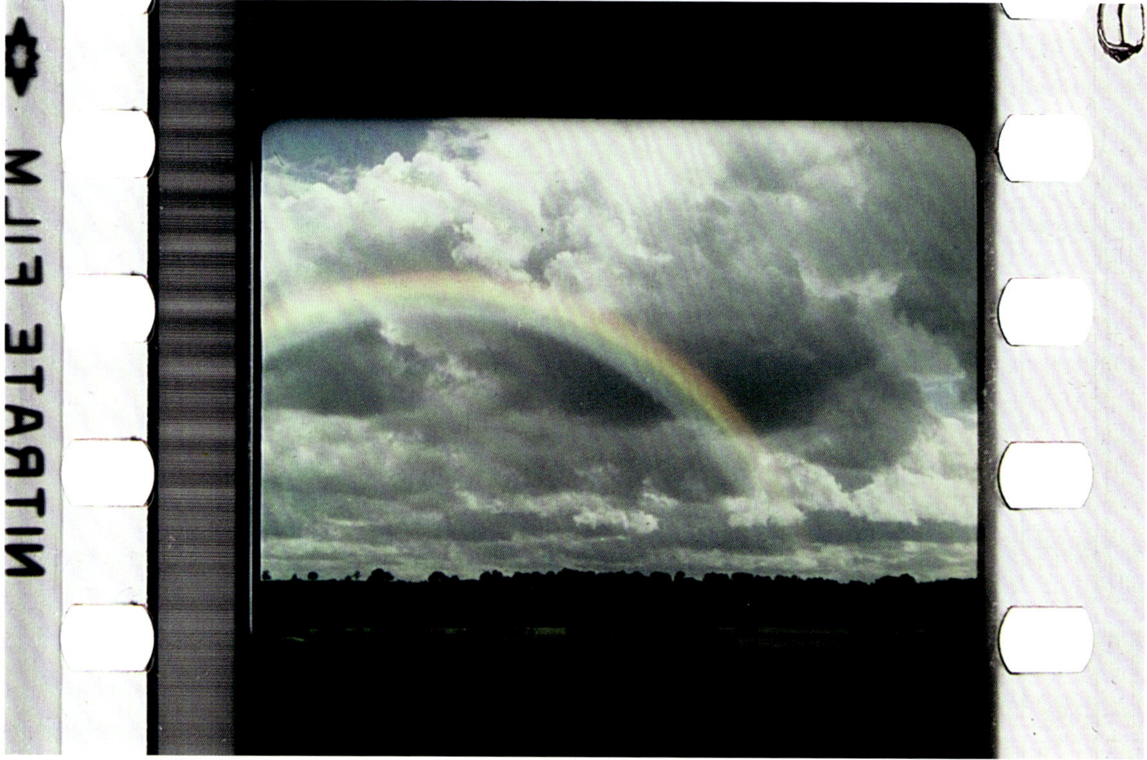

1 *This Is Colour* (UK, 1942; dir. Jack Ellitt).

2 *This Is Colour* (UK, 1942; dir. Jack Ellitt), photograph of Technicolor dye-transfer print by Kieron Webb. Courtesy of the BFI National Archive.

Introduction

THE RAINBOW'S GRAVITY

In the opening sequence of the short British documentary *This Is Colour* (1942; dir. Jack Ellitt), a brilliant rainbow fills the screen, hovering above the landscape like a resplendent mirage (fig. 1). These translucent hues shimmer and glint, appearing radiant against the cloudy grey sky typical of a British summer. Each colour is luminously rendered yet the rainbow has an ethereal quality, becoming indistinct and almost invisible where it meets the thin strip of verdant countryside that skirts the bottom of the screen. This rainbow is spectral in both senses of the term, at once prismatic and phantasmagoric. Its quivering colours have an evanescent beauty, reminding the viewer that despite colour's visual allure, its gorgeous effects are temporary. With only the slightest change in the weather, the smallest shift of the sun, these colours will be gone.

This Is Colour was made at a time when the majority of films were still black and white, rendering this image of a rainbow a particularly novel spectacle. Under the guise of educating British audiences about their nation's pre-eminence in the field of colour science, the documentary takes the subject of colour as a pretext for many such dazzling moments. Colour is used here to intellectually inform and visually delight, giving this rainbow a didactic function in addition to its visual appeal. In the words of the film's chief (male) narrator, the rainbow demonstrates a key chromatic principle, that 'colour is light and light is colour', as the tints of this rainbow are merely the effect of white light refracted through raindrops. These colours are not material or physical substances, but an illusory, optical effect. This conflation of colour and light would have been all the more evident to audiences in the cinema, as the rainbow would have appeared as an elusive apparition floating above their heads, suspended in the air, made from nothing more solid than the light of the projector beam itself.

Yet as much as the narrator insists that these colours are immaterial, the production of this rainbow was contingent on very tangible material processes. It is both a sparkling projection made from light and also, as an image on a filmstrip, a physical object made from celluloid, gelatin and synthetic dyes (fig. 2). Its colours are the product of the messy, toxic and fetid work of industrial photochemistry, their chromatic brilliance the result of the physical labour of printing, processing and dyeing film on a massive scale. The surface of this rainbow is coloured with chemical substances derived from the polluting industries of coal and gas. They sit suspended in an emulsion made from the skin and bones of slaughtered cattle. While the rainbow on screen is impalpable and fugitive, the rainbow printed on the filmstrip is solid and concrete. This rainbow can be touched and handled, transported and stored; it has a scent and texture as well as a price. As a physical object this rainbow is deeply enmeshed in the material networks of energy, chemistry and industrial agriculture.

This particular filmstrip, fabricated at the height the Second World War, was also embroiled in the dangerous mechanics of warfare. Imperial Chemical Industries (ICI), Britain's largest chemical conglomerate and the chief supplier of chemical weaponry to the British government, both sponsored the production of *This Is Colour* and furnished Technicolor Ltd with the dyes necessary to colour the release prints at its London laboratory.[1] The knowledge and skills that made ICI leaders in the field of colour chemistry were also crucial to the company's production of explosives and gases necessary for combat, revealing the very close affinities between dyeing and death in Europe at this time.[2] The colours of the rainbow in the opening scene are therefore far from intangible illusions. The materiality of this rainbow makes these colours active participants in the political, military and economic operations of the British state at a time of national crisis. While this rainbow may appear weightless, in fact it has a profound gravity.

I use the term 'gravity' very deliberately here. It reveals my interest in the physical weight and heft – the gravity – of something that is often understood as an ephemeral, optical phenomenon – the colours of the rainbow. While a great deal of writing, from the foundational philosophical work of Johann Wolfgang von Goethe and Ludwig Wittgenstein to more recent academic studies, has focused on colour's intangibility as a sensational experience, here I am interested in its material realities.[3] To speak of the rainbow's gravity is to invoke the density, hardness, texture and mass of the raw substances that constitute colour. It is to recognise the heavy industry involved in colour's production – the onerous work undertaken by human hands and automated machinery in laboratories and factories. Understanding colour through its physical gravity reveals the inseparability of its making and its meaning, bringing to light how its beautiful effects are made possible and the political realities they create. To manufacture colour is to animate networks of labour, to stimulate the flow of capital and to enact environmental degradation on a global scale. It is, as ICI's sponsorship of *This Is Colour* demonstrates, to understand colour as an imperial chemical industry. To claim the rainbow has a gravity is therefore not only to imply that colour has a literal weight. It is also to metaphorically invoke colour's seriousness, its gravity, as a political as well as an aesthetic phenomenon.

This book is about the magnitude of colour's importance, the gravity of the rainbow, during a period when its material fabrication underwent radical change. During the long century covered here, between 1856 and 1968, new processes for chemically synthesising and mass-producing paints, inks and dyes emerged in tandem with the new chromatic mass media of print, photography, film and television. These novel techniques for making colour revolutionised the visual environment of the modern world. Colour saturated artists' palettes in the form of new pigments, seduced consumers through brilliantly rendered advertisements and circulated as lustrous photographs in colour magazines. Homes, shops and offices were enlivened by the presence of brightly coloured new goods, while colour also transformed the surface of the body through painted lips and fingernails, as well as fashionably dyed garments. The introduction of colour to film and television rendered novel media forms that had become quotidian and banal. Across this period, artists, advertisers, designers and filmmakers turned to new colour technologies to forge the aesthetic environments of modernity. As *This Is Colour* celebrates with nationalistic fervour, many of these colour innovations originated in, or were industrialised by, Britain.

It is unsurprising that Britain emerged as a centre for modern colour-making. The nation's long-established monopoly on the extraction of pigments and dyes from its vast empire, combined with its rampant industrialisation, made it an ideal locus for modernising and mass-producing colour from the mid-Victorian era. Across the nineteenth and twentieth centuries, Britain pioneered a series of new, industrial colour technologies: revolutionary synthetic dyes in 1856, three-colour photography in 1861, colour television in 1928 and nearly two hundred patents for early colour film processes before 1930. Britain also boasted the world's largest colour printing press and ink factory at the turn of the twentieth century, one of the most technologically advanced colour film laboratories by the mid-century, and more hours of colour television broadcasting than any other European nation by 1968. Britain therefore held unprecedented control over the material fabrication of the colours that defined modern visuality. If the rainbow had a gravity during this period, then the centre of that gravity was Britain.

By transforming the materials and techniques for colour-making, these innovations also imbued colour with new meanings. Mass produced and mass consumed, colour aestheticised technological transformation, scientific innovation and the new economic realities of consumer culture, rendering these societal changes as discernible, visual components of the material world through colourful goods and mass media. Colour's capacity to intensify and vivify the sensory environment also seemed to match the perceptual fissures that characterised modernity – the automation, acceleration and electrification of everyday modes of existence. As a sphere where the changes wrought by industrial modernity were highly visible, colour enabled the implications of these changes to be surveyed. These new colour technologies not only reflected the societal changes that characterised modernity but also created an aesthetic arena where these conditions could be negotiated, celebrated and contested.

The affinities between these modes of aesthetic, sensory and socio-historical transformation are neatly expressed in Sarah Street and Joshua Yumibe's concept of 'chromatic modernity', which articulates how colour captured and mediated these transformative societal changes through a profoundly optical phenomenon.[4] As Street and Yumibe describe in their work on the prismatic culture of the 1920s, to think of modernity in chromatic terms is to foreground the absolute indivisibility of the visual and cultural transformations that shaped the experience of the modern, and to elevate colour as a crucial site for understanding them. Here I extend Street and Yumibe's formulation of 'chromatic modernity' to establish new pathways for thinking about the chromatism of nineteenth- and twentieth-century culture more broadly, sharing their understanding of modern colour not as a particular aesthetic of bright and vivid hues but as a driver for the social and political conditions of modernity itself.

Certainly, Britain's modes of chromatic modernity shared many features with other nations of the Global North in the nineteenth and twentieth centuries, where colour was similarly industrialised, synthesised and commodified.[5] But Britain's status as the world's largest modern imperial power forged unique cultural dynamics that lent a specific tenor to the twinned modernisation of colour and culture there. In the mid-nineteenth century, when this book begins, Britain controlled a global network of colonies from which it extracted colour in the form of raw pigments, minerals and dye crops. These materials were crucial to the textile industries upon which Britain's industrialisation was partially predicated. But colour had also lubricated the brutal economy of slavery that bolstered Britain's prosperity into the nineteenth century, entangling its production and circulation with the apparatus of racial capitalism. Indeed, it was the long historical entanglement of colour and empire that made possible the industrial expansionism that established Britain as a major centre for the mass production and consumption of colour from the mid-Victorian era.

Britain was pivotal to what Geoff Quilley and Kay Dian Kriz dub the 'economy of colour' that forged the early conditions of modernity in the Atlantic world.[6] The globalised networks for the circulation of colourful goods, as well as the enforced displacement of people of colour that facilitated the manufacture of these goods, comprised an economic system essential to Britain's ascendant status as a geopolitical power. The British colonial control of colour braided together the histories of Asia, Africa, Europe and the Americas through this trade in dyes and textiles, but also cemented the identity of enslaved and colonised subjects with colour itself.[7] At this same time, European naturalists and anthropologists were erecting racial categories based upon the essentialising and abstracting hues of white, black, red and yellow, establishing skin colour as the defining visual signifier of race, despite the fact that these hues do not correspond with the actual tonalities of human skin. This codification of racial types through chromatic categories affirms Richard J. Powell's assessment that 'the science of colour is never entirely separate from a sociology of colour'. What Powell calls the 'shared racist underpinnings' of 'new world racial classifications and hierarchies [and] the pseudo-scientific analysis of skin pigmentation' produced the idea of skin colour as a stable, visible signifier of racial type.[8] While this conflation of colour and racial identity was an emergent and much debated practice in the eighteenth century, by the mid-nineteenth century skin colour was taken as a natural, innate and fixed marker of racial difference.[9]

The British Empire played a major role in conflating these ideas of colour and racial identity through its barbarous dynamics. By the eighteenth century, Britain was using colourful textiles and dyes to purchase enslaved people on the west coast of Africa, who were themselves forced to cultivate dye crops in the Caribbean. These dyes were then used to colour fabrics for sale back in Europe or Africa, completing a circuit characterised by colour, commerce and racialised violence.[10] This 'economy of colour' was at once contingent on the circulation of chromatic materials but also on the people of colour upon whose labour and lives the British Empire thrived, entangling their histories with the chromatic produce they were forced to cultivate and for which they were traded. This history, linking colour to imperial commerce and racialised systems of exploitation, is not merely a preface to the modern forms of British colour examined in this book, but the absolute foundation upon which the specific conditions of chromatic modernity in Britain were established. As the work of Anna Arabindan-Kesson and Natasha Eaton has also shown, Britain's modes of chromatic modernity and colonial modernity are inseparable.[11] These imperial meanings of colour were instrumental in the formation of modern colour media technologies, as colour's deep links with the mechanics of empire and the fictions of racial difference it perpetuated produced the unique circumstances through which chromatic modernity emerged in Britain.

The history of modern colour in Britain is therefore a profoundly international and imperial tale, and its course was determined by the vicissitudes of empire, as any change to the production or consumption of colour in Britain had ramifications not just at a national level but also on a global scale. Therefore, while the focus of this book largely remains in the colonial metropole of Britain (and in particular England), the specific forms of chromatic modernity developed there are shown to be inextricable from the colonial exploitation of Africa, from Indian struggles for political independence and from the dynamics of Commonwealth migration.[12] Following Priya Jaikumar, this book takes up the proposition that the modernity of Britain was formulated by and through its dynamic relationship with its empire, rendering their cultural histories indissoluble.[13] To construct a history of British modernity through colour is therefore to recognise the inherently global nature of the nation's visual culture, and to contribute to the expanding field of 'global British' art histories, which reckon with the legacies of colonialism and imperialism as constituent elements of British visual culture.[14]

Despite these deep historical links, there remains no comprehensive account of Britain's role in fabricating modernity's chromatic worlds, nor a thoroughgoing assessment of colour's significance to British visual culture in the modern era. While the development of specific colour media has been historicised, and the look and style of certain decades explored, no single study has investigated how colour itself cultivated a distinctly British paradigm of the modern.[15] The embeddedness of colour within the larger project of Britain's modernisation from the 1940s has been critically examined by Lynda Nead in her work on post-war visual culture, which she frames as 'the emergence of the nation from grey into a brightly coloured future'.[16] Yet, across the nineteenth and twentieth centuries, colour repeatedly made and remade the visual and material environment of the nation in ways that articulated different possibilities about that future. The constant transformation of the very look of Britain redefined the visual and political terms in which it could be imagined across a century of profound social change.

Given that colour was one of the most pervasive and insistently visual dimensions of the modern experience, what were the implications for British visual culture of the nation's primacy in the sphere of modern colour-making? If the materials and technologies used to make colour were crucial to its meaning, then how did Britain shape both the aesthetics of modern colour and its wider cultural implications through these new technologies? If colour articulated the experience of modernity, then how did these colours not just resurface the appearance of the modern world but craft its social and political realities as well?

These are the questions this book takes up through a close analysis of Britain's five most significant chromatic innovations across the spheres of paint, print, photography, film and television. With a chapter dedicated to each of these media, I examine the impact of these new technologies through a range of alluring objects: radiant paintings by esteemed Victorian artists, vivid print advertisements, scorching inter-war fashion photographs, glorious Technicolor films and the prismatic programmes of the BBC's early years of colour television. Through these objects I reveal how the material and technical demands of new colour processes gave a very distinctive appearance to colours that made them identifiably modern and British.

This intermedial history, which places objects of high and low culture into a single discursive space, traces an original narrative of modern British visual culture only discernible through this chromatic lens. While scholars have routinely focused on colour's relationship to modernism, foregrounding avant-garde and abstract practices, my approach in this book is informed by the work of Lisa Tickner and David Peters Corbett, who argue that modernism was only one response among many to the conditions of modernity.[17] Here, popular, vernacular and mass culture are understood as crucial sites for examining how social processes of modernisation transformed Britain's visual environment.

As the following case studies reveal, these new colours were not perceived as modern because they were necessarily more vibrant or brilliant than traditionally made hues. Instead, new manufacturing techniques transformed other formal, haptic and material qualities of modern colour – it had a changed texture, grain and surface quality; it was distributed differently on the page and screen; and it threw up new technical problems of contrast and spatiality. Through close analyses of the technologies used to fabricate colour and their resulting surface effects, I construct a meticulous narrative of how the formal, visual qualities of modern colour evolved over this long century in dialogue with the cultural, social and political upheavals that defined modernity in Britain. In other words, I am interested in what Jennifer Y. Chuong has eloquently dubbed 'the politics of technique'.[18]

Therefore, rather than arguing that these new chromatic technologies forged a coherent British palette for modernity, this book shows how the diversity of visual effects they produced enabled colour's cultural meanings to be constantly redrawn in line with evolving ideas about the terms of modernity in Britain. The result is a kaleidoscopic history of modern British visual culture, which, like the view through a kaleidoscope (another British chromatic apparatus), delights the eye with its glittering and luminous hues yet is also fragmented, as its patterns and shapes constantly change and reform.[19] This kaleidoscopic history reckons with colour's polyvalent meanings, as well as the multiple different ways modernity took shape, as an experience fractured along lines of class, gender and race. Indeed, it foregrounds why colour, a substance whose meanings were always contingent, protean and mobile, became such an ideal vehicle for thinking through the contours of modernity, a historical phenomenon and sensational experience whose terms were always under negotiation.

Precisely because colour was understood as such a crucial signifier of the modern, the transformed qualities of colour produced through new technologies emerged as flashpoints for debates about the nature of larger social and cultural issues that constituted the nature of British modernity. Each new colour technology created a distinct sphere where the terms of what it meant to be British and to be modern could be reviewed. These new colour media did not simply reflect the changing circumstances of modern Britain, therefore, but became drivers for and participants in the crucial debates of this era. As I explore here, these debates, which revolved around issues of labour, gender, empire and racial difference, were critically articulated through colour.

In short, this book reveals how Britain modernised colour and in turn how colour modernised Britain. It shows how the nation pioneered the techniques that redefined modernity's colourful aesthetics and how those aesthetics intersected with the social, cultural and political transformations that characterised the nation during a century of deep change. Beginning with the British invention of ground-breaking synthetic dyes in 1856 and ending with the BBC's conversion to full colour broadcasting in 1968, this book examines a long century during which the visual appearance and cultural meanings of colour were significantly transformed by British technologies. Over the decades considered here, the material transformation of colour made it a site for thinking through other kinds of social transformation. These transformations encompassed changes to the nature of work, and particularly the gendered division of labour in the increasingly automated environments of industrial Britain; the shifting status of British colonial power through the expansion and dissolution of the empire; and new ideas about racial identity stimulated by patterns of Commonwealth migration set in motion by decolonisation. These new forms of chromatic meaning were all articulated through and informed by the material and technical specificity of the chromatic technologies developed in Britain over this century.

The Chromatic Material Turn

The materialist approach adopted here advances new ideas about where and how colour generates meaning in the visual arts. Certainly, to see the material fabrication of colour as indistinguishable from its cultural functions is an idea familiar to art historians. Since Pliny, the material origins of colours as precious stones, scarce minerals and rare botanical elements have been understood as integral to their meanings and used to interpret the iconographic value of certain hues, especially in painting.[20] The use of ultramarine made from costly lapis lazuli to paint the robes of the Virgin Mary, compared with Indian yellow pigment derived from cow urine for the drapery of Judas, offers a well-known example from Christian art. But it is only with the recent 'material turn' in the humanities that this approach has been expanded beyond a conventional focus on pigments and dyestuffs to animate the wider networks of labour and technology in which the material production of colour is situated.[21]

Since the turn of the millennium, the incorporation of ideas from anthropology and science studies into art history has opened up new ways of thinking about the links between making and meaning. The work of Alfred Gell, Tim Ingold, Jane Bennett and Bruno Latour, among others, has been absorbed into art historical discourse, offering novel ways of conceptualising the role that materials and techniques play in visual culture.[22] Among art historians these new approaches have advanced re-evaluations of the political agency of artistic materials as well as the technologies and tools used to produce them.[23] They have reconsidered the assumed inertia of materials, like colour, and imbued them instead with the capacity to transform the physical and social environments in which they exist. The idea that colour has affordances that can actually shape the conditions of a society, rather than just reflecting its tastes and aesthetic desires, is crucial to my project here.[24] Yet it is because art historians have such a long-standing interest in the materiality of colour that it has become such a fertile subject for these new forms of materialist investigation. For art historians interested in how (to borrow Ann-Sophie Lehmann's term) 'materials make meaning', colour presents an obvious area of investigation.[25]

In light of the recent material turn, in addition to the pigmentary substances that were historically understood to make up colour's material quiddity, a host of new avenues have been opened up for investigation. The way that chromatic materials are mined or farmed, the systems by which colour is stored and circulated, and the tools and implements used to mix and apply it can now be understood as equally legitimate sites for interpreting chromatic meaning. The recent materialist work on colour views it as an important imperial commodity, the result of global networks of labour, markets of exchange and processes of transportation that render its physical realities integral to interpreting its social meanings.[26]

Yet much of this work within art historical circles has focused on colour before the nineteenth century.[27] From 1856, new chemical processes pioneered in Britain enabled the artificial synthesis of many pigments and dyes, disturbing long-established global networks of exchange as well as orthodox techniques of manufacture. Through their industrial manufacture and chemical simulation, these colours supposedly lost many of the conventional meanings they had historically carried through their concrete links to the natural world and human craft.[28] But, through their embeddedness within different economic and industrial networks of production, I show that their meanings were not eroded, but reformulated. Indeed, it was precisely because the materiality of colour was critically recomposed that it was able to become a signifier of the novel sensations and conditions of modernity. This book's project therefore begins where many art historical studies of chromatic materiality conclude, at the moment colour's physical composition underwent its most radical reformulation in the mid-nineteenth century.

The expansive approach to materials and techniques elicited by the material turn has also drawn film and media scholars to consider how photographic media and moving images can be examined through a similar lens. This approach is particularly suited to a discipline already familiar with the idea that its objects of study are the industrially authored products of both human and technological actors. But, in addition to the long-standing interest in technology that has animated media studies, the material turn has helped scholars to interrogate mass media's reliance on extractive mining (for the silver necessary to photography and film, and the copper and gold crucial to the electronics of broadcast media), industrial farming (for photographic-grade gelatin and the cotton used as a substrate for film) and the chemical industry (for the nitric acid, alcohol and methanol necessary to make celluloid).[29] Such approaches clearly intersect with exciting new eco-critical approaches in film and media studies, which demand more space than it has been possible to allocate here.[30] This book engages with the work of these scholars informed by the recent material turn, and productively extends their thinking to the broad field of visual media through which British chromatic modernity emerged. While extensive work has been done to construct rich material and technical histories of various colour media (principally film and photography), the aim here is not only to describe how these technologies work but also to demonstrate that the meanings of these different cultural forms inhere in the very act of their physical fabrication.[31]

As demonstrated by the rainbow with which this Introduction began, colour is not just a material substance but also a sensory phenomenon. Colour is felt and experienced as much as it can be touched and handled. Colour can simultaneously be a powder, a liquid or a solid mass, as well as what literary scholar David Kastan calls 'pigments of the imagination'.[32] Colour is both a physical property located in an external set of stimuli and an embodied sensation produced through a system of emotional and cognitive responses. These are not mutually exclusive categories. Colour's fraught status as a material trace in the world that can elicit multiple, shifting mental sensations is what has made it such an object of fascination for artists and scholars alike. It is for this reason that so many recent studies of colour have focused on the philosophy and psychology of colour perception as a defining paradigm of modernity that changed the way we sensed and experienced the world.[33] Perhaps unsurprisingly, many of these analyses have emerged from literary studies, where the textual description of colour in poetry and prose can be decoupled from the messy materiality that attends its manifestation in visual media such as painting and print.[34]

My focus on the material is by no means intended to preclude an interest in these sensory and psychological dimensions of colour. It is because of colour's affective capacities that it became so crucial to the systems of mass consumerism, high art and popular entertainment examined here. Yet privileging colour's ephemeral, sensual qualities can render invisible the concrete processes by which colour is made, and mask the tangible political and social impacts those processes have. To cathect upon the experience of colour in the mind is to overlook the physical effects it has in the world. While, as Wittgenstein famously claimed, 'colours spur us to philosophise', it should not be forgotten that colours also spurred us to colonise, industrialise and monetise.[35] Colour certainly formed one of modernity's sensory ruptures, but these sensational effects were produced by and through other kinds of economic, imperial and geopolitical transformations that were equally vital in forging the conditions of the modern world.

This materialist approach is particularly urgent for our present time. At a moment when the increasing digitisation of visual culture claims to (spuriously) dematerialise its physical realities, while actually catalysing serious environmental damage and exploitative labour practices, it seems especially important to remain attentive to the material realities of phenomena that announce their intangibility.[36] The digital 'cloud' in which we store our data is as insistent upon its transience as the rainbow with which this introduction began. It is no coincidence that the material turn emerged in the humanities at the same moment as the digital revolution – that at a moment when visual culture seemed to dematerialise into data, scholars became even more acutely attuned to the politics of physical matter. What is at stake in attending to the rainbow's gravity is not just a reckoning with modern processes for making colour but a need to remain vigilant to systems that hide very real processes of exploitation behind discourses of transience and intangibility. This book is populated with alluring objects whose surfaces simultaneously conceal and render visible the orchestration of raw materials and human labour that made the production of colour an intensely politicised practice in Britain, forging the nation as a crucial locus for uncovering how colour's meanings inhere in its materiality.

1856–1968: A Chromatic Century, from Coal to Colour Television

Crafting a history of modern British visual culture through a chromatic lens means departing from established chronologies. By beginning in 1856 and ending in 1968, this book establishes a new set of cultural coordinates through which to map this period and narrate its history. While the periodisation of this century is marked by technological innovations, beginning with the synthesis of colour from coal and ending with its electrification through television broadcasting, this narrative is not one of technological determinism. Instead, this material and technical history advances new ideas about the drivers of modernity's visual paradigms in Britain. This book shows how the evolution of one of the most fundamental aspects of aesthetic experience (colour) was inseparable from the formation of the modern nation (culture). This is not so much a book about colour *and* culture (to borrow the title of John Gage's seminal study) as it is about how colour *makes* culture – specifically, how British colour technologies cultivated a distinctly British mode of modern visuality.[37]

This history begins in 1856 because this year has accrued a near mythic status in narratives of modern colour, which locate Britain at the centre of the most significant chromatic revolution of the modern world: the synthesis of colour from coal. This has become a watershed moment that divides the history of colour between the traditional, historical techniques that had existed for centuries and the new industrial manufacturing methods that would define colour in the future. It was in 1856 that the story of Britain's modernisation of colour, and colour's modernisation of Britain, began.

This significant moment in Britain's chromatic history is vividly recounted in *This Is Colour*. The film begins its heroic tale of British enterprise with a pasto-

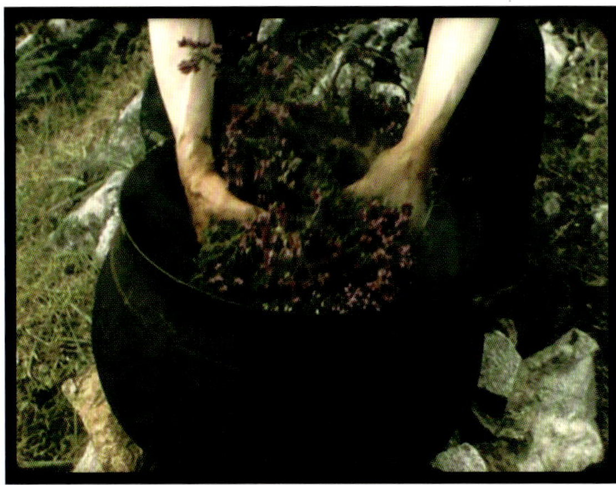

3 Hebridean colour-making in *This Is Colour*.

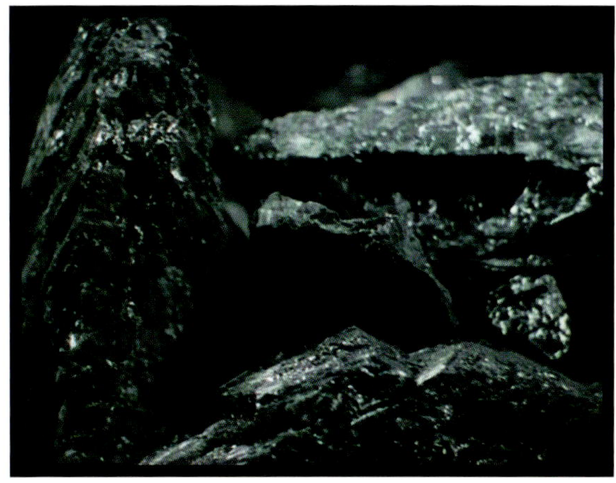

4 Synthesising colour from coal in *This Is Colour*.

ral scene in Scotland. The camera tracks across a Hebridean hillside – a landscape symbolic of an ancient, pre-industrial Britain – and follows the hardy labour of two figures who gather organic materials in the craggy hills. They scrape moss from rocks, pull up grass, harvest ferns, wrench lily roots from ponds and amass heathers, all of which are loaded into a steaming cauldron nestled among boulders, with implications of alchemy and witchcraft (fig. 3). As the narrator explains, this was how colour was made for centuries, through arduous physical work and the complex, even mysterious manipulation of natural substances. The film presents these pre-industrial modes of colour-making as local, artisanal and traditional despite the fact that, as just noted, the production of colour was a profoundly global and imperial industry in the nineteenth century, contingent upon enforced and enslaved labour, and other forms of imperial violence in British colonies overseas. Dyes like indigo, grown under brutal conditions in Bengal, or pigments like Mummy brown, manufactured from human remains exported from north Africa, were as much part of the Victorian palette as the natural dyes for Scottish tweed we see manufactured in this sequence.[38]

Yet the traditional forms of colour-making shown here would be disrupted in 1856, the narrator of the film explains, when William Henry Perkin, a teenage chemistry student in London, 'discovered' a new source of colour in coal.[39] The screen is filled with a close-up of glistening black hunks of rock, which sparkle seductively like jewels as though alluding to the chromatic richness contained within (fig. 4). 'It was from coal-tar … the useless residue of the gas industry', we are told, that Perkin extracted what would become the world's first mass-produced synthetic colourant.[40] The camera lingers on the shimmering black surface of a pool of coal-tar, lending glamour to what was in reality a noxious, sticky, black waste material (fig. 5). In the next shot a man's hand triumphantly holds aloft a test tube of Mauve, the vivid purple textile dye Perkin distilled from coal-tar (fig. 6). Mauve forever transformed colour's history and made Britain the epicentre of that transformation.

The profound significance of Perkin's innovation is not exaggerated by *This Is Colour*. While dyes had formerly been derived from natural substances and produced using manual skill, deep botanical knowledge and tacit techniques passed down through history, from 1856 colour would increasingly become mass produced, chemically synthesised and machine made. While Britain already sustained colonial monopolies on colour, principally through dye-crop plantations, these new chemical hues consolidated the control

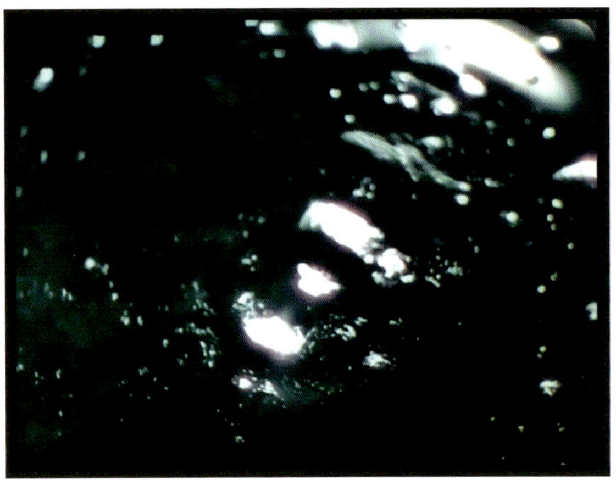

5 A pool of coal-tar in *This Is Colour*.

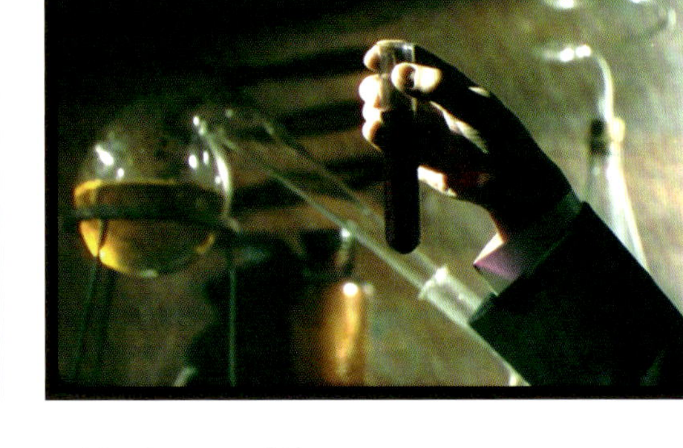

6 The discovery of Mauve in *This Is Colour*.

of colour into its laboratories and factories. Coal-tar colours therefore attenuated Britain's dependence on overseas agriculture and the exploited labour necessary to sustain it.

That the first colour Perkin synthesised was Mauve, a vibrant shade of purple, was particularly significant.[41] Purple textile dyes had been among the most expensive to produce, their manufacture contingent upon the complex processing of costly, imported natural substances, principally lichens sourced from coastal regions of Africa and India or remote European mountain ranges.[42] Perkin's Mauve instead made purple a cheap and ubiquitous colour, famously causing a mania for the shade among the fashionable bourgeois of the 1860s as he rendered this once-exclusive hue affordable to the middle classes for the first time.[43] Mauve therefore decoupled colour from stable signifiers of class, shifting the social status of this colour through its new physical fabrication.

This Is Colour celebrates how Mauve catalysed the industrialisation of colour with sequences showing scientists synthesising all manner of hues in the laboratory and holding up test tubes in myriad shades, followed by scenes of workers mass-producing these colours as dyes and pigments in factories. The manufacturing sequences are captured with high angles and long shots to emphasise the enormous scale of chromatic production. Dried pigments are then piled up in glimmering heaps ready for export, while liquid colour cascades and oozes through this vast industrial space (fig. 7). Colour spurts out of metallic tubes and is churned in enormous tanks, which are agitated by loud, whirring machinery – a marked contrast to the diminutive cauldron, stirred by hand, that opened the film (fig. 8). *This Is Colour* makes clear why 1856 has become a defining moment in the history of colour that separates old forms of colour-making (organically derived and artisanally crafted) from modern techniques of chromatic manufacture (artificially synthesised and industrially produced).

The film then highlights the many applications of Perkin's synthetic colours for contemporary audiences. Textiles and ceramics, plastics and stationery, magazines and postcards, and fashionable accessories and home furnishings are all shown in the audacious hues made possible by Perkin's innovation. The products are arranged in brilliant spectrums, reminding viewers of the rainbow with which the film began, as though modern science had harnessed its colours for mass consumption, rearranging its hues for a host of new chromatic effects (figs 9 and 10). The quick editing of this sequence, which cuts rapidly between attractive displays of tableware, telephones and wrapping paper, reinforces how the expanding palette

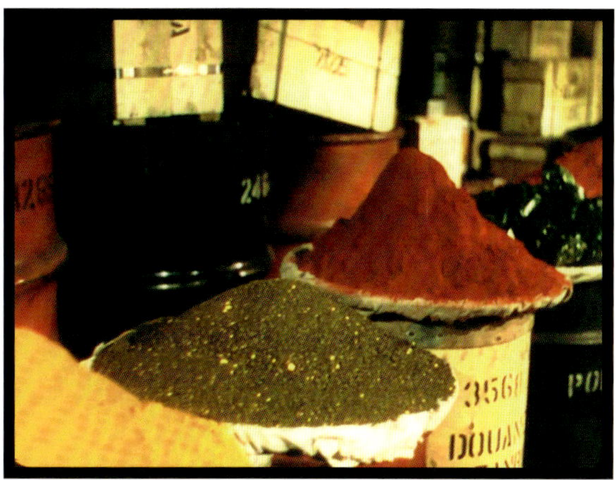

7 Industrial pigment-making in *This Is Colour*.

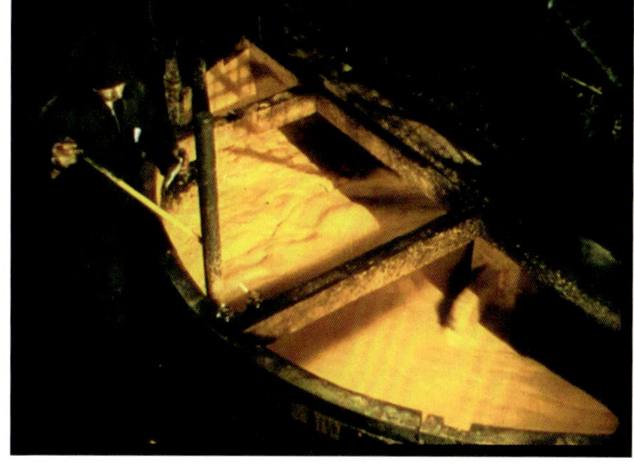

8 Industrial dye-mixing in *This Is Colour*.

of synthetic colours heightened and accelerated the sensory qualities of modern life.

Conspicuously, this section of the film is voiced by a female narrator, who describes how these colourful items can brighten up the home as well as one's personal appearance, revealing the profoundly gendered associations of colour.[44] The film draws upon the long history of colour's supposed femininity, ossified into Western aesthetic discourse since Renaissance debates about the relative merits of *disegno* versus *colore*, which rhetorically pitted masculinist notions of form and intellect against the womanly interest in surface and affect.[45] The deeply held conviction that the application of colour, as a form of ornamental decoration, was linked to and thus trivialised as a kind of cosmetic, informed the modern uses of colour. This meant that women were routinely employed as colourists in various spheres, from ceramics to film prints. Indeed, the range of choice celebrated in this sequence speaks to colour's rhetorical conflation

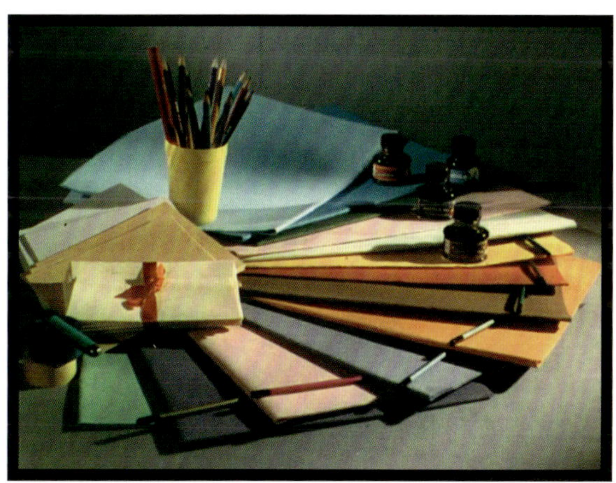

9 Colour commodities in *This Is Colour*.

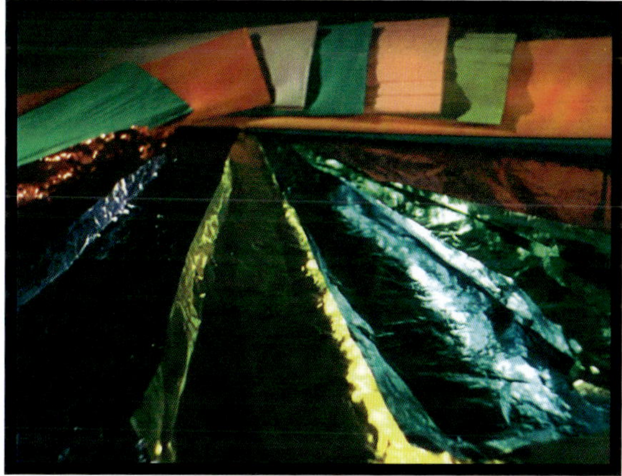

10 Colour commodities in *This Is Colour*.

with femininity, as the propensity to constantly alter one's visual appearance had long been understood as one of the shared characteristics of women and colour. The use of colour, in the narrator's words, to 'catch the eye' in hues that are 'pretty' illuminates the way in which modern women were encouraged to use colour as a form of seduction, constructing their identities, and indeed their personalities, through the consumption of colourful new goods.[46]

Despite the myriad items showcased here whose radiant hues rely upon coal-tar dyes, curiously the film elides the fact that these chemical colourants were instrumental to the development of colour photography and cinema. The mass production of coal-tar dyes was a necessary precondition for the development of chromatic mass media, as these substances were the colouring element in the printing and dyeing processes that defined colour film and photography from the late nineteenth century until the digital era. As already described, coal-tar colours manufactured by ICI are what lend *This Is Colour* its hues, as these synthetic chemical dyes are the colouring agents of this filmstrip itself. The film therefore not only narrates the history of colour's modernisation in Britain since 1856 but also is itself a material product of the processes it dramatises.

As *This Is Colour* demonstrates, Perkin's synthesis of colour from coal in 1856 had wide-reaching implications across aesthetic, environmental and social dimensions – implications that continued to shape the look of the world, as well as its geopolitical organisation, well beyond the mid-nineteenth century. This innovation transformed understandings of social class, redefined imperial trade networks and eroded colonial monopolies. It completely altered the appearance of the modern world through the application of coal-tar dyes to all manner of consumer goods and also made possible the emergence of new colour media in the form of photography and cinema. That this innovation took place in Britain made colour critical to its identity as a modern, industrialised nation, as the heroic retelling of Perkin's discovery over eighty years later in this film demonstrates. The fact that colour was the subject of this morale-boosting documentary, made at the height of the Second World War, reveals how colour was a source of national pride at times of crisis.

But the coal-tar dyes valorised here were only the beginning of the many new innovations for modernising colour that would emerge in Britain over subsequent decades. These chapters examine how Britain pioneered new methods for mass-producing modern oil paints and storing them in tubes, industrialised chromolithographic colour printing on an unprecedented scale, invented the new Vivex process for colour photography, sustained a Technicolor film laboratory that serviced the entire globe, and became the first European nation to broadcast colour television on a regular basis. While not all of these chromatic technologies were contingent upon Perkin's chemical discoveries in 1856, they forged its legacy, consolidating Britain's status as a global power in the production and circulation of modern colour.

Although 1856 therefore marks a crucial rupture in chromatic history, signalling the dawn of a new era of modern colour, there were also important continuities that need to be acknowledged. It is true that Perkin's discovery disrupted the conventional material links between colour and empire, but it did not sever this connection entirely. In fact, Mauve was itself a product of imperial enterprise, as Perkin invented the dye while trying to synthesise quinine, an anti-malarial drug in high demand by the British East India Company.[47] Modern colour was born from the demands of empire and continued to shape imperial interests over the century that followed.

While the physical extraction of colour from the colonies became increasingly rare in the twentieth century, the production and consumption of colour continued to be managed by the same imperial prerogatives. Colour remained a spectacle of imperial power, a weapon for sustaining racial hierarchies and a commodity crucial to Britain's newly evolving forms of global commerce. Colour was vital to the gradual reconfiguration of Britain's relationship to its empire from the late nineteenth century, when imperial statecraft gradually came to be configured less in terms of governance and more in terms of marketing and commerce. Whether in brightly hued advertisements for imperial produce or Technicolor films celebrating British military power, colour commodities became a way for Britain to imagine its continued global hegemony through decades of imperial decline.

By 1968, when this book concludes, there was no aspect of modern British visual culture that had not been transformed by colour. Colour had seeped into the spheres of print media, advertising, photography and cinema, and by 1968 it had become a regular feature of BBC television, broadcast on a daily basis into British homes. This book ends before the digital and cybernetic revolutions that remade colour's meanings once again, which Carolyn L. Kane takes up in her study of 'chromatic algorithms' from the 1960s and are the subject of ongoing research by Lida Zeitlin Wu.[48] But 1968 did not merely mark a moment of chromatic saturation in British visual culture, concluding a process that had been set in motion in 1856. If the chromatic revolution of the mid-Victorian era was particularly salient for its imperial ramifications – the way it transformed Britain's relationship to its empire through the medium of colour – then 1968 marked a similarly significant reformulation of these terms.

By the 1960s the flow of colour into the metropole was understood less in relation to material substances and more in regard to the Commonwealth subjects from the West Indies, South Asia and Africa who were invited to relocate there. Because colour as chromatic hue and as a racial designation were collapsed into a single discursive framework, discussions of colour played an especially important role in mediating the process of decolonisation and Commonwealth migration that shaped life in Britain following the Second World War. As Lynda Nead has incisively examined, the linguistic slippage between colour-as-hue and colour-as-race was inescapable in post-war Britain, when the enhanced presence of people of colour was read alongside the enhanced chromatism of the visual environment.[49] The pervasive idea in the 1960s that Britain was becoming increasingly colourful reflected both changed understandings of British racial identity and a new sensory environment transformed by colour media. This post-war moment and its fraught debates over the place of colour in British culture were the result of the much longer colonial and imperial tradition already described, which forged colour as the principal way of thinking through racial difference.

While 1968 is understood as a year of revolutionary left-wing political change in Europe, in Britain this year marked the apotheosis of rightist institutional complicity with systems of anti-Black racism, espoused in Enoch Powell's notorious 'Rivers of Blood' speech and its legal legitimation in the Commonwealth Immigration Act, designed to limit the number of Commonwealth citizens of colour who could migrate to Britain. Thus, 1968 was a year in which British citizens fully embraced colour in its commercial and materials forms, not least through regular television broadcasts, but it was also a year in which many White Britons vitriolically espoused an opposition to colour as a synonym for racialised forms of Commonwealth migration. The year 1968 is therefore less of a conclusion to the narrative of colour's modernisation examined here and more of a significant point of connection between the history of chromatic modernity in Britain in the previous century and its expression in the most urgent issues of our current moment.

At present, British cultural, political and educational institutions are attending to and reckoning with the legacies of empire, exploring how it continues to shape the attitudes and experiences of Britons in the twenty-first century. The year 1968 marks an important moment for reflecting upon precisely these dynamics, as a year in which places imagined as the peripheries of empire were drawn into a new proximity with the metropole through processes of migration. Concluding with this moment forces attention upon how imperial entanglements overseas in the eighteenth and nineteenth centuries had concrete and tangible impacts on the social and cultural fabric of life at home in Britain well into the twentieth century. The British Empire is shown here to be less of a historical phenomenon than a force that continued, and continues, to shape British life.

Colour-as-Hue, Colour-as-Race

While the conflation of colour as a hue and as a marker of racial difference was critical to the specific contexts of Commonwealth migration in the 1960s, the intertwining of racialised and chromatic discourse recurred throughout the decades under consideration here. Precisely because race was formulated and fictionalised as a system of classification based on colour, all new colour media produced crucial arenas where these imagined categories of difference could be perpetuated and reinforced or opposed and resisted. The major technological shift examined in this book, from monochrome to chromatic media, from black and white to colour, therefore cannot be conceptualised outside this lexis of race. To discuss the material construction of colour media is to discuss the material construct of race itself.

As already noted, by the nineteenth century colour had become the definitive system of racial classification, whereby abstract colour terms ('black', 'white', 'red', 'yellow') were assigned to people of different origins (African, European, American, Asian), despite the fact that their skin tones did not resemble these hues. Indeed, as Richard J. Powell suggests, the chromatic basis of such 'racial hypotheses' reveals their 'abstract, conceptual dimensions and their impulse to gauge visually'.[50] Colour thereby facilitated a formulation of race as a visibly discernible form of *difference* necessary to the project of dividing human types into supposedly fixed categories. It is precisely because colour can 'activate a feeling of visual difference' that Nicholas Gaskill suggests it endures as the dominant lexis for discussing race even today.[51] If race is, as Vron Ware and Les Back describe, an unreliable 'index of human difference', then colour is a fittingly unreliable system for its articulation; both require the formulation of seemingly secure terms (such as 'black', 'white', 'red' and 'yellow') to describe what is in fact a relational, culturally articulated and contingent state rather than a biological reality.[52]

My attention here to the conflation of colour-as-hue and colour-as-race is therefore not intended to reify the idea of race as a biologically determined fact legible through skin colour. As Anne Anlin Cheng argues, the colour of skin is merely one property among many that has been tied to 'the process of race making', and she suggests alternative ways of reading the relationship between the surface of the body and its racialised presentation.[53] But, by focusing on colour, the aim here is to remain vigilant to the multiple and pervasive ways colour emerged as an instrument of racialisation from the nineteenth century.

Indeed, the recent debates around the capitalisation of the terms 'Black' and 'White' have in part been motivated by attempts to separate out the meanings of these racialised and chromatic terms. For instance, the decision in June 2020 by the Associated Press and some editorial style guides to recommend the capitalisation of 'Black' when it is used in 'a racial, ethnic or cultural sense' and the lowercasing of 'black' when referring to 'a color, not a person' spoke to the clear fact, as Kwame Anthony Appiah states, that 'everyone knows that black people aren't literally black'.[54] These editorial decisions, largely precipitated by the growing momentum of the Black Lives Matter movement in the wake of George Floyd's murder in May 2020, were explained as a way of articulating an understanding of race as a socially constructed, historically situated, politically resonant and collectively experienced mode of subjectivity distinct from the more troubling formulations of race as a biologically situated marker – that is, the imagined blackness of Black skin designated by the lowercase term 'black'.[55]

For these reasons, this book capitalises 'Black' when referring exclusively to racial and cultural identities, although it recognises that this is not a uniformly accepted practice and has been understood by some as essentialising and limiting.[56] Yet, given that so much of this book is dedicated to exploring the interwoven histories of colour as a racialised and aesthetic phenomenon, it is important to recognise both the points of difference and the sites of conflation between these meanings.[57] It is for this reason that this book also capitalises 'White' when used as a racial designator, a far less accepted practice due to its historical adoption by White supremacist groups. Yet retaining the lowercase term can also naturalise Whiteness as a racial category and overlook the social formulation of its fiercely guarded boundaries. As Nell Irvin Painter and Eve L. Ewing argue, retaining the lowercase 'w' can reproduce the idea of White people as an unraced group, problematically perpetuating what scholars including Richard Dyer, bell hooks, Vron Ware and Les Back have described as the imagined invisibility and normativity of Whiteness.[58]

For the purposes of this book, capitalising both 'Black' and 'White' (except in quotations, where the author's own decisions around capitalisation are followed) allows both terms to be recognised as socially constructed racial identities. This practice also helps to clarify the discussions of complexion central to this book's arguments, because just as Black skin is not literally black, nor is White skin literally white. There are moments in the following analyses, however, when the chromatic and cultural meanings of these terms are completely inseparable – when Black skin is literally rendered black with ink, or the use of white paint, or paper, or textiles, becomes a proxy for White skin itself. In these instances, where the meanings of these racial and chromatic categories have been inextricably mapped onto one another, the lowercase is used.

'Black' and 'White' are not the only colour terms deployed as racial markers of course, and, as numerous scholars have highlighted, cathecting on this particular binary risks overlooking the multiple and nuanced ways that ethnicity, indigeneity and nationality inform ideas about 'race' beyond a paradigm of White supremacy and anti-Black racism.[59] Critical explorations of how racialised identities are forged through chromatic terms such as 'brown' and 'yellow' have highlighted the insufficiency of what is often referred to as the Black/White binary.[60] As Anne Lafont has shown, 'Black' and 'White' became the most pervasive chromatic binary for expressing racial difference as this juxtaposition invoked the notion that people of European origins and those of African descent occupied opposite ends of a spectrum of human value, and thereby legitimised the enslavement of one group by another.[61] Expressing racial difference as a binary in this way can therefore reproduce the idea of racial difference as a fixed and polarised fact rather than a relational and contingent position.

Yet the Black/White binary is a particularly important paradigm when considering the relationship between media aesthetics and racial epistemologies. As the term 'black and white' also signals an absence of colour when used in the context of visual media (black and white television, black and white photography etc.), it imbues these greyscale images with a racialised charge. While 'Black' and 'White' as racial designators are metaphorical and abstract labels, in monochrome media it becomes possible to literalise the racial binary between Blackness and Whiteness as an aesthetic binary between black and white hues. In the period under consideration here, the introduction of colour to black and white media therefore simultaneously threatened to pluralise and confuse the imagined fixity of this dichotomy while also promising a more accurate way of ostensibly locating racial difference through skin pigmentation, no longer conveyed through a palette of greyscale.[62] By ascribing colour to all bodies, these chromatic technologies disturbed the imagined distinction between Whiteness (a supposed absence of colour, rhetorically linked with European identity) and colour (grouping together people of radically distinct origins).

The various case studies considered here therefore speak to what Alice Maurice has defined as an established trope in American media history: that the difference between old and new media has repeatedly been spectacularised as a form of racial difference, particularly between White and Black bodies.[63] Colour technologies offered an especially privileged sphere for such operations, because colour was already understood as a tool for distinguishing and differentiating between these culturally constructed racial groups. As is revealed throughout this book, the difference between the absence and presence of colour in visual culture was explored through the imagined absence and presence of colour on the body: the supposed *colourlessness* of White people and the imagined chromatism of people of colour, and particularly people racialised as Black.

The importance of skin colour to the evolution of the chromatic media under discussion in this book can therefore not be over-emphasised. The fidelity and sensitivity of any colour process, whether paint, print or photography, was tested by its ability to correctly capture flesh tones. As Jacqueline Lichtenstein describes, in the history of painting 'the depiction of flesh has always been the colourists' triumph' as the nuance, liveliness and subtlety of skin were so difficult to render without the animacy lent by colour.[64] This discourse extended throughout the evolution of colour print and subsequent photographic media, which were all measured by their capacity to accurately render skin. The emphasis on flesh tones was typically shrouded in discourses of naturalism – the idea repeated across the various cultural sectors considered here that viewers measured the accuracy of a colour technology by its ability to faithfully capture the colours of the skin.

Yet, repeatedly, when artists, broadcasters or advertisers wanted to show the capacity and potential of a new colour system, they turned to people of colour as the subject matter most suited for this task because their skin was already imagined as a locus of colour. This book is replete with examples, from the stereotyped African bodies used to showcase the expanded palette of Victorian colour printing (as discussed in Chapter Two) to the imperial subjects of British India who were used to highlight the chromatism of colour cinema in the inter-war decades (as discussed in Chapter Four). There were clearly ideological as well as technological imperatives behind this practice, which reveals how completely interlocked were the histories of making colour and of constructing racial identities. For it was the ability not just to accurately depict flesh but to make visible and distinct the differences between various kinds of flesh that was the marker of any successful colour technology. In other words, while people of colour were used as test subjects to demonstrate the chromatic range and possibilities of a new media, in this way their presence helped to produce the idea of Whiteness and reinforce its primacy.

In some ways these new colour media were exploiting a well-established trope from the history of painting, whereby artists juxtaposed a White subject with a person of colour (typically a Black attendant or enslaved person) in order to highlight the beauty and brilliance of the sitter's White skin – activating the very idea of Whiteness through its juxtaposition with 'colour' (whether in the form of a person of colour or exoticised items like birds, fruit or flowers).[65] This topos repeats across these chapters, which describe how people of colour were used to demonstrate the expanded possibilities for colour in a manner that did not displace the centrality of Whiteness as an ideal but reinforced it by contrast. Although featuring a range of skin tones was vital to measuring and testing chromatic media, White skin was deemed the most important hue of all, yet it could only be understood and rendered visible in relation to its rhetorical opposite: colour.

This is made evident by the fact that failures in new chromatic media were routinely framed as problems of racial confusion: that a paint rendered White skin too dark, or that colour television distorted pink flesh tones so they appeared brown. A successful colour technology was one that could properly capture and distinctly identify a full gamut of skin colours without any ambiguity over who was White and who was not. Yet by placing skin tones on a spectrum rather than fixing them in a binary, colour media routinely posed the problem of blurring and eroding the distinction between White people and people of colour. In order to re-establish a clear hierarchy between these types, new colour media systematically turned to explicitly racist content in their early demonstration moments to reinforce the hierarchies of racial distinction. What David Batchelor calls 'chromophobia', the broad prejudice against chromatism in Western culture, routinely manifests in British culture as explicit forms of racism – as a fear and hatred of people of colour perceived as a contaminating threat to ideals of White purity.[66]

From the anti-Black humour of Victorian advertising to the use of blackface minstrelsy on colour television, again and again the expanded spectrum of colour made possible by chromatic media was perceived as a threat to Whiteness, which was stabilised and shored up by denigrating, stereotyping and otherwise demeaning the (typically) Black bodies on display. Scholars including Richard Dyer, Kara Keeling, Lorna Roth, Tanya Sheehan and Genevieve Yue have all explored how, in Keeling's terms, 'anti-black racism adheres in the [film] apparatus', considering how various media technologies are calibrated around the successful reproduction of White identities, often at the cost of other skin tones, by White engineers, artists and technicians.[67] But, as this book demonstrates, racism was also incorporated into the content of colour images as a way of staving off the perceived threat of contamination, colourisation and distortion of Whiteness that colour in the form of hue and in the form of racial difference seemed to pose.

However, because British colour media were so routinely used as an apparatus of racism, a practice with long roots in imperial and colonial ideologies, colour also became a tool of resistance against these systems. This is explored in the greatest detail in the discussion of colour film in post-colonial India in Chapter Four, which demonstrates how Indian filmmakers instrumentalised colour film technology as an act of political defiance against the British regimes that had used colour for so long as a weapon of colonialism. This idea is then revisited in the coda on Chila Kumari Singh Burman's 2020–21 neon installation at Tate Britain, to consider how colour might operate as an instrument for social change amid calls to decolonise British institutions precisely because of colour's long and established relationship in Britain with forms of imperial and racialised violence.

Chapter Breakdown

The following chapters, unfolding in chronological order between 1856 and 1968, forge a new history of British visual culture that reveals colour to be central to both its aesthetic trajectories and its political formations. Each chapter examines a new technique for making colour across the respective fields of paint, print, photography, film and television, revealing these technologies as agents of both aesthetic and political change.

The opening chapter, titled 'The Texture of Capitalism: Oil Painting and Industrialisation in the Nineteenth Century', reveals the impact new techniques for manufacturing 'artists' colours' (or oil paint) had upon painterly practice in Victorian Britain. It shows how the mass production of these colours from the mid-nineteenth century made painting a medium that was used to critique the changing nature of labour under industrial capitalism. The host of new technological innovations that modernised paint-making from an artisanal craft into an industrial process at this time did not change the hue or saturation of colours, however, but radically altered their texture. The texture of colour therefore became central to debates about the degenerative effect of capitalist modernity on painting in particular and British society more broadly. The chapter focuses on the Victorian painter George Frederic Watts, who mobilised the texture of his paints to articulate an anti-capitalist, moral aesthetic through his paintings. Placing his work in dialogue with the Pre-Raphaelite painter William Holman Hunt and the Aesthetic Movement artist James Abbott McNeill Whistler, this chapter situates Watts's work within broader dialogues about art and labour paramount to artistic discourse at this time. This chapter offers a new approach to questions of 'modern colour' in painting, by offering a haptic and textural model for thinking through the chromatism of modern British art.

The second chapter, 'The Complexion of the Chromolithograph: Colouring Skin in Late Victorian Print', considers how the new colour printing technology of chromolithography changed the way racial difference materialised in print through depictions of skin in late nineteenth-century advertisements. Chromolithography was the first affordable technology for mass-producing colour images; it was industrialised in Britain on an unparalleled scale and transformed the realm of print advertising. It was widely used to promote imperial goods resulting from intensified colonial expansion and the heightened commercial exploitation of Africa from the 1880s. Colour became a tool for enhancing the visual appeal of these products to potential customers, but it also gave printers an expanded palette through which to exploit racial difference as part of these advertising campaigns. Yet the addition of colour to a formerly monochrome medium raised a host of questions about the relationship between skin colour and racial identity. How was it possible to render White skin in a variety of hues without it becoming, in the racist terminology of the time, 'coloured'? The technique of chromolithography also lent a distinctive surface pattern, or complexion, to the surface of these prints – a spotted and dotted configuration that complicated ideals of Whiteness and its supposed purity and colourlessness. How did this spotty surface pattern intersect with ideas about skin colour and discoloration linked to understandings of disease and dirtiness bound up with class and labour, as well as ideas about desirable and undesirable coloration dictated by the racial hierarchies of Victorian beauty standards? Through a close examination of advertisements for Pears' soap, this chapter reveals how the surfaces of these colour prints became a space for materialising ideas about British racial identity in an era of colonial expansionism.

The third chapter, 'Modern Women, Modern Colours: Madame Yevonde and the Feminisation of Photography between the Wars', explores how the British Vivex process of colour photography reformulated ideas about gender and labour in the inter-war years, when women were gaining new forms of political, professional and social freedom. The chapter focuses on the pioneering work of Madame Yevonde, a committed suffragette and feminist campaigner who became one of the most successful colour photographers of the inter-war period through her radiant celebrity portraits and vibrant advertising commissions. At a time when photography was dominated by black and white images and male practitioners, Yevonde's dazzling works troubled the hegemony of both. Her photographs raised questions about colour's capacity to feminise photography – debates that intersected with broader societal anxieties about the increasing presence of women in the workforce following the First World War. Through close analysis not only of the subject matter and aesthetics of Yevonde's works but also of the material processes conducted by female staff at the Vivex laboratory, this chapter shows how colour articulated the value of women's work at a time when female labour was fiercely opposed and devalued.

The fourth chapter, 'Decolonising in Technicolor: Chromatic Imperialism and Post-War Colour Cinema in Britain and India', interrogates how the dyeing technique used at London's Technicolor film laboratory helped Britain to imagine its sustained global hegemony during the transition from empire to commonwealth. In particular it considers the role this technology played in articulating Anglo-Indian relations following Indian independence in 1947. The British Technicolor laboratory was an international hub for processing colour film from the 1930s to the 1960s, dyeing film shot all over the world. This gave Britain unparalleled global control over the aesthetics of colour cinema and its economic market. The nation's control of this dyeing process had acute resonances in India, where Britain's colonial regime had historically operated through the violent management of dyes and textiles. Technicolor's system for dyeing film – a potent echo of dyeing fabrics – therefore became a highly politicised technology in Anglo-Indian relations. Although a newly independent India began regularly making colour films in the 1950s, Britain's continued control of the dyeing process that imbued these films with their colours heightened the importance of cinema as a contentious site for expressing Indian and British post-colonial identities. This chapter explores these themes through a close reading of *Jhansi Ki Rani* (India, 1953; dir. Sohrab Modi), the first Technicolor film made by an Indian director, which was printed at the London Technicolor laboratory. A historical epic that revisits India's First War of Independence (also called the Indian Revolt of 1857), *Jhansi Ki Rani* is a particularly compelling case study for considering how political power is articulated through colour film, both through its colour design and through the material and technical processes used to print and dye film itself.

The final chapter, 'The BBC's Colour Problem: Race, Migration and Colour Television in the 1960s', reveals how the BBC's conversion from monochrome to colour television broadcasting intervened in debates about Commonwealth migration and British racial identity in the 1960s through the charged categories of black and white and colour. It takes up what were problematically framed as two related 'colour problems' in the 1960s. Colour – as a synonym for racial difference – was routinely expressed as a 'problem' by the popular media in the post-war period, which formulated migration from the West Indies, South Asia and Africa as a catalyst of societal unrest. From 1967, the BBC's conversion to chromatic broadcasting raised a related 'colour problem'. Due to the high cost of colour television sets and the limited geographic reach of the colour broadcasting signal, when the BBC launched its colour service in 1967, the majority of viewers would have watched this historic moment in television history in black and white. The technical difficulties of broadcasting simultaneously in colour and monochrome made the accurate rendition and standardisation of flesh tones a particular challenge for engineers, make-up artists and designers, making skin colour and, by extension, racial difference central to the BBC's 'colour problem'. This chapter explores how the BBC's attempts to resolve its technological 'colour problem' therefore intersected with and participated in the larger ideological and political 'colour problem' of late 1960s Britain, when these shared discourses about the integration and regulation of colour made television a space for dramatising the fraught negotiations between black and white and colour at this time.

A brief coda, 'Neon Futures', examines how the major themes of chromatic modernity narrated throughout this book continue to shape British art and culture today. Through a reading of Chila Kumari Singh Burman's installation of neon sculptures at Tate Britain, *Remembering a Brave New World* (2020–21), this concluding chapter explores how colour's inextricable connections to racial identity, gendered labour, migratory politics and the legacies of British colonialism resonate powerfully in our contemporary moment. It reveals how Burman's use of colour to disrupt the white façade of Tate Britain exemplifies a strategy of decolonising by re-colourising, describing how her work illuminates colour's capacity to defamiliarise spaces, institutions and histories that are problematically framed as uniformly White. Examining her use of digital technologies to design the work and the use of silicon in its material fabrication, the coda emphasises the continued importance of remaining vigilant to questions of materiality in the digital era.

These chapters advance a new understanding of colour that shows it to be inseparable from the aesthetic developments and ideological entanglements of British visual culture. These case studies take up some of the most urgent questions facing Britain today, revealing their origins to be dyed deep in the very fabric of the nation. The political realities and historical legacies of empire are shown to have instructed one of the most pervasive dimensions of visual experience, while the problematic construction of Britain as a grey or colourless nation is unveiled not just as a question of taste but as a deeply racialised and ideological project. The case studies brought together here reveal colour in its many material and political guises to have been crucial to constructing a distinctly British form of modernity. These chapters therefore offer a model for examining the gravity of the rainbow in today's culture as well as our recent past.

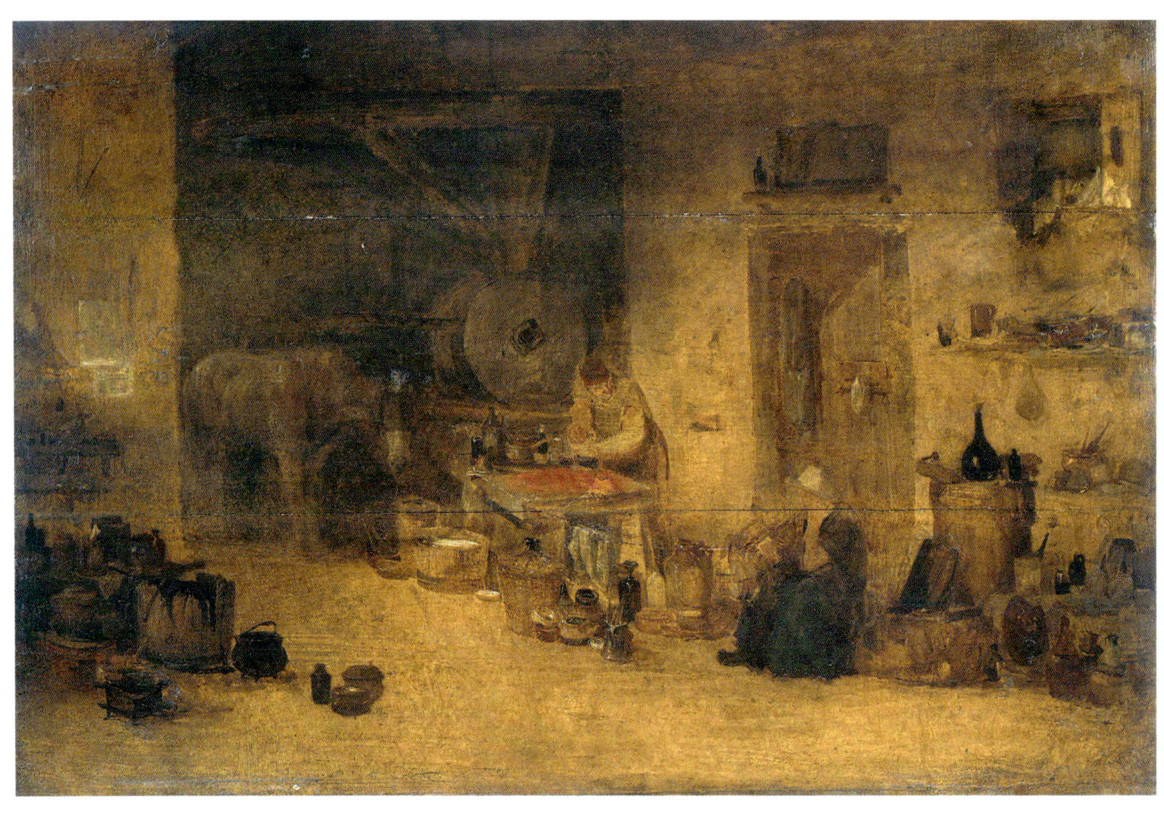

11 J. M. W. Turner, *An Artists' Colourman's Workshop*, c.1807, oil on wood, 62.2 × 91.4 cm. Tate.

1

THE TEXTURE OF CAPITALISM

Oil Painting and Industrialisation in the Nineteenth Century

An Artists' Colourman's Workshop (*c.*1807), an unfinished painting by J. M. W. Turner, offers a glimpse into the craft of colour-making in the early nineteenth century (fig. 11). At the centre of this tenebrous interior, a figure stoops over a slab as he grinds dry pigments and oil to make paint. His head is tilted upward in conversation with the figure seated beside his workbench, but his hunched posture and firm grip on the muller make clear his physical engagement with the demanding task at hand. Although these pigments have already been ground by the donkey-drawn mill seen in the rear of the workshop, he must refine them even further to transform them into paint. He keeps a cask of oil nearby should he need to add more vehicle to his mixture, as he requires precisely the right amount to ensure the paint is neither too viscid nor too fluid. Jars, bottles, flasks and cauldrons litter the floor and counters, containing myriad nostrums to add to his paint, perhaps to make it dry more quickly, brush more smoothly or shine more seductively. A book labelled 'Old Masters', perched on the shelf above the door, is close at hand for reference on such material matters. Amid the smoky, golden yellows and the murky, earthy browns that permeate the scene, the vivid red paint streaked across the grinding table makes clear the fruit of the colourman's labours, as its dazzling colour leaps out at the viewer from the centre of the work, imbuing the scene with a sense of alchemical magic, of something precious emerging from the gloom.

This scene is consistent with accounts of how colours were made and sold in this period. Some artists certainly continued to make their oil colours fresh in the studio at this time, but many purchased them premixed from their colourman, who ground together the pigments and oil and stored these paints in small animal bladders to keep them moist. It is possible that Turner based this scene on the workshop of James Newman, a London-based colourman who was known for the high quality of his 'Indian red', among other colours.[1] As the name of this pigment suggests, British colourmen at this time imported materials from all over the empire.[2] It was not merely pigments like ochre sourced from India that contributed to the imperial character of colour at this time, but also the binders, varnishes and resins necessary to make paint, whether copal imported from Sierra Leone and the Niger, dammar from Singapore and Ceylon, or gum arabic extracted from trees in Sudan.[3] The British colourman's workshop was furnished by the extractive economy of empire, and the workshop became the place where these raw substances were transformed into lustrous paints.

However, by the end of the nineteenth century, the scene Turner depicts would have been exceptionally rare, as few colourmen still made paints this way. The continued use of the singular term 'colourman' elides the fact that many of these colour-makers were no longer small firms run by individuals but were industrial-scale businesses operating factories for mass-producing colours. Even within Turner's lifetime, new technologies transformed colour-making from an artisanal craft into an industrial process, and, by the time of the artist's death in 1851, this transition was well advanced. From the 1840s steam-powered mills enabled colourmen to grind pigments and paints on a massive scale, improving the shelf life of these colours through storage in collapsible metal tubes. From 1856 and William Henry Perkin's synthesis of colour from coal (as discussed in the Introduction), the trade developed a host of new, artificial pigments, transforming the colourman's identity from herbalist to industrial chemist. The colourman's reliance upon imperial trade networks for raw organic materials was vastly reduced by the ability to fabricate materials chemically in a laboratory. By the closing decades of the nineteenth century, therefore, colour-making was largely automated, mechanised and industrialised, and the range of colours that were commercially available to painters seemed to have doubled.[4] By the late Victorian era, paint-making was a fully modern enterprise.

The impact these modern tube colours had upon nineteenth-century painting is a well-rehearsed narrative. In the words of the French painter Pierre-Auguste Renoir, 'without paint in tubes there would have been no Cézanne, no Monet, no Sisley or Pissarro, nothing of what the journalists were later to call Impressionism'.[5] The increased portability of ready-mixed colours available to buy in tubes enabled artists to work more freely *en plein air*, and a host of new chemical shades meant they were able to enliven their canvases with the brilliant effects of natural daylight, producing the kinds of chromatic effects that became synonymous with the Impressionist movement and the emergence of modernist painting in Europe.[6] Art historical accounts of this period remain largely obedient to Renoir's assessment – that by ushering in a new era of convenient, chromatic brilliance, these modern paints helped to produce modernist painting.[7]

The applicability of such theories to British contexts seems vividly demonstrated by John Singer Sargent's *Carnation, Lily, Lily, Rose* (1885–86), a work painted largely outdoors during the precious twilight hours of a summer and autumn spent in Worcestershire (fig. 12).[8] With the American painter having developed a close friendship with Monet in Paris, his canvas reflects a similar approach to conveying the atmospheric immediacy of contemporary life in all its rich tints. The canvas seems to radiate light and colour, both from the glowing amber lanterns the girls illuminate with tapers and from the lively hues of the flowers that festoon the scene. The intensity of these yellow, pink and crimson petals is enhanced by juxtaposition with the girls' white gowns, whose frilled collars echo the opening of the lilies that surround them. Sargent captured the scene by painting *en plein air* daily in the dwindling light, a process enabled by the portability of his easel and his box of tube paints, which included materials manufactured by Winsor & Newton, one of the largest industrial colour-makers in Victorian Britain. In addition to more traditional colours, Sargent enlivened his canvas with a host of recently developed synthetic, artificial and chemical pigments such as cadmium red, lemon chrome, viridian, synthetic ultramarine and cerulean blue.[9] The modernity of the subject – a fleeting moment of contemporary bourgeois life – is compounded through its materials: the products of heavy industry, synthetic chemistry and capitalist commerce.

Yet to suggest that this kind of heightened radiance was a logical or necessary outcome of these modern colours is to overlook the plurality of reactions evidenced by painters at this time. Modernism was only one response among many to the technological, social and political upheavals that shaped the nineteenth century, as Elizabeth Prettejohn and Tim Barringer's work on Victorian art has routinely demonstrated.[10] Yet the vibrant palette of Impressionist painters and their followers, brilliantly evidenced in *Carnation, Lily, Lily, Rose*, has come to define the modernity of colour in rather too narrow terms as an aesthetics of immediacy, of heightened sensory response and of optical intensity. This focus on a particular kind of chromatic modernity has overshadowed other ways that artists could use modern colours, not only to celebrate the vivacity and effervescence of contemporary life but also to critique the often detrimental societal transformations that

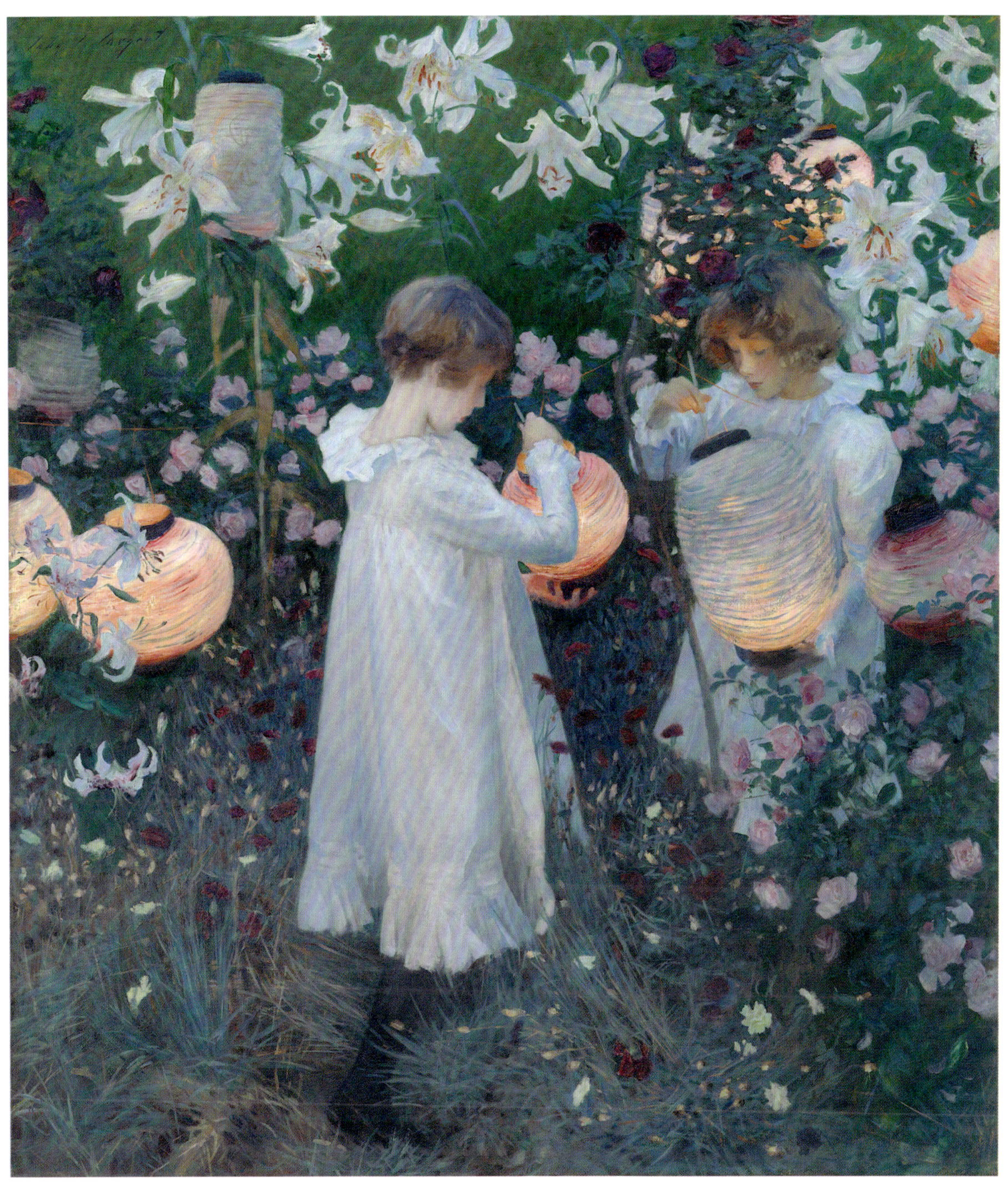

12 John Singer Sargent, *Carnation, Lily, Lily, Rose*, 1885–86, oil on canvas, 17.4 × 15.4 cm. Tate.

accompanied technological, industrial and capitalist modernity.

Moreover, while art historians have primarily focused on the aesthetics of modern colour – its brightness, hue and saturation – one of the most important ways mass-produced paints affected painters had more to do with their haptic and textural dimensions than their optical properties. As evidenced in painters' manuals of this period, artists did not believe it was the appearance of colour that had changed with the industrialisation of its manufacture, but rather its purity, longevity and texture. While many artists remained indifferent towards industrially made colours, some, particularly in Britain, were vocal in their rejection of these modern paints as these new techniques of manufacturing, processing and packaging colour radically affected the permanence, stability and materiality of paint, placing these issues at the centre of debates about modern colour at this time.

These changed properties of modern colours meant that some artists continued to prefer artisanally made, hand-ground and organically derived materials – a choice easy to read as a conservative backlash against the onslaught of technological modernity and a rejection of modernist practice. But this disavowal of industrial colours marked a conscious and explicit engagement with the conditions of contemporary life, which had potent ethical and political dimensions at this time. As Carol Jacobi notes, there were moral as well as material concerns that attended the emergence of modern paints.[11] Because it was through the materiality of their paints that artists became aware of the impact industrialisation had upon their practice, these issues of purity and temporality, but especially texture, became flashpoints for debates about the effect of capitalist modernity on painting in particular, and on society more broadly.

As David Peters Corbett observes, the materiality of a painting's surface was where the specific forces shaping its historical, social and political contexts were physically registered.[12] Following Corbett, this chapter suggests that it was not just the iconography of urban life, or the formal innovations intended to capture the perceptual ruptures of this accelerated century, but the materiality of colour and paint itself that offered a platform on which artists could negotiate, interrogate and in some cases protest the adverse effects of modernity *qua* industrial capitalism on society at large. This chapter explores how the texture of painted colour became a critical site where artists articulated their attitudes towards industrial capitalism, focusing on the artist George Frederic Watts.

Watts is best remembered as 'England's Michelangelo', a name given to him by Frederic Leighton, president of the Royal Academy in the closing decades of the nineteenth century.[13] This nickname suggests both Watts's esteemed position in Victorian society and his identification with the art of the past. As a painter of allegorical, symbolic and mythological subjects who based his style and technique upon that of Italian High Renaissance models, it is unsurprising that Watts disliked modern, mass-produced colours. But for Watts, who self-consciously fashioned himself as a living Old Master painter, the effects of industrial modernity were most acutely experienced through the materiality of his colours. When systems of mass production altered the texture of the paints with which he worked, it was through his materials that he chose to contest the pernicious effects of industrialisation most vociferously. This examination of how Watts politicised his use of colour begins by exploring the technical reasons why the mass production of oil paint transformed the texture of paint in the late nineteenth century, focusing on Watts's colourman, Winsor & Newton. The chapter then examines how Watts rejected the greasy texture of industrially made paints and mobilised especially dry, coarse paints to enact the anti-capitalist, anti-industrial politics of his paintings through the materiality of his colours.

The Texture of Capitalism

The intimate still life *Mound of Butter* (1875–85), painted by the French realist Antoine Vollon, may seem an unlikely work to begin an assessment of the impact that the mass production of oil paint had upon painting in Britain (fig. 13). Yet *Mound of Butter*

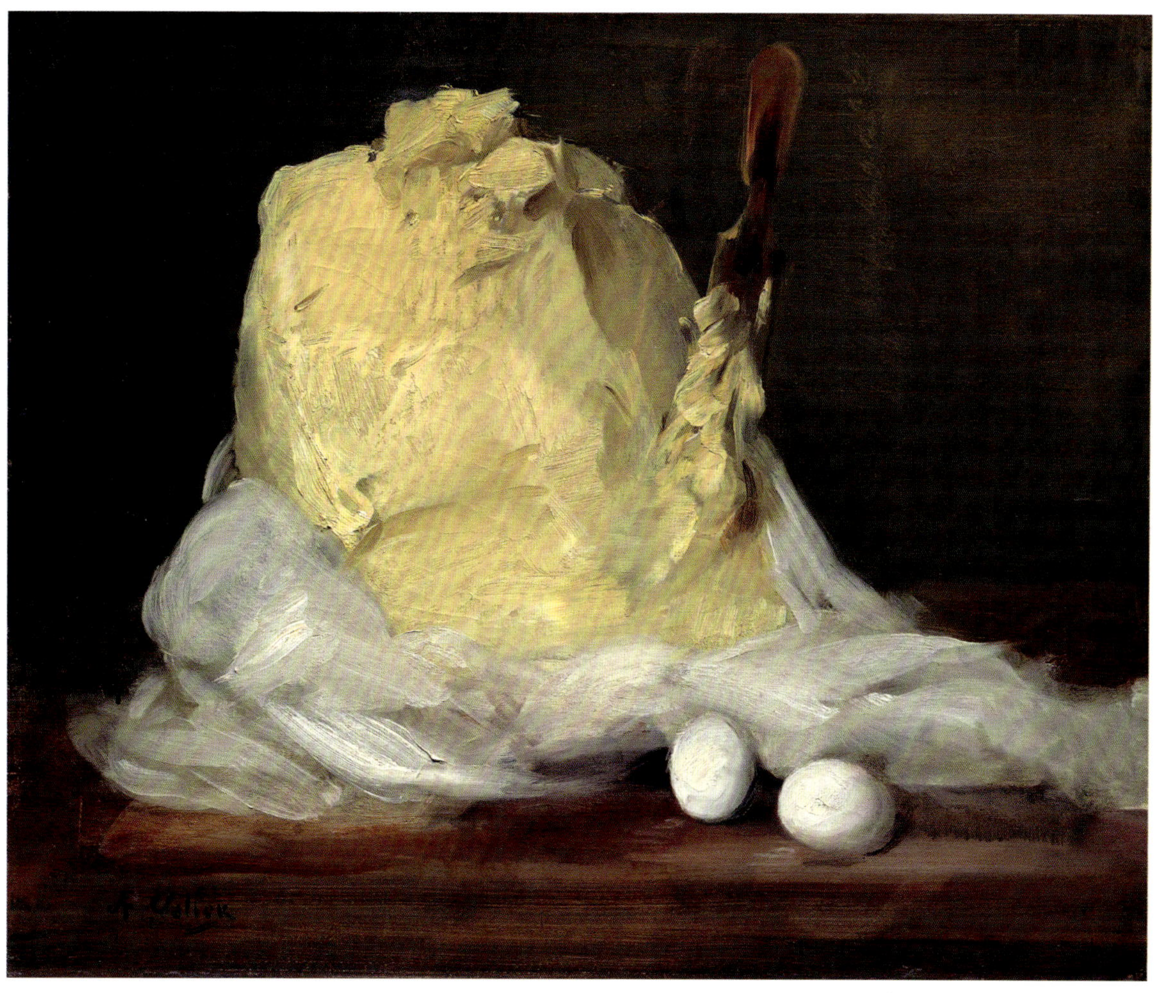

13 Antoine Vollon, *Mound of Butter*, 1875–85, oil on canvas, 50.2 × 61 cm. Collection of National Gallery of Art, Washington, DC.

encapsulates what was felt by many artists (both British and French) to be one of the most significant new characteristics of mass-produced oil colours. It was not that they had a distinctive appearance but a specific material consistency – a new texture, frequently characterised as that of fresh butter.[14] This new texture was produced through a nexus of related technological advances necessary to make paint on a large scale, from how the paint was ground and stored to the kind of additives used in its manufacture.

The conflation in Vollon's work between paint and butter makes clear the smoothness of this mass-produced substance. The lively diagonal smears of paint created with both paintbrush and knife show the effects possible with this slick new paint. The fluidity of industrially produced paint meant it was pliable enough to work easily under the brush (evidenced here by the brush marks that remain in the surface of the paint, most visibly in the lower left corner of the muslin), but it was also more full-bodied than hand-ground paint and could be applied just as well with a palette knife (which Vollon used liberally to manipulate his paint here, particularly the flat areas of colour on the butter mound itself).[15] This painters' tool is echoed in Vollon's painting in the form of a butter knife, which scoops up gobs of butter in the same way the artist did his paints, spreading colour on the canvas in the way he might butter bread.

Yet while Vollon revelled in the new possibilities of buttery, mass-produced paint, other painters disliked this texture, finding it too homogenous, oily and slick compared to artisanally manufactured colours. For instance, Frederic Leighton complained about the 'greasiness and slipperiness' of his paints.[16] This was a problem because many painters believed greasiness to be injurious to the long-term stability and permanence of colour, as excess oil could yellow, crack or darken, resulting in dramatic changes to a work's appearance and longevity.[17] Furthermore, industrially made colours were frequently less pure than those made by hand, as they were more prone to so-called sophistication – that is, adulteration by the addition of impure and fraudulent substances that would further erode the quality of the colours.[18] The new texture of industrially manufactured paint therefore came to represent the other more insidious ways that the mass production of colour detrimentally affected painting. This homogeneous, oily, buttery consistency, what I call here the 'texture of capitalism', was a physical manifestation of the effect of industrialisation upon painting.[19]

Concerns about the purity and stability of colour were particularly acute in nineteenth-century Britain. After the establishment of the National Gallery in 1824 and the expansion of its collection in the 1840s, visitors could directly compare paintings executed by the previous generation of British academicians with those by Old Masters, as well as paintings by Italian and Netherlandish artists of the fourteenth and fifteenth centuries. It was widely noted that the colours of early Netherlandish oils and Italian temperas seen in the National Gallery were fresher, brighter and more sound than more recent works by Joshua Reynolds and Turner, perhaps England's most famed colourist.[20] In particular Jan van Eyck's *Arnolfini Portrait* (1434), acquired by the National Gallery in 1842, was considered the paragon of durable, vivid colour, and his technique was much discussed in technical manuals at the time.[21]

Looking again at *An Artists' Colourman's Workshop*, it is possible that its warm patina was not an intentional evocation of the golden age of Dutch painting by Turner, but the results of an unintentional darkening and yellowing of the painting's surface. Although Turner was famed for the brilliance of his works, like many painters of his generation he added unstable substances such as beeswax, megilp and bitumen to his colours to improve the handling qualities of his paints.[22] By the mid-nineteenth century faults were already emerging in paintings by the most celebrated artists of the previous century.[23] These paintings began to wrinkle, darken, yellow, crack, fade and flake, precisely because of these material experimentations with colour.

Rather than reading Turner's painting as a nostalgic reverie for the lost craft of colour-making, it should perhaps be understood as an illustration of the material experiments that produced such catastrophic effects in subsequent centuries. After all, it was in imitation of the Old Masters that painters like Turner experimented with their colours, in attempts to replicate the chromatic effects of painters like Titian.[24] Although Turner was considered one of the most original and inventive colourists of his age, his material craft was shaped, often in misguided ways, by these historical precedents.[25] Perhaps the book on the colourman's shelf contains such unsound advice regarding Old Master technique, and the vessels scattered about the room may be filled with the volatile additives that would have resulted in the overall gloominess of the picture. To put it another way, perhaps the painting records the means of its own demise.

The demonstrable material decline of academic paintings from the previous century, and the enduring brilliance of medieval and early Renaissance works seen in the National Gallery, provoked Victorian painters to think more seriously about the quality of their own colours, an acute problem when painters had a decreasing degree of control over their materials. The rise in academic training and the decline of the apprenticeship system meant that by the mid-nineteenth century, painters knew little about grinding or mixing colours, and increasingly relied upon commercially available, ready-made paints. This combination of new technologies for making colour, unease regarding the permanence and purity of colour, and a lack of technical knowledge among painters produced a unique set of cultural circumstances into which modern, industrial colours emerged in Britain. These various anxieties, about purity, stability and control, converged on the question of texture.

It was Watts's colourman, Winsor & Newton, that helped to transform the texture of paint in Britain. Established in 1832, the firm owned industrial-scale factory premises for manufacturing and processing many of the raw pigments used in its paints and was responsible for two major technological shifts in colour-making in the 1840s. First, the firm introduced mechanical pigment and paint grinding and, second, although it did not invent collapsible metal tubes, it was responsible for commercialising this invention and enabling its widespread adoption in Britain and beyond.

Grinding was necessary to reduce pigments to a powdery consistency and to combine that powder with oil to make paint (although rarely did paints solely comprise oil and pigment). As evidenced in *An Artists' Colourman's Workshop*, pigments were traditionally ground by hand using a slab and muller, a laborious activity that required a sound knowledge of every colour's material properties, as each required a different degree of grinding: dense pigments needed intensive work while others were inherently soft; some could be ground endlessly fine while others dulled through overgrinding; and some were absorbent, mixing well with oil to produce a glossy sheen, while others were gritty and unabsorbent, producing more matte colours. The resulting texture, finish and hue of the colour depended to a large extent upon how it was ground.

Ideally artists wanted paints that were the correct consistency for sitting on a palette – fluid enough to apply with a brush but not so thin that they would run. When made by hand, each paint had a different consistency depending upon the grinding requirements of its pigments. But this individuated treatment became difficult when manufacturers began grinding pigments and paints on an industrial scale. The steam-powered grinding equipment introduced to Britain by Winsor & Newton in 1844 economised on the cost of skilled labour and enabled manufacturers to grind much larger volumes of pigments into much, much finer particles.[26]

However, the intensity of some colours could be compromised by overgrinding. Therefore some firms, such as Charles Roberson & Co., the primary colour supplier to the Pre-Raphaelites, persisted with hand-grinding their pigments and paints. A Roberson catalogue published as late as 1907 describes how colours 'ground by hand under the muller give superior results over those ground by machinery; [we] therefore continue to retain the old and more costly system, and are thus able to give direct attention to the requirements of each colour'.[27] This continued artisanal approach to grinding colours produced numerous distinct textures in contrast to the homogenised smoothness of mass-produced paints all ground to the same fine consistency.

Once paints were no longer made fresh in the studio immediately before use but were ground in large volumes at commercial factories, it became vital to increase their shelf life so they did not dry prematurely. Bladders were of limited use as the paint frequently dried, separated and hardened inside, especially once the bladder had been pierced with a tack to release the paint. Although Winsor & Newton briefly used glass syringes, they were costly and prone to breaking. The invention of collapsible metal tubes in London in 1841 by the American painter John Goffe Rand significantly retarded premature drying, and Winsor & Newton purchased this patent from the artist, selling its own paint in tubes and licensing the technology to other colourmen.[28] The firm was responsible for popularising this enormously significant innovation, which British painters swiftly adopted. But, in addition to mechanised grinding, tube storage further homogenised the texture of paint and threatened its purity.

While some pigments naturally produced colours that were dense, gummy or thick, this storage system demanded a standardised consistency that was easily squeezable from the tube but not so fluid that it would drip from the palette. Although mechanical grinding helped to make the paint smooth, it could also make some paints too liquid, so colourmen restored body to the paint using additives such as wax, tallow and petroleum jelly, as well as adding extra oil to enhance brushability.[29] These additives and extra oil gave industrially made colours the necessary standardised texture and prolonged shelf life that were demanded by tube storage, but they also made it more greasy and slick.

The smeary, oily homogeneity of these paints frustrated many artists, who habitually squeezed their colours onto blotting paper before use to absorb excess oil.[30] One painters' manual from 1892 complained that industrially manufactured colours used an 'exaggerated quantity' of oil, speculating that because oil was cheaper than pigment, manufacturers 'merely concerned with the commercial side of the industry' used an unfavourably high oil-to-pigment ratio to cut costs.[31] The author mockingly suggested manufacturers might push this economising logic to its limit, eliminating pigment altogether and simply using synthetic dyes to 'tint a kilogramme of gluten made from wax and oil and have superbly tinted colours of a very consistent paste'.[32]

The use of additives to give paint body and prevent drying severely eroded the purity and permanence of these colours. For instance, Winsor & Newton's scientific director, John Scott Taylor, was puzzled to discover that other colourmen used additives in their white lead paint to prevent it from hardening in the tubes, given that such additives would also inherently darken the colour over time. He suggested that 'if an artist finds his white lead go hard in the tubes, let him by all means treasure the brand; it will be the best, perhaps, he can get in these degenerate days'.[33]

'Vilely Sophisticated'

Manufacturers did not only use additives to improve the shelf life of paint. The increasing separation of labour involved in colour-making, combined with artists' growing ignorance about their paints, created possibilities for manufacturers at any point in the long supply chain to tamper with materials without painters realising. This was a problem for a small firm like Roberson. The company prided itself on its artisanal approach – not only hand-grinding its colours but also using traditional recipes from the esteemed British herbalist and colour-maker George Field.[34] However, as a small-scale firm without the resources to manufacture its own raw ingredients, it relied upon wholesale suppliers for many of its materials (not just pigments but also varnishes and oils), only grinding and mixing colours in-house.

Roberson's reliance on wholesalers made the firm vulnerable to the widespread culture of adulteration and substitution, which thrived upon lengthening supply chains, as dispersed responsibility for the purity of materials made it hard to pinpoint precisely where adulteration had occurred. Manufacturers might use 'extenders' to dilute the purity of colours and economise on production costs (for instance, brick dust was added to madders for this purpose), or colour-makers could bulk out the weight of paint using cheap materials such as sand and chalk.[35] One of the most serious problems was the substitution of genuine expensive pigments with cheaper, less stable alternatives.

The increased availability of synthetic pigments (both organic and inorganic) in this period exacerbated this problem.[36] While 1856 had been a landmark moment for the chemical synthesis of colour with Perkin's ground-breaking discovery of Mauve, the Victorian era was not the first time painters could access synthetic or artificial pigments. Indeed, methods for manipulating colours had been known since antiquity, and new chemical colours, such as Prussian blue, had been available since the eighteenth century.[37] But the major developments in inorganic chemistry precipitated by Perkin's discovery, combined with the industrial infrastructure to manufacture and distribute these substances, made it appear in the nineteenth century that the market was flooded with new chemical colours.

Paint-making was particularly affected by the concurrent technological advances in the dye industry engendered by Perkin's industrialisation of coal-tar or aniline dyes. These synthetic colours, which had revolutionised textile dying, soon migrated into the colourman's trade and were incorporated into artists' oil colours.[38] These brilliant dyes fostered a new era of luminescent artists' colours but were extremely prone to fading. One 1893 painters' manual described how these aniline colours 'are merely stains, and although very bright and fascinating, are totally unfit for the painting of pictures, and soon fade away altogether'.[39] Although some colourmen explicitly advertised their colours as aniline derived, others would illicitly lace their paints with coal-tar dyes to (temporarily) enhance their saturation, leaving them prone to deterioration over time. As Arthur Church – the first professor of chemistry appointed to the Royal Academy – noted in his 1890 artists' manual:

> During the nineteenth century the progress of synthetical [*sic*] chemistry placed at the disposal of the picture-maker a long series of pigments – good, bad and indifferent – so that the chances of introducing dangerous and fugitive colours have been enormously increased. It is to this increase in the number of pigments, and to their greatly extended range of composition ... that one should attribute in great part the frequent deterioration of modern paintings.[40]

Although the burgeoning use of synthetic colour is often characterised as a brightening of the artist's palette because some of these synthetic colours were notoriously garish, it was difficult to distinguish organic and synthetic colours by sight alone.[41] This proved problematic when unscrupulous colourmen either replaced stable, costly pigments with less permanent and trustworthy colourants or used aniline dyes in place of organic materials, with catastrophic effects for the longevity of painted colour. This practice of tampering with the contents of paint, the so-called sophistication of colour, was not necessarily new in the nineteenth century but was understood by artists to be the result of surrendering control of their colours to a commercial trade invested in profiteering rather than quality. From the moment oil colours could be purchased in bladders, painters worried that manufacturers might adulterate their paints to save costs – or, in the words of one painters' manual from 1795, that commercial colours were 'either not genuine, or [...] vilely sophisticated'.[42]

These issues of adulteration and sophistication were most forcefully brought to the attention of Britain's artistic community from the 1880s through the campaigning of the painter William Holman Hunt. An original member of the Pre-Raphaelite Brotherhood, Hunt was the only member of the group who adhered to its principles for the rest of his career. From the foundation of the Brotherhood in 1848, Hunt cultivated a deliberately historicising approach to his materials in explicit rejection of the academic training he received at the Royal Academy Schools in the 1840s. Rather than the rapid, loose handling and fatty paints advocated by 'Sir Sloshua' (as the Brotherhood nicknamed the academy's first president, Joshua Reynolds), Hunt followed the exacting, patient practices of fourteenth- and fifteenth-century painters, meticulously applying thin layers of paint with fine brushstrokes and laying vivid, pure colours over white grounds to give his works an enhanced luminosity. Hunt believed not only that his technique was more sound than that of the academy but also that it conveyed the spiritual value of honest labour, reinforcing the moralising and religious themes of his paintings.[43]

However, Hunt's late career was dominated by perceived threats to these principles from the industrial manufacture of colour. He became acutely aware of the issues of sophistication when in 1873 he experienced great difficulty with a tube of Roberson's orange vermilion while completing work on *The Shadow of Death* (1870–73) (fig. 14).[44] The painting shows Christ as a thewy young man stretching with exhaustion at the end of a hard day labouring in the carpentry workshop, the setting sun illuminating his bronzed skin and simultaneously throwing his shadow

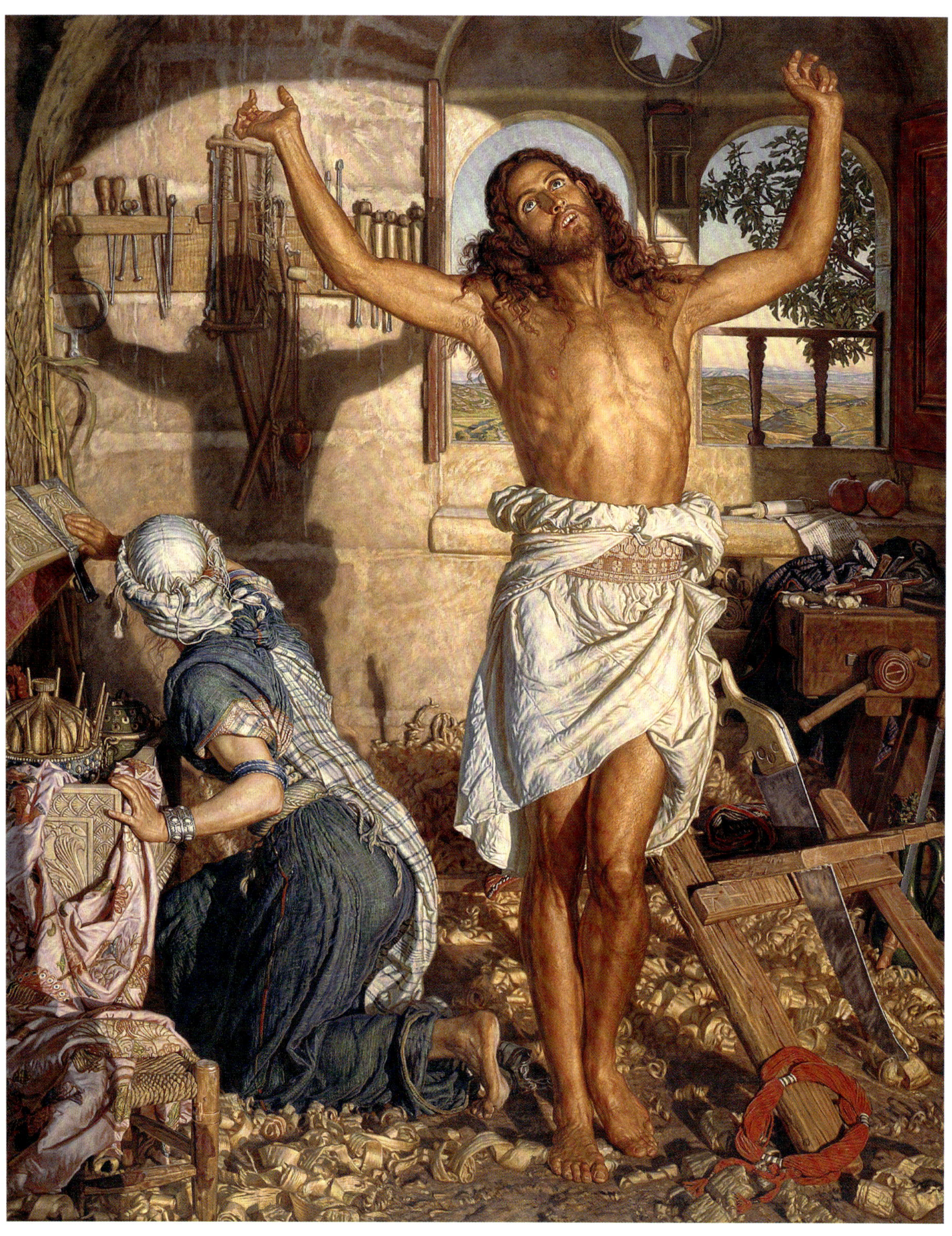

upon the wall behind him, in morbid anticipation of his crucifixion. Hunt selected Roberson's orange vermilion, which he had hoped 'to be particularly delicate', to capture the correct skin tone for Christ.[45] He also purchased madder carmine from the firm, as he noted a little pink was required 'for fair flesh'.[46]

As Shalini Le Gall describes, Hunt was particularly sensitive to the tonality of the flesh in the painting as critics had condemned his previous representations of Christ as too dark.[47] Hunt clearly wanted to convey a flesh tint reflective of rugged, open-air labour performed beneath the sun of the Middle East, but he also wanted to avoid the racialised connotations of Christ appearing as anything other than White. He anticipated that his selection of orange vermilion and Madder Carmine, both mixed with zinc white, should produce the desired effect.

However, upon application these colours rapidly dulled and darkened. Hunt described his dismay in various letters, writing 'I was overwhelmed with confusion at seeing that all my flesh painting went black', claiming it 'blackened so rapidly ... that I nearly went crazy'.[48] Hunt later characterised the unpleasant effects of this discoloration, describing Christ's 'leaden-hued veins', a face that appeared 'dirty and smeary' and skin 'the color of old leather'.[49] Hunt's pejorative description of these dark flesh tones as unclean, unattractive and deathly in appearance clearly reflects perceptions about the superior beauty, cleanliness and vivacity of light skin that permeated the British imperial imagination (taken up at length in the next chapter). But Hunt also registers what emerges in this book as a defining trope of British approaches to colour: that perceived defects with chromatic technologies are articulated as a form of undesirable racial othering. As the colour of skin was consistently used as the benchmark for the chromatic fidelity of any colour process, it was upon the skin that attention to defects, faults and problems centred.

14 William Holman Hunt, *The Shadow of Death*, 1870–73, oil on canvas, 94 × 72.6 cm. Manchester Art Gallery.

Hunt's problem with the skin colours illuminates how easily chromatic discourse tips over into racial discourse. Indeed, looking back to Sargent's *Carnation, Lily, Lily, Rose*, it is clear that the title of the work refers not only to the flowers on display but also to the delicate pink flesh tints of the young girls, literally pink like roses and carnations (the latter a flower whose name derives from the Latin word for 'flesh') and metaphorically white like lilies.[50] Hue, tint and tone were not merely facets of the colour of skin; these optical qualities inflected racial identity, social standing and, for Hunt, moral character. The negative associations Hunt assigns to darkened skin are particularly salient with regard to the depiction of Christ. When Hunt describes his frustration 'at finding flesh which I had thought at first pure and sweet prove dull and heavy in a few days', he reflects the double meanings of purity and sweetness as both aesthetic and moral virtues.[51] For him, the darkening of Christ's skin into what he called a 'dull dirty brown' simultaneously compromised the figure's spiritual and racial purity.[52]

However, Hunt could not believe the fault was with the colour itself; assuming the error must lie with his own technique, for months he continually scraped away and reapplied the paint in the hope the colour might not deteriorate.[53] Eventually suspecting the colours themselves, Hunt sent the orange vermilion for scientific analysis.[54] His speculation that the paint was, in his words, 'adulterated with 10 per cent of villainy', was validated – although it proved to be 10 per cent lead, perhaps suggesting to him the description of Christ's 'leaden-hued veins'.[55] This motivated Hunt to investigate whether the madders had perhaps been laced with synthetic dyes. In a letter in 1875 he wrote, 'I have strong reason to think that the Madders of the market are made of Coal-Tar. I am pursuing this now and won't I come down like a thunderbolt upon the trade if I prove right!'[56] Hunt was indeed proved right about the presence of synthetic aniline dyes in Roberson's madders, although it is unclear whether Roberson adulterated these colours or if the firm received tainted materials from its wholesale suppliers. Nevertheless, Hunt began acquiring samples from every colourman in London to discover how widespread the problem of colour adulteration was, maintaining that only one manufacturer in London sold genuine madders, while the rest peddled fraudulent substitutes.[57]

Hunt pursued this issue for the rest of his career, with the 1880s marking a flurry of campaigning from the artist. Through letters to *The Times* and a lecture delivered at the Society of Arts (reproduced in its journal), Hunt spread the word about the 'pestilential aniline dye'.[58] He advocated for the regulation of artists' materials, better technical training for painters, and the need to catalogue historical and rare pigments lest they should disappear altogether in the current climate of material fraud. Hunt held the commercialisation of the trade and 'wholesale makers' to blame for this lack of quality, as he believed the distance between producer and consumer, mediated by long supply chains and industrialised networks of transport and transaction, meant colour-makers cared little about the reception of their products by artists, whom they would never meet face to face.[59] For Hunt, once 'the real skill of the workshop was handed over to the tradesman', the material safety of painting 'was doomed'.[60] But he also believed painters held responsibility for the declining quality of colour, as their indifference regarding the longevity of their materials encouraged indifference among colourmen. Hunt argued that neither painters nor manufacturers cared if colours deteriorated in the immediate or distant future, as once both had made their profits, they were indifferent to the legacy of their works.

The impacts of Hunt's discoveries upon his own painting practice have been widely explored, most extensively by Carol Jacobi.[61] But his campaign is worth recounting here as it makes evident how concerns of both a moral and a material nature converged on the surface of painting at this time, when the commodification of colour rendered artists vulnerable to deception and fraud in the name of profit. For Hunt, the impurity of paint reflected an impurity of character among both manufacturers and artists, a form of moral deviance shaped by profiteering. As Hunt's intervention makes clear, an aversion to modern oil paints was far from a simplistic rejection of technological modernity, but demonstrated a deep awareness both of how industrial commerce affected the material qualities of paint and of how these changed material qualities reflected the insidious values of the market. These issues seemed particularly acute for painters in Britain, where several of these technological transformations to colour first originated.

Hunt's campaign for pure, unadulterated colour resonated strongly with his friend Watts, whose own concerns about the contents of his paints were exacerbated by Hunt's findings. Watts was particularly concerned about these links between the commodification of paint manufacturing and the resulting damage caused to the longevity, stability and consistency of colour – concerns that intersected with his political and moral objections to industrialisation more broadly. Watts cathected these concerns upon texture, as the most palpable evidence that processes of mass production negatively affected the art of painting. It was therefore through texture that Watts tackled this issue, cultivating an idiosyncratic consistency to his paints to enact a moral objection to the texture of capitalism.

'The Slimy Qualities I So Much Hate'

The unusual texture of Watts's paints puzzled and fascinated contemporary viewers. Critics variously described his strange surfaces as 'rocky, dry, and crumbled', 'heavily forged' and 'corrugated'.[62] Repeatedly, critics noted that the physical qualities of Watts's paints were atypical for the period, a departure from the 'smooth consistency of ordinary oil-paint', as the *Pall Mall Gazette* stated.[63] Some struggled to find a suitable vocabulary to describe the odd materiality of Watts's painting. George Moore found himself unable to capture its effects in words, claiming, 'I can think of nothing else but the rind of Stilton cheese.'[64]

In part, it is the variety of surface textures of Watts's paintings that makes them difficult to characterise – some are gritty and rough like sandpaper, others are powdery and dry resembling chalk, while others have surfaces coated in solid, thick and hard paint piled up in clotted mounds.[65] This coarseness and dryness of surface were the result of Watts's unusual painting technique, an attempt to eradicate oil almost entirely from his practice recounted at length in the biography written by his wife.[66] Watts applied very absorbent grounds to his canvases to suck oil from the paints applied on top and would use especially lean paints (that is, pigments bound in very little oil) to avoid excess grease. Sometimes he applied these paints thinned down with benzene, allowing the weave of the canvas to permeate the surface of the painting, but elsewhere he worked up dense layers of thick impasto. Insisting on each layer drying completely, he left paintings to dry in direct sunlight for weeks in a purpose-built greenhouse in his garden. Once they were dry, he rubbed them with potato or onion to eradicate remaining oiliness, and burnished the paint with a rhinoceros-horn palette knife to harden it before applying more paint.

Watts arrived at this unusual system through a combination of historical revivalism and technical prudence. He had not received rigorous academic training but worked as an assistant in a sculptor's studio from an early age and attended the Royal Academy Schools sporadically before an extended stay in Italy in his twenties, a period he considered his true artistic education.[67] This time, between 1843 and 1847, spent principally in Florence, sparked his lifelong engagement with the Italian Renaissance, enabling him to study Italian painting and sculpture first hand. Historical frescoes fascinated Watts and he studied the technique intensely, but the Venetian school of oil painting also entranced him. His own methods were principally derived from his studies of Renaissance painting and fresco technique, facilitated by a newly available body of technical information on historical painting methods.[68]

Watts's travels in Italy in the 1840s confirmed for him that the most enduring works of art were those displaying little gloss or sheen: monumental frescoes with their matte surfaces and sixteenth-century Venetian painting, particularly the late work of Titian, with its dry, open brushwork. His close friend and biographer Emilie Isabel Barrington described how the painter intentionally modelled his practice on Titian's late style, which he studied through a translated account of the painter's technique.[69] Many elements of Watts's practice are indeed attributable to his reverence for Titian: his slow pace, allowing the weave of the canvas to enliven the surface; the dryness of the paints skimmed across the canvas; and the ambiguous degree of finish.[70] But, as conservator Carol Willoughby describes, his method also operated as a form of fresco executed in oil paint, as Watts (mistakenly) believed his absorbent grounds would operate like the wet plaster in fresco, binding the colours permanently to the support.[71]

It would be easy then to resolve the material idiosyncrasy of Watts's paintings by suggesting these surfaces are symptomatic of his nostalgic, historicising style, evidence of his desire to emulate the works of the Italian Renaissance that he most admired.[72] However, the appearance of Watts's paintings cannot simply be understood as historical revivalism, and scholars primarily understand his use of especially coarse, dry colours as an attempt to ensure the material safety of his paintings.[73] Watts regarded oil as the enemy of stable painting because it was often responsible for the cracking and yellowing of a painting's surface. Watts had direct experience of these problems when his early works suffered extensive craquelure due to paint drying insufficiently between layers (fig. 15).

Through these early technical problems and his failed attempts at creating frescoes, Watts became particularly attentive to the durability of his materials.[74] He would only use colours he believed were absolutely stable, frequently enquiring about the suitability of certain pigments with his supplier, Winsor & Newton. He corresponded regularly with Henry Newton, the artist who co-founded the firm, and subsequently with Scott Taylor, its scientific director. Watts requested that Winsor & Newton should only offer him colours that were '<u>quite pure and permanent</u>', noting that 'if I ask for any that are not in this category <u>never</u> send them'.[75]

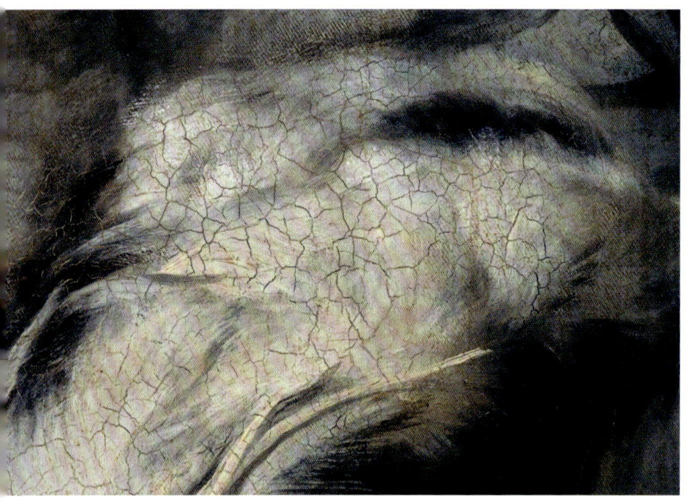

Watts was deeply aware of the culture of substitution and adulteration rife in the colour trade, not least through Hunt's campaign, and explicitly avoided colours prone to fading or tampering. In one instance Taylor had to convince Watts about a sample of rose madder, noting that 'it is so pure and vivid that had I not made it myself from pure Madder root I should have felt convinced that it had been doctored up with an aniline dye'.[76] However, Watts was most concerned about the oily character of industrially manufactured paints. From 1871 he began to request colours of 'a stiffer or at least more solid nature' than those he typically received from the firm, insisting that the 'colour should be … as dry as may be convenient'.[77] He hoped for colours 'free from the slimy qualities I so much hate', qualities that were the direct result of machine-grinding and tube storage.[78] Newton tried to highlight the benefits of more moist, pliable paints to Watts, explaining that when 'pigments are very, very finely ground in oil till they assume the smoothness of butter, the oil is not so likely to leave the pigments and float … which was the case before the powerful grinding machinery used by Winsor & Newton was invented'.[79] Yet Watts insisted his pigments must be ground to an especially coarse consistency, with very little oil.

These hand-ground paints became known as Watts's 'Special' or 'Stiff' colours, and they helped the painter to produce the rough surfaces contemporary viewers found so noteworthy.[80] Taylor described how he prepared these colours by hand with 'a small model-mill' in his laboratory; he wrote to Watts to endorse this technique, noting that 'modern colors, in many cases, have all the life taken out of them by being ground perfectly smooth and buttery and … in this way the most precious qualities of pigments are now lost'.[81] However, Watts's consistent demands that his colours be ground ever more coarsely and with decreasing amounts of oil meant they eventually became so intractable he could not work them on the canvas, and he admitted in a letter to Taylor that 'we have a little over shot the mark'.[82] He found conventional paintbrushes ineffectual when faced with these recalcitrant paints, and instead deployed alternative instruments (palette knives, paper knives, toothbrush handles and his fingers) or used brushes worn down to rigid stumps, writing to Winsor & Newton asking for brushes 'as stiff as if made of wire'.[83] According to Barrington, Watts claimed that, of all the tools for applying paint, 'the best of all … was the finger', and his habit of applying these stiff paints with his hands betrays his dual identity as a painter-sculptor.[84] Indeed, he explained to Taylor that he wanted to use his colours 'almost like modelling clay'.[85]

Watts's painting *The Sower of the Systems* (*c.*1902) renders visible his painting practice, whereby artistic creation is presented as physical work done with the hands (fig. 16). Through this dynamic figure, draped in robes not unlike the artist's own painting smock, Watts parallels God's fabrication of the universe with his own act of pushing paint manually around the canvas. Watts uses the muscular stance of the body, whose torso twists dramatically in an exaggerated lunge that spans almost the entire width of the canvas, to highlight the physical effort required to

15 George Frederic Watts, *A Wounded Heron* (detail), 1837, oil on canvas, 91.4 × 71.1 cm. Watts Gallery Trust.

16 George Frederic Watts, *The Sower of the Systems*, c.1902, oil on canvas, 122.6 × 91.4 cm. Art Gallery of Ontario, Toronto.

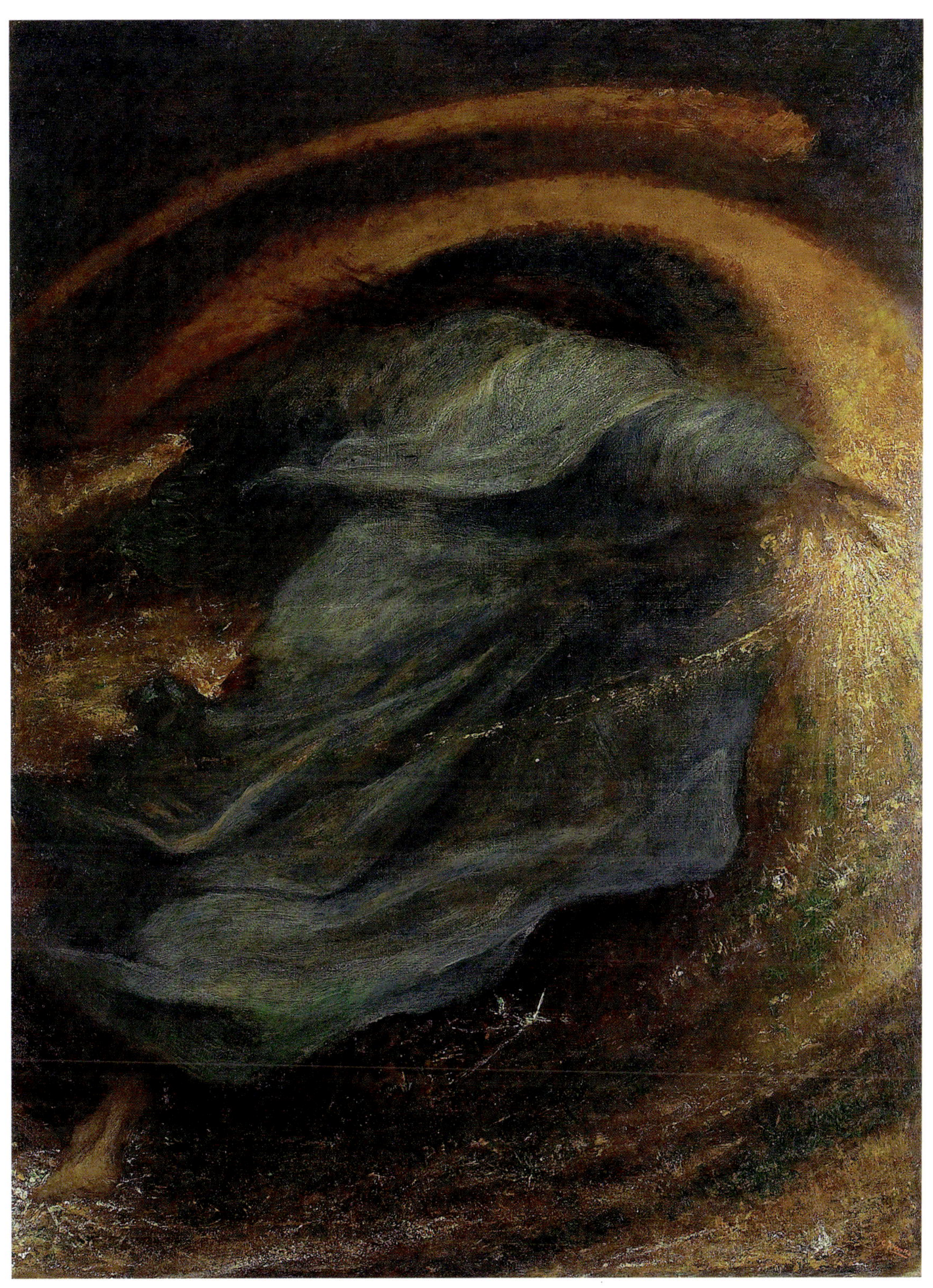

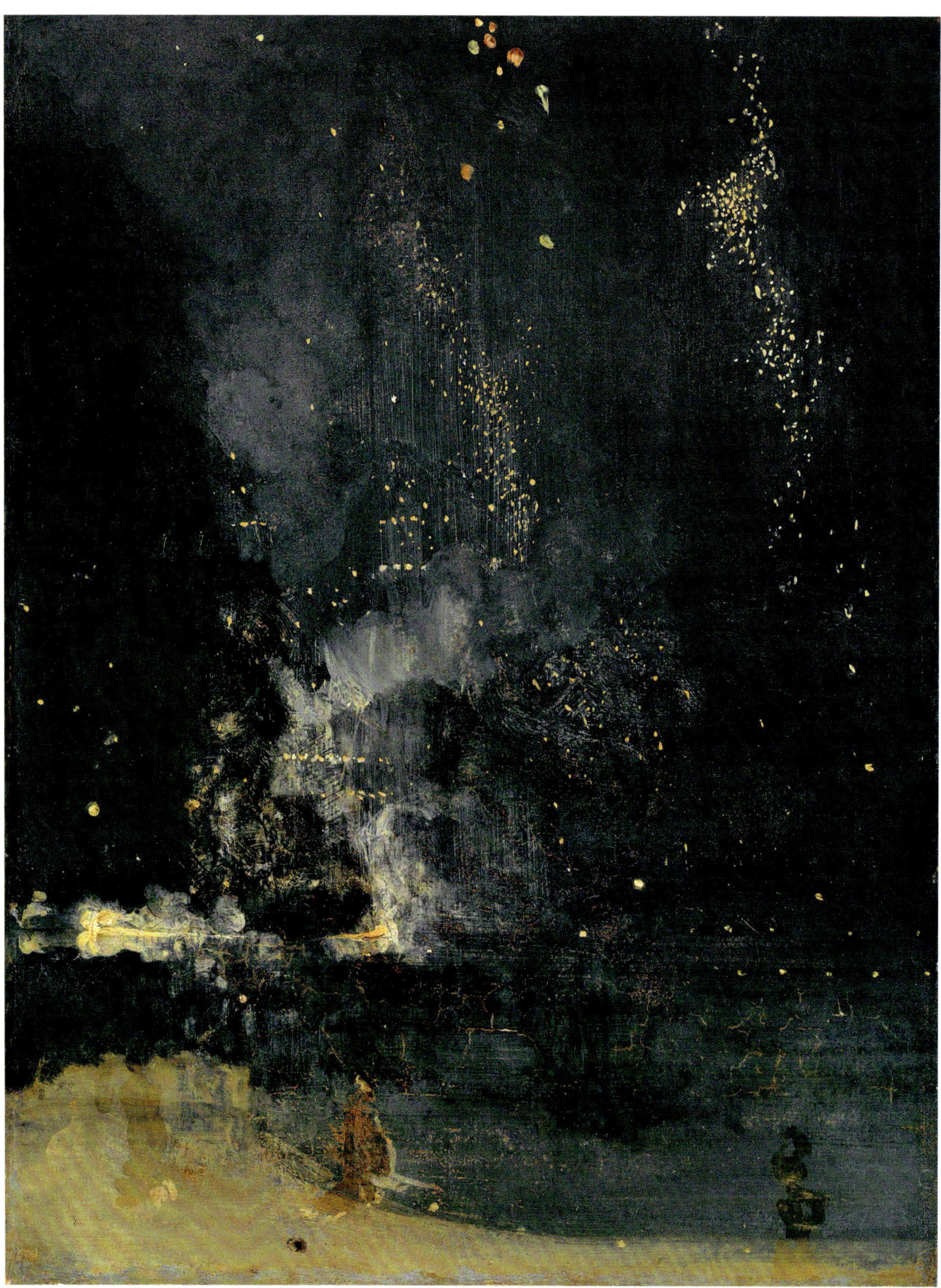

marshal his materials into a semblance of order and meaning.[86] With fingers outspread and taut, and arms at full extension, the figure summons every ounce of strength to drag and push the stuff of creation in looping orbits through the air with his hands. Paint is treated here as a physical substance – a raw material that must be manipulated and modelled with the hands in much the same way Watts worked with clay in his sculptural practice.[87]

The work also highlights the gendered nature of chromatic labour at this time. By emphasising the physical strength demanded by the act of creation, *The Sower of the Systems* not only invites a comparison with Watts's practice of labouring to apply his coarsely ground paints but also imbues the technique with an enhanced sense of rugged masculinity. This affiliation between essentialised ideas of masculine physicality and the rough, heavily worked surface of the canvas stood in stark contrast to the supposed effeminacy implied by the so-called licked surface of academic painting at this time. This finish was most famously associated with the work of Frederic Leighton, whose glassy, perfectly smooth paintings drew profoundly gendered criticism, variously described as conveying 'a peculiar look of feebleness of the sugar-candy kind', with one reviewer linking its 'qualities of softness [and] smoothness' with 'languor, luxuriousness and effeminacy'.[88] While Chapter Three explores the gendered connotations of working with colour more extensively, this link between the slick polish of Leighton's work (which effaced any evidence of the brush) and an implied effeminacy (connected to physical weakness and delicacy of touch) illuminates how for contemporary viewers, the gritty solidity of Watts's heavy paints and their laboured application on the canvas conveyed a masculine vigour. But the heavy impasto and dry scumbled paint here also speak to a wider ethics and politics of materiality in the late nineteenth century. These dry paints, harder to produce and apply than industrially made colours, put Watts's practice into dialogue with broader concerns about the relationship between art, labour and morality in Britain at this time.

17 James Abbott McNeill Whistler, *Nocturne in Black and Gold, the Falling Rocket*, *c.*1875, oil on panel, 60.3 × 46.7 cm. Detroit Institute of Arts.

The Moral Aesthetics of *Mammon*

At the very moment Watts began requesting his stiff colours in the 1870s, John Ruskin was involved in a public dispute about the liquidity of paint. Of course, Ruskin's notorious accusation that James Abbott McNeill Whistler's painting *Nocturne in Black and Gold: The Falling Rocket* (fig. 17) was akin to charging 'two hundred guineas for flinging a pot of paint in the public's face' is not typically understood as a tirade against thin paints in themselves.[89] This comment, which provoked the infamous libel trial of 1878, was an invective aimed at a market-driven culture in which artists minimised effort and maximised profits, earning sums disproportionate to the labour expended on their paintings.[90] However, the liquidity of Whistler's paints in Ruskin's metaphor – so runny it must be stored in pots not tubes, so thin it can be thrown like water – is vital to his argument.[91] For Ruskin, the ease with which Whistler's paints could be manipulated spoke to the debasement of painting, as to Ruskin, a work of art that involved no 'work' could never truly be art at all. This link between texture and the morality of labour is vital to understanding Watts's use of coarse paints. For Watts, the greater labour his colourman invested in grinding his colours was replicated in the extra effort required to work them on the canvas, endowing his materials with a moral potency he leveraged to reinforce the political messages of his paintings.

Watts's understanding of artistic labour as a moral and ethical issue was profoundly informed by his social and intellectual circle, which counted leftist political activists, social reformers, and socialists proper among his friends and sitters, including William Morris, Walter Crane, Thomas Carlyle and

Ruskin himself.[92] Contemporary critics noted the impact of these thinkers upon Watts, describing how 'echoes of Carlyle … of Ruskin, seem to haunt all his work'.[93] Watts was deeply committed to their shared belief in the dignity of labour and its potential for spiritual nourishment, and was similarly troubled by the danger posed to these values by the dehumanising culture of work under industrial modernity. Watts, like these contemporaries, was particularly concerned about the industrialisation of manufacturing, believing that purely in the name of profit, mechanisation and automation both eroded the quality of the resulting products, as well as the workers' pleasure and pride in their work. Watts expounded these views through a series of essays he published in the 1880s, making explicit his belief that artisanal labour served the spiritual wellbeing of workers while mechanisation, in the service of financial gain, eroded their humanity.[94]

His 1889 essay 'The National Position of Art' powerfully demonstrates Watts's indebtedness to Ruskin's values, where he decries the fact that beauty and human decency are consistently scarified to convenience and profit. He protests against the displacement 'of the skilled workman's eye and hand' by 'mechanical aid', claiming that 'machinery is the most deadly foe to art and beauty'.[95] His emphasis that 'heart and conscience, is never absent from hand-work, however rude, and is never found in machine-work, however perfect' begins to illuminate the political and moral significance of his insistence upon the stiffly hand-ground paints that were so arduous to apply.[96]

Undoubtedly *The Stones of Venice* (1851–53) tied together the ethics of labour and the aesthetics of colour for Watts, as Ruskin's volumes both expounded the beauty of Venetian colouring through ekphrastic prose and exalted the nobility of the labour that produced them, contrasting the dignity of the gothic Venetian craftsman with the 'signs of slavery' found in industrial England.[97] In the most famous passage of *The Stones of Venice*, titled 'The Nature of the Gothic', where Ruskin potently expounds his belief in the ethics of labour, he explicitly mentions colour-making, noting that 'the painter should grind his own colours; the architect work in the mason's yard with his men; the master-manufacturer be himself a more skillful operative than any man in his mills'.[98] For Watts, Ruskin politicised his existing love of Venetian colour, moving his appreciation of Titian out of the purely aesthetic sphere and into a moral realm.

Watts's conviction about Ruskin's principles of ethical labour encouraged him to support the establishment of the Guild of St George, a school Ruskin founded to teach traditional craftsmanship in opposition to the onslaught of mass-produced, factory-made goods. Offering Ruskin a tenth of his annual income for the project, Watts described his support as a 'protest against Mammon worship'.[99] Mammon, a personification of wealth and greed described in the New Testament, appeared frequently in Watts's writing, as he saw Mammon as the new god of a contemporary wealth-obsessed nation.[100] His wife recalled that Watts once joked that he should sculpt a statue of Mammon in Hyde Park, where 'he hoped his worshippers would be at least honest enough to bow the knee publicly to him'.[101]

Watts's description of Ruskin's project as a protest against Mammonism underscores his belief that the moral production of art and the accumulation of material wealth were mutually exclusive. Watts maintained that 'while Mammon, the deity of the age … cold and unlovely, without dignity or magnificence, the meanest of the powers to whom incense has ever been offered, sits supreme, [then] great art, as a child of the nation, cannot find a place; the seat is not wide enough for both'.[102] Watts's *Mammon, Dedicated to His Worshippers* (1884–85), held in the collection of the Tate Gallery (fig. 18), and the smaller work by the same name (fig. 19) at the Watts Gallery in Compton (c.1885), literalise this sentiment through their subject matter, but the smaller canvas also enacts a potent critique of Mammonism through the very coarseness of its colours.

Its composition modelled on Renaissance papal portraits, the painting depicts Mammon seated in glory upon his skull-topped throne. Cradling money purses in his lap, a common attribute found in allegories of avarice, he crushes 'humanity' (personified as nude, White figures – one male, one female) beneath his hefty feet and monstrous hands.[103] With a meaty neck, heavy brow and indifferent frown, his gargantuan proportions give him a demonic presence. Mammon wears a golden crown decorated with coins and sprouts ass's ears like those of King Midas, whose wish to transform everything he touched into gold rapidly became a curse. Apollo punished Midas with these unsightly ears because the king preferred the sound of Pan's pipe to the music of the god's lyre and was therefore evidently deaf to the true beauty of art, preferring the earthly and coarse to the heavenly and transcendent.

This unusual conflation of Mammon and Midas undoubtedly alludes to Carlyle's 1843 tract *Past and Present*, where the author rails against 'Midas-eared Mammonism', comparing the present condition of industrial England to that of the cursed, avaricious king: 'full of wealth in every kind, yet dying of inanition'.[104] He calls for 'giant LABOUR … noble LABOUR' to take its rightful place as 'King of this Earth' upon 'the highest throne' thereby 'leaving Mammonism … on the lower steps'.[105] Watts inverts this hierarchy to reflect his dismal view of contemporary British society, showing Mammon triumphant while bodies litter the steps below. Although the location of the painting is indistinct, a theatrical red curtain lifts to reveal the fires of hell burning in the distance, further imbuing the work with a religious didacticism.

The smaller painting initially appears to be a preparatory sketch for the larger canvas due to its loose handling, its unfinished quality and the small difference in composition: the bound foot. This detail reveals that Mammon suffers from gout, an ailment precipitated by gluttonous overindulgence, often represented as a bloated man with bandaged feet recumbent in an armchair. However, the smaller work has frequently been exhibited as an autonomous painting, and art historians have suggested that it delivers a more biting critique than the larger Tate version.[106]

Watts worked on several versions of the same painting simultaneously, selecting one for exhibition but continuing to work on the others endlessly, considering each a different experimental solution to the same formal and conceptual problems. Indeed, Watts's wife recorded in her diary that the artist was still 'piling up the hideousness of *Mammon*' a year after he first exhibited the larger work.[107] The distinctive handling of paint in the Compton *Mammon* is therefore not a sign of its preparatory status but integral to its meaning.

In comparison to the Tate canvas, the plasticity of the Compton painting is remarkable, as Watts pushes the expressive potential of his stiff colours to the limit. Mammon's gold brocade convulses with dense brush marks where the paint is raised into blunt ridges, replicating the effect of folds in the fabric through its weightiness (fig. 20). The knee of Mammon's outstretched leg is a maelstrom of thick, uneven colour, piled up in heavy clots (fig. 21). Watts creates the impression of swirling drapery at Mammon's feet by skimming a brush loaded with dry colour across the canvas, leaving behind broken dashes of green paint (fig. 22). The highlights of the crown are picked out in scumbled areas of white, like beads resting on the canvas's surface (fig. 23). The female figure's skin is rough and caked, evidently the uppermost application of many layers of paint beneath (fig. 24).

Varnishing has unfortunately lent the painting precisely the glossy finish Watts wanted to avoid. Watts was ambivalent about varnish, valuing its protective capacity but loathing its sheen, and he experimented with additives to reduce its reflective qualities.[108] It is therefore difficult to ascertain whether Watts planned the varnishing of the Compton *Mammon*. Yet, unlike in many of his other paintings, which have been coated in thick homogenising layers of varnish by subsequent collectors and restorers, by no means does the varnish here detract from the painting's overall crustiness, instead giving it an almost unpleasantly haptic quality.[109] The cragginess and crumbliness of these paints, which so perplexed contemporary viewers, seem to find their true meaning here, as the

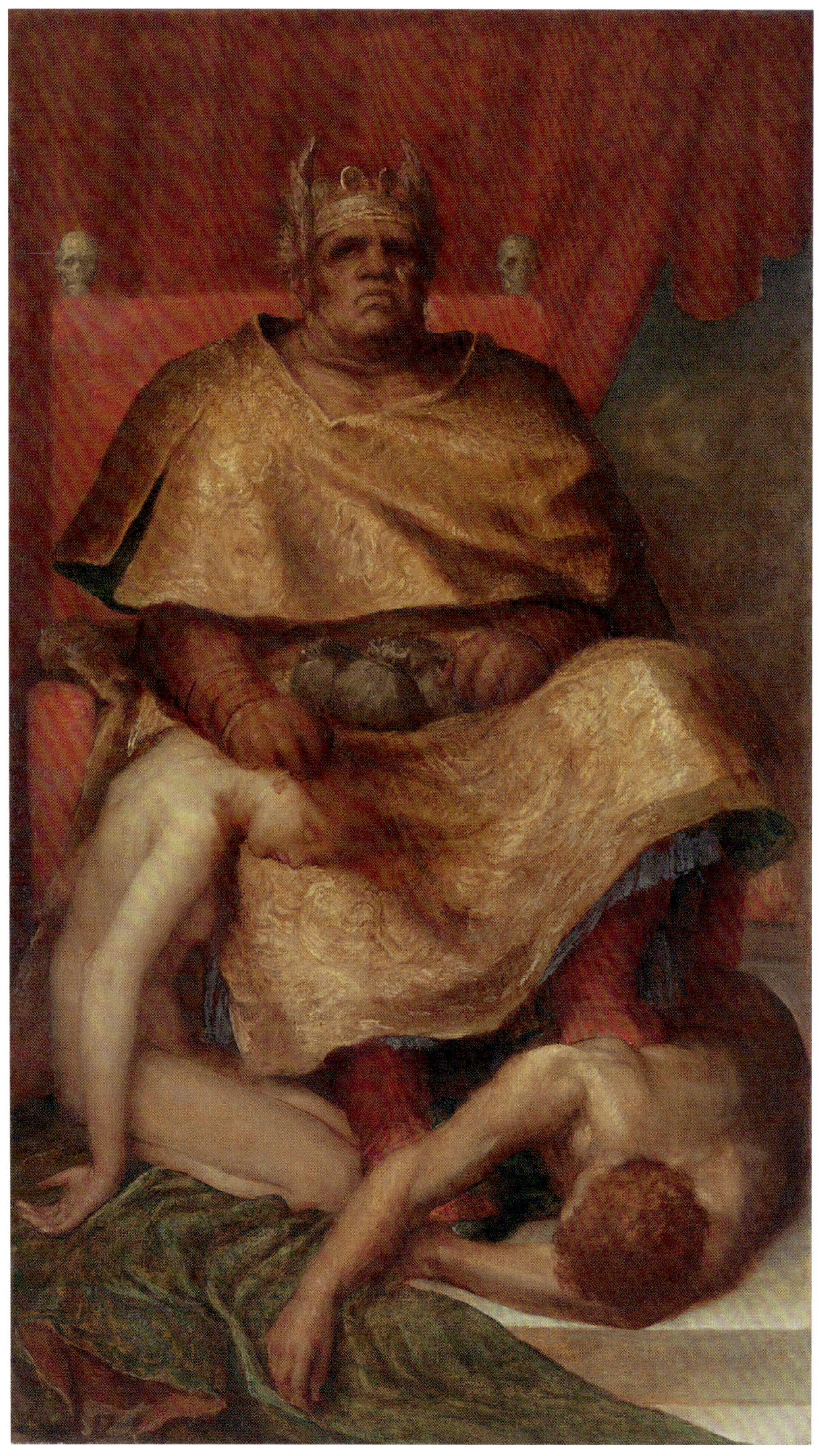

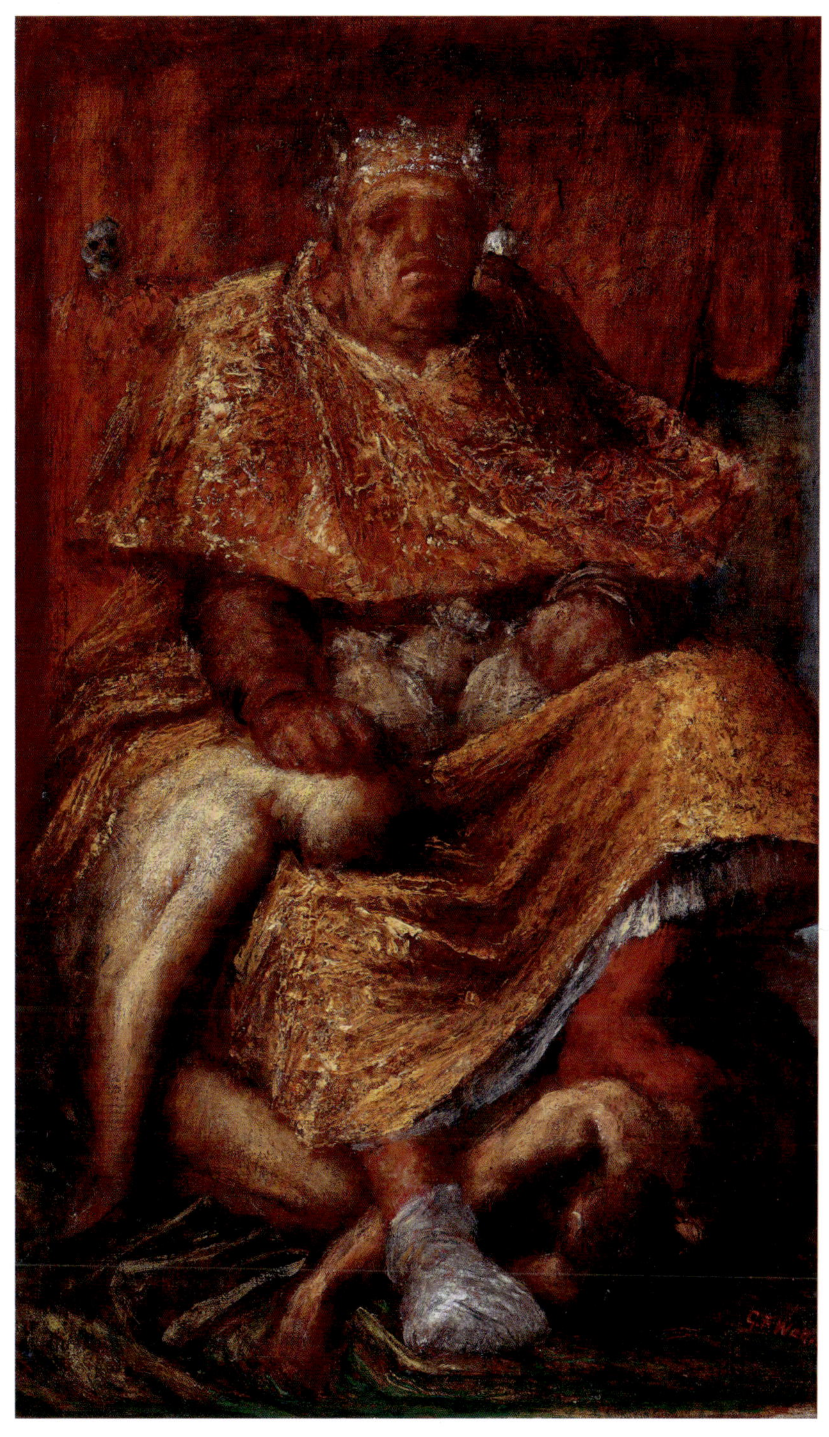

18 George Frederic Watts, *Mammon, Dedicated to His Worshippers*, 1884–85, oil on canvas, 183 × 106 cm. Tate.

19 George Frederic Watts, *Mammon, Dedicated to His Worshippers*, *c.*1885, oil on canvas, 53.3 × 30.5 cm. Watts Gallery Trust.

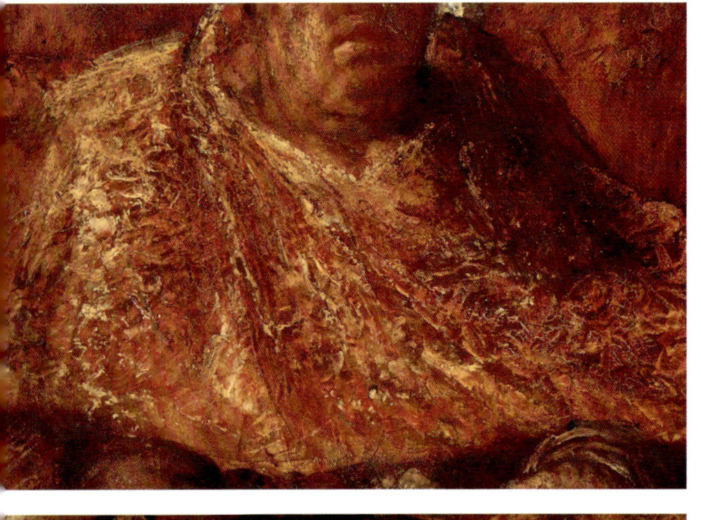

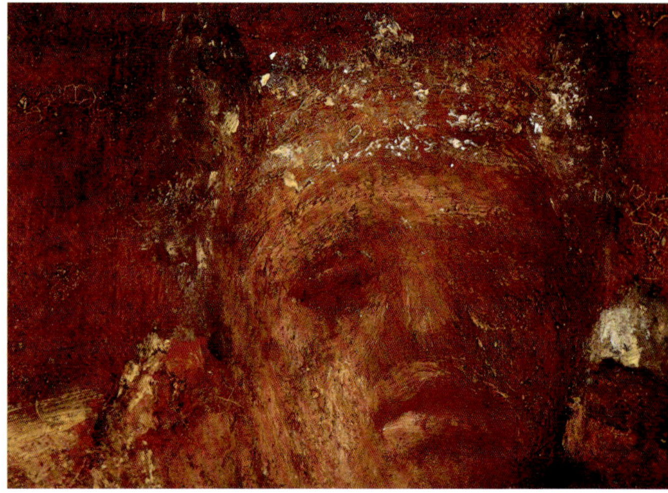

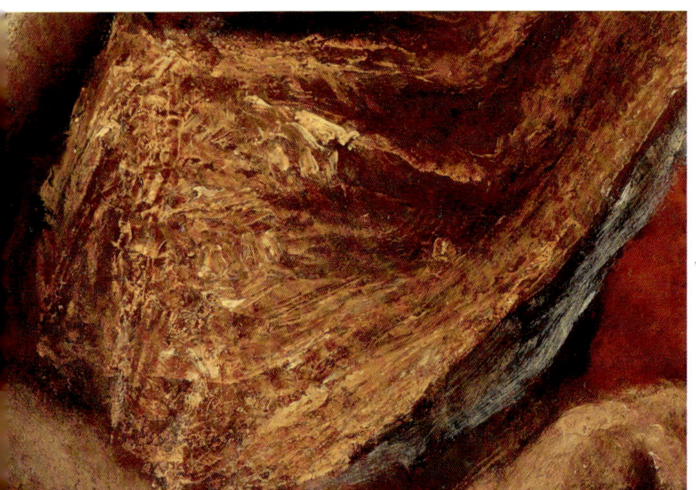

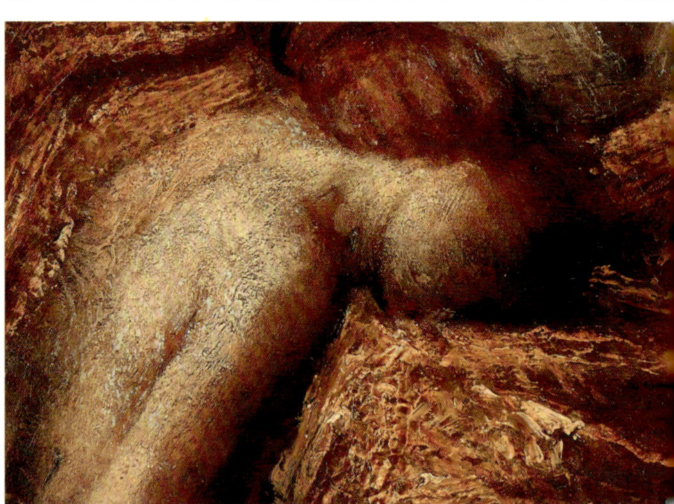

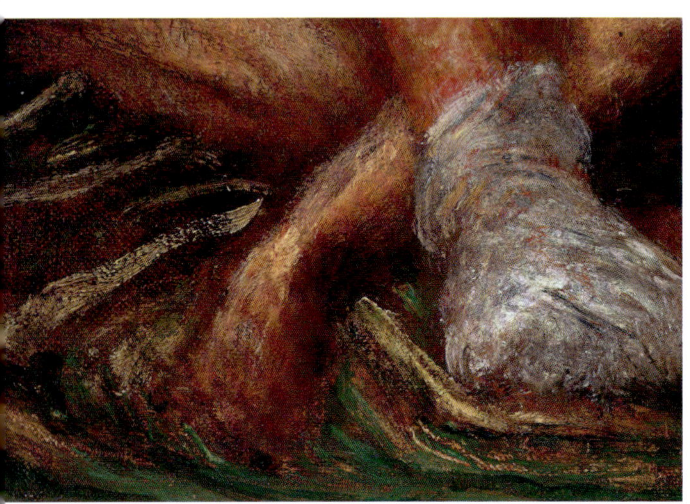

20 Detail of fig. 19 showing gold brocade.

21 Detail of fig. 19 showing knee.

22 Detail of fig. 19 showing swirling drapery at feet.

23 Detail of fig. 19 showing highlights on crown.

24 Detail of fig. 19 showing female figure's skin.

crude, unrefined surface of the painting heightens the grotesqueness of the subject. The texture of these paints imparts an affective power to the work, as Mammon seems all the more repugnant for his rough handling, offering a true rebuke to the idealised, beautiful effects possible with glossy, slick, commercial oils. While Watts certainly exploited the decidedly unappealing consistency of his paints to convey Mammon's 'unloveliness', he also enabled his materials to enact the anti-capitalist argument of the painting.

By showcasing the very stiffness of his artisanally made paints in a work that critiques the evils of industrial capitalism, Watts made clear the link between his aesthetics and his ideology. Here, the coarseness, dryness and density of these colours render visible the labour involved in both their manufacture and their application. They manifest both the demanding, time-consuming technique of hand-grinding the pigments and the taxing work of applying them to the canvas. Some painters squeezed their colours directly from the tube or exploited their paints' pliability to work in a quick, spontaneous manner, producing a lively impasto (as demonstrated in Vollon's *Mound of Butter*), but the plasticity of Watts's work imparts a very different temporality to his painting. These colours evidence the dignified labour of applying colour slowly, carefully and arduously, thereby activating the political agenda of the painting's subject.

It is possible to understand the Compton painting as a damning indictment both of the corrupting effects of capitalism upon society in general and of the malignant effects of industrial modernity upon painting more specifically. To do so makes a more nuanced and historically precise reading of its iconography possible. The double valence of Mammon as Midas is a particularly fitting critique of the contemporary colour trade, as it pointedly highlights the perils of alchemical desire. Watts parallels Midas's ruinous cupidity with that of unscrupulous colourmen, who also wished to transform base materials into more expensive substances. Watts suggests that just as Midas starved from lack of food or drink as he turned everything he touched into gold, colourmen would bring about similarly disastrous effects in their attempts to turn coal-tar into ultramarine, brick dust into madders and sand into pure white paint. The fate of Midas operates as a warning here to those who similarly seek wealth through a debased form of transubstantiation. The fact that the painting is dedicated to Mammon's worshippers makes clear its mode of address as a cautionary tale to those who do not heed its message.

The moneybags in Mammon's lap, as previously noted, are a long-standing feature of allegories of avarice found throughout the history of Christian art, typically signalling the bearer's miserly spirit as well as the immorality of materialism (fig. 25). The purses here, of course, demonstrate Mammon's sinful accumulation of wealth through the sacrifice of virtue and innocence. Yet these plump purses also bear a striking resemblance to bladders of paint, which were similarly tried with string at the neck (fig. 26). This visual slippage between paint and money invites us to imagine further ways in which the painting could reflect upon the corrupting influence of capitalism upon art. Because bladders marked the first moment when painters surrendered control of their materials to a commercial industry, the money-purse-as-paint-bladder suggests a damning equivalence between colour and capital. This visual echo invokes the avaricious colour-makers who treated paint as a means to riches rather than improving its production for the benefit of art, which Watts understood as a crucial tool for social progress. This richly suggestive parallel evocatively counsels against the conflation of paint and profit, upon which Mammon's kingdom is based.

The physicality of the smaller painting, its grotesque plasticity worked as much with the fingers as with the brush, invites us to wonder whether Watts considered the work as a kind of sculpture made in paint. Perhaps he viewed this canvas, which is much more corporeal than the larger work of the same name, as the public monument to Mammon he quipped he would erect, a physical testament to Mammon's growing cult in modern Britain. If modern oil paints embodied the texture of capitalism, then Watts's painting here embodied something altogether different – a moral aesthetics, rendered

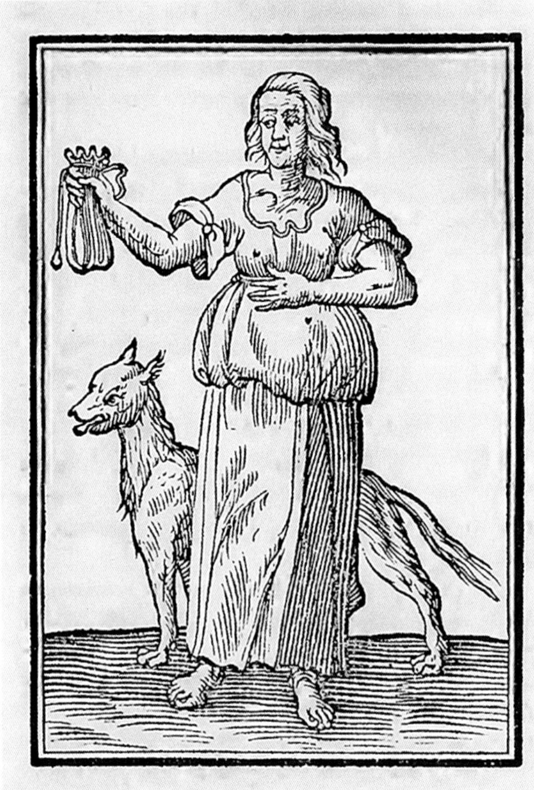

25 Cesare Ripa, *Iconologia, of uytbeeldingen des verstands* (Amsterdam: Pers, 1644), p. 169. Collection of the Sterling and Francine Clark Art Institute Library.

26 Illustration of a paint bladder from Pierre Louis Bouvier, *Manuel des jeunes artistes et amateurs en peinture*, 2nd edn (Paris: F. G. Levrault, 1832), pl. III, fig. M. Collection of the Getty Research Institute.

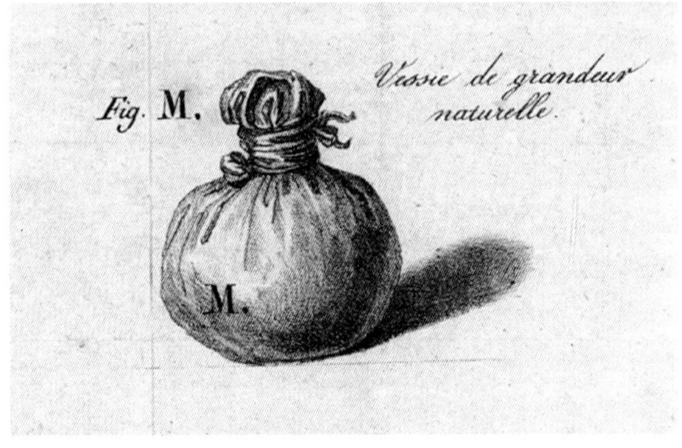

visible and physical through the very materiality of his paints.[110]

Comparing *Mammon* to *Carnation, Lily, Lily, Rose*, these two paintings could not seem more distinct. Sargent's work embraces the possibilities of modern oil paint to produce a radiant celebration of the contemporary social world. By combining his chemical colours with gelled megilp, Sargent enabled his artificially pigmented paints to flow freely under his brush, dry rapidly on the canvas and lend a glossy sheen to the finished work.[111] Despite the painting's bucolic setting, the work's rapidity of execution (facilitated through its materials) and the vivacity and intensity of its sensory impressions (generated by its artificial hues) seem to imbue it with a privileged relationship to the accelerated, technologised and synthesised culture of modern life. On the other hand, Watts's painting – a didactic mythological allegory captured in dry, crumbly paints, painstaking applied – captures little of the vivacity and lightness that imbues Sargent's painting with its modern atmosphere. Watts rejects every expedience exploited by Sargent, refuting the moral and spiritual corruption he believed accompanied such conveniences.

Yet the juxtaposition of these near contemporary works of art, made using paints manufactured by the same firm, illuminates a crucial point: the modernity of colour was by no means communicated purely by a particular palette or style of painting. Although idiosyncratic, Watts's approach demonstrates an equal investment in and cognisance of the contours and conditions of the modern experience in Britain, an awareness he politicised through his colours. Watts's colours clearly had a profound political gravity, in addition to their dense, textural materiality. While Watts's work certainly does not participate in the formal language of modernism in the same manner as Sargent's, his painting evidences a spirited engagement with the terms of modernity through colour itself.

From works that occupied the most elite circles of Victorian visual culture, Chapter Two now turns to objects in a radically different sphere of cultural production: print advertising. The objects under consideration are equally engaged in questions of profit-making, colour and industrialisation, yet they demonstrate a very different approach from that expressed by Watts. While Watts used colour to articulate his distaste for commercial profiteering, the next chapter considers how colour also became a tool for a particular imperial form of racialised commodity capitalism contingent upon techniques of mass production and consumption.

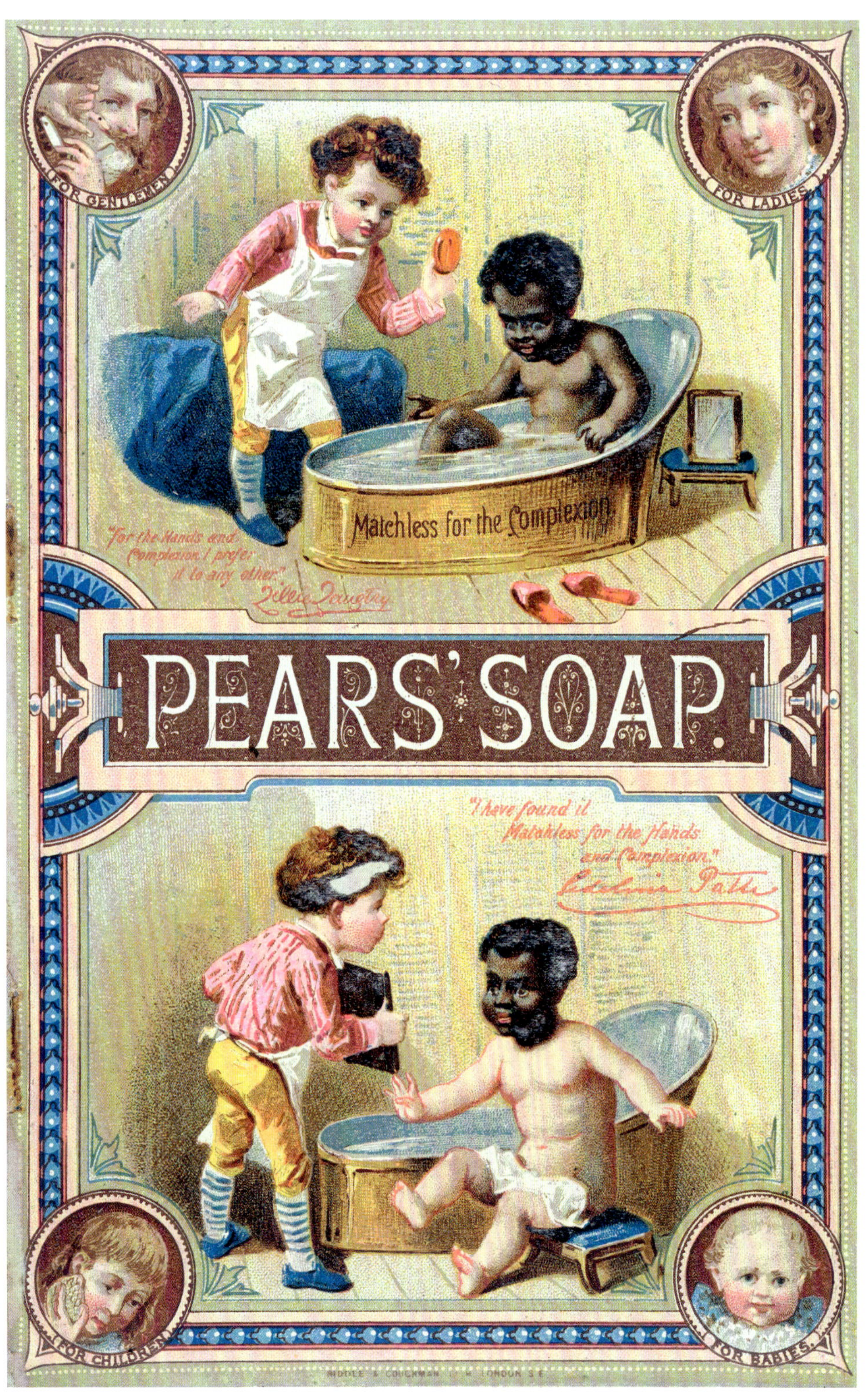

27 Pears' soap advertisement, 1889, chromolithograph. Wellcome Collection, London.

2

THE COMPLEXION OF THE CHROMOLITHOGRAPH

Colouring Skin in Late Victorian Print

A promotion for Pears' soap printed in 1889 illuminates the multiple functions of colour in Victorian advertising (fig. 27). It presents two scenes bifurcated in the centre by the Pears brand name, framed with an ornamental border rendered in various hues of pink, russet and blue. In the top scene a White child, dressed in an apron as though playing barber, offers soap to a nude Black child seated in a golden bath.[1] The White child is dressed in a striking outfit comprising a magenta shirt, yellow britches and blue-and-white-striped socks, a combination whose gaudiness is exacerbated by his mop of auburn ringlets and rosy cheeks. The soap he brandishes, captured in rich orange, appears like a bar of glowing amber, forming a chromatic counterpoint to the puce slippers the Black child has discarded on the floor. The bathing child stares with some trepidation into the grey-blue surface of the water, but, in the lower panel, this expression changes into shock.

Now seated on a stool beside the bath, its blue upholstery replacing the pink slippers that previously occupied the spot, the Black child nearly topples over with amazement, his arms and legs akimbo. Dressed in nothing but a small white towel, revealing bare arms, legs and chest, the child is alarmed to see his reflection in the mirror held up by the other child, which reveals a dramatic change to the colour of his skin. While his (presumably unwashed) face retains its original coloration, the rest of his body, cleansed with the soap, has changed from a warm brown tone to a creamy peach hue. The message of the advertisement is unambiguous: Pears' soap is such a powerful cleansing agent it can even wash Black skin White.

Colour is used here to catch the consumer's eye, not least as the advertisement employs such bright, garish tones. Colour was believed to seduce the viewer, impose itself upon their mind, and render the advertiser's messages more powerful and memorable than when consumed in black and white. The glowing bar of soap, the colourful clothing and furnishings, and the ornamental border all serve to enhance the visual allure of the page and draw the consumer's interest. Yet it is also the different skin tones on display here that forge part of the advertisement's chromatic appeal. In fact, the entire premise of the advertisement is that the soap enables a dramatic chromatic transformation, changing the colour of the child's skin and, with it, his racial identity.

Conflating Black skin with dirt and poor hygiene, and White skin with purity and cleanliness, the advertisement's meaning relies upon racist assumptions about the virtues of these skin colours, where Blackness is framed as an undesirable layer of grime that should be removed, and Whiteness as the appealing, immaculately cleansed surface beneath. This was a highly conventional theme that appeared in soap advertisements across Europe and America at the time and that had its roots, as Jean Michel Massing has explored, in the long iconographic tradition of 'washing the Ethiopian'.[2] Derived from Aesop's fables, this proverb suggested that to try to wash the colour from Black skin was to labour in vain or attempt the impossible. It was often linked to the biblical passage about the immutable nature of morality in Jeremiah 13.23: 'Can the Ethiopian change his skin or the leopard his spots?' Inverting this centuries-old tradition, these soap advertisements did not depict washing Black skin as useless but instead suggested that through purchasing the right brand of soap, transformations of a hygienic, aesthetic and moral character could indeed be possible, metaphorised as a transformation from Blackness to Whiteness.

Yet, while these skin tones may be referred to as 'Black' and 'White', these terms are racial taxonomies and not actual hues; they are socially constructed and culturally contingent, reducing a wide spectrum of skin pigmentation to an essentialised and abstract binary. The reductive nature of these terms is made abundantly clear by the materiality of the print itself and its striking use of colour. The 'White' skin here is by no means the same hue as the white apron or white towel, and the 'Black' skin is captured in many colours, but none of them are black. White skin is represented through a number of hues – fuchsia, eggshell, buff and coral – while the Black skin is rendered in hues of chestnut, ash, lemon and blue. While colour was a vital tool for advertisers, used to charm and attract consumers, it evidently also gave printers an expanded chromatic vocabulary through which to explore and exploit racial difference as part of these advertising campaigns, capturing skin tones with a new degree of chromatic variety that added to the visual impact of the print and the potency of its racist message.

This advertisement has been subject to a great deal of scrutiny by historians of Victorian visual culture, understood as a paradigmatic example of what Anne McClintock calls the 'commodity racism' that characterised advertising of the late nineteenth century, particularly in Britain.[3] This new cultural form emerged in the second half of the nineteenth century through the promotion of imperial commodities – those goods whose production was contingent upon the extractive economy of empire and the industrial infrastructure of domestic manufacturing. The confluence of colonial expansion and industrialised production at this time, particularly the intensified commercial exploitation of Africa from the 1880s, saw major growth and diversification of the kinds of consumer goods available for purchase in Britain, with the markets for products such as soap, cocoa and tobacco (all derived from African sources) growing exponentially at this time.[4] Intensified competition not only between domestic producers but also with German and American manufacturers created the need – for the first time – for the systematic branding of products as well as ever more alluring and persuasive advertisements, which drew for their appeals upon nationalistic, colonial and imperial themes. As McClintock suggests, the double valence of the term 'empire builders' to describe the newly created profession of the advertiser makes clear how the increasingly visual sphere of print promotions was crucial to bolstering Britain's imperial and economic health.[5]

These advertisements displayed the distant spaces of empire as home to industrious workers harvesting the abundantly rich goods for consumption in Britain (such as cocoa beans from West Africa or tea leaves from India) or imagined how goods made in Britain could be exported to these exotic locales to be consumed by colonial subjects (such as soap arriving on the African coast). Visualising and exploiting racial difference became central to the visual idiom of Victorian advertising, which routinely used stereotyped and caricatured representations – typically of Black bodies – to sell products.[6] The advertisements enabled the spread of racist ideology in a popular, accessible and aestheticised manner on a scale previously unseen. As Anandi Ramamurthy describes, despite its low cultural status, advertising of this era demands close scrutiny precisely because it was where the colonial, imperial and profoundly racist values of this new era of British consumerism were most potently articulated, widely circulated and unambiguously expressed.[7]

This Pears' soap advertisement, reproduced in various iterations in the late nineteenth century, has been foregrounded in discussions of commodity racism and imperial consumerism.[8] Soap was a product of an extractive colonial economy, its cheap manufacture contingent upon coconut and palm oils manufactured on imperial plantations in West Africa, South East Asia and the South Pacific; however, as a product intended to cleanse and purify, it also performed ideological work, linking literal cleanliness with the symbolic, moral and racial cleansing central to the imperial programme.[9] Additionally, the soap industry was a crucial driver of an increasingly image-centred form of promotion at this time, with Pears emerging as a leader in the field of pictorial advertising, spending unprecedented sums on visual advertising campaigns that frequently drew upon racist imagery for their impact.[10]

But, until the closing decades of the nineteenth century, these advertisements were predominantly printed in black and white. Although printers had numerous techniques for printing colour at their disposal, such prints remained a relative luxury due to the additional time and labour expended upon their production.[11] From the late nineteenth century, however, colour became an increasingly common feature of commercial prints. This was due to the expansion in chromolithography, a printing technique that involved no carving or etching but produced prints from the flat surface of a stone matrix. Although the process was invented in the eighteenth century, it was not practicable economically on a large scale until the 1860s, when steam-powered presses and ready-made inks enabled the affordable mass production of colour images for the first time, revolutionising the aesthetics of popular print.

Chromolithography found its primary use in the promotion, packaging and advertising of consumer goods, and would be indelibly linked with the commercial sphere in Victorian mass culture. If the promotional bluster circulating in the Victorian era is to be believed, Britain was a global leader in industrialising this printing process, home to the world's largest colour press (in Leeds) and the world's largest printing-ink factory (in Edinburgh).[12] Chromolithography was therefore a distinctly industrial practice in Britain. While in France, commercial chromolithography became a site of modernist experimentation for artists such as Jules Chéret and Henri de Toulouse-Lautrec, its use in British artistic circles was always marginal compared to its monopoly in large-scale commercial printing.[13] As an 1892 article on colour from the *British Lithographer* put it, the process was primarily known for its 'cheapness, gaudy prints and rapidity of execution'.[14] Chromolithographers printed prismatic labels for cigar boxes, flamboyant show cards for tooth polish, dazzling advertisements for detergent, bright leaflets for cosmetics and kaleidoscopic box wrappers for baby food. Chromolithographic prints were therefore a visual symptom of a new era of mass production and consumption that characterised capitalist modernity in Britain and the emergent commodity culture of the second half of the nineteenth century. If, as literary historian Thomas Richards argues, advertising of this era helped to produce 'a specifically capitalist form of representation' in Britain, then chromolithography was the visual technology through which it took shape.[15]

The 1889 Pears' soap advertisement exemplifies the close ties between the new technique of chromolithography and the emerging culture of commodity racism that underpinned British consumerism. Historians have rigorously scrutinised the racist ideology embedded within advertisements of this period, paying particular attention to soap as the quintessential imperial commodity.[16] However, the function of colour, as well as the material and technical construction of these images, has been largely overlooked. Undoubtedly this is because these advertisements, although often originally printed in full colour, conventionally trade upon the racial binary of Blackness and Whiteness, a binary that seems to retain its legibility when reproduced in the literal palette of black and white typically used by academic journals and historical textbooks. Yet, as this chapter demonstrates, the difference between printing Black and White skin tones as a polarised binary and representing them as part of a colourful spectrum comprising many hues implies fundamentally divergent ways of understanding racial difference. Through colour printing, the racial taxonomies of Blackness and Whiteness accrued not just different aesthetics but different meanings – ones that were fundamentally bound up with the techno-material processes of colour printing.

Chromolithography is one of several media examined in this book where the transition from black and white to colour was demonstrated through the spectacular display of the Black body, a display that produced and reinforced fictions of White superiority. As Anne Lafont has described in relation to eighteenth-century printing techniques, from the earliest moment it was possible to work in colour, printing became a way of examining racial difference and was 'immediately associated with the exploration of anatomy and not incidentally with African anatomy'.[17] Chromolithography was thus only the latest iteration of this well-established trope, that new colour media became tools for visualising racial difference, but did so on an unprecedented scale. As the first technology for mass-producing images in colour, chromolithography changed the way skin materialised in print, and ultimately the values and properties that it signified. This was not only because Black and White skin were now rendered in a variety of hues but also because chromolithographic printing lent a very distinctive surface pattern, or complexion, to these prints.

I use the term complexion here as it most accurately reflects this chapter's concern with both colour and surface appearance. Mechthild Fend has argued that the term is especially useful for considering the materialisation of skin colour in visual art, as the complexion of the human face and body comprises a mixture of hues combined together, as in painting or print, and has an aesthetic and social value directly linked to the skin's texture, inflected by the manner in which it is rendered on the canvas or printed page.[18] As is evident from the Pears' soap advertisement, chromolithographs had a recognisable complexion, which covered the surface of the print in spots and dots of coloured ink (fig. 28). This effect was produced by stippling, which was by no means a new technique nor uniformly employed by all lithographic printers, but became the form of mark-making that would characterise mass-produced commercial chromolithographs of the closing decades of the nineteenth century in Britain, at a time when commodity racism dominated popular advertising.

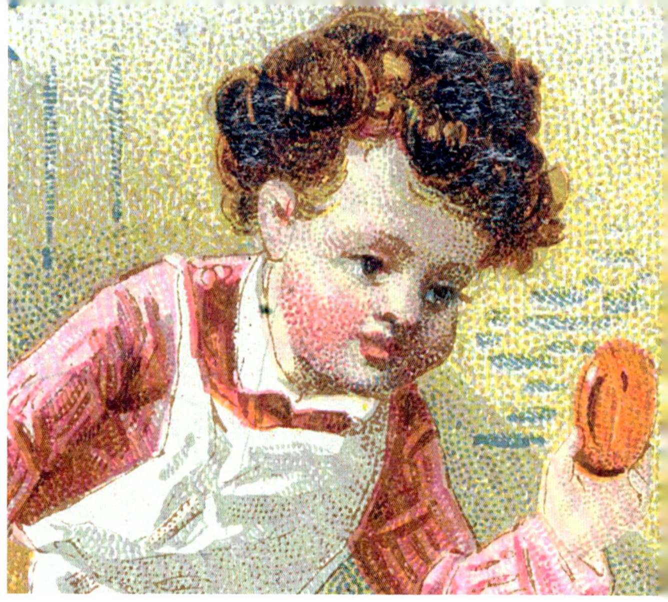

28 Detail of fig. 27 showing spots of coloured ink.

The complexion of the chromolithograph becomes particularly salient in considering advertisements for products aimed at the skin, whether soaps, lotions or powders, which operated as critical sites for shaping ideas about the desirable and undesirable colour of skin. Perhaps more than any other kind of product, these advertisements exploited racial difference to promote and sell an ideal of Whiteness to British consumers. As this Pears advertisement demonstrates, such images foregrounded the issue of the complexion. Here, the bath is emblazoned with the Pears slogan 'Matchless for the Complexion', words drawn from an endorsement by the Italian opera star Adelina Patti. Her praise for the soap is quoted here below that of transatlantic stage performer Lillie Langtry, underscoring the link between a good complexion and these contemporary idols of White femininity. Similarly, the reverse of the advertisement carries an endorsement that the product is 'A Speciality for the Complexion Recommended by Sir Erasmus Wilson, F. R. S. late President of the Royal College of Surgeons of England'. Wilson, who died in 1884, was a leading London dermatologist responsible for promoting skin as the seat of health in the human body. He was well known to the public through his campaigns around sanitary reform as well as his widely read publications on skin health and beauty, which promoted skin cleanliness, hygiene and routine bathing.[19]

Yet the complexion of the chromolithograph, which rendered skin spotted with colour, does not sit comfortably with such paradigms of healthy, clean, beautiful White skin promoted by Pears and Wilson. While this chapter has already described the cleansed White body in the lower panel of the Pears advertisement as 'immaculate', close scrutiny reveals it to be quite the opposite, as the torso presents a highly maculated surface, swarming with flecks, specks and spots of different hues, gathered in clusters under the armpits and dappled in patterns all down the child's flank. This distinctive complexion raises a host of questions about how chromolithography materialised skin and skin colour in print, not least in advertisements such as this, which foregrounded the issue of complexion. How did the printer negotiate the challenge of colouring White skin without it becoming, in the racist terminology employed at the time, 'coloured'? What were the implications of covering White bodies in coloured spots, with their negative aesthetic connotations for ideals of healthy and beautiful skin? If the iconography of this advertisement invoked a biblical passage – 'Can the Ethiopian change his skin or the leopard his spots?' – then how could the spotty complexion of the chromolithograph avoid such conflations between animal and human coloration?

This complexion also invites speculation about how chromolithography troubled the established values of Black and White skin in print. When coloured inks were expensive and time consuming to produce, how could the printer imply the different values of Black and White bodies when both were rendered in spots of multiple colours? When brown inks were made from prized organic substances such as madder, or metals and minerals such as copper and manganese, and combined with myriad other hues to capture the various shades that characterise representations of Black skin, did this contradict the denigration of Black skin at the heart of the advertisement?[20] At a time when advertising placed such a high premium on skin tones and complexions, and when skin tones and complexions were so bound up with racial difference, what were the implications of covering both Black and White bodies with spots and dots of colour? How did this surface pattern intersect with ideas about skin colour and discoloration linked to understandings of disease and bodily pollution, about cleanliness and dirtiness bound up with class and labour, and about desirable and undesirable coloration dictated by racial hierarchies and Victorian beauty standards? These related and overlapping discourses converge, this chapter argues, on the surface of the chromolithograph, as the most pervasive form of mass-produced colour image at the end of the nineteenth century.

The chapter answers these questions by interrogating this particular Pears' soap advertisement further, taking it as a paradigmatic object for exploring the relationship between the complexion of chromolithography and the wider discourses around skin colour and race in Victorian England. In doing so, the chapter demonstrates that chromolithographic printing developed a privileged relationship to depictions of skin, as the process exhibited a distinctly cutaneous logic in its materials and techniques. More broadly, however, this chapter contributes to a recurring theme of the book – that new colour media exploited the display of people of colour, and particularly Black bodies, to demonstrate their chromatic appeals, while simultaneously reinforcing an imagined supremacy of Whiteness through the racist content of these images.

How the Chromolithograph Got Its Spots

By the time this chromolithographed Pears advertisement was printed in 1889, lithography was approaching its centenary. Lavation was a particularly poignant subject to capture through the lithographic process, as soap, water and washing were all crucial to the technique. Lithography required a thick slab of limestone, a finely grained surface described in printing manuals as covered in 'pores' – the tiny pockmarks and pits that lent the substance its natural texture.[21] The capacity of the pores in the lithographic stone to trap grease, in much the same way the pores of the human skin retain dirt and grime, was what fundamentally made the process work.

At its simplest lithography involved laying a design on the surface of the stone using a pen or brush loaded with greasy drawing ink containing lampblack, wax and soap. The grease from the ink had to sink down into the pores of the stone to stop up those areas that were to print. Printers added black pigment to this drawing ink in order to see their work on the stone but subsequently had to remove the colouring so it would not appear in the final print. The stone was therefore coated with gum arabic to protect un-inked areas, before the black pigment was lifted from the surface chemically using turpentine. The stone now carried the design captured solely in grease. The stone was then washed with water, which was repelled from the grease through its natural antipathy to oil but absorbed into the un-inked areas of the stone. A roller charged with similarly greasy printing ink was then passed over the design, and the ink would adhere only to the grease, as it was repelled by the wet areas due to its antipathy to water. As an article of 1904 described it, the process was predicated on 'the affinity of one greasy body for another'.[22] The printing ink comprised pigment, varnish and other additives such as beeswax, tallow, sperm oil and soap, which helped to make ink greasy enough to resist the water but fluid enough to be applied to the stone.[23] Paper was then laid upon the stone and pressure applied in the press to transfer the inked design to the page. To produce a chromolithograph – that is, a print in multiple colours – the image was divided into its respective hues, with one colour allocated to each stone. Each was printed in succession, in register, on a single sheet, where the separate ink layers were recombined into a single full-colour image.

Soap was a key material of lithographers due to its emulsifying properties, which made the greasy inks workable on the stone.[24] These emulsifying qualities are also what makes soap a useful aid in washing the human body. The naturally sebaceous surface of the skin attracts grease and repels water in much the same way as the lithographic stone, but soap makes grease miscible with water so it can be washed away. This made lithographers wary of using too much soap in their inks, as it could cause their design to be removed from the matrix completely when the stone was washed. But the similarity between the natural oils of the skin and the greasy consistency of lithographic ink also meant that printers had to be extremely careful not to touch the matrix with their hands, as any fingerprints would register in the final print. Soap therefore operated as a potent connection between the printed Pears advertisement and the product it advertised, entangling both in the material networks of empire through these imperially manufactured oils and forging an analogy between the surface of the printing matrix and that of the body.

The original process of lithography had been invented in Germany by printer John Aloysius Senefelder in 1795, while Godefroy Engelmann patented 'chromolithographie' in France in 1837, as the chromatic variation on Senefelder's technique.[25] Engelmann's innovation relied upon theories and techniques established around 1700 by the German printer Jacob Christoph Le Blon, who demonstrated that by overprinting three colours (red, yellow and blue, sometimes with the addition of black), printers could reproduce a near complete spectrum of hues.[26] As Mechthild Fend observes, through Le Blon's technique, 'skin colour [was] not only represented but mimicked', as the process, contingent upon the layering of hues and mixing of coloured fluids, mirrored eighteenth-century understandings of how the body was pigmented.[27] Yet, as Fend notes, while Le Blon placed particular emphasis on skin and flesh tones as the benchmark for successful polychrome prints, he did not speak of skin in general but of Whiteness in particular, placing this subject at the centre of technical concerns for generations of printers.[28]

While chromolithographers often relied upon more than three colours, the basic principle of separating hues onto distinct matrices and then printing them in register were unchanged from Le Blon's trichromatic mezzotint system, as was their interest in White skin as a test case for the quality of their prints.

Chromolithography initially gained favour among printers due to the ease with which the matrix could be marked. Before the introduction of the steam-powered lithographic press in the 1860s, almost any mark artists could make on paper using a brush or pen could be easily reproduced on the lithographic stone, whether they desired crisply hatched lines, sloppy washes of ink, or flicked and spattered spots. In the hand-press era the greasy lithographic crayon (a solid stick of ink) allowed for the kind of direct and spontaneous mark-making that was difficult to replicate in other print media that required carving or engraving lines into the matrix, and was almost identical in nature to drawing. Soft, gradated marks could also be produced by dragging the crayon sideways across the stone to give subtle tonal variation. These effects were largely contingent on the use of grained limestone, typically imported from Bavaria but also quarried in the west of England.[29] The similarity between the pock-marked surface of the stone and the natural texture of the human body made the process ideally suited to representations of skin. As historian Mieneke te Hennepe notes, before the adoption of photography, hand-pressed chromolithographs were the preferred method for illustrating manuals on cutaneous medicine due to both the delicate colouring and the fine textural quality of the process.[30]

This is demonstrated in a hand-pressed chromolithograph by Hullmandel & Walton in an 1853 reprint of Wilson's *Portraits of Diseases of the Skin* (1848), which illustrates an outbreak of acne rosacea (fig. 29).[31] At this time colour printing was still a highly skilled and expensive process, reserved largely for elite audiences, as demonstrated here in the use of coloured lithography for a specialist medical text, where colour was essential to the accurate identification of cutaneous afflictions. The hatching of the woman's shoulders makes clear how lithographic crayon could closely resemble the immediacy of drawing, lending a sketch-like quality to the edges of this print, while the extremely delicate granular surface of the stone lends a naturalistic texture to the skin, captured with the very fine shading of colours that characterised this era of lithographic printing. The woman's neck, for instance, perfectly captures the surface texture of soft, smooth skin, which is not completely slick like the surface of glass but very minutely indented with tiny apertures, most visible when captured in the gentle shading on the right, which lends a gauzy, smoky tonality to her throat. Her face demonstrates why this process was ideal for illustrating dermatological texts, as it enabled the subtle gradation between the hues of the skin, from the healthy areas of peachy pink to the reddened patches affected by rosacea, and the yellow tone of the pustules that dominate her complexion. The delicacy of this colouring is enhanced, by contrast, with the grey tones used to capture her clothing and bonnet, enabling the viewer to focus their attention upon the coloration of the face alone. While the presence of such a lace bonnet in portraiture, as Angela Rosenthal suggests, might echo the beautiful transparency and delicacy of White skin, here this framing device only conveys the delicacy of the mark-making, as its cellular structure mirrors and emphasises the carbuncular appearance of the woman's face, exacerbating its unpleasant appearance.[32]

That this print was made by trapping grease in the pores of the stone, which attracts coloured pigments suspended in oily ink, also creates a potent echo of the malady depicted. As Wilson describes, acne was caused by excess oil in the pores attracting, in Wilson's terms, 'dust and smoke of the atmosphere', which irritated skin, leaving it discoloured, black, red or even violet, and causing these colourful eruptions to cover the face.[33] The coating of the stone's pored surface in these oily materials, which attracted other oily colours, reproduced on the matrix the greasy complexion manifested in the print.

However, the introduction of steam-powered printing in the 1860s radically changed the surface texture of chromolithography and the established

and gradation altogether and use only blocky, solid areas of tessellating hues – what was known as the flat-colour style. While this technique was ideal for reproducing two-dimensional subjects, especially those featuring abstract and geometric patterns of interlocking colour, it was of little value to chromolithographers, who needed to convey depth, volume and tonality in their work.[37] The solution was therefore to stipple the surface of the stone with fine dots of greasy ink, essentially reproducing the fine network of pores that trapped grease slightly below the surface with spots that carried grease on the face of the stone. The newly smoothed texture of the lithographic stones therefore produced the opposite effect in the resulting chromolithographs, which were now peppered with spots, dots and specks. The stippling technique could create the impression of transitions between areas of light and shade, or between colours, through optical mixture – the process by which closely spaced dots are automatically mixed when perceived by the eye.

This practice was not contingent upon recent developments in colour theory, nor was this style of stippling related to the contemporary development of neo-impressionism. It is often mistakenly suggested that the writing of Michel Eugène Chevreul and Charles Blanc must have been instrumental in developing this style of chromolithographic marking, as this technique was predicated on a similar system of optical mixture to the one that neo-impressionists painters experimented with in the 1880s under the influence of these theorists. However, the notion that two colours mixed in the eye to create a third had been used by artists and designers for centuries, particularly in textile manufacture.[38]

Nor was this stippling process new to colour printing. Stipple had been particularly poplar as an engraving technique in Britain since the eighteenth century, as it gave subtle variations of tone to a print by incising or punching small pocks into a metal plate. When the plates were coloured by hand, the resulting delicate surface effects were similar to hand-press chromolithography, and this laborious technique sustained some popularity into the nineteenth century.[39] Chromolithographers of the hand-press era also used stippled marks, particularly for printed books in the 1840s, but the process was not widespread until the final decades of the nineteenth century due to the expansion of steam-powered printing.[40]

An 1893 diagram illustrating an article on colour theory in the *British Lithographer* perfectly demonstrates the way in which stippled colour enabled the transition between hues, as minute dots of one colour gradually disperse and mix with those of others (fig. 31). This had the aesthetic benefit of facilitating gradated shades and subtle half-tones, as well as the economic benefit of reproducing the full spectrum of hues using a limited number of colours. Here, nine identifiable inks produce twenty distinct shades marked on the colour wheel, demonstrating how stippling could expand the chromatic range of the printer while also enabling tonal modelling through colour. In keeping with the commercial nature of the printing process, this educational diagram also doubled as an advertisement for inks. It is clear that the chromolithographic printer had to strike a balance between the use of premixed inks and the creation of colours through mixing on the page, with the optimum balance determined by the quality, speed and cost of the job.

But stippling was a laborious, manual process that involved painstakingly marking the stone using the tip of a pen or brush, and it was a job often assigned to a specialist member of staff at the press. The skill, cost, pace and tedium of this process led printers to adopt a technique known as 'Day's Patent Shading Mediums', also known as 'Ben Day dots' or, in Victorian printing terms, the 'mechanical tint'.[41] An American, Ben Day initially patented his mechanical tints in New Jersey in 1879 but finalised an English patent for them in 1882. These mechanical tints were flexible, transparent sheets made from glycerine and gelatin

31 'Spectrum Analysis of White Light', chromolithograph, *British Lithographer*, vol. 2, no. 11 (June–July 1893). British Library, London (LOU.EW S1437).

Printed with A. B. Fleming & Co[s] Lithographic Inks.
CHEMICAL WORKS: CAROLINE PARK: EDINBURGH.

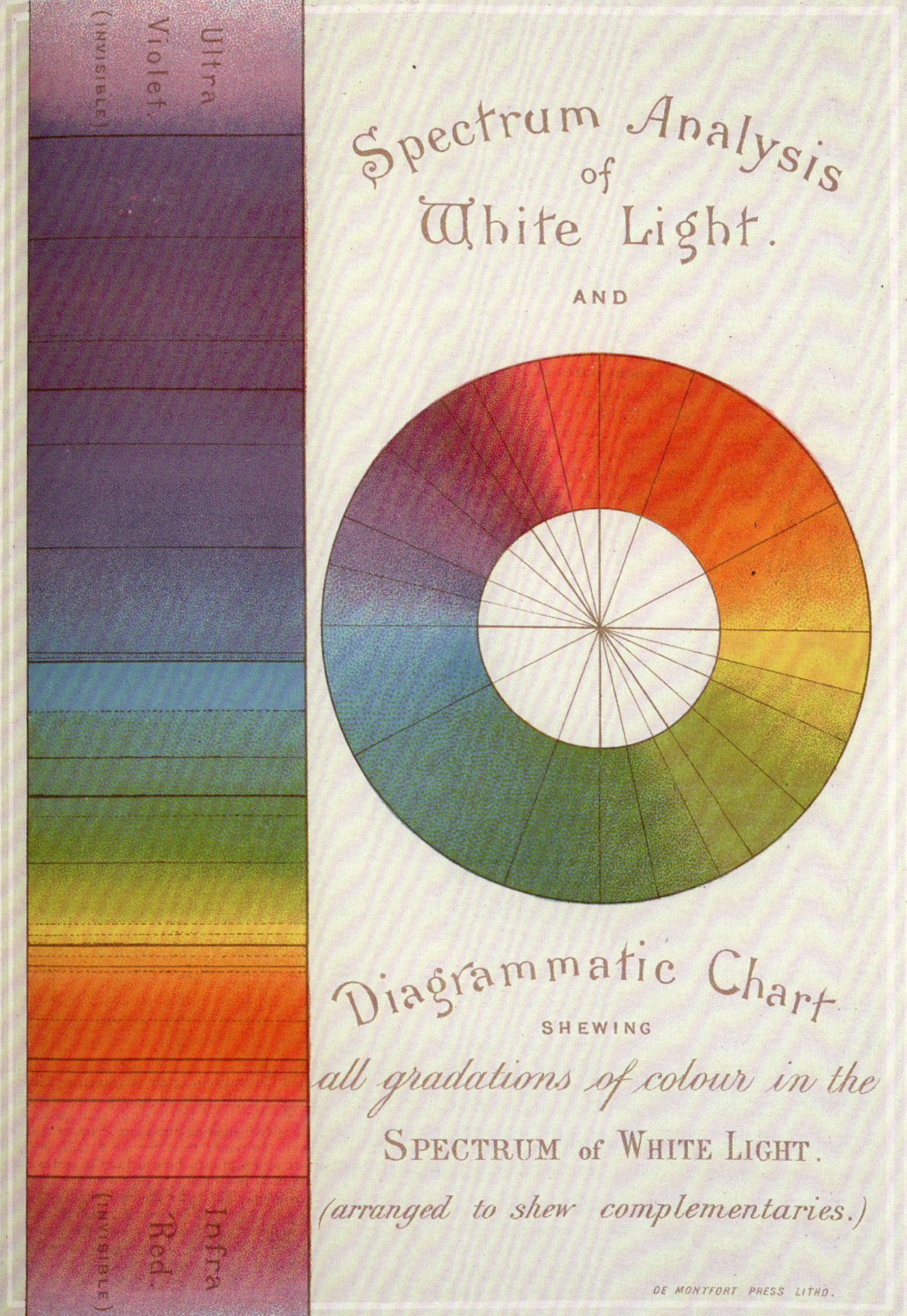

Printed on Chromo Paper Supplied by SMITH & Mc LAURIN, JOHNSTONE, SCOTLAND.
211 C. D. Crown, at 17/6 per ream. Subject to a liberal discount.

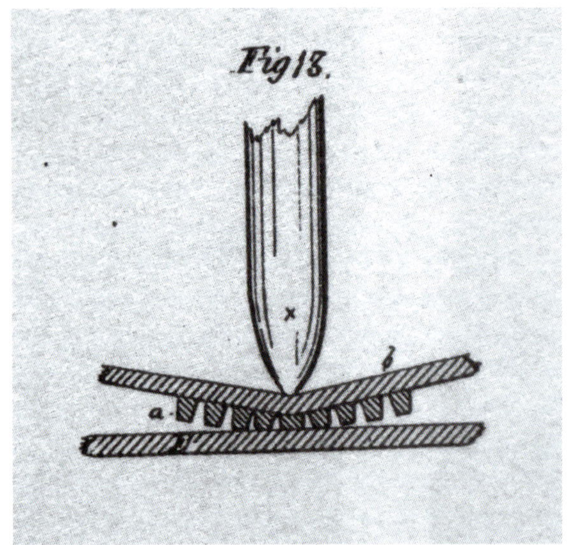

32 Detail from Benjamin Day's US patent no. 214 493 of 22 April 1879.

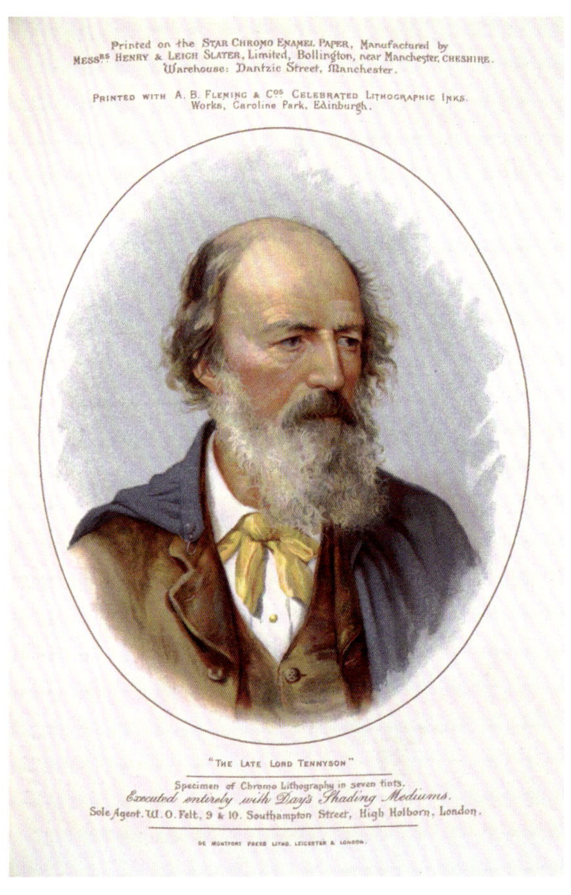

33 'The Late Lord Tennyson', chromolithograph, *British Lithographer*, vol. 2, no. 12 (August–September 1893). British Library, London (LOU.EW S1437).

moulded with raised dots; the sheets could be inked on the raised side and then rubbed on the reverse to transfer the ink to the stone (fig. 32). As one lithographic manual from 1885 celebrated, the speed, precision and repeatability of the process produced effects 'unattainable by hand labour'.[42] Rather than purchasing mechanical tints, British printers had to lease them at considerable cost annually from W. O. Felt in London, the only officially licensed Ben Day agent in Britain, rendering the technique the preserve of major industrial and commercial printers who could afford these fees.

The *British Lithographer* included a special supplement on the process in 1893 demonstrating the effects that it could achieve and encouraging presses to adopt the system as a 'new departure' for fine stipple work.[43] The journal included a portrait of the poet Lord Alfred Tennyson (fig. 33) as well as the colour separations that would be overprinted to produce this completed image 'executed entirely with Day's Shading Mediums' (figs 34–40).[44] These colour separations illustrate the fizzy, speckly complexion of the process and how the accumulation of these tiny dots, when printed close together, produced new chromatic effects. But the separations also reveal the order of colour printing in chromolithography, which ran from the lightest to the darkest hues, typically beginning with yellow and ending with black. As the *British Lithographer* describes, the order of printing here was 'yellow, flesh, red, first grey, second grey, first brown, second brown'.[45]

'Flesh' refers to the salmony shade of peachy pink advertised as 'flesh tint' by ink-makers, and which was allocated its own discrete stone in the printing.

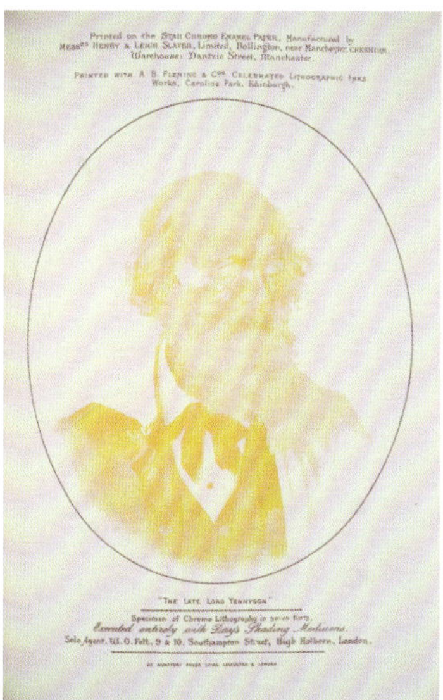

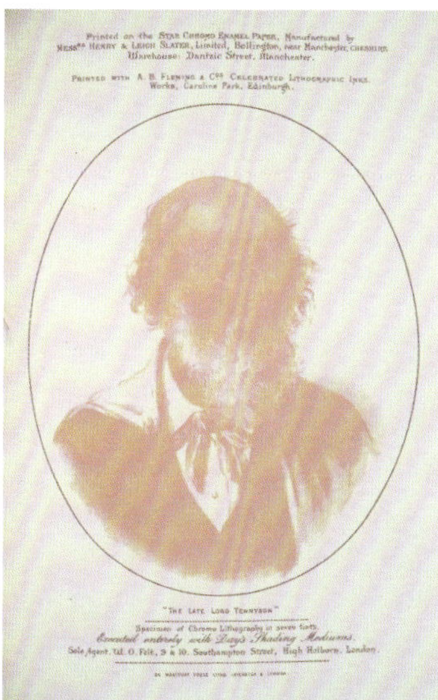

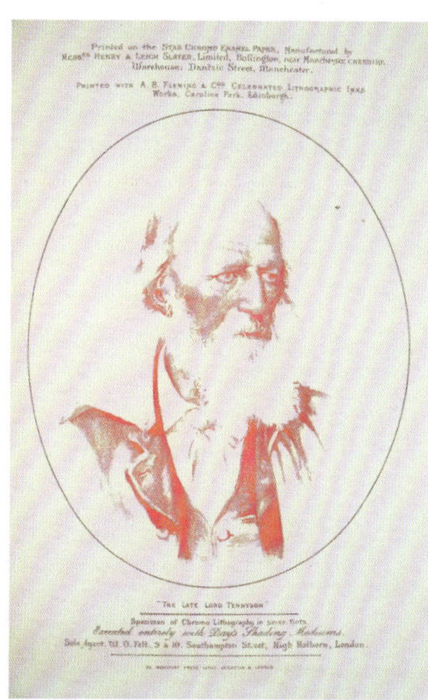

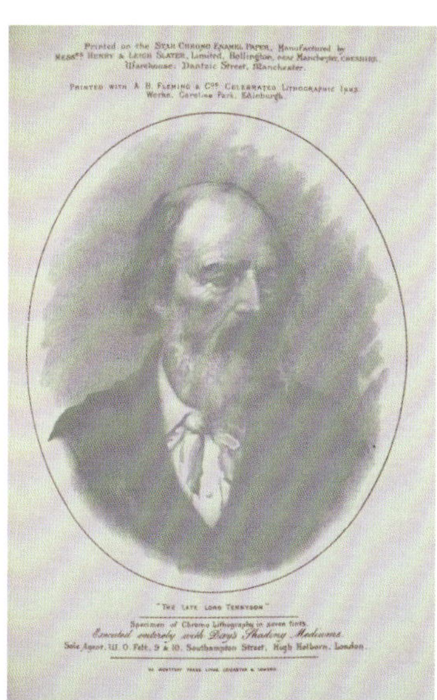

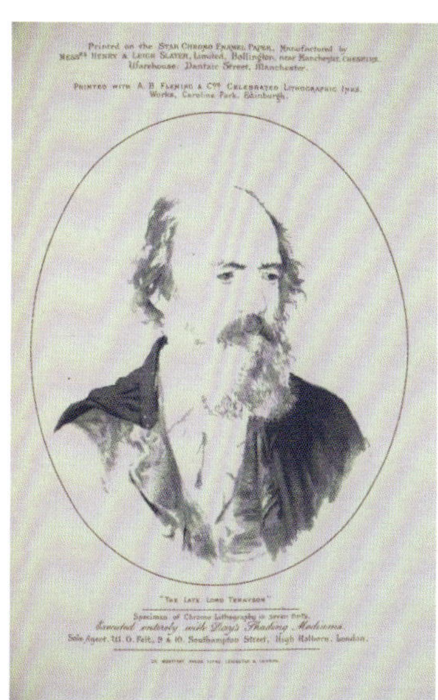

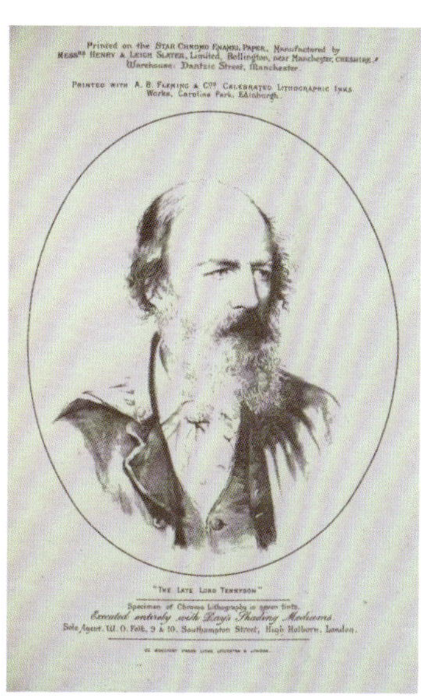

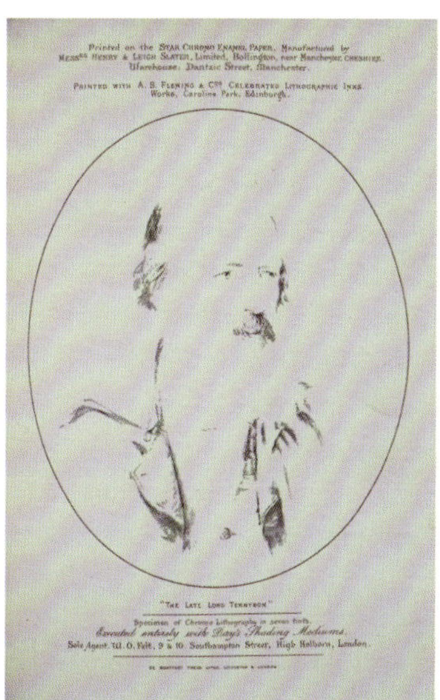

34–40 Chromolithographed colour separations showing yellow, flesh, red, first grey, second grey, first brown and second brown captured in Ben Day shading mediums. *British Lithographer*, vol. 2, no. 12 (August–September 1893).

Clearly 'flesh' was not only used for capturing the tones of skin. Here it also undergirds the hues of the jacket, tie and hair. Nor was 'flesh' the only colour allocated to skin, as red, yellow and grey also constitute the face's palette. It seems curious that printers would pre-mix a tint that needed such routine modification with other colours. But the description of this peachy hue as 'flesh' reveals the racial assumptions built into the process, where all skin was assumed to conform, at its base, to this hue.[46] Although in practice it was clear that White skin tones comprised several colours, the ideal of White skin as a single, uniform, pale pink could be upheld by the idea that 'flesh' could be reproduced through a single ink. The use of the mechanical tint, with its highly regulated surface pattern, also makes the separate layers of printing even more discernible. When considered at close range (as one might a page in a magazine as opposed to a poster), the dots comprising the skin tones do not seamlessly blend into a unified colour but retain their discrete character. The colours are evidently stacked on top of one another, revealing 'flesh' to be the base of the print and an ideal of Whiteness to undergird this construction of colour.

Dots were not the only pattern reproduced by these special shading mediums, as closely spaced lines, or hatches, were also available, and some mechanical tints replicated the randomised and asymmetrical style of hand-stippling. Yet the highly regulated appearance of these dots, as demonstrated in the 1893 diagram and the Tennyson portrait, came to characterise the surface of mass-produced chromolithographs, betraying the industrialised nature of their manufacture and application. In 1884 the *Printing Times and Lithographer* reported that it had 'been objected by handworkers, that some of the effects were too mechanical in appearance', perhaps because the mechanical tint rendered all too visible the industrialised labour involved in making these images, which were the product not of a single artist but of a group of workers – some skilled, some unskilled – using labour-saving devices to economise on costs.[47] In other words, this new complexion made the capitalist separation of labour visible on the print's surface as a separation of colour.[48]

This complexion of small, regular spots typified commercial chromolithography, its distinctive aggregation of colour resulting from the demands of speed, automation and cost-efficiency. Through its very surface appearance, chromolithography was revealed as a cheap, commercial process, indelibly linked with the techno-material systems of mass production that characterised the consumer age of late Victorian Britain. When mapped onto the complexion of human skin, the complexion of the chromolithograph also imbued the body and face with further negative connotations.

Spots, Grease and Colourful Complexions

The spotty complexion of chromolithography, which covered faces in greasy dots of colour, ran counter to many established conceptions about the appearance of beautiful, healthy White skin that companies such as Pears promoted through their products. These ideals of Whiteness were formed through the expanding beauty culture that accompanied the profusion of consumer products aimed at the skin, as well as the development of dermatological medicine, a field driven by the work of Wilson. Wilson was a key figure for Victorian understandings of the skin both in the specialist field of cutaneous medicine, a discipline he helped to establish as a discrete field of practice, and in popular conceptions of healthy, beautiful skin, through his various popular manuals on skin health, which were routinely quoted in contemporary beauty advice. Wilson's name became even more familiar to the Victorian public through his endorsements of Pears' soap, as featured on the reverse of the 1889 advertisement. Although not officially associated with the firm (and supposedly receiving no financial benefit from its use of his endorsement), Pears exploited his recommendation of the product in a journal article of 1868 and subsequently cited it widely to lend medical credibility to the company's claims about the soap's benefits for the complexion.[49] Wilson is therefore a critical figure in connecting the specialised field of cutaneous medicine with popular understandings of the relationship between colour, skin, health and beauty.

As Wilson explained in his numerous publications, colour was critical to interpreting the health of skin. The skin was understood as the interface between the internal operations of the body and its external environment. Its coloration, or discoloration, therefore gave vital clues to the efficiency and wellbeing of the physical systems contained within, as well as the quality and wholesomeness of an individual's surroundings. But colour was also considered vital to the aesthetic and visual appeal of skin. Popular discussions of the skin's appearance were both racially determined, through ideals of Whiteness, and heavily gendered, linking the skin's beauty to a woman's romantic and sexual allure. As Francis Pears (grandson to the firm's founder) stated in his 1859 publication *The Skin, Baths, Bathing, and Soap*, a text that draws liberally upon Wilson's work, the 'complexion is the great charm of woman' as 'neither the eye, the hair, the figure, nor the manner, exert an influence in love, compared to that inspired by the fairness and perfection of the skin'.[50] As the visible boundary between the interior and exterior of the body, skin was the site where women projected their most appealing qualities, and, as the primary organ of sensation, it was also intimately linked with the eroticised promise of touch. As the author of the 1893 manual *Beauty Culture: What Dermatology Has to Do with Beauty* stated, the skin was like a fine garment worn to enhance a woman's loveliness, attractive for both its colour and texture, possessing a 'softness of velvet' rendered in 'the delicate hues of the lily and the rose'.[51]

This description typifies discussions of the ideal qualities of beautiful Victorian skin, which were consistently framed in racialised and gendered terms, as the ideal complexion was believed to be soft and tender, blemish free and pink in colour. As one 1897 beauty manual succinctly stated, 'all women are anxious to possess a white, fine, skin, tinted with the rich glowing colour which is indicative of perfect health and free from the pallor and the eruptive diseases of the skin'.[52] This 'glowing colour' was linked to the healthy circulation of blood beneath the skin, which lent it a rosy hue, visible due to the translucence of the skin's surface.[53] As Francis Pears insisted, the 'fresh and ruddy colour' that characterised healthy skin was intimately linked to an individual's vigour. Too little colour indicated indolence and left skin looking wan and sickly; too much colour and skin acquired what Pears described as the 'colour of those who spend much of their lives in the open air' – in other words, the negative class associations of working outdoors.[54] The 'delicate hues of the lily and the rose' indicated an appropriate moderation of open-air exercise and bodily and mental activity, but without the taint of physical labour – a formulation of untainted Whiteness familiar from John Singer Sargent's painting *Carnation, Lily, Lily, Rose*, discussed in the previous chapter.

The coloration of White skin could therefore indicate an individual's class status, but also moral virtue, as gluttonous indulgences such as alcohol, caffeine and greasy foods could affect the purity and hue of skin. An 1897 beauty manual attributed the 'sallowness and want of colour that is characteristic of French, Italian, and Spanish women' to 'their unwholesome diet, and to the large amount of coffee which they consume daily', linking 'the matchless purity and freshness of complexion' that supposedly characterised British women to their bourgeois values of measured restraint, and their wholesome lifestyles.[55] Wilson similarly linked clean, healthy skin to national character, suggesting that the popularity of cleansing the body with soap and water in the bath was 'especially and characteristically British'.[56] That an individual's complexion reflected the values of the nation further reinforced the established links between clean, White skin and British imperial values that underpinned Victorian soap advertisements. This in turn linked the civilising mission of empire to the consumption of soap, and cleansed, White skin to the virtues of discipline, morality and decency.

To maintain an ideal complexion it was crucial to ensure skin was free of blemishes and the 'eruptive diseases of the skin' that indicated poor health ('indigestion, constipation, nervous irritability') or poor lifestyle ('habitual potations of wine, spirits, beer!').[57] These spots, plooks and pimples were believed to be caused by the body expelling noxious substances through the pores of the skin, rendering indulgences visible on the face of the consumer. But the skin could similarly be affected by materials absorbed through the pores from the atmosphere, what Wilson identified as 'poisonous gases, miasmata, and infectious vapours' – again, suggestive of the polluting environment of the urban metropolis and proximity to industrial labour.[58] Returning to Wilson's discussion of acne rosacea, illustrated earlier in a delicately coloured print, Wilson described how this cutaneous affliction, which he notes was far more common in women than men, was caused by 'sedentary employment and mental fatigue', 'excesses in diet or stimulating drinks' or indeed the 'abuse' of certain substances 'employed as cosmetics'.[59] The woman's greasy, spotty, reddened complexion, Wilson suggests, is the product of vanity, intoxication and laziness. Spotty skin was therefore not merely a medical disorder but indicative of a failure of character, a weak physical constitution, low social standing and unwholesome morals.

It is clear when examining the 1889 Pears' soap advertisement how easily the addition of colour to give a healthy appearance to skin could, when conveyed in the dotted complexion of the Ben Day dot, give skin an unappealing surface. Closely examining the White child in his apron – or, indeed, the consumers captured in vignettes around the border – the way in which their cheeks are captured in clustered spots of fuchsia is clearly intended to capture the healthy flush of blood in their cheeks. Yet, rather than a delicate bloom of colour, the spotted complexion of chromolithography renders these faces as though covered in measles. The face of the baby in particular is almost engulfed in these brilliant pink pimples, swamping the face in a gaudy hue, while the face of the child in the apron is teeming with spots of the same alarming magenta shade as his shirt, covering his skin in a flurry of blemishes.

Of course, the dangers of overloading White skin with colour were not only that it implied gluttonous habits or a toxic environment, or carried connotations of working-class labour, but also that it threatened to destabilise an individual's racial identity. The fascination with maintaining an appropriately pink tone for White skin, which structured contemporary beauty and sanitary culture, reflected anxieties about the links between skin colour and racial classification that were firmly established by the nineteenth century. Such concerns became especially fraught on the surface of the chromolithograph, where skin tones that were essentialised into a rhetorical binary of Black and White were now materially rendered in colour. However, the divergent ways in which Black and White skin were printed in chromolithography continued to produce an identifiable difference between them in order to maintain the supremacy of Whiteness consistent with its rhetorical value in European scientific and cosmetic culture.

Flesh Tints and Pigment Granules

Before looking again at the chromolithographed Pears' soap advertisement to see how the use of colour changed the rendering of Black and White skin, it will be helpful to first demonstrate how different values were accorded to these skin tones in monochrome printing. Helpfully, Pears' soap reproduced this particular advertisement in both black and white and colour, and an 1884 monochrome wood engraving of the same subject offers a useful comparison with the chromolithograph (fig. 41). This advertisement was clearly based on the same source material as the later chromolithograph, as the content is almost identical, save for the floral border, undoubtedly included to invoke associations of the English rose complexion of pale White skin (which returns again in discussions of

41 Pears' soap advertisement, wood engraving, *The Graphic* (December 1884). British Library, London (C.188.c.52).

THE GRAPHIC CHRISTMAS NUMBER, 1884

For improving & preserving the complexion.

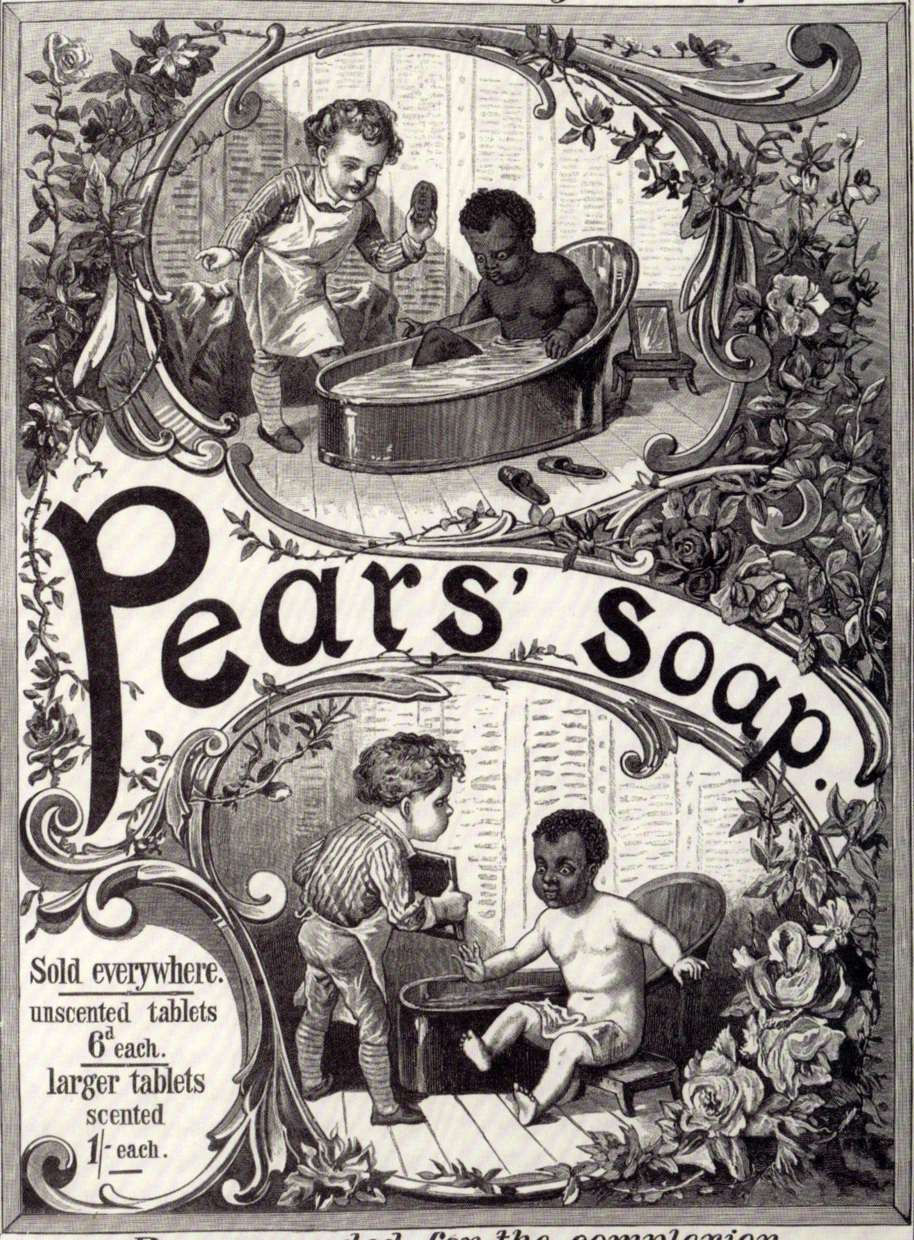

Recommended for the complexion.
by Madame Adelina Patti & Mrs Langtry.

ture. He shaped thinking about the skin's exterior – its sweat ducts, pores and hair follicles – as well as its interior, in particular where colour pigment was located in the body and how it coloured the skin.[70] Wilson's work marked an intensification of research undertaken in the previous century, when the diversity of skin pigmentation found among different peoples fascinated and baffled European scientists, who tried to understand why and how the body produced these colours. This medical research was driven by, and profoundly informed, attempts to better taxonomise and classify different racial groups undertaken by anthropologists and natural scientists – work critical to legitimising the project of European colonialism and the enslavement of African people, as Anne Lafont has discussed.[71] Although much debated, skin colour increasingly became the model for identifying and hierarchising racial types, and by the mid-nineteenth century it had become the principal way racial difference was understood and represented.[72] Wilson's research was deeply preoccupied with exploring racial difference through the coloration of skin and his consideration of healthy and unhealthy, and desirable and undesirable forms of pigmentation therefore cannot be disentangled from such racial implications.

By the time Wilson was practising medicine, dermatologists had moved away from theories circulating in the previous century – that coloration was based on the mixture of fluids contained within the body or the effects of the local climate – proposing instead that colour was solely determined by pigment cells found within the skin itself.[73] In the nineteenth century skin was understood to comprise a series of connected layers: the bottom layer, the cutis or 'true skin', comprising 'white fibrous tissue'; the middle layer or 'rete mucosum', the mucous network, where pigment resided; and the top, transparent layer, the epidermis, which had a coloured appearance due to the pigments contained below.[74] While the coloration of fluids such as blood running through the skin could influence its colour, the chromatic appearance of skin was imposed by the cells carried in the mucous network, described by Wilson as 'pigment granules'.[75]

Wilson emphasised that White skin was not 'perfectly colourless' but instead contained pigment granules that were 'extremely slight' and 'pale' in colour compared to the skin of what he termed 'the darker races'.[76] The pigment granules of dark skins were larger and more abundant, producing their dark coloration through their cumulative chromatic effect. Wilson noted that, when examined individually, these pigment cells 'offer very little indication of the depth of colour which is produced by their accumulation; some have the hue of amber, while others scarcely exceed the most delicate fawn', noting that 'the depth of colour of the deep stratum of the negro' is produced by the quantity of these 'coloured granules', which leave Black skin with 'a mottled appearance' as they are 'scattered through its texture'.[77]

This description neatly aligns with the depiction of different skin colours rendered in the chromolithographed advertisement (see fig. 27). White skin here is not colourless, but is coloured by 'granules' – dots of hue (pink, grey, yellow) that are dispersed loosely across the body's surface. The White skin tones here are certainly maculated, but the density and quantity of colours are markedly different from those comprising the Black skin tones. The tonality of Black skin is configured through the accumulation and compound effect of these coloured 'granules', more numerous and darker in colour than in White skin, and resulting in the kind of 'mottled' effect that Wilson describes, a phrase that accurately captures the surface appearance of mechanical tints when tightly overprinted, as seen on the seated child's face. Furthermore, Wilson's description of the layers of the skin comprising a 'true skin … chiefly composed of white fibrous tissue' overlaid with pigment is explored here in both the content and aesthetics of the advertisement. The supposed humour of the image in fact hinges upon the revelation of White skin lying just below a Black surface, which also reflects the material construction of these flesh tones, as printers placed dark pigments on top of the pink 'flesh tint' of White skin, which was always among the first colours printed and which itself sat upon the literal white surface of the paper beneath.

Jennifer Roberts and Mechthild Fend have both described how printing, which produces colour through the accumulation of layers, replicates the structural logic of skin.[78] But here, in the Pears' soap advertisement, the complexion of the print also stages the pigmentary mechanics of skin described by Wilson, mirroring his description of skin colour as an accumulation of coloured granules, through the speckled colours that cover its surface. My suggestion is not that the print intentionally reflected contemporary scientific ideas about the composition and coloration of skin, but rather that the way chromolithographs constructed colour reinforced and popularised ideas about pigmentation that were also circulating in medical science. Both these artistic and scientific conventions therefore mutually informed perceptions of racial difference at this time. As Fend notes, the term 'pigment' moved from artistic culture into medicine rather than the other way around, indicating that understandings of the body's colour had long been shaped by ideas about colour from painting and print.[79] As Richard J. Powell notes, because pigment 'can either be an artificial substance such as liquid paint or pulverised matter … used for colouring [by artists], or it can be a naturally occurring substance in the tissue of animals, plants and other organisms that gives them colour', the term forges a powerful confederation between aesthetic and biological functions of colour, particularly as it relates to racialised understandings of human skin.[80]

These differences of colour and complexion, so visibly rendered in chromolithography, were understood to relate to other physical properties of the skin, which reflected the general disposition of the individual. The idea that darker skins carried what was described in Victorian dermatological studies as an 'abundance of the colouring matter' produced the perception that Black skin was more dense and opaque than White skin, an undesirable characteristic when the skin's translucency was of the utmost importance to ideas about beauty, intelligence and emotional sensitivity.[81] Wilson explicitly connected opacity to unhealthy skin, as any loss of transparency and 'the production of an excess of pigment' would render skin dull.[82] The transparency of skin was not merely an aesthetic preference, however, but, as Angela Rosenthal describes, had been understood since the eighteenth century as a 'precondition of emotional legibility', as the skin's capacity to register and express the internal sensations of the body, as well as its inner moral and intellectual character, was contingent upon its transparency.[83] The perceived density of Black skin, in contrast to the idealised translucency of Whiteness, therefore implied a lack of sensitivity of both an emotional and a physical nature, and was perceived as a barrier to assessing the inner qualities of character, in Lafont's terms producing 'an emotional opacity that led to invisibility and, consequently, to mistrust'.[84] As Lafont illuminates, these assumptions about the opacity and insensitivity of Black skin, developed in the previous century, were seen to give medical credibility to theories of White supremacy, historically legitimised the enslavement of Africans and shaped tenets central to the development of scientific racism in nineteenth-century Europe.

That this Pears' soap advertisement trades upon the removal of colour from the Black body as a means of improving the complexion reflected beliefs current to scientific racist thought, which proposed that as human beings evolved socially and mentally their skin carried less pigment. An 1879 tract by the surgeon William Sharpe, *The Cause of Colour among Races and the Evolution of Physical Beauty*, argued for instance that an 'intensity of colour' marked the 'lower races', framing skin pigment as a kind of protective layer that shielded individuals from the ravaging elements that Sharpe imagined typified the primitive conditions of a life lived outdoors in Africa, Asia and 'the tropics'.[85] Sharpe proposed that the 'luxuries of civilised life have enabled man to dispense with pigmentary colouring', proposing Whiteness as the product of societal and intellectual evolution, developed over time as a mark of cultural superiority.[86] He did lament that even among White Europeans 'a certain muddiness of complexion and general coarseness of the skin' marked the 'retrogressive and descending grades' of society, which he compared with 'that dusky turgescence which is the result of disease'.[87] Sharpe's suggestion that the density and intensity of pigmentation carried on the skin could change dependent upon the moral, social and intellectual capacity exhibited by an individual clearly intersects with the chromatic and racial transformation at the centre of the Pears' soap advertisement, where the cleansed White body emerges from the bath with less coloured pigment on its surface. To some contemporary viewers, this reduction in skin pigment would have suggested that the uncivilised Black body had been improved by the consumption of imperial commodities and the participation in ritual cleansing through what Wilson called the 'characteristically British' act of bathing.[88]

The chromatic superfluity that typified the complexion of chromolithographed Black skin therefore reinforced such associations, rendering the surface dense, inscrutable and thick with pigment. But Sharpe's comments also demonstrate how fragile ideas about the complexion of White skin were at this time, when colour carried connotations both of an undesirable racial othering and of disease, and a 'coarse' texture could signify a lack of cultivation. While White skin was not colourless either in medical discourse or in chromolithographic prints, the quantity and quality of colour carried on the skin's surface were of crucial importance to reflect the kind of beautiful, healthy, clean White complexions promoted by Pears. Any excesses of colour carried on the surface of the White body therefore threatened the ideals with which Whiteness was associated, a particular problem for White sufferers of what Wilson called 'chromatopathic' diseases.

'Chromatopathic Affection or Derangements of Colour of the Skin'

Wilson wrote at length on the use of skin colour to diagnose diseases. Any changes to colour on the surface of the body could indicate problems occurring within, reflecting a poor constitution and general disturbances to the nervous system. Different hues implied specific ailments: yellow skin revealed liver problems, green skin signalled irritations in the abdomen and blueness suggested 'morbid chemical combinations' in the blood.[89] Certain conditions were named for their chromatic characters and the particular tints they lent to skin, including 'xanthopathia' (yellowing), cyanopathia (blueness) and chloasma (from the Greek 'becoming green').[90] These 'chromatopathic' diseases, these 'derangements of colour of the skin', firmly linked colourful skin with ill health.[91]

But colour itself could also be toxic to the body. Wilson recalls numerous patients whose skin was severely damaged by contact with poisonous colours. He describes the ill effects of aniline dyes upon the skin, recounting a patient who had worn socks 'originally striped with purple, and the impression of the purple stripes was made visible on the legs of the patient in the form of dark red bands that resembled burns'.[92] He also describes a factory worker employed making the colourant 'Schweinfurt green' whose body was overcome with ulcers and papules due to the high content of arsenic in the pigment, noting that 'house-painters, plumbers, and workers in certain oils, pigments, and metals' were likely to suffer similar fates.[93]

Ink-makers were especially vulnerable to this kind of affliction as they were constantly exposed to pigments in powdered form, which could easily be inhaled. Inks for powered presses had to be ground especially fine in order not to clog these high-speed machines and could easily become airborne when ground to a dust.[94] This danger was further exacerbated by the fact that, because ink-making involved boiling oil, fires were a constant risk. As one worker for Mander Brothers' ink factory in Wolverhampton recalled, in 1871 a fire at the factory caused the firm's pigments to disperse throughout the city in this manner, and 'the street, houses and chimneys, and all the pavements [were] covered with red, black, blue, white, green, while many other coloured minerals were scattered about by the wind. The poor people could not keep the diversified colour out of their dwellings with all their efforts.'[95] At a time when colours contained highly poisonous pigments

– emerald green, for instance, comprised arsenic and copper – the dispersal of these toxic substances in the air was disastrous. One contemporary printer noted that emerald green was 'so deadly a poison … that it is almost cruelty to employ any one on this kind of work'.[96]

If this chapter speculated earlier that the colours used to print Black skin carried more value than the soot-filled black inks, then they also carried higher toxicity. One of the reasons that black became a ubiquitous colour in printing, aside from the ease with which it could be ground, was because black pigments (wood, bones, plant matter) are largely non-poisonous.[97] Coloured inks had to be specially sanitised if used for printing medical supplies (these 'antiseptic' inks were patented in the 1880s) and some were fragranced with oils to mask their toxic odours when used for packaging aromatic products such as perfumes.[98] The coloured inks that captured the varied tones of Black skin, therefore, may have been more expensive than black ink but also carried additionally noxious and toxic properties. But such associations would also trouble representations of Whiteness.

Indeed, the kinds of skin irritation produced by these colours and the pathological discolorations described by Wilson would have been most visible on light skin, forging Whiteness as a medical norm for dermatology, a practice still troublingly in place in medical education today.[99] Yet Wilson frequently described these chromatic shifts resulting from disruptions to the body's regular functions in racial terms. For instance, xanthoderma, a pathological yellowing of the skin, resembled in Wilson's terms 'the yellow complexion of certain of the races of mankind', which reveals how despite the abstract nature of the chromatic terms applied to different racialised groups in the eighteenth century, medical science confused these aesthetic and racial descriptors.[100] But the idea that chromatopathic diseases could result in a kind of racial transformation was most potent in discussions of the pathological darkening of White skin. Wilson invariably compared these changes of physical appearance to racial metamorphosis among his White patients, describing a 'fair' young man who due to his skin condition 'entertained the apprehension that he was turning into a negro'; a natural brunette whose skin changed colour so that she 'had the appearance of an East Indian'; and another woman whose malady meant that she 'had the appearance of a mulatto rather than that of an inhabitant of our climate'.[101]

The converse situation, as imagined in the Pears' soap advertisement, of Black skin becoming White, was framed by Wilson less as the result of a dangerous malady and more as a curious, and even propitious, disorder of pigmentation. For instance, in his lectures on dermatology, Wilson recalled a story from the eighteenth-century French naturalist Georges-Louis Leclerc, Comte de Buffon, involving a French 'negresse' cook named Françoise, who was 'born in Virginia, and as a child, was perfectly black'.[102] Françoise's skin gradually began to lighten, until by the age of forty her skin became, according to Wilson (citing Buffon), 'as soft and transparent as that of the most beautiful European, and permits the colour of the blood-vessels to be seen through it'.[103] Wilson described Françoise as 'a perfect albino', a term implying both the scale of her pigmentary transformation, which covered almost her entire body, and the supposedly agreeable qualities of her new appearance, a perfection of texture and hue.[104]

Albinism was the one skin condition routinely discussed in relation to Black skin rather than White, because in Wilson's terms the condition was 'less remarkable in the Europeans than in the African' due to the striking visual contrast between darkly pigmented skin and skin lacking any pigmentation at all.[105] As Anne Lafont describes, European medicine and scientific thought were fascinated by albinism precisely because it suggested the visual slippage between racial identities, supposed by physicians, anthropologists and natural historians to be rigidly fixed and biologically determined categories – rather than culturally constructed labels.[106] But it was not only the 'perfect albinos' who transitioned completely from Blackness to Whiteness that captivated the European imagination, but those whose bodies simultaneously displayed the appearance of Black and White skin at the same time. Of particular relevance for a consideration of the relationship between such cutaneous disorders and the complexion of chromolithography is the frequency with which those exhibiting partial albinism were described as spotted, dotted and dappled in appearance.

This particular preoccupation is especially relevant to a further exploration of the Pears' soap advertisement, which curiously, instead of showing the complete transformation of the bathing child from Black to White, shows only a partial change in colouring, leaving a Black face on a White body. Historians have interpreted the child's Black face in various ways. Anandi Ramamurthy reads it as an allegory for British colonial interests in Africa, whereby the child represents 'the body politic, with the head remaining Black or African, but the body or the state coming under white or European control'.[107] Others, including Tanya Sheehan and Henry Louis Gates Jr, suggest that in keeping with its Aesopian origins, the child's true identity, inseparable from the visage and visually marked by race, cannot be altered by any form of civilising process and must remain Black in order to highlight the immutability of racial difference and ultimately reinforce the superiority of whiteness.[108] In addition to these astute readings, this chapter echoes Sarah Amato's suggestion that this advertisement also draws, in a far more literal and explicitly visual way, upon the contemporary fascination with the pigmentation of bodies and those of people with albinism in particular.[109] It is not proposed here that this child's Black head and White body literally represent a case of partial albinism or 'achroma' (vitiligo in contemporary terms). Instead, this advertisement uses the transformative chromatic potential of colour printing to exploit the contemporary preoccupation with the transformative chromatic metamorphoses exhibited by such diseases, which captivated the public imagination.

Albinism and achroma were established sources of visual sensationalism in nineteenth-century popular culture. These pigmentation disorders were not merely objects of medical scrutiny but also public fascination and mass entertainment. Indeed, the case studies Wilson uses to describe these conditions in his publications are typically not of individuals he met through his medical practice but of people whose atypical pigmentation had made them fairground curiosities, stage attractions and subjects of public exhibition earlier in the century. Typically these were children born to enslaved parents, suggesting to Wilson that the condition was particularly prevalent 'among negroes recently exported from Africa', lending the pigmentation disorder further connotations of abject, dehumanised status in Victorian Britain.[110] For example, Wilson discussed the case of George Alexander Gratton, popularly labelled the 'Beautiful Spotted Negro Boy' and described in contemporary accounts as 'beautifully covered over by a diversity of spots'.[111] Gratton was born in 1808 to enslaved African parents in the British Caribbean colony of St Vincent, but he was purchased as an object of curiosity in Bristol by the British showman John Richardson in 1809 and exhibited as a public attraction until the child's untimely death in 1813.

An 1809 print reproducing Daniel Orme's painted portrait of Gratton of the same year demonstrates how the child's spotted colouring dehumanised him in the public imagination (fig. 43). The print further illuminates some of the associations of spotted skin later in the nineteenth century, when chromolithography brought such complexions into the mainstream graphic vocabulary of advertising. Here the child sits naked in an idealised tropical mountain landscape atop a large green tortoise and beside a piebald dog, whose irregular constellation of brown spots amid white fur matches Gratton's skin pigmentation, an archipelago of brown patches amid large expanses of cream-coloured skin. The print invites the viewer to compare him with these animals – a exotic curiosity like the tortoise, a subservient spotted creature like

43 P. R. Cooper, *George Alexander Gratton*, after the painting by Daniel Orme, published 11 November 1809, hand-coloured etching and stipple, 29.8 × 22.5 cm. National Portrait Gallery, London.

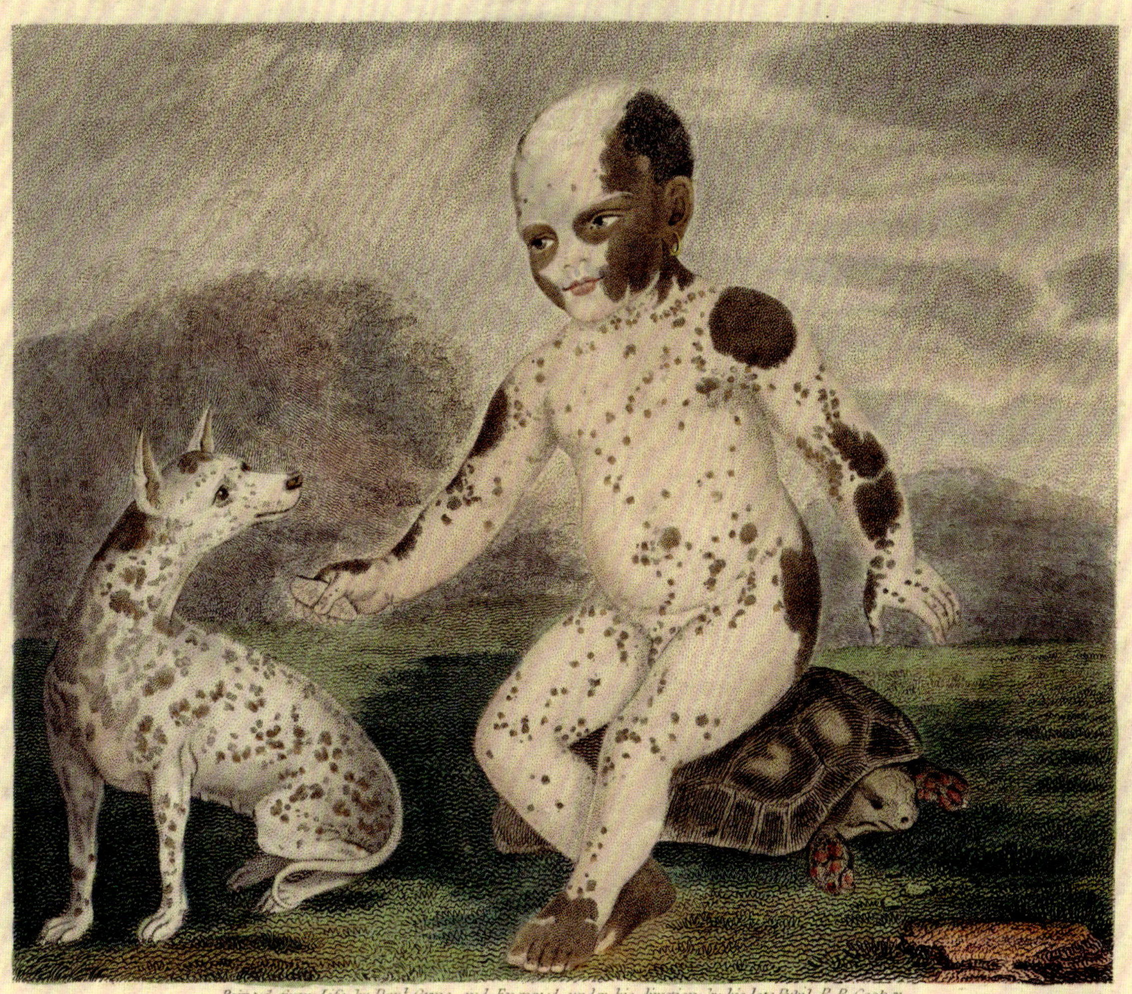

Painted from Life by Danl. Orme and Engraved under his direction by his late Pupil P. R. Cooper.

THE PORTRAIT of GEORGE ALEXANDER,

An Extraordinary Spotted Boy,

from the

Caribbee Islands in the West Indies.

Published Novr. 11. 1809. by Richd. Gretton Esqr. London. and Sold by D. Orme. 308, Oxford Street.

the dog. Wilson similarly compared partial albinism to coloration found on animals, suggesting that those afflicted with the condition can be 'likened to a dappled or piebald horse' or even 'spotted insects'.[112]

Gratton's complexion is not just imitated by the dog's coat, however, but by the surface of the print itself, produced through a combination of hand-coloured etching and stipple.[113] While the vibrant, linear zigzags of the grassy hill have been engraved, the flecked dots that cover the surface of Gratton's body have been stippled. The 'spotted' nature of his appearance is therefore captured not just through the brown patches of pigment painted onto his skin alongside the larger creamy areas of pale pink and grey-blue, but also through the minute, stippled dots of black and grey ink that engulf his entire body with minuscule speckles. While there is a huge diversity of marks here, it is the spotted effect of Gratton's skin that is reproduced as a surface logic across the entirety of the print, which gives the image its busy surface teeming with minute marks. The effect is closely related to that of the spotted complexion of chromolithography, which was similarly suited to capturing skin tones afflicted by what Wilson described as a 'spotted condition'.[114]

The subject of partial albinism and its association with animal coloration was particularly current in late Victorian London, as Sarah Amato has shown.[115] In early 1884 the American showman P. T. Barnum displayed a Burmese elephant in London Zoological Gardens for a number of months; he proclaimed it to be completely 'white' but visitors noted that it instead displayed a 'mottled appearance' combining white patches with its ashy grey.[116] Speculation about the animal's coloration in the press routinely invoked racial analogies similar to those expressed in the print of Gratton, which aligned the elephant, hailing from a British colony, to the exoticised human bodies that peopled the empire. The *Illustrated London News* suggested that the elephant exhibited a condition found 'both among negro human beings and brute animals' where 'there is a partial absence of the dark colour matter in the epidermis, and this sometimes presents the appearance of light-coloured patches'.[117] Such

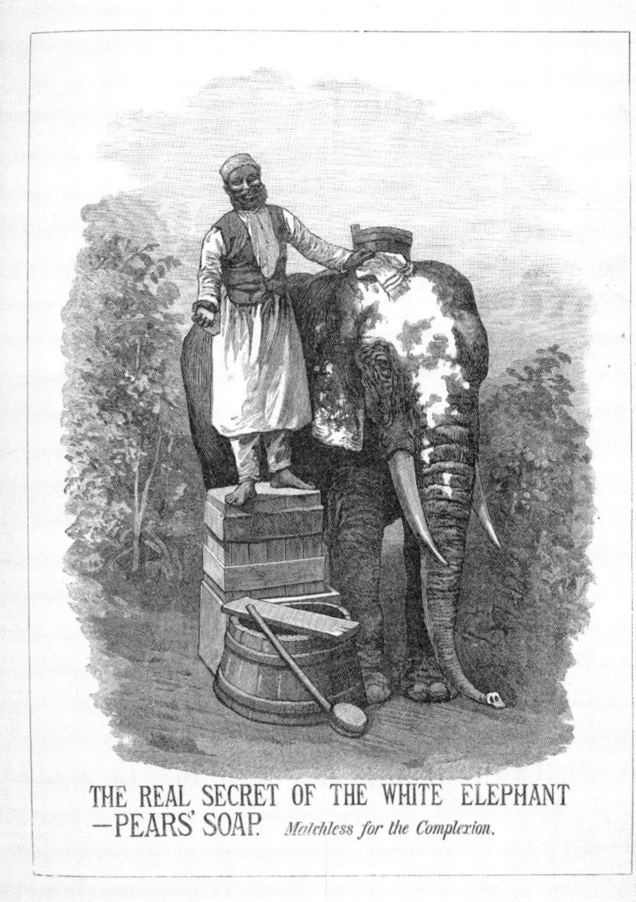

44 Pears' soap advertisement, wood engraving, *Illustrated London News*, 1884. British Library, London (P.P.7611).

conflations of non-White bodies and non-human animals clearly echo the analogies drawn in the earlier print of Gratton and highlight how his 'spotted' skin tones bestialised the afflicted individual in the popular imagination. Eager to capitalise on this public interest, Pears released an advertisement suggesting that the elephant's white spots were the result of washing with the firm's soap (fig. 44), imagery Amato has astutely linked to the Pears advertisement of the Black child scrubbed White, which was produced in *The Graphic* that same year.[118]

These associations established in the public imagination between, on the one hand, the 'mottled' and 'spotted' appearance of animals and, on the other, the appearance of partial albinism on Black skin would have been even more potent in the 1889 Pears' soap advertisement, where the surface of the bathing child's skin is captured in the spotted and mottled complexion of chromolithography. The unresolved mixture of pigment on the surface of the print and the surface of the body would have suggested to the Victorian imagination a chromatic instability and resulting racial limbo, confirmed by the Black face on the White body. But it would also have invoked animalistic associations through the pervasive linking of varicoloured bodies and varicoloured beasts in nineteenth-century visual culture (dogs, insects, horses, elephants). Shortly after this print was made, Rudyard Kipling would cement these associations between Black skin and the spotted coloration of animals in his story 'How the Leopard Got His Spots', which implied that the cat's dark spots had been transferred from the skin of an Ethiopian when he touched the leopard with his fingertips.[119]

Just as the stippled and engraved print exploited the granular surface of the matrix to highlight the spectacular appearance of Gratton's skin, so too does this chromolithograph heighten the spectacular display of the spotted appearance of the part-Black, part-White body. In this way, the printed advertisement invites the associations accrued in Victorian mass culture and medical science that perceived the spotted body as a curiosity skirting the limits of racial boundaries and the limits between the human and non-human. The curious retention of the Black face on the White body imbued the image with a host of additional meanings that may have been lost through a 'perfect' racial transformation from Whiteness to Blackness.

Such associations compounded those already manifested on the surface of the print in the chromolithograph's spotted complexion of colourful pigments – a complexion that problematically presented White skin as excessively oily, polluted, morally compromised and racially othered, and Black skin as opaque, toxic, diseased and bestial. By no means were these implications limited to soap advertisements, or to advertising in general, and considerations of other forms of chromolithographic printing (such as sheet music, artistic reproductions, maps and educational prints) would undoubtedly yield additional meanings to those suggested here. But this particular advertisement – so intimately connected to the material networks of empire; the exploitation of commodity racism; the expansion of cutaneous medicine; the ecological, pathological and ideological implications of black and coloured inks; and a long iconographic tradition of derogatory Black representation – serves as a paradigmatic object for interrogating how chromolithography transformed the aesthetics of commercial printing. Chromolithography did not simply make coloured advertisements cheaper, brighter and more vivid; its distinctive complexion of maculated hues also informed the perception of human value, class, beauty and racial difference as articulated through colour. As the most prolific form of colour printing in the age of imperial consumerism, chromolithography profoundly shaped understandings of race, racial difference, skin and skin colouring at a time when the physical and economic health of the British imperial body was contingent upon shoring up these racialised hierarchies.

Chromolithographic Legacies

The success of any new chromatic technology, as already discussed in the Introduction to this book, was contingent upon two things. The first was exhibiting people of colour as a mode of spectacular chromatic display, thereby demonstrating the chromatic possibilities of a technology through a spectrum of racial difference. The second was reassuring White audiences that this expanded spectrum would not destabilise the primacy of Whiteness. Chromolithography, this chapter has suggested, was not entirely successful in this undertaking. As the chromolithographed Pears' soap advertisement demonstrates, despite attempts to reinforce the beauty and cleanliness of White skin through the subject matter and iconography of the print, the absolute imbrication of

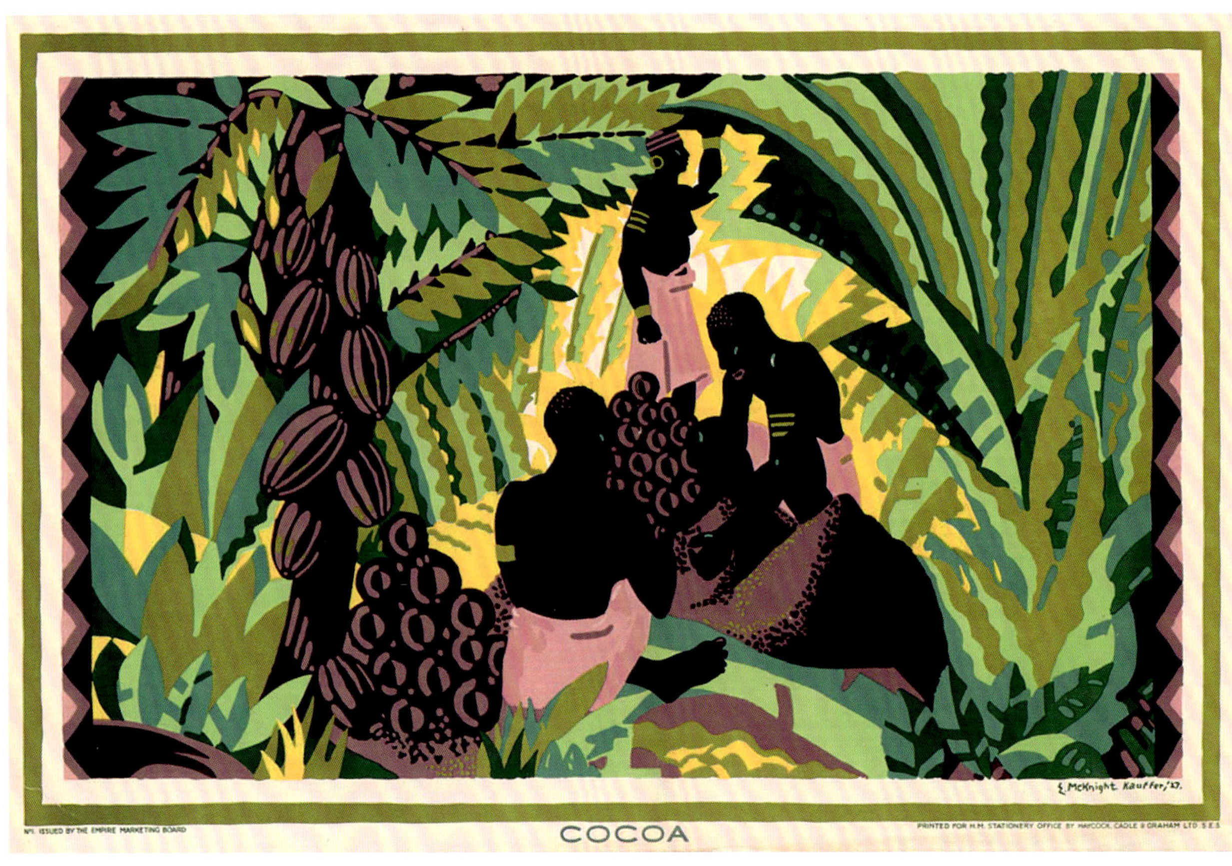

45 Edward McKnight Kauffer, 'Cocoa', chromolithograph, from *One Third of the Empire Is in the Tropics*. Library and Archives Canada / Department of Industry, Trade and Commerce fonds (ICON142381).

the White body with spots of colour, which carried negative connotations of disease, labour, toxicity and racial othering, ensured that this printing technique would be denigrated as debased and crass. That chromolithography occupied such a low status among artistic media (and still occupies this status in art historical scholarship) is not merely due to the speed with which it was printed, the gaudiness of its hues or the reproductive nature of its imagery but also due to its failure to sustain an idealised form of Whiteness.

Yet chromolithography found a fitting afterlife in the inter-war period, when it was used extensively by the Empire Marketing Board (1926–33) to encourage British consumers to buy more imperial goods, whether pineapples from Singapore, tobacco from Rhodesia (now Zimbabwe) or oranges from South Africa. Chromolithography was ideally suited to this campaign, launched in 1926, as the process's identity was intimately linked with the production and consumption of imperial commodities. These chromolithographed posters absolutely cemented the conflation of consumerism and imperialism that had emerged in the second half of the nineteenth century – of which the Pears advertisement is such a vivid encapsulation. Yet these new colourful posters emerged as Britain's imperial status gradually transitioned from one of colonial governance contingent upon an extractive economy of raw materials to a system of (supposedly) consensual and mutually beneficial commerce, a topic explored in greater length in Chapter Four, on colour film.

While these posters similarly traded upon the vivid appeals of colour to the consumer's imagination, they bear no trace of chromolithography's distinctive late Victorian complexion, which so confused the clear boundaries between Blackness, Whiteness and colour. A poster promoting cocoa created by the Anglo-American artist Edward McKnight Kauffer clearly embraces the aesthetic of the flat-colour style, comprising simple planes of solid, tessellating hues (fig. 45). This style lends itself to the primitivist modernist aesthetic, cultivated here through geometric abstraction and radical simplification of form, echoing the use of the flat-colour style in the Orientalist work of Owen Jones. This style exploits the long-held association of bright colour with the tropical spaces of the empire and the people of colour who laboured and lived within it, vivifying, exoticising and othering the bodies on display here, who are framed within a generalised verdant scene captured in teal, lime, olive, yellow and pink. But the Black skin of these cocoa harvesters is not rendered in the multiple colours and spotted complexion that characterised late Victorian chromolithography. Instead, Black skin is presented as a flat field of black ink, rendered even darker by the stark juxtaposition with bright yellow palm leaves, the uniformity of its surface (alleviated only by small blue highlights where the skin seems to glint in the sun) and the russet-coloured sole of an upturned foot. If the complexion of chromolithography troubled the relationship between Blackness, Whiteness and colour, forcing a consideration of how this reductive binary of Black and White as racial taxonomies translated into a spectrum of actual hues, then this poster essentialises the Black bodies depicted here into abstracted patches of black ink.

But chromolithography would soon be replaced by the enhanced veracity of photo-lithography, and eventually colour photography itself (the subject of the next chapter). The stone matrix would be replaced with gelatin and the hand of the lithographic artist with the photographic plate. Photo-lithography and colour photography would enable what Victorian printer W. D. Richmond described as 'such a variety of soft graduations' that 'in lithography and engraving would be impossible'.[120] While there were economic benefits to automated image-making in photography, the enhanced capacity to render subtle shifts in coloration, and gentle transitions between hues, would ultimately render the technique preferable to chromolithographic printing, as it was better suited to sustaining the idealised complexion of blemish-free, soft White skin. But, as the next chapter considers, the application of colour to the skin carried profoundly gendered connotations in addition to those of racial identity, which forged a distinctive context for colour photography's emergence as a mass medium in the inter-war decades.

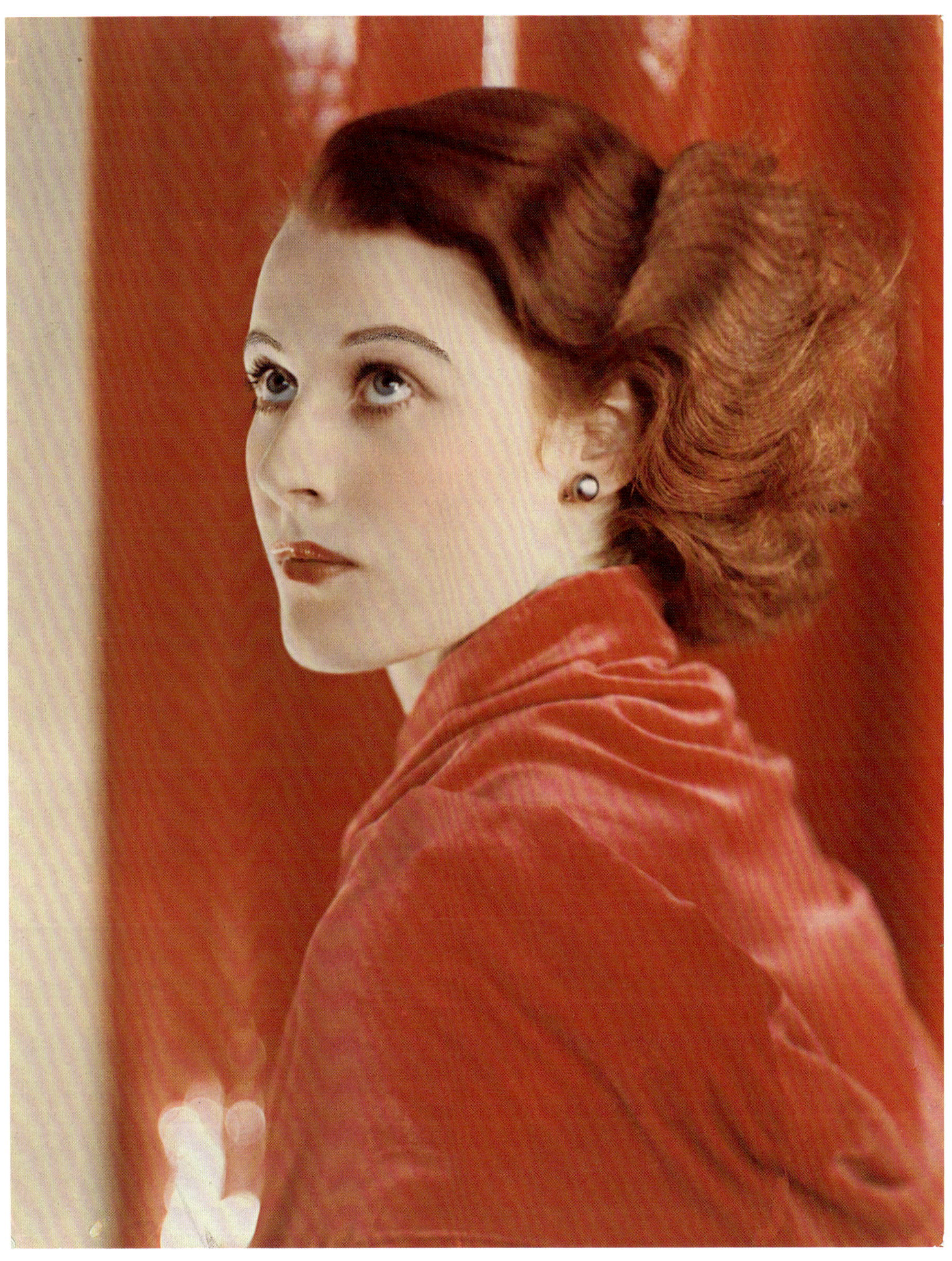

46 Madame Yevonde, *Joan Maude*, 1932, 35.6 × 27.8 cm, Vivex colour print. National Portrait Gallery, London.

3

MODERN WOMEN, MODERN COLOURS

Madame Yevonde and the Feminisation of Photography between the Wars

A striking photographic portrait of the actress Joan Maude, taken in 1932, illuminates the vital role colour played in constructing new female identities in inter-war Britain (fig. 46). Draped in a scarlet jacket, her lips coated with a ruby gloss and her face framed by a shockwave of fiery auburn hair, Maude's appearance is constructed by the sensational effects of colour. Each distinct shade of red harmonises with the folds of vermilion fabric billowing behind her like a stage curtain, alluding to her professional work in the theatre. The gentle rouging of her peachy skin indicates the attention paid to the hues with which her face is painted and powdered as part of the overall composition. Her cheeks reflect a rosy tint that complements the more powerful reds of her lips and clothes as well as the sorrel tint of her pencilled-in brows. These carefully orchestrated chromatic effects demonstrate the inseparability of colour from the forms of self-presentation that constituted popular understandings of modern femininity at this time, through clothing, cosmetics and other fashionable forms of display.

The potent chromatism of Maude's appearance presents a bold image of the 'modern woman', a new type much debated in the popular press of the inter-war decades, understood as a product of the rapid societal shifts taking place after the First World War.[1] As more women, and particularly young women, sought educational opportunities, professional fulfilment and new kinds of leisure pursuits outside the conventional spheres of domestic labour and family life, they became symbolic of the social transformations destabilising hierarchies of gender and social class in the 1920s and 1930s. The modernity of these women was measured through their appearance, whether worn on the body as bright, fashionable clothes (purchased with their own wages), painted on the face as colourful cosmetics (in a manner only just becoming socially acceptable) or dyed into their (typically short) hair. Because a woman's looks were a metric of her modernity, colour became a crucial tool for displaying and celebrating her new financial independence, participation in mass culture and departure from outmoded social conventions. It was through her appearance that the modern woman made visible the changing conventions of her gender in these years, making the supposedly trivial concerns of fashion and make-up newly politicised modes of display at this time.

Colour photography played a crucial role in mediating these new feminine identities. The end of newsprint restrictions in 1918, combined with developments in rotogravure colour printing, meant that colour photographs superseded the chromolithographed illustrations explored in the previous chapter to become an increasingly common presence in popular print media in the 1920s and 1930s.[2] Women's magazines and periodicals had long embraced colour as an essential element in fashion and beauty coverage, with *British Vogue* including a colour supplement since its launch in 1916, but this practice expanded in the inter-war years. Magazines dedicated to the glamorous lifestyles of the metropolitan elite, such as *The Bystander*, *The Sketch* and *Tatler*, often exploited colour pictures on their covers from the 1920s, while British film magazines such as *Picturegoer*, targeted largely at female fans, exploited the growing colour film market through the inclusion of colour photography.[3] The expansion of women's 'colour weeklies', such as *Woman* in the 1930s, as well as the extensive use of colour advertising in titles for younger female readers, such as *Miss Modern*, further cemented the links between colour photography, mass culture and female consumption.

The 1932 portrait of Maude, a successful stage and screen actress who would later appear in Technicolor cinema, highlights the glamour associated with colour portraiture as well as its capacity to transform women themselves into visually appealing commodities for mass consumption.[4] As Rita Felski argues, it was precisely this status both as consumers and as objects of consumption that gave women such a privileged status as symbols of modernity. However, this also meant these specifically feminised forms of modernity were devalued as compromised by capitalist and patriarchal ideologies.[5] Certainly, Maude's portrait highlights how colour was inseparable from commodified and sexualised presentations of modern femininity, as the different textures of her silky wrap, thick wavy hair and glistening lips heighten the sensuality and eroticism conventionally linked with the colour red. The portrait reflects the positive new associations of colour with feminine modes of modernity while also perpetuating the negative historical associations of colour with demonised aspects of femininity – its links to cosmetic superficiality, deceptive charm and the dangers of sexual allure. Colour was an appealing new way of expressing modern social attitudes, but it could also invoke criticisms of duplicity, artificiality and sexual profligacy that had to be carefully navigated.

The portrait is particularly significant for considering colour's relationship to modern female identities in the inter-war period, as it was one of the first colour images exhibited by pioneering photographer Yevonde Cumbers, known professionally as Madame Yevonde. Yevonde included the portrait in her 1932 exhibition at the Albany Gallery in London, which she claimed was the first show of colour portraiture ever staged in Britain.[6] As her debut colour exhibition, the show celebrated her use of the new Vivex colour photography system, only patented in Britain four years previously. Yevonde would use Vivex exclusively for her colour work during the inter-war years. The striking novelty and modishness of the exhibition secured her identity 'among the leading and most up-to-date exponents of photographic portraiture' – as the *Photographic Journal* claimed in its review.[7]

At a time when professional photography was dominated by male photographers and by black and white images, Yevonde's scorching colour portraits questioned the hegemony of both. As part of a growing cohort of professional female photographers in the inter-war decades, Yevonde's Vivex work therefore sparked debate about the feminisation of photography at this time. Colour became critical to these debates as it was a complex procedure that carried a high degree of masculine professional cachet, yet its links to fashion and cosmetics also demeaned it as a feminine concern. Yevonde's commercial success as a colour photographer, with her work dominated by portraits of fashionable women as well as commercial goods aimed at female consumers, sparked anxieties that colour, with its feminine appeals, could disrupt the historically masculine sphere of photography. While women had always been a pervasive presence in photographic circles, Yevonde's vibrant colour work marked a particularly powerful challenge to the gendered norms of photographic practice at this time.[8] It was precisely the combined effect of Yevonde's gender and her chromatism that made her work doubly disruptive to these established conventions – conventions that Lindsay Smith and Bettina Gockel have shown to be formulated around a presumed absence of women and colour from the field.[9]

Such debates reflected a broader visibility gained for women in a host of male-dominated professions at this time. Following the First World War, when many British women had assumed new jobs in order to fill labour shortages, the artificiality of the distinctions that separated men's and women's work were highlighted, creating various newly acceptable, but fiercely contested, professional opportunities for women. Yevonde's status as the foremost colour portraitist of this period made her work a visual barometer of the changing gender of labour in inter-war Britain, highlighting the role colour played in redefining men's and women's status in society through their work. This chapter examines how Madame Yevonde's Vivex photographs use colour to reflect upon and engage with the feminisation of photography, labour and modernity in the inter-war years, both through their content – as representations of modern women, wearing colourful new fashions and cosmetics and displaying new codes of behaviour – and as the products of female labour.

The focus here is on colour's gendered implications of the creative labour of a White female photographer whose work was produced and consumed within the most elite circles of British society. But the questions raised by her work – regarding the gender, and colour, of labour in inter-war Britain – are bound up in those of racial and sexual identity, which have been richly contextualised by historians of the period.[10] Of course, race and sexuality cannot be neatly de-coupled from discussions of gender, and are critical interlocutors for the feminisation of colour explored here. However, the focus in this chapter remains on the two dimensions of Yevonde's work that were perceived as marking her difference (her status as a woman and her work in colour) as opposed to those that marked her continuity with dominant photographic practice in Britain (her Whiteness, her heterosexuality and her class position).

Yevonde's work feminised photographic practice not simply because of the long aesthetic tradition that denigrated colour as a feminine concern but because the processes and technologies that she used to make colour photographs spoke to specific historical concerns around the automation and feminisation of labour in general at this time. The Vivex process, associated both with Yevonde's photography and with the feminised labour of the women who worked at Vivex's laboratory, carried gendered connotations that made it a crucial site for negotiating new ideas about women and work in the 1930s, articulated through these dazzling photographs.

'Could a Woman Have Done That?'

Yevonde viewed her photographic practice as an expression of her feminist politics, intimately connected to the urgent concern of women's equality. Having joined the suffragettes in 1910 at the age of seventeen, she was eager to participate in this thriving feminist movement. However, she was anxious about the escalating militancy of the Women's Social and Political Union at this time, as its tactics of civil disobedience and criminality conflicted with the bourgeois values of her middle-class upbringing in south London. She recalled in her autobiography that 'I would cheerfully have burned churches, destroyed letterboxes and embarked on a career of wickedness and violence in order to claim political freedom, had it not been for the horror of prison, hunger strikes and forcible feeding'.[11] While Yevonde sought to positively further the suffragettes' feminist agenda, encompassing greater educational, professional and social freedoms for women as well as voting rights, she did not wish to participate in the illegal activities, violent strikes and other forms of physical protest that characterised factions of the movement at this time.[12] As a White, middle-class woman in metropolitan London, Yevonde found other means of expressing her interest in women's liberation, viewing a professional career as a way of liberating herself from the cycles of female oppression, subservience and domesticity she saw as endemic to women's lives in her suburban surroundings.[13]

Yevonde was inspired to pursue photography after seeing a 1911 advertisement for a studio assistant in *The Suffragette* magazine placed by the movement's portraitist Lena Connell, but she ultimately took up an apprenticeship with society photographer Lallie Charles, whose portrait studio was based in Lon-

gence of colour photography intersected with understandings of the gendered labour of photography at this time.

Yevonde's lecture, reproduced in the *British Journal of Photography*, elicited a slew of correspondence debating which sex produced more capable photographers, much of it exuding a fervent misogyny and repeating highly conventionalised ideas that a women's inferior physical and intellectual capacity meant she should occupy herself solely with domestic labour. One correspondent commented that:

> Women photographers are merely a passing fad ... as much out of place in our community as women barbers or police. But we shall have to endure them for a time, just as we have to put up with influenza and rheumatism. If we have patience, the whirligig of time will bring its revenges upon them and compel them to play the part in life nature intended them to do, and nurse babies rather than grievances.[31]

Other male correspondents noted that women lacked both the rugged physicality and the scientific expertise demanded by the manual and technical process of the 'man-founded profession' of photography.[32] One recalled an incident 'in the old wet plate days' when, in order to produce survey photographs, he had had to carry his materials – 'darkroom tent, silver bath, collodion, iron developer, water tank "and all"' – for several miles, rising at four in the morning to ensure he could capture the plates and develop them 'on the spot' before sensitising, printing, toning, fixing, washing and mounting them before delivery by one o'clock. He concluded, 'Could a woman have done that? I think not.'[33] Highlighting the taxing physical labour necessary to take photographs as well as the complex chemical knowledge required to process them, the correspondent insisted photography was a profession unsuited to women. However, a female correspondent suggested such a concern with photography's complex materiality was long out of date, noting that while women had practised photography for generations, now thanks to 'modern conveniences ... photography is not the messy job it was in my father's time and its simplicity today is an inducement for any lady to take it up'.[34]

These responses to Yevonde's lecture illuminate some of the key issues that structured debates around women and photographic labour in the inter-war years, as well as broader debates in British society about women and work in general. The suggestion made by Yevonde and her supportive female correspondent – that photographic skill was shifting away from technical expertise towards a more feminised interest in aesthetics, a shift facilitated by new technologies that removed some of the mechanical and chemical complexities of photography – echoed broader debates about the deskilling and feminisation of work in the inter-war years.

These issues became particularly urgent in the 1920s and 1930s as the First World War had forced significant disruptions to conventional ideas about appropriate male and female occupations. During the war, many women on the home front had filled positions left vacant by men, undertaking waged manual work in manufacturing, agriculture and the military sector. Yevonde herself temporarily closed her photographic studio in London to undertake agricultural work as a land girl. But for some women the war created an opportunity to enter photography, as female receptionists and assistants were promoted to studio managers and camera operators, overseeing these businesses while their male owners were at war.[35] Shortly before the conclusion of the war, the *British Journal of Photography* reported that as women had taken up the posts left vacant by men, 'a large class of well-trained women photographers has thus been created capable of commanding good wages who are not likely to relinquish their professions'.[36]

These photographers were among the increasing numbers of women moving into paid work outside the home, whether in factories or offices, who attenuated the logic of a gendered division of labour in British society. These changes to women's professional standing were coupled with other kinds of legal reform that redefined the status of women in the immediate post-war period, chief among them changes occurring in 1918 and 1919 including new voting rights for some women and the ability to become lawyers, civil servants and Members of Parliament.[37] While marriage bars were still in place for most occupations, throughout the 1920s and 1930s young women increasingly moved into waged labour outside the conventional realms of domestic service, becoming a conspicuous new presence in the British workforce.[38]

The inter-war decades also saw a recession for heavy industry in Britain and its empire, as shipbuilding, coal, cotton and steel slumped following the First World War. This was compounded by the effects of the depression and mass unemployment from 1929, which eroded opportunities in these male-dominated labour sectors. However, the consumption of branded commodities (of the kind considered in the previous chapter) coupled with the expansion of mass production methods created new kinds of work, particularly for women, who became especially prevalent in the manufacture of electrical goods and cars, as well as domestic consumables such as pre-packaged food items. Young women in particular presented a cheap and un-unionised workforce that became increasingly visible on the shop floor in the 1930s, whether in the factory or in retail environments. The growth of machine production, conveyor-belt assembly lines and other kinds of Fordist automation created more part-skilled or unskilled work for unmarried girls, who were popular with employers as they could be paid lower wages than adult men.[39] While employment in a photographic studio was not the same kind of assembly-line production as factory work, the employment of women and girls was still seen as a way for photographers to cut production costs in these industries.[40]

The inter-war years were therefore marked by a pervasive anxiety (particularly among working-class men) about the feminisation of the workforce, engendered in part by the automation of sectors that previously required either skilled work or heavy physical labour.[41] While concerns over the mechanisation of labour were not new to these decades (and even predated George Frederic Watts's disquiet about industrialisation, explored in Chapter One) and had always carried gendered assumptions about the manliness of physical work, in the inter-war years these arguments became acutely framed in terms of gender in response to the growing female workforce emerging after the First World War. As Adrian Bingham describes in his study of the period's popular press, a lexis of 'invasion' permeated discussions of women and work, with tongue-in-cheek suggestions in the *Daily Mail* that it would soon be necessary to establish a 'Men's Rights Defence League'.[42] The acute response to Yevonde's lecture from vitriolic male correspondents is therefore legible as part of this wider resistance to the related automation and feminisation of labour in the inter-war years.

These concerns about technical skill and the gender of photographic labour would be further exacerbated by the growth of colour photography in the 1930s and in particular the Vivex process used by Yevonde. The complexity of working in colour ensured it carried a high degree of technical prestige (associated with the masculinist discourses of professional photographers), yet the emergence of the new Vivex colour process, designed to simplify certain aspects of colour work, raised questions about the gendered nature of chromatic labour. Given that colour was already strongly gendered in the public imagination, linked with the female spheres of fashion, cosmetics and other forms of beautification, Vivex opened up debates about whether colour photography, like portraiture, should be 'entirely a woman's profession'.

The Automatic Paintbox

The chemist Douglas Arthur Spencer patented the Vivex process through his firm Colour Photographs Ltd in 1928, releasing the system on a commercial basis a year later.[43] Vivex entered the market at a moment when photographers had a range of systems available to them – by 1932, Spencer estimated, there were 250 systems from which to choose.[44] The complexity of these systems had evolved significantly since the earliest demonstrations of colour photography by Scottish physicist James Clerk Maxwell in

1861.[45] Yet many of the theoretical principles underlying Maxwell's work still informed photographic practice in the inter-war period, each contingent on the separation and recombination of colours.

By this time colour processes were divided into two types: the complex subtractive processes that produced colour through the mixture of pigments in the form of a print, and the simpler additive systems that produced colour through the mixture of light in the form of a transparency. These two systems carried distinct limitations and connotations of class and gender, which were framed around questions of skill and aesthetics. Understanding the implications of these technologies is crucial for situating Vivex and Yevonde's work within the context of photographic labour at this time.

Subtractive processes, including the British Autotype (available from 1919) and Spencer's Vivex system, required the photographer to record colour information on three separate plates using coloured filters, which were then recombined through printing, as each image was either pigmented or dyed its respective colours and reassembled to form a single full-colour image. These processes, also called 'assembly' systems due to the need to reassemble the image in register from three negatives (in a manner not unlike a chromolithograph), proved challenging even to skilled photographers. Colour printing demanded specialised equipment, knowledge of colour chemistry and an advanced degree of technical skill. However, such systems gave rich saturation and a high level of control over the finished image, including the chance to retouch photographs – noted as especially important for fashion photography that demanded the manipulation of the female form. For these reasons, and their reproducibility as paper prints, photographers favoured subtractive systems for professional and commercial work.

Additive colour processes, on the other hand, removed much of this technical complexity but were limited in other respects. Several were suitable for amateur use, including the Autochrome (from 1907) and Dufaycolor (from 1935), which required only a single exposure of a specially designed plate that was overlaid with a colour screen filter. However, these systems had long exposure times and desaturated colour, and produced only a single positive as a transparency, which required a special lightbox or projector for viewing and exhibited visible grain when enlarged. Although much more convenient and less technically complex than subtractive systems, additive technologies were therefore unviable as commercial techniques.

The distinction between these processes – between amateur and professional, between additive and subtractive – was also implicitly gendered, with female photographers far more prevalent among the amateur practitioners using these additive systems. These distinctions were by no means rigidly fixed, as evidenced by Yevonde's contemporary Agnes B. Warburg, an amateur photographer who co-founded the Royal Photographic Society's Colour Group in 1927 and worked across a host of colour processes, from the simpler Autochrome and Dufaycolor systems to the highly complex subtractive assembly systems such as Raydex and Tri-Colour Carbro.[46] But the division between the waged labour of the commercial photographer and the hobbyism of the amateur (like Warburg) was drawn along distinctly gendered fault-lines and reflected in the technologies used by these respective groups.

It is important to reiterate that amateurs such as Warburg were a distinct class of photographer from the so-called button-presser. Colour had remained outside the purview of the snapshot photographer as it was too complex and expensive for a truly untrained user. Kodak's release of its Kodachrome film in 1936 did herald the beginning of colour snapshot photography, but, until this time, even amateur work in colour demanded a significant understanding of photographic technology.[47] These colour amateurs occupied a status above the 'button-presser' due to their technical curiosity, understanding of photochemical techniques and specialised equipment. As Carol Armstrong describes, upper- and middle-class women had always been especially well represented among these amateur photographers, as the medium carried few of the institutional or

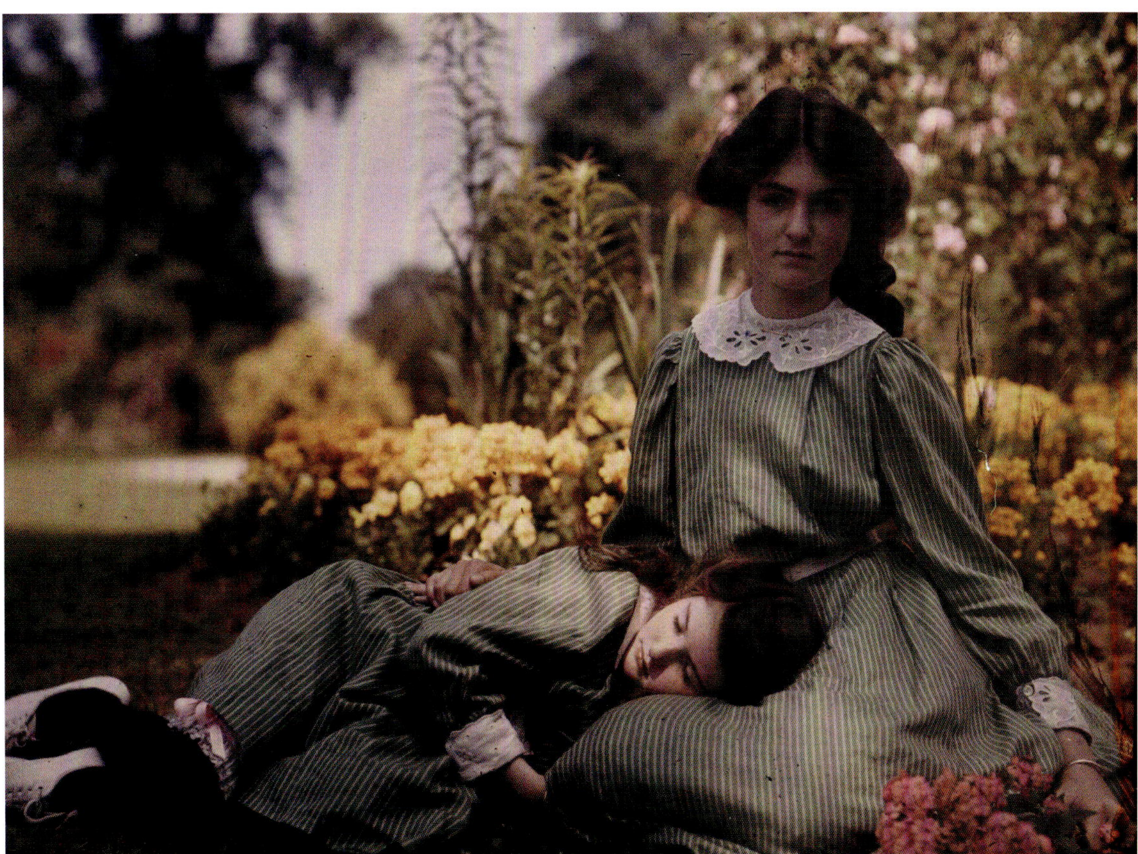

48 Etheldreda Janet Laing, *Iris and Janet Laing*, 1914, 3¼ × 4 in, Autochrome transparency. Science and Media Museum, Bradford.

education barriers that barred women from other creative pursuits, and it could be undertaken in the domestic space of the home by anyone with the time and capital to invest in its equipment.[48] But the additional cost of working in colour made it a form of photographic practice reserved for the wealthiest of experimenters, like Warburg, who came from a family of bankers and (without marrying or working) remained financially independent throughout her life. Colour therefore added a class dimension to the already gendered division between amateur and professional photography witnessed at this time. Furthermore, the difference between the technologies used by amateurs and professionals aestheticised these distinctions.

The technical limitations of amateur processes such as the Autochrome and Dufaycolor produced a very distinctive aesthetic of muted tones, soft focus and, in the case of Autochromes, a typically diminutive size (4 × 3¼ inches) that lent itself to conventionalised feminine descriptors.[49] A review of Autochromes from the 1925 Royal Photographic Society demonstrates the gendered language used to describe these works even when they were made by men, as the reviewer praises one 'perfect little autochrome', noting another is 'quiet and so restrained in colour', while others he praises for their 'delicate' and 'charming' tints.[50]

The gendering of these aesthetic qualities is illustrated by a pre-war Autochrome by amateur photographer Etheldreda Janet Laing (fig. 48). This double portrait of her two daughters, shot in the grounds of Bury Knowle Manor House in Oxfordshire, where the family lived, features many of the tropes that would become conventional for Autochrome work and

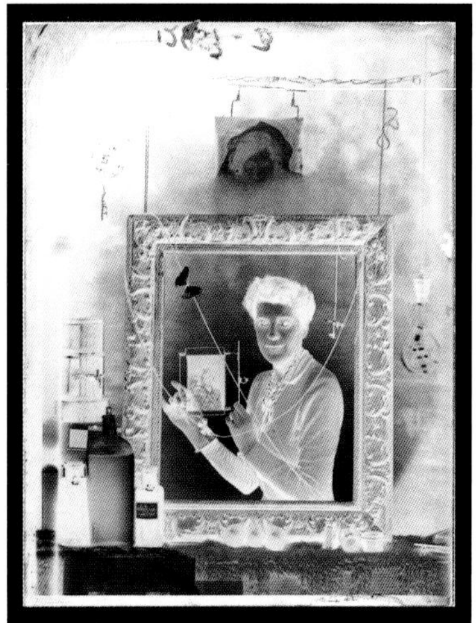

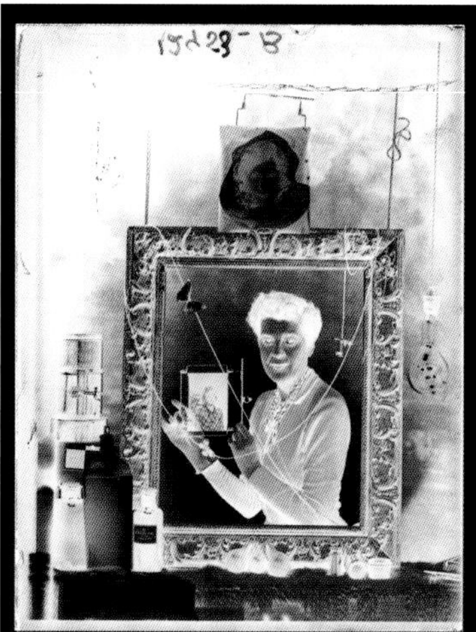

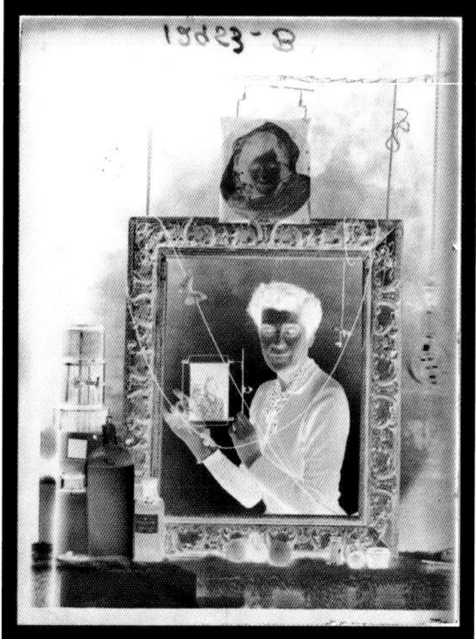

49 The three glass plate colour separation negatives for Madame Yevonde, *Self Portrait* (see fig. 65). National Portrait Gallery, London.

highlights how the process became associated with upper-class, amateur female photography. The screen process was not especially sensitive given the density of the filter through which light had to pass, and it therefore worked best with bright light, long exposures and vivid subjects. Sunlit floral studies, like Laing's festooning borders, feature heavily in Autochromes of this period, as the natural hues of flowers captured in broad daylight reproduced especially well. The languid poses of the children would have prevented blurring during the long exposure, but they also reproduced conventions of female passivity, as the forced stasis of these girls renders them ornamental objects like the flowers they sit beside, draped in green as though they, like the plants, are a naturalised form of decorative colour. The short focal length of the Autochrome give a softness to the photograph's background that renders the blossoms a dreamlike haze, while the loss of light renders their hues muted, restrained and gentle. This leisurely subject reflected the time spared by the photographer, freed from the demands of waged labour to capture the slow, delicate hues under the sun of a summer's afternoon.

The subtractive Vivex system – with its bold, saturated colours, glossy prints and crisp faces lit by bright studio lights – evidenced a radically different aesthetic from these pastel reveries. Autochromes are easily described as 'pretty', a term that Rosalind Galt explains has profoundly gendered connotations of sweetness, minuteness and fussy ornamentation.[51] Yet Yevonde's Vivex photographs seem to occupy an altogether different aesthetic order, with sharp geometry and rich colours. Yevonde also had her Vivex photographs printed at the large size of 15 × 12 in (38 × 30 cm), nearly fourteen times larger than an Autochrome, to establish their status as commercial artworks for display rather than as sentimental keepsakes.[52] However, in developing the Vivex technology, Spencer had incorporated certain aspects of amateur processes to make colour work easier and more accessible to a larger number of photographers, and thereby expand his market. The Vivex process therefore crucially shifted the task of printing and registering prints from the photographer to the manufacturer.

The system, a modification of the Carbro technique, required photographers to capture three exposures onto discrete quarter-size (3¼ × 4¼ in; 8 × 11 cm) glass plates (fig. 49). Each plate was covered with a different colour filter of red, green or blue, which enabled colour to be recorded as tone

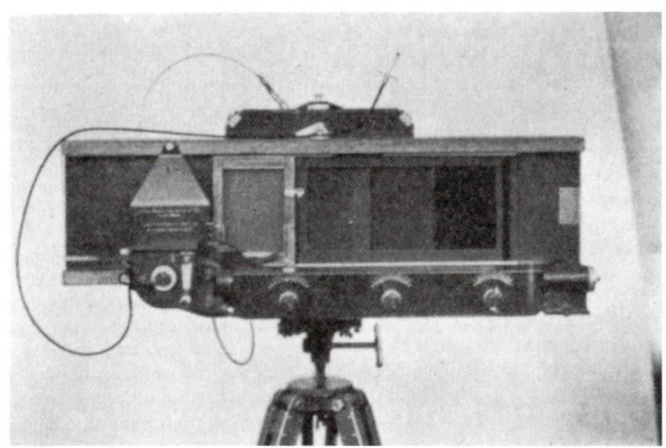

50 Vivex repeating back camera, illustrated in D. A. Spencer, 'Recent Developments in Colour Photography', *Journal of the Royal Society of Arts*, vol. 88, no. 4545 (1939): 168.

51 Filters for the Vivex automatic repeating back camera, *c.*1935, possibly owned by Madame Yevonde. Royal Photographic Society Collection, Victoria and Albert Museum, London.

on the black and white plate. Capturing these three exposures could either be done with a repeating back camera (figs 50 and 51), which exposed each plate in turn, or through a single-exposure Vivex camera, as Yevonde documents in her vivid self-portrait of 1937 (fig. 52), although she used both systems in her practice. Weighing 5.5 kg, the Vivex camera was heavy and cumbersome, as indicated by Yevonde's flexed bicep revealed by her short sleeves as well as her firmly gripped fist, perhaps a playful nod to the performative masculinity of handling weighty photographic equipment boasted by correspondents to the *British Journal of Photography* and the supposed 'daintiness' required by cameras for women. Yevonde revelled in the physical challenges of the system, describing 'the enormous lenses, heavy cameras … monstrous arc lamps and immobile studios' as 'quite wonderful'.[53]

Certainly, photographers using the Vivex system devised printing instructions for the laboratory so their photographs would reach desired levels of density and saturation. They could also ask for amendments to the images after they had initially been processed. For instance, Yevonde might indicate to the laboratory the correct hair colour for her sitters when she sent her images for processing (noting their hair colour as 'fair' or 'dark' on the envelopes containing the plates), and she similarly requested amendments to skin tones after receiving her prints (describing the flesh of the Earl and Countess Mountbatten of Burma as 'too dark' in their 1937 portrait, presumably in order to sustain ideals of Whiteness for the imperial couple, who would go on to become viceroy and vicereine of India).[54]

Yet it was the Colour Photographs Ltd laboratory in Willesden that was responsible for carrying out the complex printing process. Laboratory workers transformed the three plate negatives into bromide paper positives, which were then each pressed, still

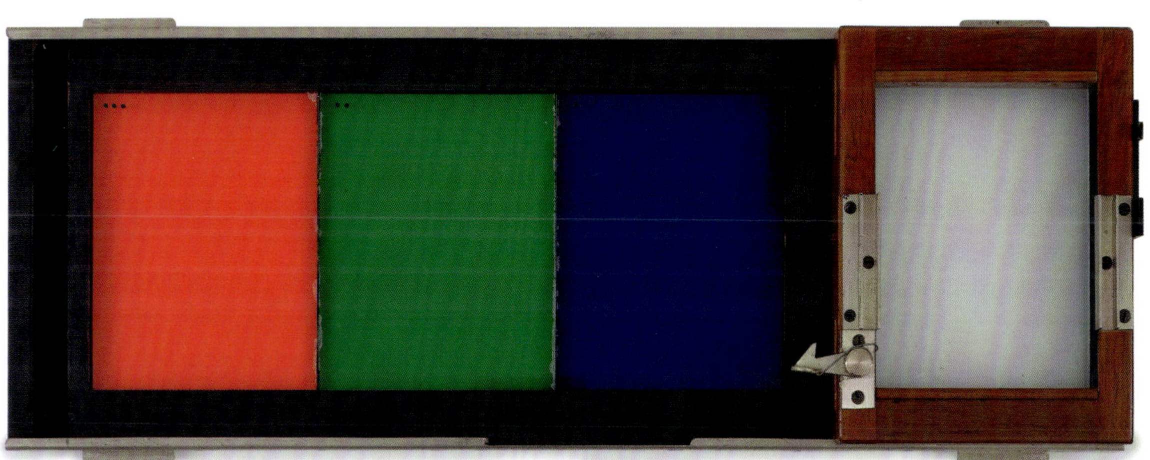

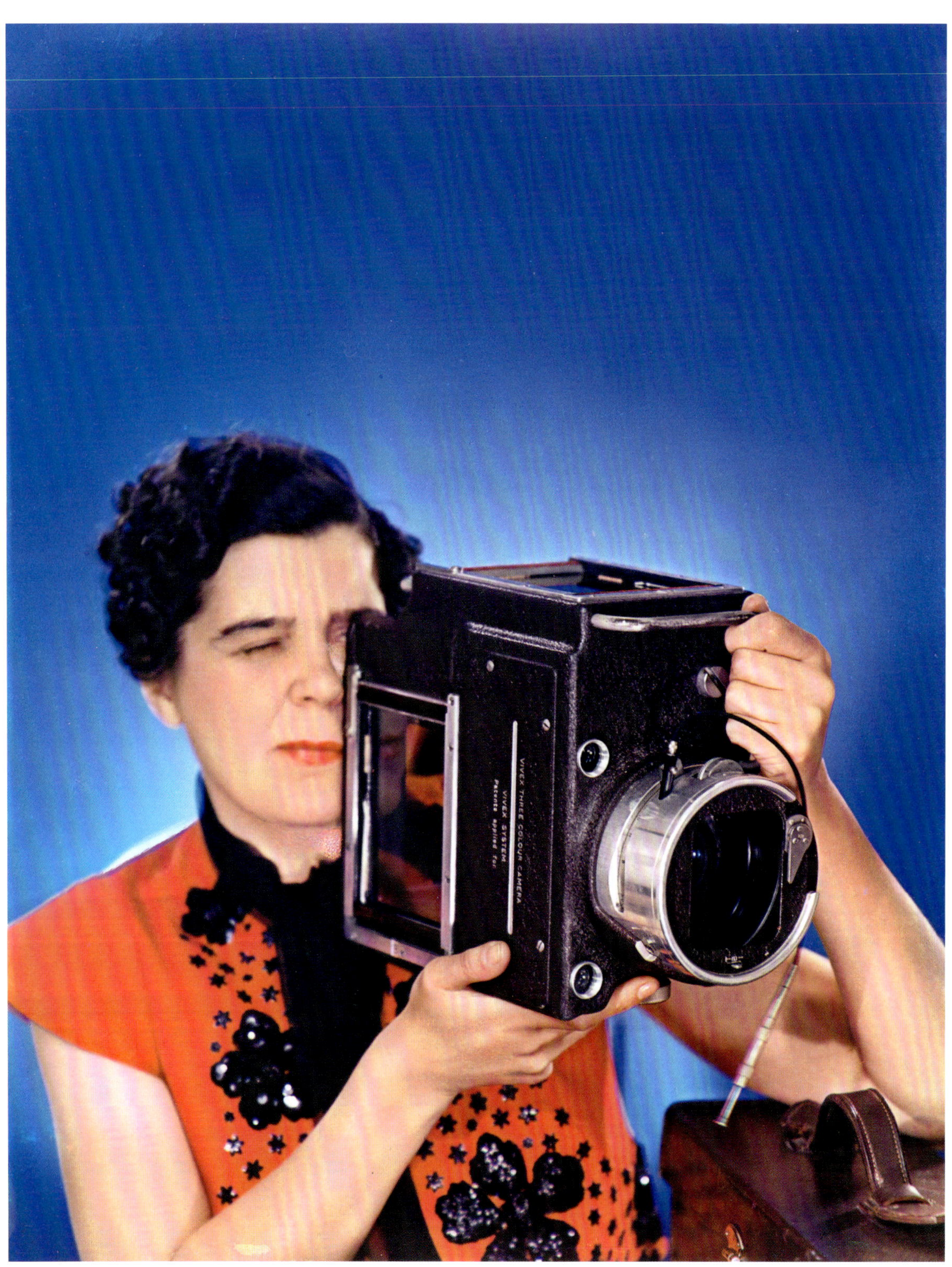
VIVEX THREE COLOUR CAMERA
VIVEX SYSTEM
Patents applied for

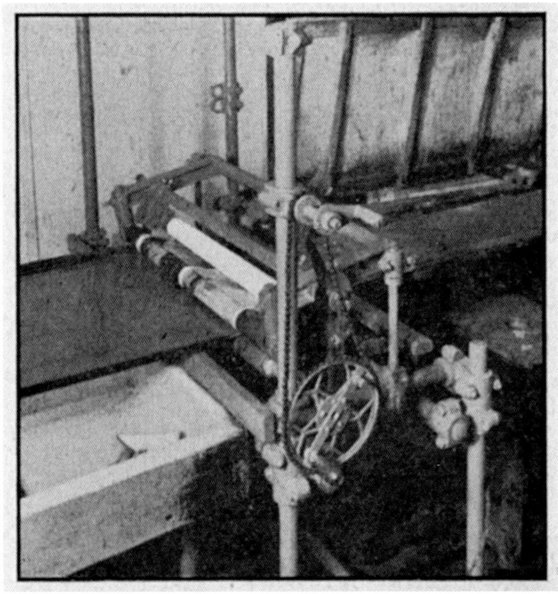

wet, against a sensitised 'tissue' of pigmented gelatin (one yellow, one cyan, one magenta). Workers used a mangle for this task of pressing together the bromide paper and pigmented gelatin tissue (fig. 53), but they subsequently peeled the images apart, leaving a colour copy of the black and white plate captured in the coloured gelatin. The gelatin was then transferred to a flexible cellophane support, subsequently washed to remove colour from unexposed areas and hung up to dry overnight, a process that left the sheets crumpled by morning. The workers in the laboratory's assembly department then transferred the layer of pigmented gelatin from the cellophane support to paper one colour at a time, the registration made easier by the stretchability of the cellophane. After the remaining gelatin was removed from the paper, only the pigmented image remained on its surface, now recombined to comprise a full-colour image. This process had to be repeated each time to produce a single print, meaning Vivex rarely executed large print runs.[55]

52 Madame Yevonde, *Self Portrait* (with Vivex Three Colour Camera), 1937, 39.4 × 30.8 cm, dye-transfer print. Royal Photographic Society Collection, Victoria and Albert Museum, London.

53 Mangle 'bringing bromide prints into contact with sensitized pigment tissue', from D. A. Spencer and F. W. Coppin, 'Basic Features of the Vivex Process', *Photographic Journal: Section B*, vol. 88B no. 4 (July–August 1948): 82.

While capturing the colour separations was a challenging task for photographers, and advising the laboratory with directions on how to balance the colour separations demanded a sound understanding of the process, the fact that photographers did not need to process and develop these images in their own darkrooms vastly reduced the complexity of the process and also made colour work more affordable. Although Spencer clearly promoted the system as a process for professionals, his description of it as an 'automatic paintbox' highlights his desire to emphasise its ease of use.[56] In a vivid echo of the debates surrounding the industrialisation of painting materials in the late nineteenth century (as explored in Chapter One), Spencer claimed that 'it was just as illogical for the colour photographer to make his own prints as it would be for the painter to make his own paints'.[57]

Vivex became the dominant system for commercial colour work in the inter-war years in Britain. Around two hundred professional photographers adopted the process, predominantly for advertising commissions, with Vivex manufacturing 90 per cent of colour photographs in Britain at this time.[58] As Spencer noted, the process was designed to allow for the mass production of colour prints to become 'a simple standardized, easily-taught drill', which created efficiencies for the laboratory and economies for the photographer, who did not need to invest in special chemicals and equipment.[59] Vivex was therefore designed both to take complex developing out of the hands of the photographer and to simplify these processes in the laboratory itself – in Spencer's terms, replacing 'human judgement by scientific measurement ... human control by mechanical certainty ... craftsmen by mechanics'.[60]

While Spencer viewed this as a means of simplifying colour, it also diminished the status accorded to colour photography as photographers no longer manufactured their own prints. Before 1932 the

Royal Photographic Society did not allow photographers to exhibit colour works they had not printed themselves. After 1932 they highlighted any prints processed by the photographer by adding an asterisk to their name in the catalogue as a mark of distinction.[61] As the complexity of processing and registering colour separations was what lent the (already feminised) realm of colour a credible masculinity, the delegation of this work to the laboratory undermined the status of the process.

The fact that this work was undertaken at the laboratory by women further threatened the masculine professionalism of colour work. As recorded in a 1935 photograph, women staffed the assembly and registration departments of the Vivex laboratory (fig. 54).[62] This was not unusual, as there were many kinds of laboratory work deemed especially suitable for female workers as these tasks drew parallels with other forms of domestic labour, or supposedly feminine concerns. Yevonde recalled that during her apprenticeship, she and two other girls 'had to rock gently' the developing dishes in the low light of the darkroom, in an unmistakable echo of rocking a cradle (ironically, perhaps, as she describes her cohort performing this task as 'three young virgins sitting in the dark').[63] She considered her other responsibilities – such as retouching photos to remove extra chins, thin the hips, enhance eyelashes, remove blemishes and smooth the skin – as a distinctly feminine skill linked to vanity and beautification.[64] Additionally, mounting prints, another aspect of Yevonde's apprenticeship, involved the use of 'a small iron' for attaching tissue, which demanded just the right degree of heat and pressure, like ironing delicate items of clothing.[65] Similarly, in her first studio Yevonde recalled 'washing the plates' in a small sink, mirroring the labour of housework with that of the studio, whereby glass negative plates stand in for dinner plates and glassware.[66]

Women also worked in the sensitometry departments of Ilford Laboratories in the 1930s measuring the sensitivity of photographic paper to light, a practice Michelle Henning links to contemporary beauty culture's interest in suntanning and the sensitivity of the skin to light.[67] At the Vivex laboratory, on the other hand, the washing and drying of the photographic sheets, which were left on a line to dry and squeezed through a mangle, clearly echoed the task of doing laundry – which reconciles this waged work with more conventional forms of female domestic tasks. Furthermore, the enhanced automation and standardisation of processes at the laboratory meant these workers were, as Spencer described, not 'craftsmen' but 'mechanics', the supposedly automated nature of their work echoing wider anxieties about women's encroachment upon male spheres of skilled labour through new technologies of mass production.[68] While the work of registering and assembling prints was clearly skilled and difficult work, Vivex's reputation as 'a factory standardised process' persisted in trade journals at this time.[69]

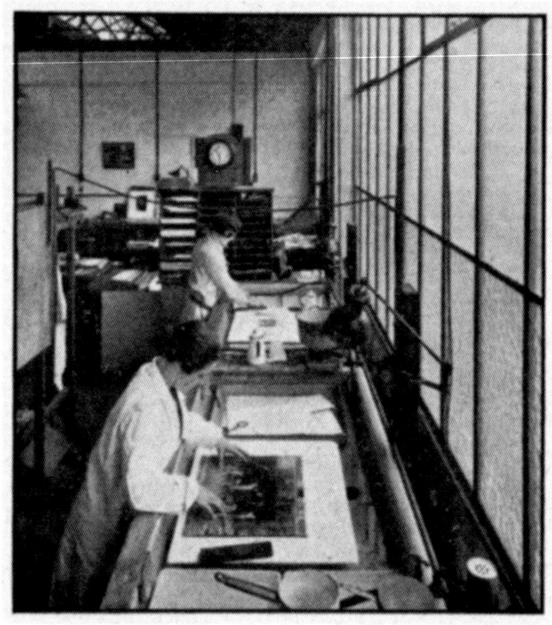

54 Women working in the assembly department of Colour Photographs Ltd. From D. A. Spencer and F. W. Coppin, 'Basic Features of the Vivex Process', *Photographic Journal: Section B*, vol. 88B no. 4 (July–August 1948): 83.

The Vivex process, which marked the arrival of commercially viable colour photography in Britain, therefore threatened to feminise photographic labour in a number of ways: through its deskilling of colour's technical complexity (linked to feminised amateur practices); the laboratory's use of female workers and automated technologies rhetorically linked to broader societal concerns about the effeminacy of inter-war work; its application in the female spheres of mass culture and consumerism; and, not least, the fact that a female photographer became the process's most visible and vocal advocate. As Bettina Gockel has argued, the increasing visibility and viability of this feminised colour photography also helped to solidify the latent masculinity of black and white practice at this time, further polarising these techniques into rhetorical binaries of colour/colourlessness, feminine/masculine and commerce/art in the inter-war years.[70]

While Yevonde claimed at a 1937 symposium on colour photography that she liked to use the Vivex process because 'it was easy. One touched a button and Colour Photographs Ltd. did the rest', such a claim was clearly a tongue-in-cheek overstatement – a riff on Kodak's slogan used to sell its automatic cameras to untrained, (typically) female, snapshot photographers.[71] Vivex was by no means this kind of simple, easy-to-use system. Yet, with this claim Yevonde laid bare how Vivex's process invited speculation over the extent to which it deskilled colour practice through automation and thereby opened up the field of professional colour photography to women. But Yevonde did not see Vivex photography as a deskilled practice. Instead, she viewed it as a realm where new skills – skills conventionally developed by women – gathered a new importance. While Yevonde had claimed that women's emotional sensitivity made them excellent portraitists, she also proposed that their skills in fashion, make-up, hair-styling and other forms of self-ornamentation made them ideal colourists.

'Why Colour?'

The ability to mix, match and combine colours was identified as a crucial skill for middle-class women in the 1930s. Beauty and fashion advice at this time routinely commented upon the new chromatism of cosmetics, hairstyles and clothing, educating women on how best to employ the new shades at their disposal. While colour had largely been absent from cosmetics until the inter-war years, as items such as rouge and lipstick had once carried unsavoury connotations of sexual licentiousness, by the 1930s beauty commentators were suggesting that these items were not just accepted facts of modern beauty but absolute necessities. The women's page in *The Express* warned in 1935 that it was 'impossible' to avoid make-up if one wanted to be seen 'under the glaring modern lights and wearing modern colours and dresses', suggesting that the vivified environment of inter-war Britain, particularly nightclubs, restaurants and dancehalls, demanded a vivified personal appearance to match.[72] The industrialisation of cosmetics manufacturing following the First World War had rapidly increased the number of products available for sale and in 1939 the beauty correspondent of *The Times* reported that 'there are an almost unaccountable number of shades available in lipstick, rouge, and powder'.[73] The influence in particular of American beauty brands like Max Factor (linked with Hollywood stardom), which were evolving to accommodate the new demands of Technicolor film, extended the palette of beauty products available for White consumers in the 1930s and these women were therefore encouraged to learn how to combine different colours of powder, lipstick and nail polish depending upon the particular hues of their skin, eyes and hair.[74] This created the illusion of an expansive, personalised palette of cosmetics despite the fact that these products only offered a narrowly prescribed range of mass-produced items designed for a small spectrum of White skin tones.

Complex charts, such as a leaflet from Max Factor's major British rival Leichner, featured regularly in beauty guides to educate women on the appropriate selection of chromatic combinations (fig. 55). Such

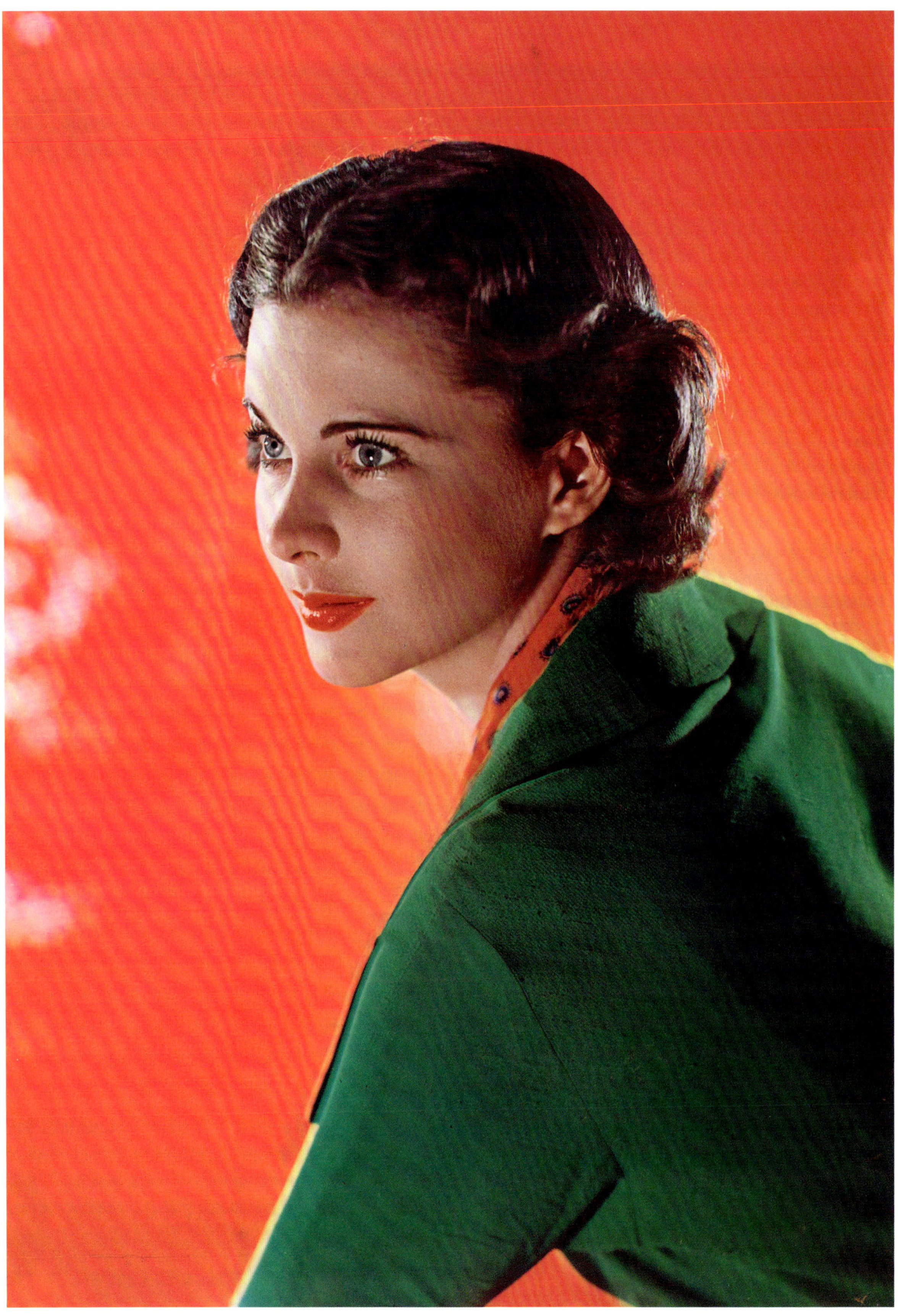

advice that 'Geranium' lips harmonised with black and 'brilliant red' clothing.[84] But, while harmony was the watchword for cosmetics and fashion, Yevonde places these matching red shades against a complementary cobalt backdrop, which makes them visibly pop through a powerful contrasting effect. She described how 'clashing contrasts are thrilling' compared to theories of harmony that advocated 'one prevailing hue'.[85] The dominant shades of red and blue are also punctuated by the dramatic blacks of her short hair, the camera and the embroidered details of her clothing, which give a punchy geometry to the portrait but also create different surface effects, from the raven sheen of her curls and the glint on the camera's metal casing to the glamorous sparkle lent by the sequined stars and flowers of her outfit.

These striking combinations of chromatic and textural effect were typical of Yevonde's style, which exploited the vivid saturation possible with the Vivex process to enrich her bold choice of colours. Her 1936 portrait of the British actress Vivien Leigh similarly demonstrates the daring combination of harmonising and contrasting shades (fig. 57). Here, the scorching red of Leigh's lipstick perfectly matches her blouse and the cloth backdrop but is starkly contrasted by the pine green of her stylish collared jacket, exposed by the dynamic twist of her torso, which reveals her back to the camera. The portrait seems remarkably proleptic, made three years before Leigh's stardom would become indelibly associated with colour through her most famous role as Scarlett O'Hara in Technicolor's *Gone With the Wind* (US, 1939; dir. Victor Fleming), a character whose chromatic name would be enriched by the notoriously vivid saturation of Technicolor's red hues. Yet the portrait does reflect the impact that contemporary Hollywood cinema and colour cinematography had upon photographic aesthetics and female portraiture at this time. A review of the 1935 Professional Photographers Association exhibition highlighted how Hollywood influenced contemporary photography, suggesting it was clear that 'Hollywood now sets the standard of feminine looks for most of the white world' as so many of the portrait photographs on display 'might have been cut out of lengths of film'.[86] Captured in the same year that Technicolor opened its British wing, a subject explored in the next chapter, Yevonde's portrait of Leigh demonstrates a keen awareness of new chromatic styles of feminine glamour cultivated through mass cultural forms (particularly Technicolor films and colour fan magazines). The striking modernity of the portrait is therefore produced through both its bold combination of fashionable colours and its dialogue with the mass culture of female consumption that characterised the 1930s.

57 Madame Yevonde, *Vivien Leigh*, 1936, 44 × 30.7 cm, modern dye-transfer print, *c.*1990. Royal Photographic Society Collection, Victoria and Albert Museum, London.

In her 1932 lecture, Yevonde described how 'when I started Colour work I said "if we are going to have Colour Photography for heaven's sake let's have a riot of colour, and none of your wishy-washy half-tinted effects"'.[87] Perhaps more than any other portrait by Yevonde, this image of Leigh reflects the photographer's riotous palette, a distinctly modern aesthetic cultivated both by the new Vivex colour technology and by modern trends in cosmetics and fashion, which linked a boldness of hue with a boldness of expression in these images of modern women, including Yevonde herself. Her deft combination of colours also celebrates the feminised skills that helped to forged these modern female identities, crafted through fashion, make-up and painted nails.

Yevonde coupled these feminised colour skills with an unusual deployment of Vivex's photographic technology to produce her distinctive style. Eager to develop new chromatic effects, Yevonde discovered ways to exploit technical flaws in the process to produce images that were not technically sound but were chromatically arresting, upholding her assertion that a preoccupation with technical precision did not necessarily produce the most interesting portraits.

In her image of Leigh, for example, the slight movement of the sitter's torso between exposures

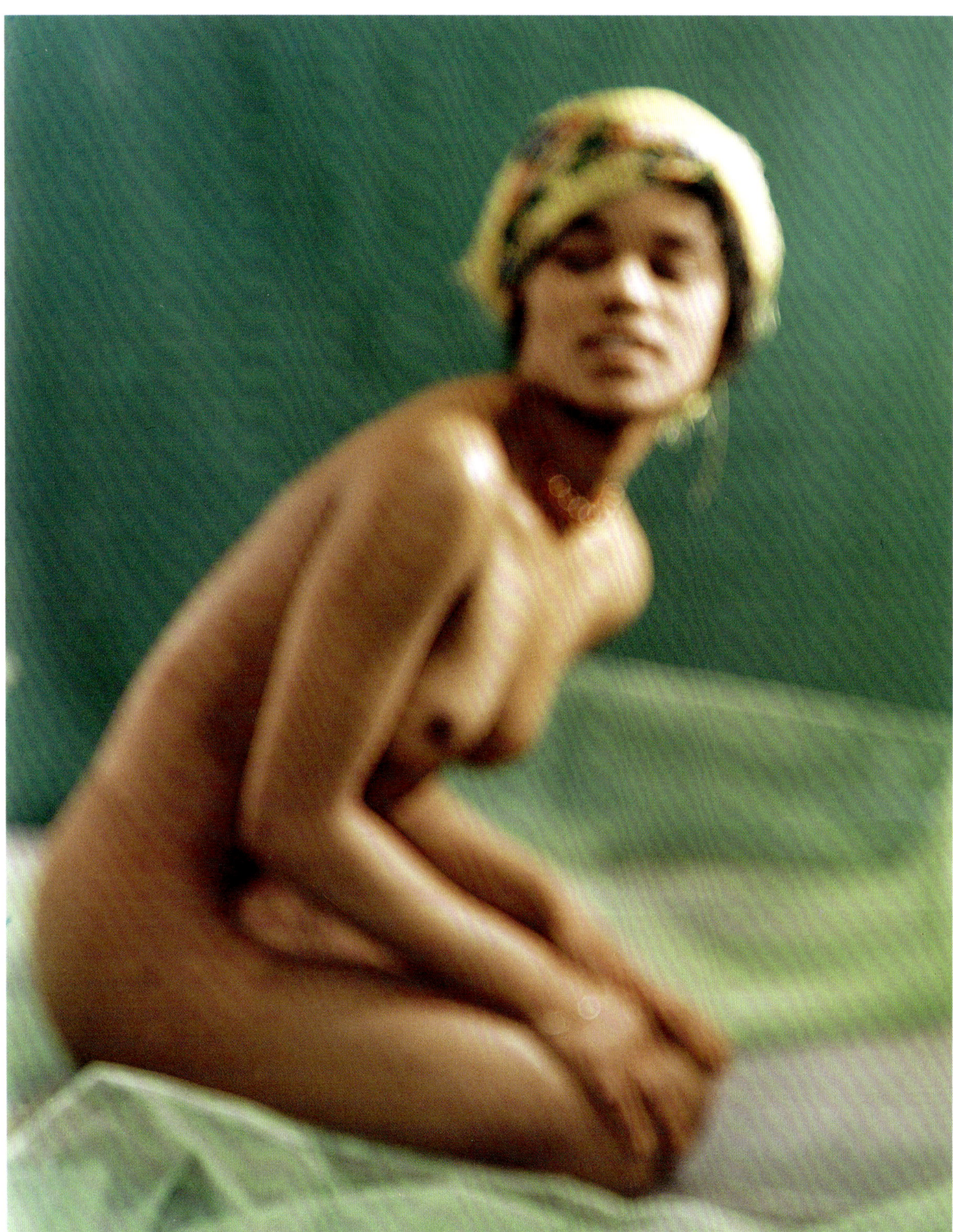

has created a fringing effect around her shoulders, visible as a bright yellow outline. This line is evidence of a technological error but gives Leigh a dramatic glowing effect, creating a film-star image radiating a celestial golden light. It would have been possible to remove this mistake by retouching the negative (a technique Yevonde used elsewhere), yet her decision to retain the error speaks to her interest in the chromatic impact of this yellow flash, which charges the photograph with an electric presence.[88]

Another aspect of Yevonde's technical practice was the under-exposure of her photographs, as the especially dense separation plates helped to exaggerate the vivid saturation of her images when they were processed. However, the laboratory would try to correct at the printing stage what it perceived to be mistakes made in the studio, as though the rich chromatism of Yevonde's work was the result of technical error rather than deliberate experimentation. Yevonde claimed her instructions to the laboratory were 'don't correct anything, just print!', while Spencer described how Yevonde's departure from conventional technical procedures meant 'many of the things demanded of us by her cut completely across the standardised procedure', as her investments lay in novel chromatic effects rather than the accuracy and precision of chromatic fidelity expected of commercial photographers.[89]

Yevonde's work disrupted and problematised automated and standardised laboratory practice, demanding close collaboration between herself and the laboratory to achieve her desired effects, where the requirements of the female photographer were realised by the labour of the female laboratory technicians. For Yevonde, Vivex did not signify a negative, feminised deskilling and automation of photographic labour but a celebratory feminised reskilling, whereby feminine colour craft in the use of coloured textiles, cosmetics and clothing produced brilliant surface effects whose rich saturation was only attainable through departures from correct photographic practice.

58 Madame Yevonde, *Gillian John (Nude Study)*, 1932, 38.1 × 30.4 cm, tri-colour separation negative. National Portrait Gallery, London.

To demonstrate her investment in aesthetics over technical perfection, in her 1932 lecture Yevonde gave the example of a nude study that she deemed especially pleasing, with 'flesh tints in all the colours of the rainbow', despite the fact that 'the negatives were put into the developer upside down'.[90] Given the very small number of nudes Yevonde executed in colour, it seems likely she was discussing her nude studies of the model Gillian John made around this time, which exhibit an extreme blur that could have resulted from the laboratory accidentally developing the colour separations through the wrong side of the glass plate (fig. 58). Yevonde's study of John illustrates what she described as the distinction between the 'pictorial' and 'photographic appeal' of her work, whereby a technical failure could produce a beautiful image, allowing the viewer to appreciate a photograph as a combination of tones and forms rather than judging it as a realistic likeness.[91] Here, the blur of the photograph both softens the curvature of John's body, echoed in the gentle bend of her elbows, and lends a dreamlike haze to the scene, where the distinction between John's body and the undulating waves of gauze surrounding her becomes fuzzy and indistinct. The warm, golden hue of John's exposed skin mediates between the sunny yellow tone of the headscarf, the lime green fabric on the floor and the richer green hue of the backdrop, while the strong directional lighting from the right ensures that the surface texture of each – the sheen on John's shoulder, the roughness of the gauze, the gloss of the oilcloth behind – is captured in sensuous detail.[92]

But this photograph also raises the question of how Yevonde's approach to colour was mediated by her understanding of skin colour as a marker of racial difference. Tellingly, as she recalled, her first formative memory of colour took place at her father's chromolithographic ink factory, where he demonstrated colour printing using an image of an 'Ethiopian slave girl'.[93] That Yevonde's earliest encounter with colour was both materialised and racialised in this way situates her approach to colour within the racialised discourses discussed in the previous chapter, whereby Black bodies were understood as a form of chromatic spectacle. Such a conflation of Blackness and chromatism (a topic taken up at length in Chapter Five) could account for Yevonde's description of this photograph of a Black model as exhibiting 'flesh tints in all the colours of the rainbow', despite the fact that John's body exhibits a conventional spectrum of naturalised golden-brown tones. Yevonde's different approaches to skin colour as she migrated between black and white and colour photography form a fascinating and unexplored aspect of her practice that warrants further attention beyond the scope of this chapter, not least as she photographed several prominent Black sitters before she began working in Vivex, including high-profile members of the entertainment industry such as Paul Robeson and Jeni Le Gon.

In her nude Vivex study, however, John's skin stands in for the kind of chromatism Yevonde would typically explore through costume and cosmetics, the surface of John's body operating as a tonal element in the composition and requiring no further adornment than a headscarf and the golden-hued jewellery around her neck and wrist. Certainly, Yevonde also used light skin in this manner. For instance, Joan Maude's pink complexion compliments the rouged and rosy tonality of her portrait (see fig. 46). But here, the nudity of the sitter suggests an elevated importance of Black skin as a locus for chromatic display that cannot be separated from Yevonde's wider interest in the surface effects of colour.

Yevonde's attention to the surface qualities of John's skin – its tonality, its capacity to reflect light – align with what Anne Anlin Cheng identifies as a modernist interest in the 'surfacism' of Black skin in the early twentieth century that extends beyond conventional discourses of primitivism.[94] As Cheng identifies in relation to Josephine Baker, the sheen and gloss of the performer's skin articulated a form of 'pure surface' that was both highly attractive to modernist artists and a crucial part of Baker's star appeal.[95] My argument is not that John wields similar agency over her appearance here, nor that Yevonde's photograph departs entirely from the primitivising tropes Cheng discusses, but that we might see in Yevonde's blurred photograph of John an investment in issues of surface that Cheng suggests were articulated in the early twentieth century through a fascination with the visual qualities of Black skin.

Surfacism was central to the aesthetics of Yevonde's photographs. This term conjures Yevonde's investment in and celebration of colour as a form of bodily adornment – whether painted lips, sparkling cloth, dyed hair or indeed colour's racialised connotations in the pigmentation of skin. But surfacism also invokes colour's negatively gendered implications associated with the forms of chromatic superficiality and feminine duplicity touched upon in the Introduction. Yevonde's interest in colour was clearly motivated by its highly feminised cultural connotations, despite the fact that these associations also contributed to pejorative attitudes towards colour in photography specifically and culture more broadly. Yet, through the subject matter and style of her work, Yevonde thematised colour's superficial femininity as one of its most appealing and powerful dimensions.

Artifice, Magic and Chromatic Labour

While this chapter has outlined the ways colour became feminised in the distinct historical moment of inter-war Britain, colour had long been understood as a gendered phenomenon before this time. As Jacqueline Lichtenstein and Rosalind Galt have explored, debates about the value of colour, from Platonic discourses to sixteenth-century Venice to the foundations of the French Royal Academy and beyond, rehearsed the same arguments about colour's subordinate status in the visual arts, as its ephemeral, deceptive and sensual charms were repeatedly linked with the sexual appeals of women.[96] A fleeting form of pure visual pleasure, liable to deceive the viewer by concealing flaws through charming hues, colour was always suspect as a compensation for another kind of lack, whether conceptual or technical, as it was a visual mode of address designed to draw the eye rather than stimulate the mind, merely creating a pleasingly artificial surface. Such arguments were repeated in the *British Journal of Photography* in 1935, with D. M. Cuthbertson warning that the 'primitive appeal' of colour photography, of 'the pretty' and 'the beautiful', distracted photographers from the technical demands of their medium, arguing that they should not allow these 'stimulating' hues to compensate for a lack of knowledge about 'focal lengths, exposure and development and so on'.[97]

Problematically gendered associations were attached to colour photography from the earliest iterations of hand-painted plates and prints in the nineteenth century, which Nicole Hudgins notes were described in contemporary discourse in highly sexualised language, as 'tainted' and 'impure' compared to 'virgin' and 'untouched' monochrome works.[98] That women often undertook this colouring work, as it offered flexible employment that could be performed at home, further cemented the associations between the superficial application of colour to the image's surface and female forms of labour, as well as the morally duplicitous application of cosmetics.

Yevonde both acknowledged and celebrated these assumptions about colour's supposedly superficial and sexual charms. Yet she viewed the surface application of colour in the form of cosmetics and other kinds of surface ornament as its most appealing dimension. Her playful rebuke of such critiques about colour's superficiality is evidenced in her use as studio props of classical busts, whose white plaster faces she frequently painted with lipstick, rouge and eyeshadow, disrupting the purity of their classical whiteness with an evidently superficial application of hue. The possible interpretations of this practice are multiple and complex, however, as Yevonde painted the faces of both the classical Greek bust of the Venus de Milo and a white plaster cast of the Egyptian Queen Nefertiti (figs 59 and 60). Adding colour to these faces with cosmetics could have been Yevonde's attempt to highlight the curious sculptural convention of reducing all flesh tones to a literal white. By adding colour to the surface of these works in the form of cosmetics, Yevonde was possibly reminding viewers that all skin (whether European or African) contains colour and that Whiteness is a bizarre abstraction rather than an accurate reflection of the hues of human skin. Alternatively, Yevonde's application of colour to these white surfaces might have been intended to imply that the ability to add and remove colour from the face was a preserve of White skin due to its imagined absence of colour, whereby the White face operates as a kind of blank canvas – a trope routinely emphasised in beauty manuals at this time. The racial dynamics of this gesture remain unclear.[99] As photography historian Lindsay Smith astutely argues, however, Yevonde's embrace of Vivex, a process where colour did not inhere in the negative but was superimposed on the finished print through a layer of pigment, speaks to the photographer's interest in colour as a surface effect, a celebration of 'the artifice of colour itself'.[100]

While the long-held suspicion of colour in Western aesthetics had formed around its instability, its propensity to change and shift, its capacity for superficial transformation – traits that had historically conflated colour with femininity itself – in Yevonde's works these feminine dimensions of colour are valorised. Given her infamous maxim 'Be Original or Die!', her attraction to colour as an ever-changing, novel sensation is entirely unsurprising.[101] Her interest in this dimension of colour was most elaborately explored in a series of portraits she made in 1935, displayed at her Berkeley Square studio that summer as *An Intimate Exhibition – Goddesses and Others*. The show featured portraits of Britain's titled aris-

Overleaf

59 Madame Yevonde, *Bust of Venus with Mask and Scorpion*, 1938, 43.3 × 31.4 cm, modern dye-transfer print, 1990. Royal Photographic Society Collection, Victoria and Albert Museum, London.

60 Madame Yevonde, *Still Life with Head of Nefertiti*, 1938, 52.4 × 32 cm, dye-transfer print, *c.*1990. Royal Photographic Society Collection, Victoria and Albert Museum, London.

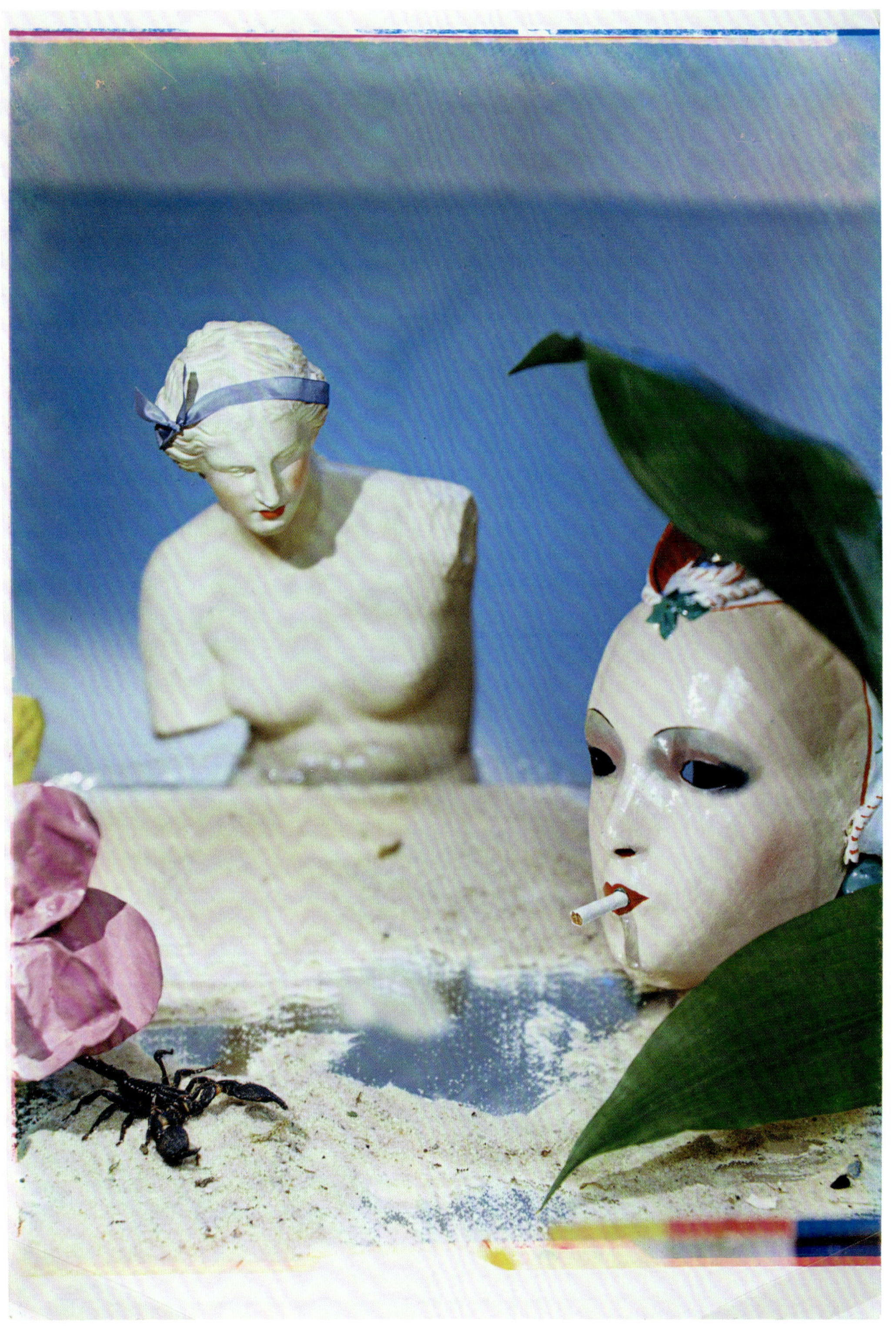

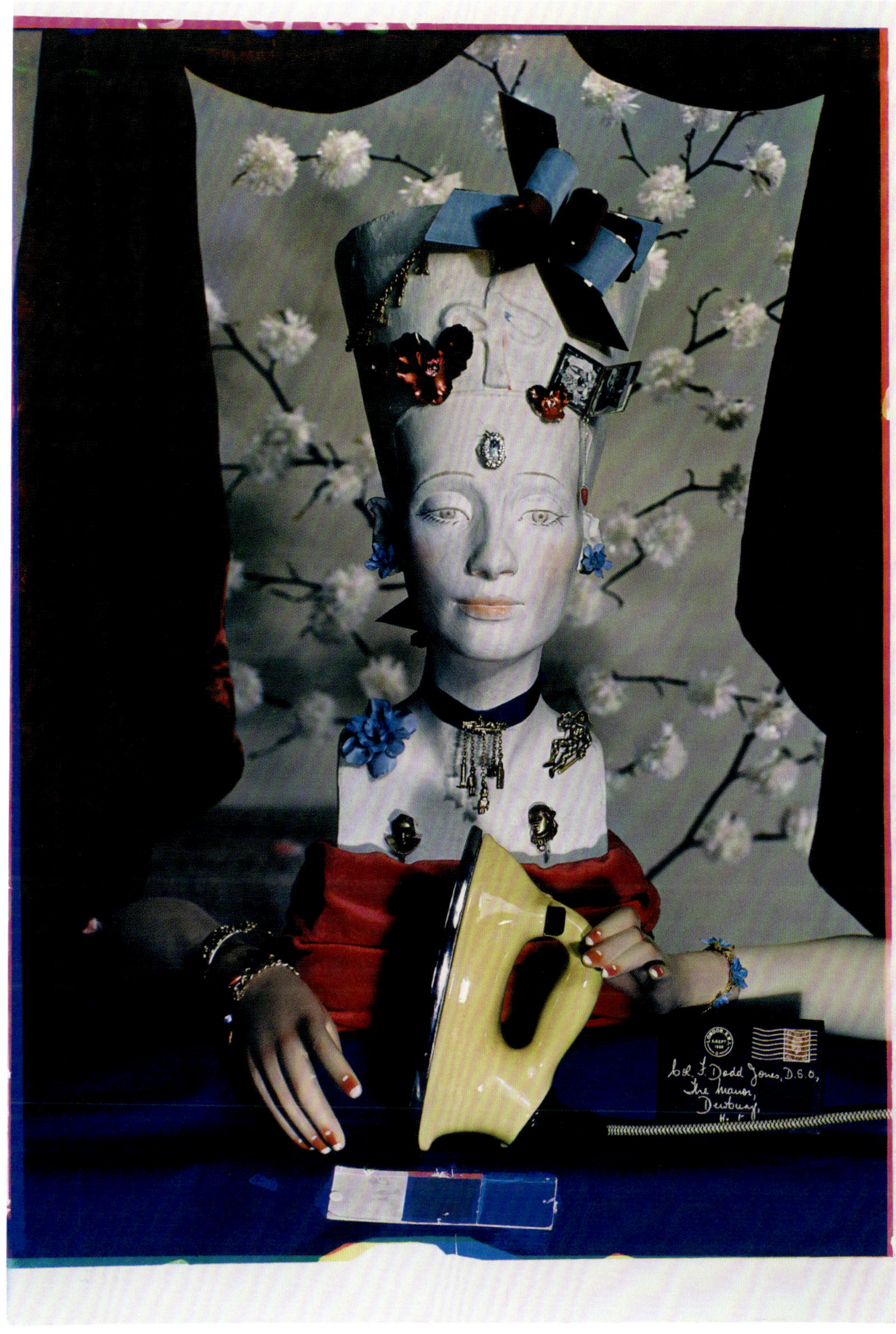
LONDON, S.W.1.
Col. F. Dodd Jones, D.S.O.,
The Manor,
Dewbury,

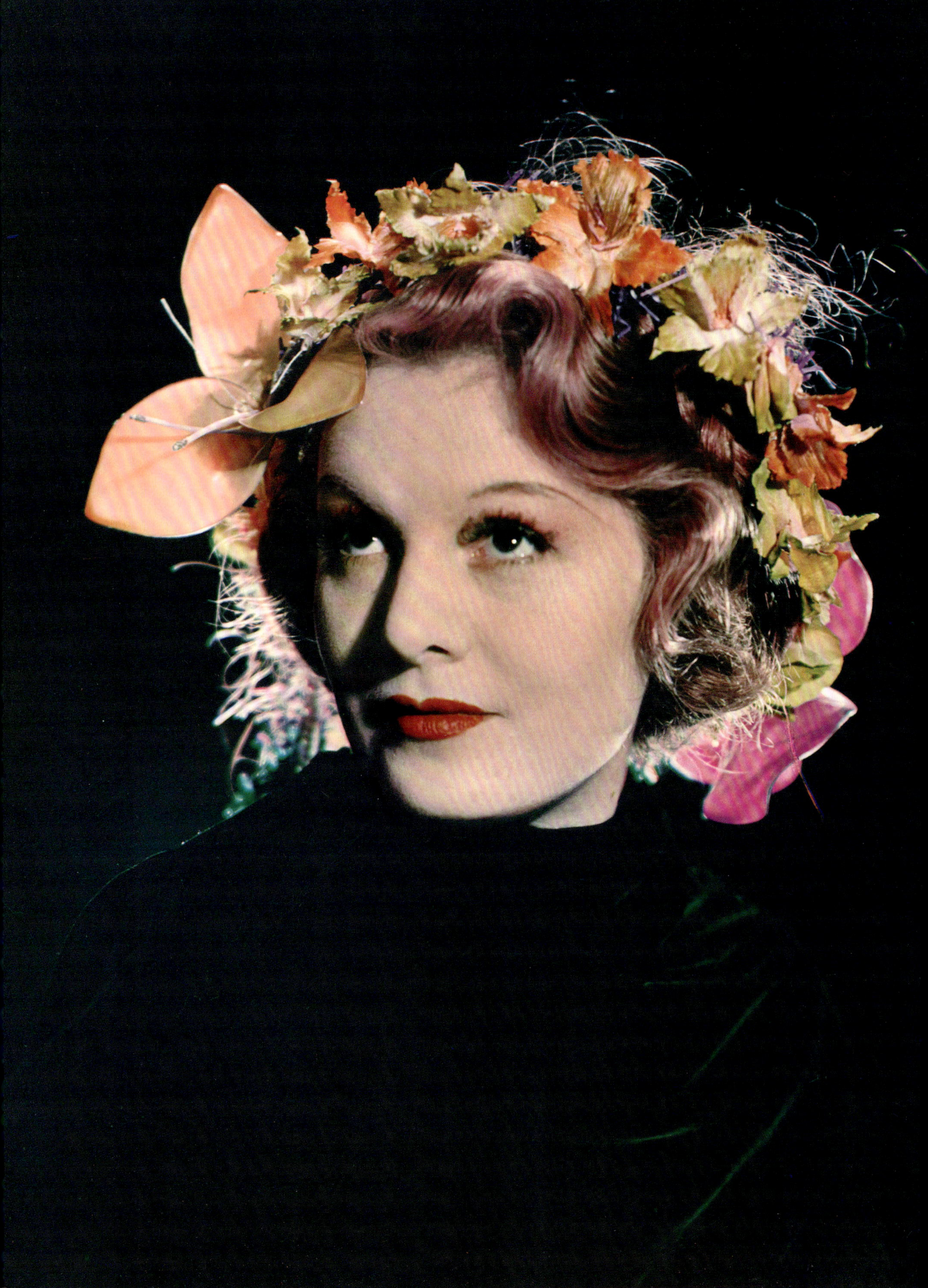

tocracy and social elite, including ladies, duchesses, countesses and viscountesses, as well as prominent actresses and the wives of politicians. The series was inspired by an exclusive charity costume ball hosted at Claridge's that March by musician and socialite Olga Lynn, where nobility, gentry and members of London's bohemian elite adopted the guise of gods and goddesses of Mount Olympus in outfits created by London's leading designers.

Yevonde took up the ball's playful conceit as the basis for her striking portraits, which both transformed her sitters into their chosen goddess but also thematised the issue of female metamorphosis through the use of colour. As a relative novelty in portrait photography, colour itself constituted a magical transformation, as these women's appearances were converted from the drab tones of monochrome (captured in the press photographs of the party reproduced in *The Bystander*) into the dazzling hues of Vivex.[102] Like Persephone emerging from the dark underworld to signify the bright arrival of spring, for Yevonde colour signified a revival and renewal of dead aesthetic tropes, a way of remaking oneself anew. Her portrait of Mrs Longdon as Persephone literalises this idea, as the sitter's face, crowned with a headdress of artificial flowers in glowing shades of primrose, marigold and fuchsia, emerges from the blackness of her surroundings as though from Hades (fig. 61). With her poppy-red lips and backlit hair, she glows like a Technicolor starlet in a Hollywood fan magazine, her identity made-over and reborn through the medium of colour.

This theme of metamorphosis dominates the subject matter and style of the series. As Smith examines, Yevonde seemed drawn to goddesses who undergo a radical physical transformation (for instance Daphne's fate as a tree or Arethusa's as a water fountain), but the series also features those goddesses whose associations with sorcery and demonic power (including Circe, Hecate and Medusa) also give them the ability to transform others.[103] The goddesses selected for the series therefore seem to trade upon the supposedly suspicious female capacity for habitual transformations of physical appearance. Yet these transformations are pointed in their artificiality. Yevonde employs patently fake props (such as Minerva's toy pistol and stuffed owl or Medusa's rubber snakes), evidently artificial fabrics (particularly the faux fur worn by Penthesilea) and wigs that cannot hide their artificiality (especially the stiff gold ringlets that cling like bathing caps to the heads of Clio and Circe), and she also invites her sitters to cultivate histrionic poses and exaggerated expressions, such as Niobe's melodramatically pained cry or Medusa's wide-eyed pouting stare (fig. 62). As Brett Rogers notes in her analysis of the goddesses, the camp artificiality of these personas speaks to Yevonde's wider interest in the construction of gender roles in contemporary society, and in particular the many guises and disguises adopted by modern women as they took on new positions and experimented with new identities, whether as workers in uniforms or sexualised starlets with painted faces.[104]

Colour becomes part of the superficial nature of these metamorphoses through the heavy application of cosmetics: the drawn-on eyebrows, painted lips, rouged cheeks and varnished nails that appear across the series. But Yevonde also experimented with the hues of the Vivex process as part of these chromatic transformations. To capture the green shade she desired for the skin of the water nymph Arethusa (fig. 63), designed to match the artificial seaweed

61 Madame Yevonde, *Mrs Longdon as Persephone*, 1935, 52 × 32 cm, modern dye-transfer print, *c.*1990. Royal Photographic Society Collection, Victoria and Albert Museum, London.

Overleaf

62 Madame Yevonde, *Mrs Edward Mayer as Medusa*, 1935, 50.7 × 40.4 cm, Permaprint dye-transfer print from original negative. British Council Collection.

63 Madame Yevonde, *Lady Bridget Poulett as Arethusa*, 1935, 42 × 27.5 cm, Vivex print. National Portrait Gallery, London.

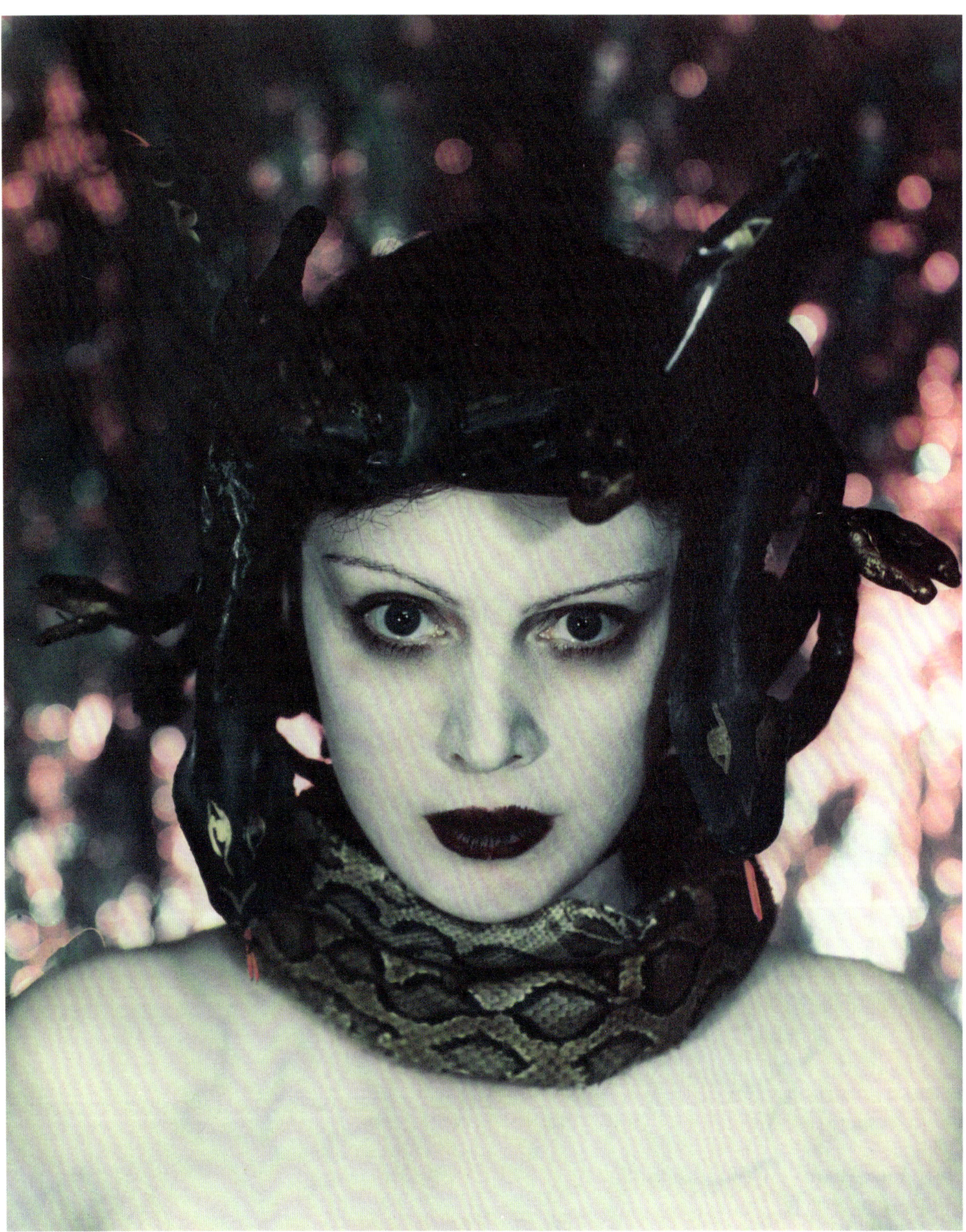

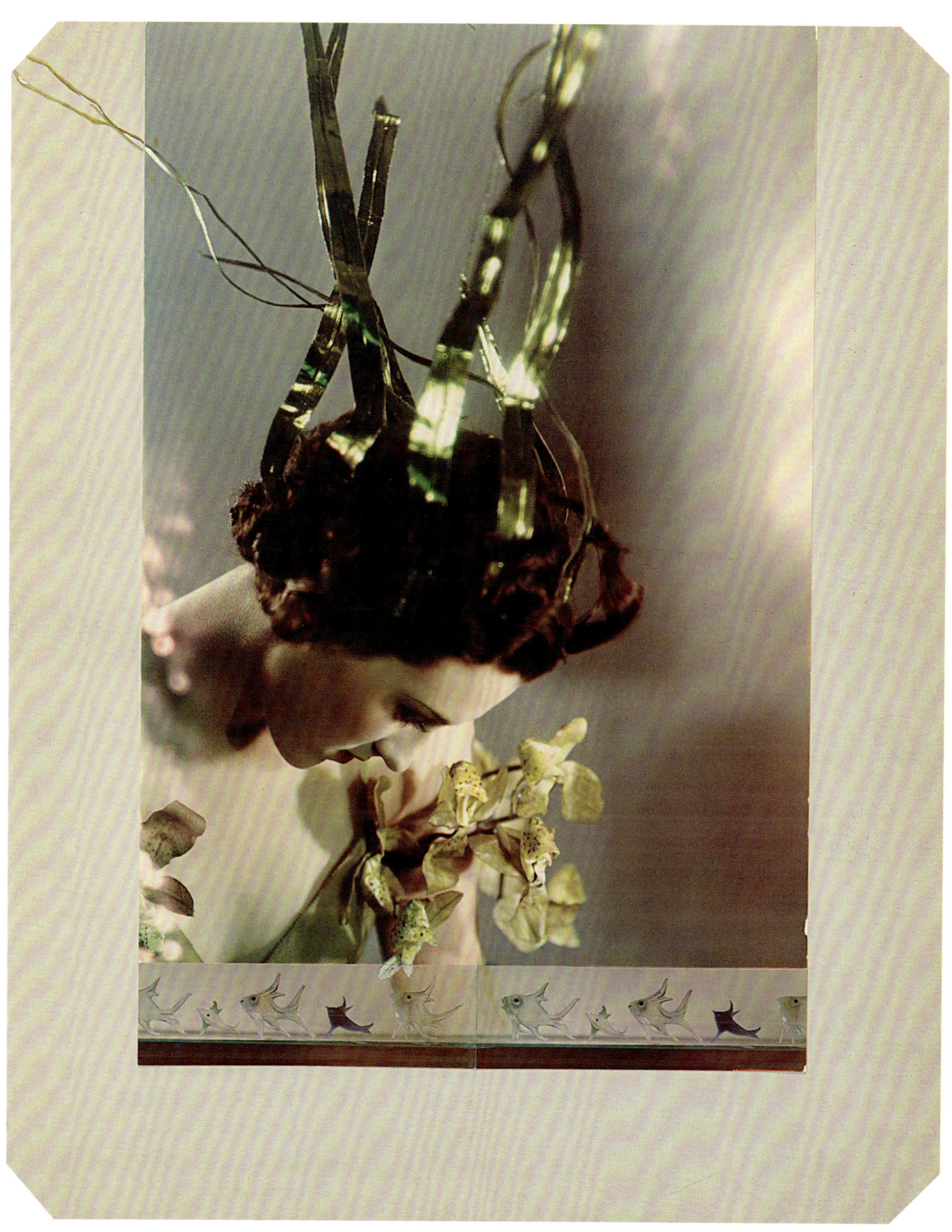

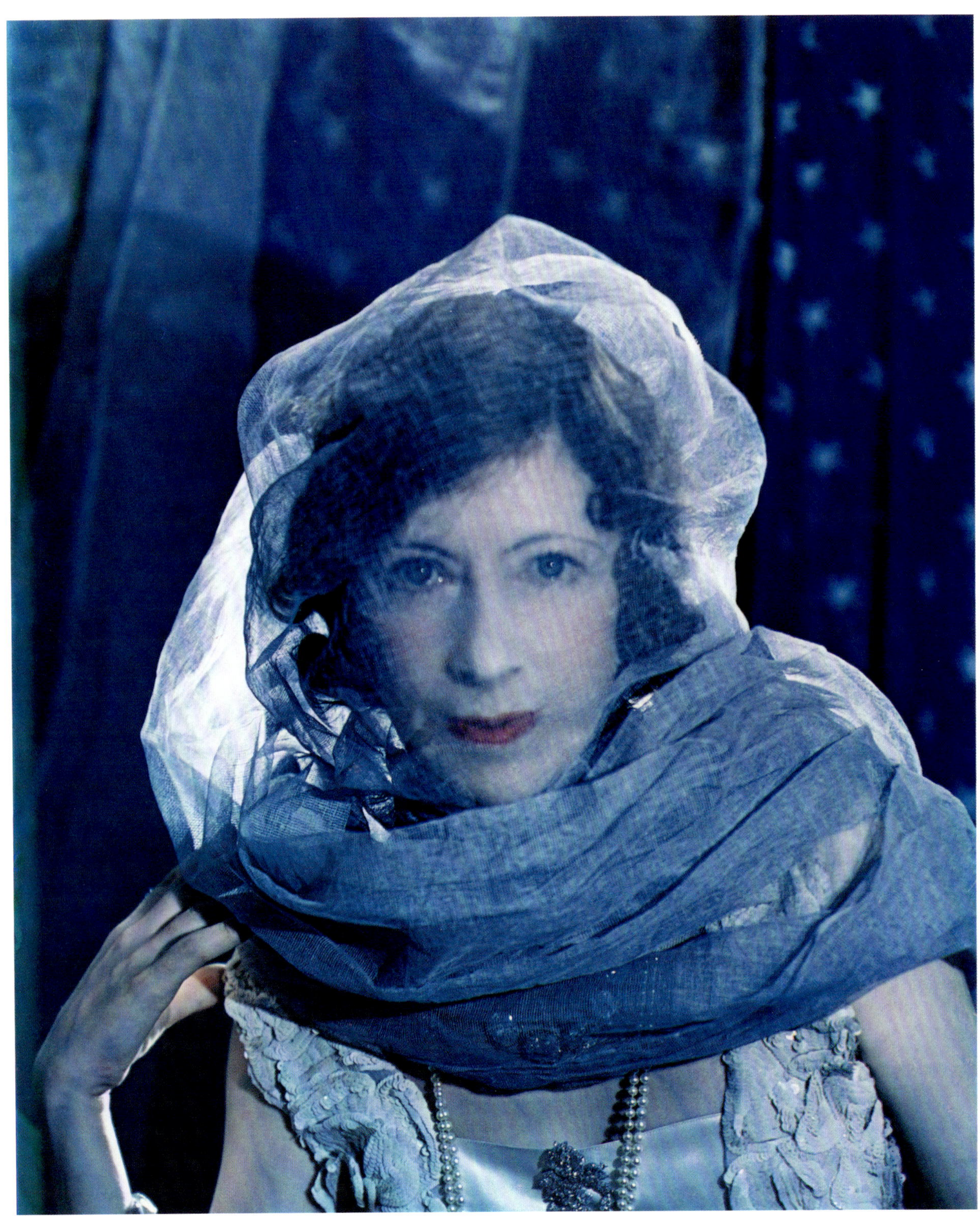

of her hair, Yevonde placed green cellophane over her lens, which she noted 'upset the balance of the three negatives pretty considerably and there were loud protests from the printers, but I achieved what I wanted … no red tones and a greenish quality in the flesh'.[105] The resulting chlorine tinge in her skin conflates her chromatic and aquatic metamorphosis as the changing hue of her skin symbolises Lady Bridget Poulett's/Arethusa's transformation into a water fountain. In several portraits (Clio, Dido, Hecate and Helen of Troy), Yevonde employed a blue filter, lending these portraits a twilight cast that operates like the veils worn by Helen of Troy and Hecate (fig. 64), as both the filters and the veils operate as translucent layers that distort and mask the faces of these women.

Goddesses such as Hecate and Medusa also invoke the perceived threat of colour that attended its shape-shifting capacity, linking its charms to those of sorcery, spells and witchcraft. Such linkages were emphasised in contemporary beauty advice that described colourful cosmetics as a kind of 'magic' whose secrets could be learned and mastered. As the 1938 pamphlet *Lessons in Loveliness* described, 'make-up magic' gave women 'influence and power', recounting how with one wave of 'the magic wand of beauty' women had 'swayed empires, inspired heroes, and acquired undying celebrity'.[106] Jacqueline Lichtenstein takes up this dimension of colour in her examination of chromatism in French academic painting, suggesting colour was also perceived as a kind of demonic magic that imbued an artist with powers of a suspect nature. Discussing Rubens's *Medusa* (1618), she aligns Medusa's powers to those of *coloris* (colour), as both have the capacity to overwhelm their viewers, who are 'surprised, arrested, seduced' by the gorgon and by colour. For Lichtenstein 'the beauty of *coloris* is Medusa's' as both threaten to overpower masculine regimes of order, operating at a level of sensuous, visual enchantment outside the control of language and intellectual reason.[107]

64 Madame Yevonde, *Dorothy, Duchess of Wellington as Hecate*, 1935, 42 × 31.5 cm, modern dye-transfer print from original negatives, 1990. Royal Photographic Society Collection, Victoria and Albert Museum, London.

Yevonde's portrait of Mrs Edward Mayer as Medusa certainly arrests the viewer with the intense frontality of the sitter's gaze and the glittering magenta curtain, which lures the viewer with its radiant sparkle. Yet the extreme whiteness of Mayer's skin, combined with her blackened lips and the slate-coloured snakes that comprise her headdress, suggests that she is not an embodiment of colour but of monochrome. Her appearance strongly resembles Yevonde's own description of the aesthetics of black and white photography, of the 'grey face' and 'black mouth' that characterised the monochrome medium and that Yevonde found so drab and unnatural. Mayer's appearance seems drained of the vivacity that animates the other sitters, where colour – in the form of artificial flowers, shells, decorative drapes, painted screen and sparkling jewels – enlivens their contrived poses. Comparing Persephone and Medusa, the levity and exuberance of Longdon's image, an explosion of life from the velvety, black darkness, is striking compared to the cool rigidity and starkness of Mayer's. For Yevonde, it is clearly not colour but monochrome that is monstrous, and Medusa's power to petrify a viewer with her deathly stare is linked not to the threatening seduction of colour but to the deathly pallor of black and white.

It is also possible to link the pronounced paleness of Medusa's skin to one of the major themes of this book, whereby new colour media announce anxieties around the status of Whiteness. The image almost parodically foregrounds the whiteness of skin in literal terms, making aesthetic and visible the abstracting idea of Whiteness as racial designation, in a manner akin to Yevonde's made-up plaster casts. It is telling that this image, which could easily be mistaken for a monochrome work, has become one of Yevonde's most often reproduced photographs.[108] The prominence of this work in exhibitions and scholarship on Yevonde suggests its capacity to ameliorate the racial-

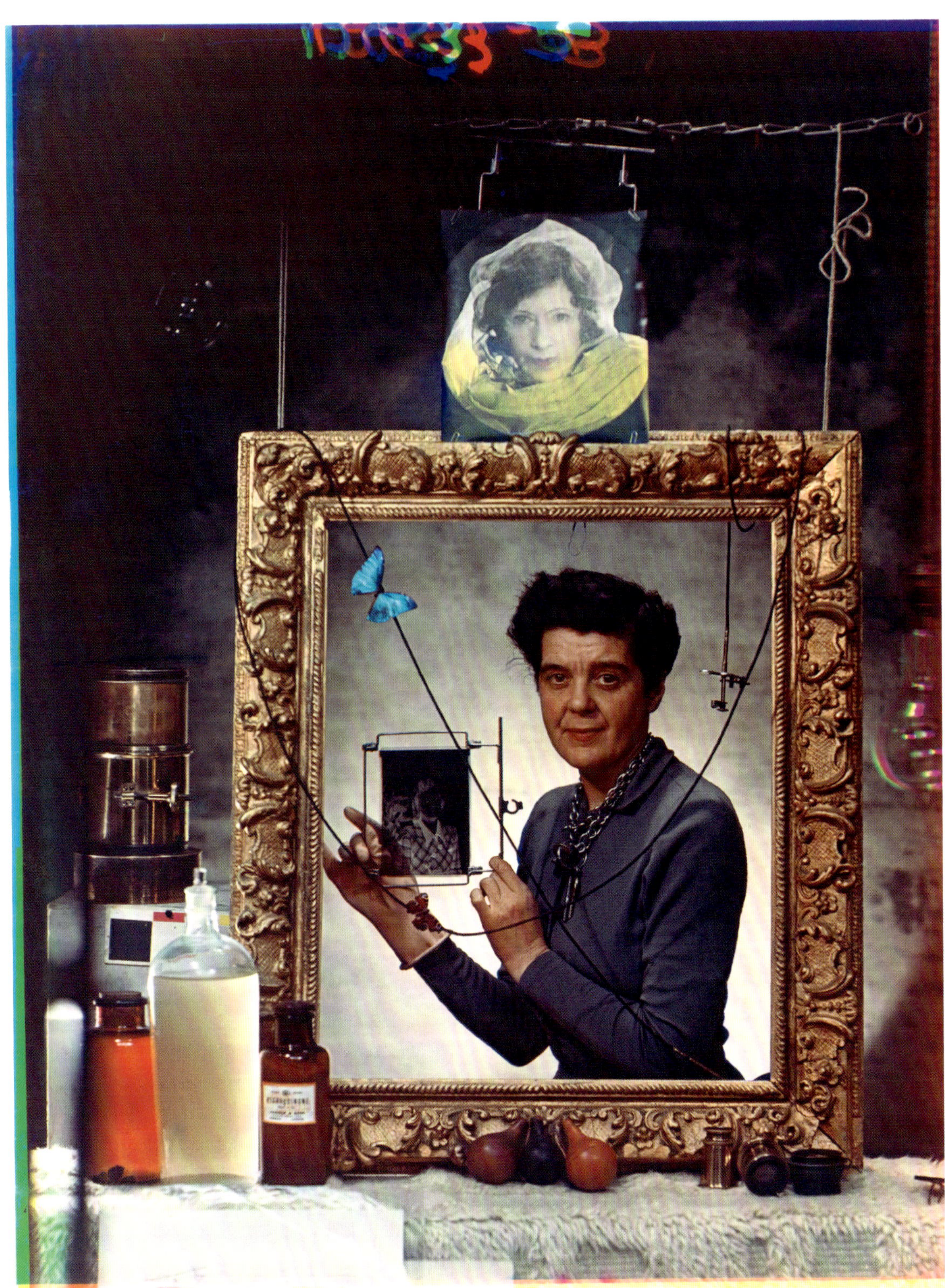

ised anxieties produced by capturing society beauties in colour, rendering acceptable the presentation of the British aristocracy as subjects of colour.

These considerations also cannot be separated from the issues of class and labour that circumscribe them. While these images of White, aristocratic women, whose lives were largely untouched by the concerns of employment, present colour as a form of magic or as a form of play, the vivid hues, theatrical lighting and large format of these photographs marked them as the product of a professional and commercial photographer. In other words, the images themselves reveal colour as a form of work. Yevonde's photography did not distinguish between these two kinds of chromatic labour, however. These photographs bring together the mechanical and chemical forms of chromatic work that characterised the photographic studio and the laboratory, with the frivolous fun of costumes and make-up that marked the social world of aristocratic fashion. These photographs represent an attempt to reconcile the privileged dimensions of working with colour, which had accrued highly valued masculinist connotations, with those trivialised feminine forms of colour craft denigrated as inane and superficial. Indeed, these varied meanings of colour converge in Yevonde's *Self Portrait* of 1940, a rich image that pointedly situates her colour work within the multiple discourses surrounding colour, photographic labour and gender at this time (fig. 65).

The spatial construction of this portrait is complex. Yevonde sits behind an empty gilt frame and captures her own image using a timed exposure (made possible by the shutter-release cables strewn across the frame), yet the composition is deliberately designed to give the impression of a self-portrait captured in a mirror. This compositional device conjures up the long history of self-portraiture in painting, which required the necessity of a mirror for the painter to capture their own appearance, thereby linking Yevonde's photography with the aesthetic tradition of painting she so admired and that she understood as a model for successful colour work. Yevonde's hope that colour photography would one day reach the status of the 'portrait painted by an imaginative artist' is here suggested through this carefully devised construction, designed to elevate photography's status.[109]

Yet the composition also speaks to the painterly convention of the female subject contemplating her own appearance before a looking glass, linked with notions of female vanity and self-absorption. Here, the inclusion at the left of photographic chemicals, whose liquids glow amber and scarlet in Winchester bottles, suggests the genre of the 'lady at her toilette', which conventionally includes cosmetic potions and powders placed before the mirror at which the lady sits.[110] The slippage here between cosmetics and colour chemicals, between the materials used to paint the face (a degraded form of feminine artistry) and those used to colour photographed faces (which carried the masculine prestige of technical skill), suggests Yevonde's attempt to disrupt the conventionally gendered divisions between these two kinds of colour craft.

This theme is also conveyed through the image suspended above the gilt frame, the portrait *Duchess of Wellington as Hecate* from Yevonde's *Goddesses* series. Yevonde appears to have hand-painted the monochrome positive in reference to historical and profoundly feminised forms of photographic colouring, adding pink to the lips and thereby connecting the application of cosmetics to the painterly application of pigment. But, unlike the 'wishy-washy half-tinted effects' Yevonde associated with hand-coloured images, the chromatism here is suitably riotous, combining the lemon-yellow streak of the gauze veil with the bright rosy pink of her sitter's mouth.

Further allusions to the professional craft of the photographer are presented by the shiny lenses below and to the left of the picture frame, which glint with a brassy sheen, lending a machine-age glamour

65 Madame Yevonde, *Self Portrait* (with image of Hecate), 1940, 37.8 × 30.5 cm, dye-transfer print. National Portrait Gallery, London.

to the composition while also suggesting Yevonde's technical engagement with her work through these pieces of specialised equipment. Combined with the chemicals, the lenses suggest a space of technical work, of scientific experimentation and laboratory craft – and, indeed, Yevonde's gesture of holding up a negative for inspection with a hand clad in a rubber glove implies the dirty labour of darkroom work. As a young apprentice in Lallie Charles's studio, Yevonde took great pride in the stains her hands received from photographic chemicals, viewing them as evidence of her earned status as a photographer.[111] The glove could similarly operate here as a boast about her regular work with the hazardous materials of photographic developing, or poke fun at the promotion of rubber gloves for domestic work, designed to keep women's hands free from the signs of labour in which Yevonde took such pride.

She holds an unidentified black and white negative of a woman's portrait in a wire frame, its inscrutability exacerbated by its greyscale tones. The murky image is rendered even duller by the proximity to the iridescent blue butterfly suspended from a wire above and the appropriately named peacock butterfly below. Here the lack of colour in the monochrome photograph is highlighted by the inherent chromatism of these beautiful butterflies, demonstrating monochrome photography, not colour, as the aberration from nature. Their inclusion thus reinforces Yevonde's belief that, contrary to the views of her peers, it was monochrome, not colour photography, that was 'unnatural'.

Yevonde herself appears at the centre of the frame, wearing red lipstick and a heavy metallic necklace. The necklace was a studio prop, previously featured as Andromeda's chains in her *Goddesses* series, but here Yevonde has added a number of large keys as a pendant. A common attribute of Hecate, known as Keeper of the Keys, these objects link Yevonde to the image of Hecate that hangs overhead. Her identification with the goddess of sorcery, witchcraft and poisons reveals Yevonde's investment in the magical and transformative powers of the photographer, not least through the bewitching charms of colour chemistry. Like the Arthurian enchantress Morgan le Fay, who used colour in the form of dye as a deadly poison, Hecate's knowledge of botanical drugs links her with the kind of alchemical knowledge Yevonde alludes to in this image, where the accumulation of chemicals, talismans and ritual objects lends an almost occultist air to the image.

Yet Hecate was also an especially apt choice for a self-portrait captured with the Vivex process. A goddess who often appears in triple form, either with three heads or three bodies, she was suited to a photographic process contingent upon the exposure of three negatives. Yevonde describes in her autobiography how she was aware of the convention that 'ancient art depicted her [Hecate] with three heads' and she therefore 'tricked the three headed effect' using the triple exposures of Vivex in an alternative version of the portrait held at the National Portrait Gallery.[112] This description both links Yevonde's photographic work with magic (a 'trick') and thematically links Hecate's sorcery with her own photographic practice (through their shared triplicity). Yevonde also thematically embeds chromatic triplication within her *Self Portrait* through the three coloured bulbs placed below the frame as well as the electric light-globe at the right, whose swinging movement during the exposures produces an 'error' that reveals all three colour separations through fringing.

The portrait therefore brings together colour's multiple meanings, conflating and confusing their gendered associations. Colour here is simultaneously a cosmetic, a chemical, a painterly pigment, a subject of scientific and technical measurement, and a tool of witchcraft, sorcery and female enchantment. It is at once part of the toxic and skilled work of the laboratory, so fiercely protected by Yevonde's male peers, and a form of superficial beautification strongly linked with forms of modern femininity at this time. Yevonde's attempt to present herself as both photographer and sorceress illuminates how her work sought to celebrate those feminised dimensions of colour that had for so long been demonised while also incorporating them into the specialised technical practice of her Vivex work.

However, this image would be one of the last Yevonde made using the Vivex process. Following Britain's entry into the Second World War, the Vivex laboratory closed permanently in 1940, due to the disruptions to trade routes, the vast dip in advertising budgets that reduced demand for colour photographs, and the deployment of the laboratory's staff into the armed forces.[113] Although Yevonde would continue to work in colour sporadically into the 1960s, her career never evidenced the same sustained engagement with colour that characterised her inter-war work. Yevonde also described how, with the start of the war, the gender of her sitters changed, as her clientele largely comprised soldiers seeking keepsakes for their families before they entered the conflict.[114] Yevonde's inter-war work therefore marked a distinct period in her career, during which colour became a critical tool for her playful and political investigations into the changing status of women and work in modern British society.

The enduring legacy of Yevonde's vivid aesthetic was perhaps not found in photography but in cinema. This chapter previously noted the proleptic quality of Yevonde's style, which anticipated the appearance of three-strip Technicolor, a richly saturated cinematic process, by a number of years. Indeed, the comparison between Yevonde's photography and Technicolor film has become a cliché in scholarship on her work, which aligns their colourful glamour and use of bold primaries as part of a shared chromatism that characterised the 1930s. But, if one of the principal arguments of this book is that the meaning of colour is inseparable from its making, then, the next chapter explores, despite their similar aesthetics, the techno-material production of Technicolor films imparted them with a new set of meanings, distinct from Yevonde's feminised photography.

. . . A credit in any language

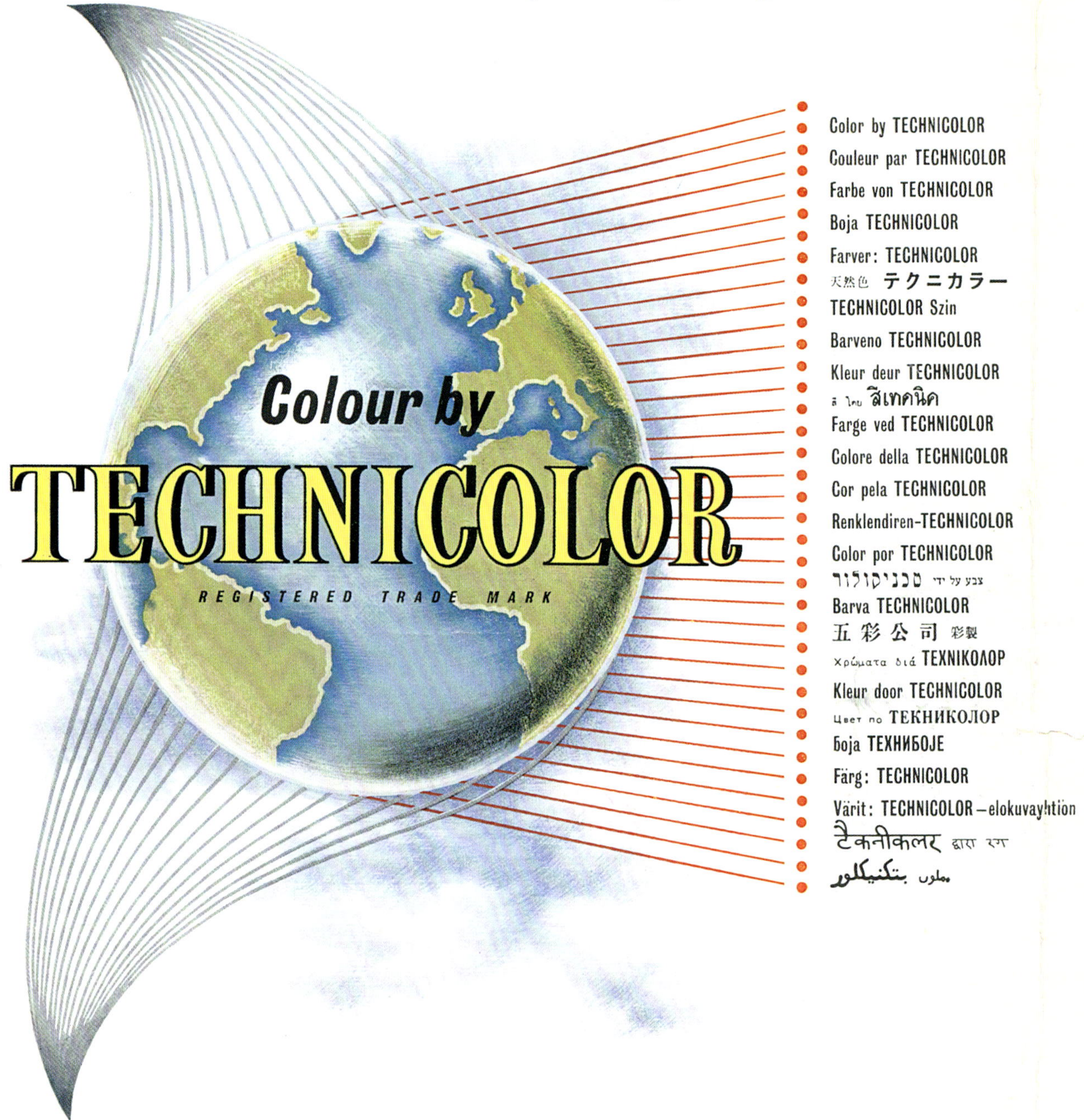

TECHNICOLOR LIMITED

HERBERT T. KALMUS, CHAIRMAN

4

DECOLONISING IN TECHNICOLOR

Chromatic Imperialism and Post-war Colour Cinema in Britain and India

The opening image of the imperial adventure film *The Drum* (UK, 1938; dir. Zoltán Korda) shows a spinning globe captured in the bright hues of Technicolor (fig. 67). As the world turns the camera zooms, allowing the viewer to appreciate the full extent of Britain's vast empire, captured in its distinctive red-pink tone. A tight close-up of the Indian sub-continent ensures the rosy hue almost entirely fills the screen. This opening sequence establishes the location of the film's action. Set in contemporary India, the film follows the manoeuvres of British military forces in the fictional Tokot region of the northwest frontier, who suppress a Muslim insurgency involved in arms smuggling.

Facing page

66 Detail of fig. 83.

67 The hues of the British Empire in *The Drum* (UK, 1938; dir. Zoltán Korda).

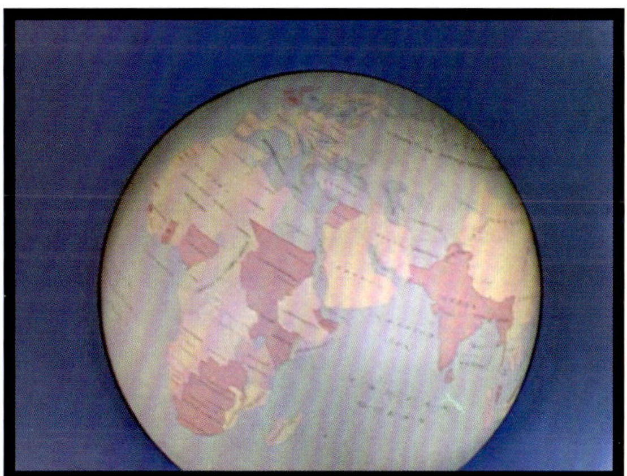

Colour is used throughout the film to celebrate and glamorise the empire, making the feats of the British forces seem all the more immediate, vivid and spectacular through the alluring veneer of Technicolor. Colour also exoticises and others the spaces and subjects of India. Dancing girls in sparkling saris, bustling markets full of colourful fruit and brightly coloured turbans that embellish busy crowd scenes – all convey Tokot as a space of riotous sensuality that warrants colonial control. That the film's Indian star, Sabu Dastagir, appears bare chested for the majority of its duration reveals how important flesh tones were to the film's design, which attempts to aestheticise the difference between colonisers and colonised through the colour of their skin.[1] From the opening moments of *The Drum*, colour is complicit in the visual regimes of empire, as the red-pink spaces of the map literally make visible the scope of Britain's power. Yet these red-pink areas do not simply mark the territories of the British Empire but also the global markets controlled by British Technicolor.

Empire was built into the corporate structure of Technicolor's British wing from the moment of its establishment. The American technology firm had been seeking a European base since the 1920s, but in 1936, and with financial backing from British investors, Technicolor opened Britain's first colour film laboratory (fig. 68) and provided four Technicolor cameras for use in British studios. These new Technicolor facilities in Harmondsworth, near London, made England the only location outside Hollywood

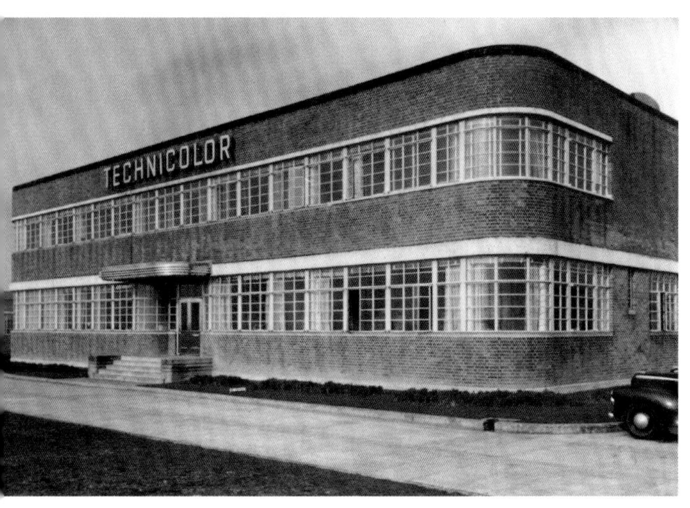

68 Technicolor Ltd in Harmondsworth, near London. George Eastman Museum, Rochester, New York.

with access to this prestigious technology at a time when Technicolor was the most advanced colour process available. The system was cumbersome, expensive and complex, yet no other technology could match Technicolor on the quality of its dazzling hues, which radiated a unique brand of prismatic glamour. While it had been possible to make films in colour for decades by this point, Technicolor was the first viable commercial system to dominate the market.[2] Between the mid-1930s and mid-1950s, Technicolor became the most desired and admired colour film technology among both filmmakers and audiences around the world. The original licence for Technicolor Ltd, as the London plant was called, laid out how the American and British firms would carve up the global market for their product. Technicolor Ltd would supply colour prints to all 'Kingdoms, Dominions, Colonies, and Mandated Countries' that comprised 'the British Empire', while the Hollywood plant would cover the rest of the world.[3] The Technicolor map that opens *The Drum* therefore reflects the territories comprising Technicolor Ltd's own empire of colour.

The conflation of the two empires pictured in *The Drum*, one a network of colonial authority operated by the British state, the other an international marketplace exploited by Technicolor Ltd, speaks to the changing nature of British imperial power at this moment. In the inter-war decades, the systems of colonial authority that structured the empire were recast as different kinds of control – economic, commercial and capitalist. While the ability to monopolise raw materials, goods and markets had always been central to the imperial project (as explored in Chapter Two), in the inter-war decades this became an explicit strategy – what historian David Harvey has called a newly emergent form of 'capitalist imperialism'.[4] While the empire was still, as *The Drum* vividly demonstrates, an organ of military and political power, it was also, as Technicolor's licence agreement reveals, a commercial infrastructure.

When Technicolor established its London branch, the reconceptualisation of the empire as a collection of free trading partners engaged in the exchange of material goods was already pronounced. The growing anti-colonial resistance movements across the British Empire and the gradual shift to self-governance among its colonies demanded that the purpose of empire be redefined. At a time when this decolonisation of the empire was coupled with economic competition from America – an emergent industrial superpower building its own commercial imperium – Britain needed to strengthen the coherence of its empire as a commercial marketplace. This new kind of economic and commercial imperialism emerged as a modern way of conceptualising empire, reflected in the establishment of bodies such as the Empire Marketing Board (1926–33), discussed in Chapter Two, which promoted intra-imperial trade in the form of fruit, fabrics and other consumables such as tobacco and tea. At the moment Technicolor Ltd was established, these different styles of imperial power co-existed, as Britain was shifting from the seat of the empire (a global system of governance predicated on racialised hierarchies, military force and aggressive territorialism) to the heart of the Commonwealth (a set of economic relations contingent on the extraction, circulation and exchange of commodities).

Film played a crucial role in negotiating the changing nature of the empire for two principal reasons. First, as a representational medium, cinema offered a space to imagine and reimagine the relationship between Britain and its empire. Whether through fiction films such as *The Drum*, which unambiguously celebrated the legitimacy of British colonial rule, or the documentaries of the Empire Marketing Board, which promoted imperial produce, cinema was a key space where popular understandings of the nature of empire were shaped. Second, as an industry and material commodity, film was an active participant in the new kinds of economic and commercial transactions that increasingly typified British imperial power. The British state created film bodies to instrumentalise its changing imperial policies, chief among them the Empire Marketing Board Film Unit and the Colonial Film Unit.[5] But the wider industry that lay beyond state control was also enmeshed in this new form of capitalist imperialism. As Lee Grieveson has demonstrated, the close ties between British filmmaking and finance capital, the industry's consumption of raw materials derived from the extractive economy of empire, its reliance upon imperial networks of shipping and transport, and its status as a British commodity exported on a global scale made it a vital actor in the new systems that characterised British economic imperialism.[6]

Scholarship on Technicolor cinema and empire has tended to focus on the first way of thinking about their relationship, as one predicated on issues of representation. The aesthetics and style of Technicolor film, as well as colour's deep links to Orientalism and racial othering, have been central to these studies, which have revealed how filmmakers used Technicolor to vivify the ideological messages of films such as *The Drum* and shore up the racist hierarchies that underpinned the colonial project.[7] India has been chief among these analyses as it so routinely featured as a subject of British Technicolor filmmaking, whether through location shooting for fiction films including *The Drum* and *The River* (UK/US/France/India, 1951; dir. Jean Renoir) and documentaries such as the *World Windows* travelogue series (1937–40), or the Orientalist fantasies of India created in the studio in *Black Narcissus* (UK, 1947; dir. Michael Powell) and *The Jungle Book* (UK/US, 1942; dir. Zoltán Korda). As India had long been understood in the imperial imagination as a colony rich with colour, having been exploited by Britain for centuries through the extraction of dyestuffs, pigments and textiles, these films took up and intensified these well-established links, forging an imperial aesthetic of India through Technicolor film.

Yet the second way of conceptualising the links between cinema and empire, as a material commodity complicit in its economic infrastructure, has yet to be interrogated in relation to Technicolor. As the opening sequence of *The Drum* makes clear through its depiction of Technicolor's vast global market, in addition to offering a space in which to picture empire, Technicolor films were commercial goods that travelled the routes of imperial trade constituting the modern consumer imperium. Technicolor cinema was not merely a process for depicting empire but also, as a desirable commodity that was manufactured and distributed from London and consumed all over the world, a participant in the very structure of that empire. As the only location within the empire with the capacity to shoot and print Technicolor films, the London facility had a monopoly on the production and circulation of the most in-demand colour process of the time, establishing England as the epicentre of film colour at a time when it was considered a scarce resource. That the laboratory's market comprised the geography of the British Empire makes explicit Technicolor Ltd's role as an agent of capitalist imperialism and of what this chapter calls 'chromatic imperialism'.

Colour had been so central to the economics of empire for centuries that its role in the new kinds of economic imperialism characterising the twentieth century seemed almost over-determined. Controlling and regulating the material manufacture of colour had long been entangled with the mechanics of colonial violence and legitimised the rampant territorialism of the British Empire. British India in particular was witness to these historical forms of chromatic subjugation, whether through the physical brutality of indigo plantations or the regulation of India's trade in coloured textiles by British authorities.[8] But, as the conventional modes of hard imperial power began to be eroded in the twentieth century, new ways of securing colour for British economic interests emerged. Colour therefore became a particularly important commodity for demonstrating Britain's continued global strength in an era of decolonisation. While colour in the form of dyes and textiles may no longer have been under the violent control of British forces overseas, Britain's continued management and monopolisation of colour markets on a global scale emblematised the nation's continued hegemony in this sphere. The ongoing British regulation of colour therefore operated as a form of chromatic imperialism that replaced the older kinds of military and colonial power that waned as the century progressed.

Technicolor Ltd was one of many organs of chromatic imperialism that emerged in the inter-war decades. The work of the British Colour Council, a textile trade body established in 1930 'to place colour determination for the British Empire in British hands', offers another example of a pervasive interest in centralising the management of global colour in Britain at this time.[9] By regulating colour nomenclature throughout the empire using appropriately British terminology, as dictated in its *Dictionary of Colour Standards* (from Post Office Red to Union Jack Blue), the British Colour Council explicitly enacted British authority over the look of the modern world and the language used to describe it.[10] Technicolor Ltd was at once part of this larger industrial and economic movement, but it was also unique. As an industrial operation trafficking in images, Technicolor Ltd not only established London as a global centre for controlling film colour but also aestheticised and glamorized the very systems that made this operation possible through the films it produced. At a time when British industry was anxious of economic competition from America, the ability to use this American technology as an instrument of British chromatic imperialism made it especially appealing.

This chapter considers how Technicolor Ltd became an agent of chromatic imperialism by locating its role within two globalised systems of power that underwent radical change across the twentieth century: the British Empire and the international film market. Technicolor was intimately connected to both, as a vehicle for imperial ideologies, a commodity of imperial commerce and the dominant force in the global colour film market. As the opening of *The Drum* reveals, Technicolor took up and operated within the territorial networks of exploitation and dependence established by the empire, while reformulating them as relations predicated on commercial and aesthetic considerations. Yet, as these twinned narratives of imperial and economic transformation unfolded against a backdrop of increased competition from American industry, the growing momentum of anti-colonial independence movements also significantly challenged the hegemony of Britain's neo-colonial networks of trade. While chromatic imperialism enabled Britain to imagine its continued global hegemony as its hard forms of imperial power waned, the lability and contingency of colour also made these systems ideal vehicles for articulating oppositional, resistant and explicitly anti-colonial ideologies among newly independent nations. This chapter therefore considers how the decolonisation of the empire reconceptualised the ideological resonances of Technicolor (an established organ of chromatic imperialism) by considering its use in Indian cinema of the 1950s.

The analysis begins in the inter-war period with the establishment of London's Technicolor laboratory in 1936, but it focuses primarily on the post-war moment for two reasons. First, this period marked an explosion in the demand for colour film facilities that invested Britain's Technicolor laboratory with enormous control over the global supply of colour film prints. Second, this period witnessed significant challenges to the integrity of empire through the accelerated process of decolonisation, which challenged Britain's colonial, military and economic powers on a global scale. Indeed, in 1952 Technicolor's Hollywood plant redrew its licence agreement with London to reflect the substantive changes that had redefined the scale and function of the empire over the preceding years.[11] Following the war, when decolonisation gained significant momentum, the diffuse and gradually disintegrating entity still called 'the British Empire' lacked the specificity necessary for this legal contract. However, Technicolor's new licence merely renamed 'the British Empire' as 'British Territory' (curiously avoiding the term 'Commonwealth') and, rather than removing nations that had won independence from British rule, added newly created independent states, such as Pakistan. As more 'Kingdoms, Dominions, Colonies, and Mandated Countries' left the official parameters of the British Empire, they forged the territory of British Technicolor's chromatic imperium. Yet it was precisely because the materials and labour of Technicolor's London plant were not reserved for manufacturing British films for British consumption that the plant became a space for negotiating Britain's position within the new structures of geopolitical power that were being redrawn at this time. By extending this chapter's analysis beyond the content of these Technicolor films to consider the material processes by which Technicolor processed and printed its materials for international actors, it is possible to trace much larger, globalised networks of exchange that illuminate the multiple and even contradictory ideological functions of colour cinema at this time.

India plays a crucial role in these interlocked histories of colour film, commerce and empire. As Britain's largest colony and one whose relationship to the metropole was forged through colonial regimes of colour control, India's independence in 1947 marked one of the most significant blows to the cogency of the empire. As Technicolor cinema had been such a crucial instrument for propagating the legitimacy of British colonial rule in India, it also became a space for rethinking post-colonial British and Indian identities. When an independent India began making its own Technicolor films in the 1950s, the technology became key to debates about how colour continued to operate as a form of British authority even after the conclusion of its official colonial regime. India therefore offers the most significant case study for exploring how Technicolor operated both as a weapon for and as a tool of resistance against British modes of chromatic imperialism.

As Jagjeet Lally confirms, understanding the relationship between colour and coloniality in Anglo-Indian contexts cannot end where Indian independence begins; instead, it demands 'an acknowledgement of the historical entanglements of colour with colonialism and its controlling and commodifying logics, and the ways in which they are reproduced and repackaged even today'.[12] Technicolor's centrality to Indian colour cinema of the 1950s is, this chapter argues, one such instance of this 'repacking' that occurred in the immediate aftermath of independence, and it reveals the legacy of chromatic imperialism into the second half of the twentieth century. Yet this chapter also points to the 1950s as an aesthetically rich and geopolitically complex era for domestic colour filmmaking in India, contributing to the burgeoning interest in the chromatic history of Indian cinema.[13] This framework is used here to analyse India's first Technicolor film, *Jhansi Ki Rani* (India, 1953; dir. Sohrab Modi), which was filmed in India but processed and printed at London's Technicolor laboratory, offering a crucial case study for considering the legacies of British colour regulation in a post-imperial nation through material networks of chromatic exchange.

Such an approach demands a radical reframing of Technicolor cinema, which views these films not only as images but also as material objects. Following Alice Lovejoy's assertion that 'politics are not only carried on celluloid ... but are also embedded in the "support" itself – in its raw materials, industrial processes and circulation', this chapter considers how the political meanings of Technicolor films inhere in their physical components and industrial manufacturing as much as the images on their surface.[14] By no means are these issues divorced from questions of aesthetics. The look of Technicolor cinema cannot be separated from the technologies used in its production. But neither can these technologies be disarticulated from their relationship with and instrumentality to British imperialist ideology. By examining Technicolor cinema through the material processes by which colour actually entered these films, namely through the specialised printing and dyeing technique used by the Technicolor laboratory, this chapter presents a new way of conceptualising the relationship between colour cinema and empire. Furthermore, by tracking the globalised networks of materials and labour that comprised Technicolor's system, it produces new historical narratives and geographic orientations for histories of twentieth-century colour cinema.

This approach also invites a reconsideration of where and how colour is produced in Technicolor film – a recognition that its palette was as much a product of industrialised labour in the laboratory as of creative labour on the studio floor. As this chapter examines, the laboratory's process for dyeing its films was central to the aesthetics, economics and geopolitics of Technicolor cinema in Britain and the wider world. By centralising the control of colour through this dyeing process at the London plant, this new form of economic imperialism forged a powerful resemblance to older forms of colonial enterprise, which were similarly predicated on the circulation of printed and dyed materials.

This materialist analysis revisits and rethinks films and filmmakers that are familiar to accounts of Technicolor's links with empire – Alexander Korda and his empire epics, for example – casting these films in a new light. But it also draws upon objects and histories conventionally left out of these narratives, notably Technicolor's short industrial films, the work of its laboratory staff, and the deep connections between British and Indian filmmaking forged through the Technicolor laboratory. By expanding the discussion of 'British' colour to include India's first Technicolor film, this chapter takes seriously Jaikumar's claim that the empire was not simply a space into which Britain exported its regimes of visual modernity but that it was in the very exchange between Britain and its empire that these regimes were constituted.[15]

'A Licence to Print Money'

Understanding how the London Technicolor laboratory came to occupy such a vital position in the global colour film market requires a precise evaluation of how this technology worked. Most significantly it demands a knowledge of where and how colour entered a Technicolor film. The single term 'Technicolor' conveniently elides the multiple processes that comprised the system, as Technicolor was not a single technology a studio could buy but a package of services, personnel and equipment leased for each film. When producers wanted to make a film in Technicolor, they had to hire a package including the obligatory rental of special cameras and cinematographers, the expertise of Technicolor's Color Advisory Service (which oversaw the use of Technicolor's process in the studio), and Technicolor laboratory services, which processed the stock and manufactured release prints. Films made in Technicolor were therefore collaborations between studios and Technicolor, with the technology firm ensuring a high level of control over the use of its process.

This was not always a happy collaboration, however. While studios desired the rich saturation only possible with Technicolor's system, they resented hiring external personnel to oversee its use. In addition to working with Technicolor staff on aspects of design and cinematography, studios also had to relinquish control of their shooting and release schedules, as Technicolor determined who worked in colour and when. In Britain, where only four cameras were available, the demand for colour could far outstrip supply, leaving producers waiting for extended periods to commence shooting. Much has been written about the friction between studios and Technicolor's fleet of colour workers, particularly between the Color Advisory Service, headed by the American Natalie Kalmus, and cinematographers, directors and other creative studio personnel.[16] Yet the camera department and Color Advisory Service comprised only one half of Technicolor's process. The place where colour actually entered these films was the Technicolor laboratory.

At its simplest, Technicolor's system comprised two parts: a camera, which separated colours in the studio, and a printing system, which recombined them in the laboratory. In some regards it was not

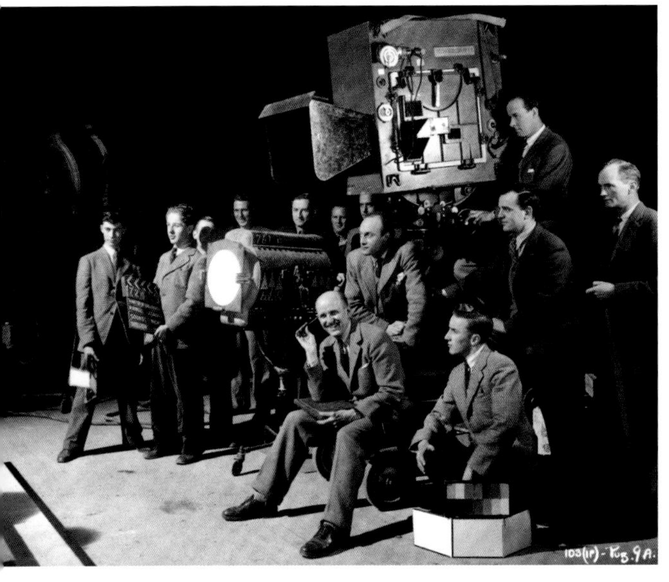

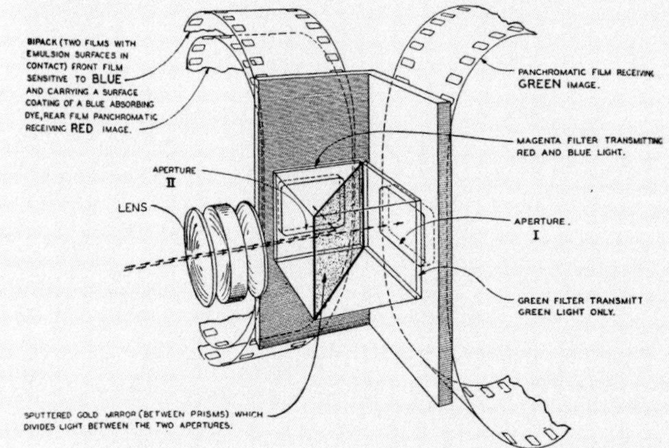
have other disadvantages, particularly as regards separating or differentiating between the various components; and some of them present difficult raw-stock manufacturing problems.

Fig. 1. Arrangement of optical system and films in the three-color camera.

69 The three-strip Technicolor camera on the set of *A Matter of Life and Death* (UK, 1946; dir. Michael Powell and Emeric Pressburger).

70 Interior of the three-strip camera showing how the prism filters light onto three strips of film. Joseph Arthur Ball, 'The Technicolor Process of Three-Color Cinematography', *Journal of the Society of Motion Picture Engineers*, vol. 25, no. 2 (August 1935): 127–38.

unlike the Vivex process of photography. However, the Technicolor camera was an enormous machine – when blimped for sound and loaded with film it weighed 64 kg (fig. 69). But its size helped to accommodate the three strips of film contained within, which lent the photographic process the name of 'three-strip Technicolor'. The camera used a prism and filters to split light into separate colour channels (red, green, blue), with the information for each recorded on three strips of black and white negative (fig. 70). The laboratory used these three negatives to manufacture a shallow relief printing block made from gelatin, called a 'matrix', which varied in thickness depending on the intensity of the colour. Each matrix was then dyed a complementary colour (cyan, magenta, yellow) (fig. 71) and sequentially pressed against a blank strip of film (also coated in gelatin) to reconstruct the three-colour image. The blank and matrix were held in contact by a pin-belt, to ensure exact registration when they were pressed together by rollers, which in turn ensured the transfer of dye from matrix to blank.[17] This gave the printing process its name: dye-transfer. That the matrix absorbed – or imbibed – the dye through its gelatin coating suggested its alterative name: dye-imbibition or simply 'IB' (short for 'imbibition'). The luminosity and saturation of Technicolor cinema were the result of this process, which coated the film's surface in pure, translucent dyes, illuminated by the projector beam shining through them.

The gorgeous hues audiences enjoyed on screen were therefore made possible by the hazardous labour of the laboratory. Although London workers described the Technicolor plant as the height of modern, automated processing, it was also toxic, humid and foul. As one worker remembered, 'it was a mucky job, the boiling of the dyes and all this used to be pretty horrific'.[18] Dyes were mixed in two-thousand-gallon vats and, despite wearing protective equipment, workers suffered from dermatitis and other forms of poisoning.[19] However, women working in the London laboratory allegedly only

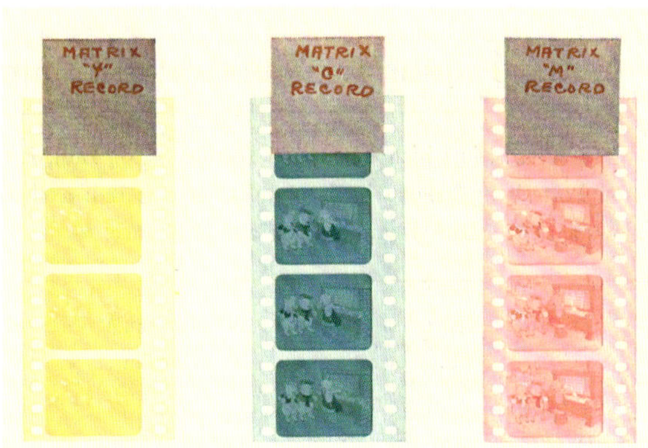

71 Examples of dyed matrices (1934). George Eastman Museum, Rochester, New York.

wore swimwear beneath their lab coats because the atmosphere in some departments was unbearably hot.[20] The laboratory's air was also full of pungent odours, but British workers were spared the olfactory affront of the Hollywood laboratory, where employees recalled experiments to purify dyes with bovine blood extracts, shrimp shells and oyster juice, which made the laboratory smell 'like a fish market'.[21] While scholarship on Technicolor typically focuses on creative work in the studio, it was this stifling, noxious industrial space of the laboratory, where a significant part of Technicolor's chromatic labour took place, that was vital to the economics, aesthetics and politics of Technicolor cinema.

Economically, dye-transfer printing made Technicolor's operation viable as, although these films were expensive to shoot, they were cheap to print. One reason Technicolor bundled its services together was because the camera department ran at a loss recuperated by profits generated by the laboratory.[22] While the production of the gelatin matrices was complex and expensive, the addition of colour to release prints involved no complex photochemical processing, just the transfer of dye from matrix to blank in a manner more akin to textile printing than photographic development. The system was contingent on an economy of scale that made the process more cost-effective for large print runs. As one Technicolor laboratory worker recalled, the process was so economical that 'after the first 25 prints, everything else was profit', a crucial factor when print runs in Britain averaged double that number and could be over a thousand.[23] Repeatedly, British laboratory staff described the IB process as 'a licence to print money'.[24]

Aesthetically, the dye-transfer process presented an enormous benefit through its colour control. The laboratory could minutely adjust each hue because they were printed separately, enabling technicians to determine the final appearance of the print in a manner unparalleled until digital colour correction. This had benefits and drawbacks, as recalled by Jack Cardiff, the celebrated Technicolor cinematographer who filmed *This Is Colour* (UK, 1942; dir. Jack Ellitt; discussed in the Introduction). The laboratory could enhance the saturation of a particular colour – he noted that the laboratory transformed an overcast sky into a brilliant blue to compensate for poor weather while filming *Western Approaches* (UK, 1944; dir. Pat Jackson).[25] However, the laboratory could reduce the intensity of a colour too. He recounted how a green tint he used on *Scott of the Antarctic* (UK, 1948; dir. Charles Frend) to give an authentic feel to faces lit by sun penetrating a tent was entirely eradicated by the laboratory, which removed it at the printing stage assuming it was a defect.[26]

Cardiff was not alone in his frustration; other British cinematographers expressed annoyance that the British laboratory had excessive control over the colour of their films. Because the Technicolor camera recorded its images on black and white stock, it was impossible for designers, directors and cinematographers to see their work in colour until the laboratory processed it. In the words of Technicolor cinematographer Oswald Morris, 'you really photographed the film blind almost'.[27] Editing similarly took place in black and white as it was too expensive to produce full-colour prints until the cut was finalised. Although filmmakers could request chromatic adjustments, the laboratory might not accommodate them. As Morris recalled, 'in the end you can't alter anything because … they've got their matrices, they're not going to change what they've got because it's cost

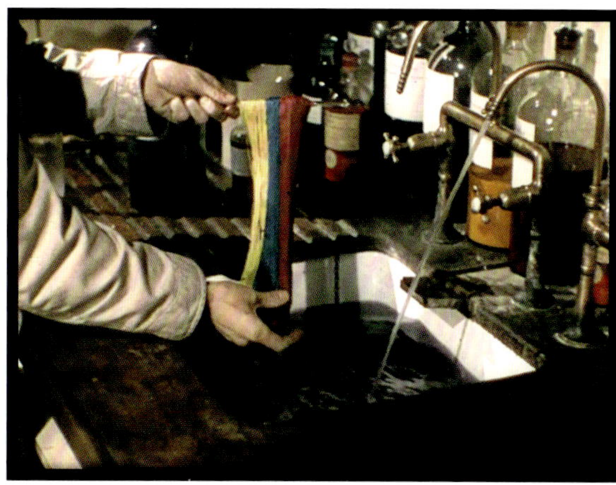

72 Dye experiments in *This Is Colour* (UK, 1942; dir. Jack Ellitt).

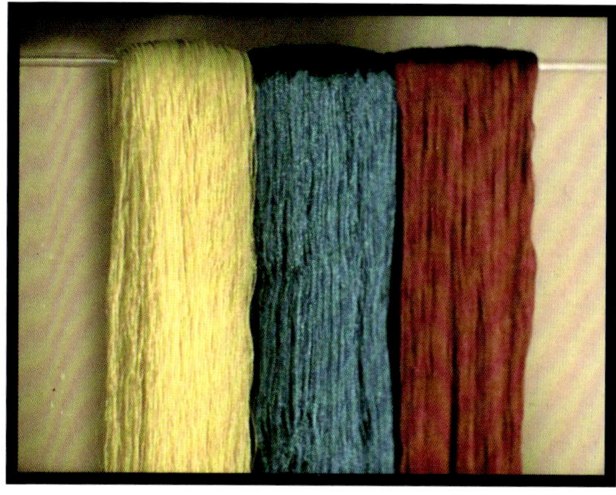

73 Three dyed strips in *This Is Colour*.

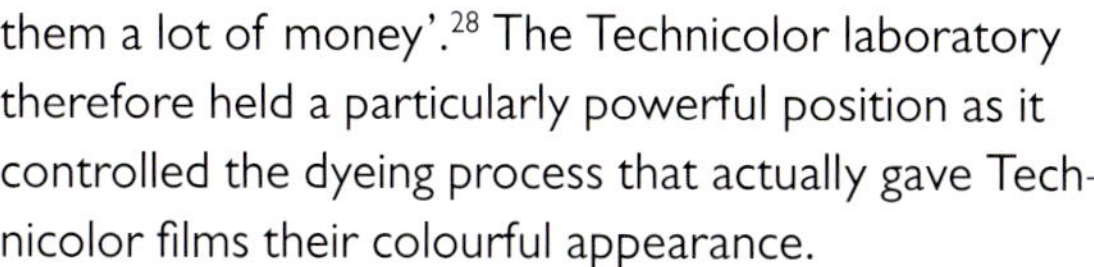

them a lot of money'.[28] The Technicolor laboratory therefore held a particularly powerful position as it controlled the dyeing process that actually gave Technicolor films their colourful appearance.

Technicolor's dyeing process carried particular significance in Britain, a nation with a long legacy of dye innovations. Technicolor was by no means a British technology; it was pioneered and patented in America and was synonymous with Hollywood filmmaking and American ideas of glamour.[29] Yet in Britain it was easy to perceive the process as a continuation of the nation's rich history of dyeing. This strategy of reframing the American colour film technology as an inheritor of Britain's dyeing heritage is made clear in *This Is Colour*. Revisiting the documentary here reveals how it conveys a nationalist approach to Technicolor cinema, despite its American pedigree.

As described in the Introduction, Imperial Chemical Industries (ICI) sponsored this short film to celebrate the history of Britain's dye industry, with its products presented as the pinnacle of this tradition. As previously outlined, the film begins with a theoretical grounding in colour science as the narrator explains the mechanics of the rainbow, revealing how this effect can be recreated in the laboratory using a prism to split white light into its various hues. The film then leads the viewer through a chronology of British dye innovations, starting with traditional methods of organic colour-making in the Hebrides, moving through William Henry Perkin's revolutionary discovery of coal-tar dyes and ending with modern industrial chemistry in the ICI laboratory. The film creates a chromatic continuity between these eras, reinforcing an unbroken lineage of British colour-making from the Hebridean cauldron stuffed with purple heathers to Perkin's revolutionary discovery of mauve to a beaker filled with a lilac solution sitting on a chemist's bench in the modern ICI laboratory. The narrator describes these ICI colour scientists as 'direct successors to Perkin', emphasising the connection between these historical and contemporary methods of British dyeing.

The sequences in the ICI laboratory comprise a series of chromatic magic tricks, whereby a chemist dips three colourless hanks of fabric into a single beaker, with each emerging a different bold hue: one yellow, one blue, one red. The chemist brandishes these three strips before the camera, inviting the viewer to assess the purity of each hue (figs 72 and 73). The high quality of the laboratory's azo dyes is then demonstrated by a scorching orange fabric filling the frame, its surface ruched and rumpled to luxuriate in the shadows and highlights of this searing chemical hue (fig. 74). Next, one of the commercial

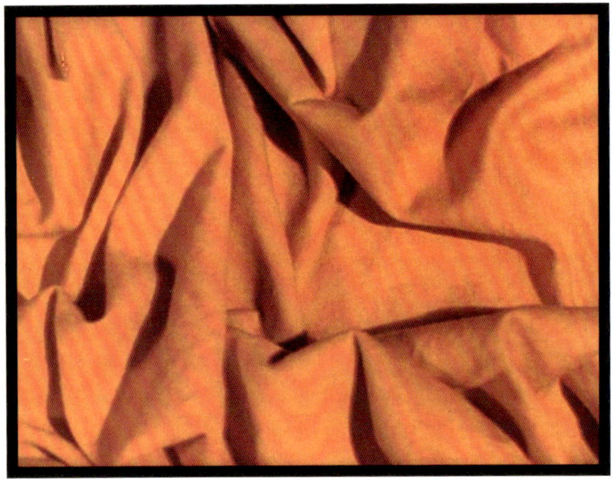

74 Textile dyeing in *This Is Colour*.

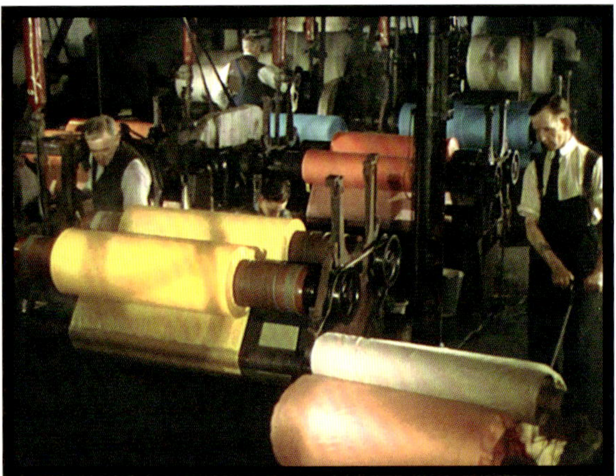

75 Rolling and pressing in *This Is Colour*.

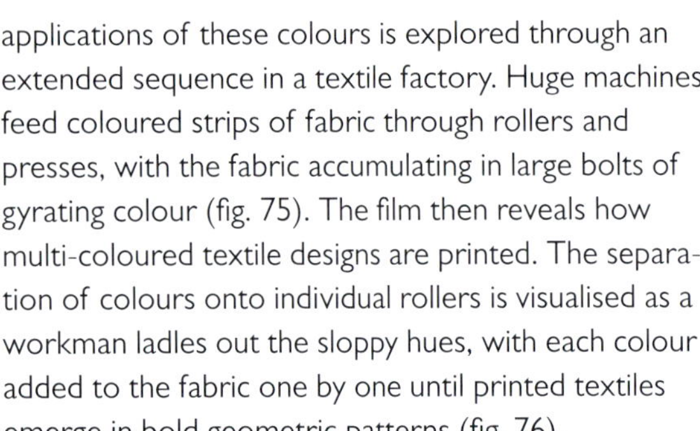

applications of these colours is explored through an extended sequence in a textile factory. Huge machines feed coloured strips of fabric through rollers and presses, with the fabric accumulating in large bolts of gyrating colour (fig. 75). The film then reveals how multi-coloured textile designs are printed. The separation of colours onto individual rollers is visualised as a workman ladles out the sloppy hues, with each colour added to the fabric one by one until printed textiles emerge in bold geometric patterns (fig. 76).

The final sequence of the film, announced by the proclamation 'Now, let all the colours dance!', relinquishes any pretence of didacticism to relish the formal delights of colour, as liquid hues squirt, run and drip across the screen. A stunningly choreographed series of shots filmed through the sides of a glass tank shows coloured dyes poured inside, producing arresting chromatic effects, such as a tornado of rosy pink liquid pirouetting before a jade backdrop (fig. 77). Yet despite celebrating colour's pure aestheticism, this

76 Printing fabrics in *This Is Colour*.

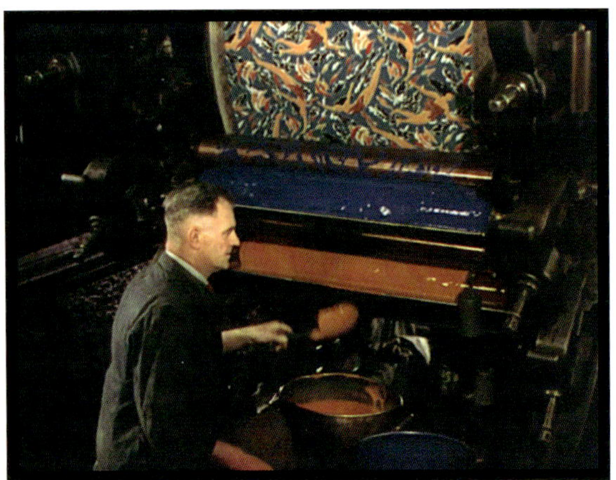

77 Imperial Chemical Industries' dyes in *This Is Colour*.

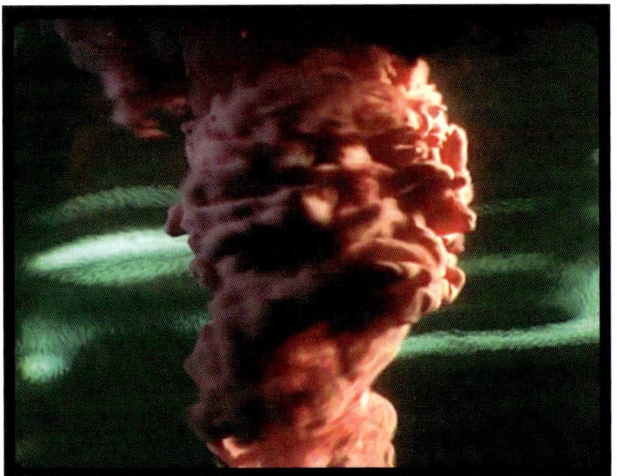

image of swirling dyes manufactured by ICI is clearly the product of, and homage to, the British industrial heritage that has been dramatised throughout the film. This sequence emphasises that the chromatic visual pleasures enjoyed in Technicolor cinema are themselves the final product of this long history of British colour innovation.

Through these sequences of dyes and dyeing, *This Is Colour* demonstrates how the American associations of Technicolor's palette could be transformed into a celebration of Britain's chromatic heritage. The endless parade of brilliant hues allowed Cardiff to revel in Technicolor's capacity for vivid saturation through his cinematography, yet the film insists that these beautiful chromatic effects are the result of British rather than American ingenuity. It places Technicolor film within this long historical lineage of British colour-making in the form of dyes and textiles, positioning cinema as the most recent iteration of Britain's mastery over, and creative use of, colour. But it was not just the film's narrative that connected Technicolor to Britain's dye and textile heritage, as the forms of colour-making shown here resonated with Technicolor's own laboratory process, which used textile dyes and industrial dyeing methods to colour its films.

Indeed, all the steps of Technicolor's process are presented here: the film opens with a prism splitting light into its component parts in the same manner as Technicolor's beam-splitting camera; in the ICI laboratory a special dyeing process produces three 'strips' in yellow, cyan and magenta just as Technicolor's processing laboratory would dye its matrices; and in the textile factory coloured prints are produced through the addition of individual coloured dyes applied through a series of rollers in a similar manner to Technicolor's dye-transfer system. The film foregrounds the technological similarities between dyeing films and dyeing fabrics – similarities further cemented by the materiality of the film itself, which was printed and dyed using ICI textile dyes.[30] The dyes best suited to Technicolor's process were aniline textile dyes for wool, cotton and silk – the dyes that, as *This Is Colour* vividly demonstrates, were famously invented by Perkin in Britain and revolutionised the global textile trade.[31] *This Is Colour* was therefore a literal product of precisely the processes dramatised in the film and a material manifestation of the historical forms of British colour it celebrates, as the textile dyes manufactured in the film's diegesis were the exact same colours as those carried on the surface of the film print itself. *This Is Colour* makes visible the material and technical processes that are typically concealed from the viewer, rendering legible the techno-materiality not of this film in particular but of Technicolor cinema in general. The overlaps presented in *This Is Colour* between dyeing films and dyeing fabrics therefore radically reconceptualise the identity of Technicolor cinema in Britain. Rather than showing the brand as an imported American process, *This Is Colour* recasts Technicolor as a local, domestic British dyeing technology.

The control of colour afforded by the IB process is important for understanding the significance of London's Technicolor laboratory within the wider world. The standardisation of Technicolor's system meant that Hollywood's matrices could be printed in Britain, and the London laboratory therefore printed both British and American films, which it also distributed around the globe. As established, the London plant supplied films within the British Empire, which in 1936 gave it a significant international scope, while the Hollywood plant covered the rest of the world. But, as Technicolor's popularity grew, Hollywood increasingly had to focus on the demands of the domestic American market. The British laboratory therefore absorbed the territories previously covered by the American laboratory, extending the reach of the London plant beyond the parameters of the empire. By the early 1950s, Technicolor Ltd supplied Technicolor prints to almost every country outside the United States.[32] As the production controller for the British laboratory recalled, 'we made prints for the world, except America … you couldn't get a Technicolor print anywhere unless you came to me'.[33] Through the dye-transfer process, an inheritor of Britain's chromatic legacy in dyeing innovations, Technicolor Ltd became the chief gatekeeper for the world's access to Technicolor film.

If Technicolor was the dominant colour film technology of the mid-twentieth century, and the dye-transfer process was crucial to the economics and aesthetics of the process, then Technicolor's London laboratory occupied a position of extreme chromatic power. Standing at the centre of this global network of printed and dyed colour, Technicolor's London plant was also imbued with an ideological resonance that the Hollywood laboratory lacked. As colour was inextricably linked with colonial enterprise and imperial economics, in particular the freight in printed and dyed textiles, the London laboratory's ability to control printed and dyed film on a global scale was deeply emblematic of a new kind of chromatic imperialism. Yet, to suggest that through these techno-material processes the London laboratory became an instrument of chromatic imperialism necessitates a further clarification of Technicolor's relationship to the British state and its interests, and how these intersected with the changing nature of British imperialism at this time. While it may have differed in terms of its methods, chromatic imperialism borrowed organisational principles, structures of labour, and patterns of resource exchange from established forms of British territorial imperialism, enabling Britain to bolster its position vis-à-vis American corporate expansionism in this period.

The Fabric of Empire

Technicolor Ltd, founded in the inter-war moment, participated in and visualised Britain's transitioning role from governmental power to globalised trader. The firm was 50 per cent owned by British interests, comprising a British conglomerate of Alexander Korda's London Film Productions Ltd, the packaging manufacture Gerrard Industries Ltd, the Prudential Assurance Company and a number of private individuals: the solicitor St George Syms and two associates of Korda, the Conservative Member of Parliament Sir Adrian Baillie and Colonel P. W. Pitt.[34] This group paid dividends to the American parent company Technicolor Incorporated, which owned the remaining 50 per cent of stocks in the British firm, positioning Technicolor Ltd between American corporate expansionism and British capitalist imperialism. Although Technicolor Ltd was therefore not officially bound to the interests of the British state and was linked to commercial operations on the opposite side of the Atlantic, through its various British shareholders it was keenly tethered to interests extending beyond Britain's film industry, to encompass its banking system, legal framework, conservative politics and the military.

Korda, a Hungarian émigré prominent in Britain's film industry, was doubly invested in Technicolor as both a shareholder in the company and a producer of Technicolor films, making him the process's greatest champion. He had initially campaigned to have the laboratory located at his new Denham Film Studios, the home of London Film Productions, but protests from the local authorities regarding toxic dyes entering the water system forced its relocation to Harmondsworth.[35] Nevertheless, Korda was known to the London plant manager as 'our best customer' – unsurprising given his financial stakes in the firm's success.[36] But Korda was also known for his sympathy with and proximity to British imperial policy. His professional and personal circles included members of and diplomatic advisers to the Conservative government and British military, and his close connections to these state interests earned him preferential standing within the British establishment.[37] Korda's use of Technicolor's system to make imperial adventure films such as *The Drum* presented an opportunity to support his own investments that was simultaneously of both a political and a financial nature.

Indeed, there are no films that more aggressively cement the bonds between imperial ideology and Technicolor cinema than those made by Korda in the 1930s, many of which were directed by his brother Zoltán. *The Drum* and *The Four Feathers* (UK, 1939), set in nineteenth-century Sudan, along with the earlier black and white picture *Sanders of the River* (UK, 1935), set in Nigeria, form what is known as Korda's 'empire trilogy'. These films were later supplemented by his Technicolor Orientalist fantasies: *The Jungle*

Book (UK/US, 1942; dir. Zoltán Korda) and *The Thief of Bagdad* (UK/US, 1940; Michael Powell).[38] But the empire epics are especially explicit in their celebration of imperialism's aesthetic splendours and moral supremacy in the form of racialised violence, military force and colonial oppression – values rendered all the more visceral through the added dimension of Technicolor.

As Jeffrey Richards argues, although these films were not officially sponsored by the state, the pro-imperial stance they exhibited earned Korda assistance from colonial officials in Sudan and India, as well as favourable treatment by censorship and regulatory boards in Britain.[39] Despite the fact that these films were not official forms of state propaganda, they were understood as such by audiences. As Prem Chowdry has shown, *The Drum* was received in India as an unambiguous vehicle of British imperial policy and was protested as such.[40] So adverse was the reaction of Indian audiences to the racism and Islamophobia displayed in this film that local authorities had to remove it from circulation to curb the protests that had engulfed uptown Bombay (now Mumbai).[41]

Korda's works are therefore privileged in accounts of colour cinema and empire, because they so transparently demonstrate Technicolor's complicity with imperial power. However, these political investments were not just conveyed through the narratives of these specific films but were endemic to the larger corporate structure of Technicolor Ltd, with Korda at its centre, and to the imperial associations of the material and technical procedures used to make them. In the same manner that *This Is Colour* made visible the usually invisible techno-materiality that underpinned all Technicolor cinema, Korda's empire films made explicit the usually tacit imperial ideology underpinning Technicolor more broadly. While Korda's epics may have more patently displayed their imperial affiliations than other Technicolor productions, these political meanings were equally embedded in films where these subjects remained submerged at the level of representation. Therefore, while Korda remains a crucial figure for the history I trace here, I refrain from revisiting the empire epics in detail, as their political implications have already been richly illuminated by other scholars.[42] To elucidate my argument, I turn instead to a short film whose relationship to empire is far less explicit and whose imperialism is more in line with the mode of capitalist globalisation that increasingly characterised Britain's relationship to its empire and Commonwealth towards the middle of the twentieth century. Furthermore, by scrutinising the material composition of the film, it is possible to elucidate the way Technicolor films *as objects* inherited the legacies of extractivism and exploitation that had typified the trade networks of the British Empire of the preceding centuries.

Queen Cotton (UK, 1941; dir. Cecil Musk), like *This Is Colour*, was one of numerous short documentaries made in Technicolor during the Second World War that enlivened screens with morale-boosting hues while also celebrating British industry and manufacturing.[43] This short fashion film, with Cardiff credited as colour consultant, simultaneously showcased Technicolor's process and the work of the recently formed Cotton Board. This textile trade body – established by the government in 1940 to stimulate British cotton exports through industrial research, exhibitions and fashion shows – was intended to shore up an industry that had historically been a key driver of the imperial economy but that was declining amid the slow dissolution of British imperial power and the challenges of the war.[44] *Queen Cotton* was part of a promotional campaign intended for overseas circulation to publicise the board's first fashion collection designed for export to South America. Unlike Korda's epics, the film never mentions the empire by name, nor does it allude to Britain's colonial or martial powers overseas, yet the empire is present here as a structuring, commercial logic that binds together the cotton goods on display and the Technicolor film displaying them.

The film opens with a panoramic view of the verdant Pennine hills in Lancashire, 'whose looms', says the male narrator, 'for two hundred years have given the world its cotton goods', and this serves to foreground the historical legacy of Britain's cotton trade in the very first moments. This pastoral image fades into a less picturesque scene, as vertiginous shots

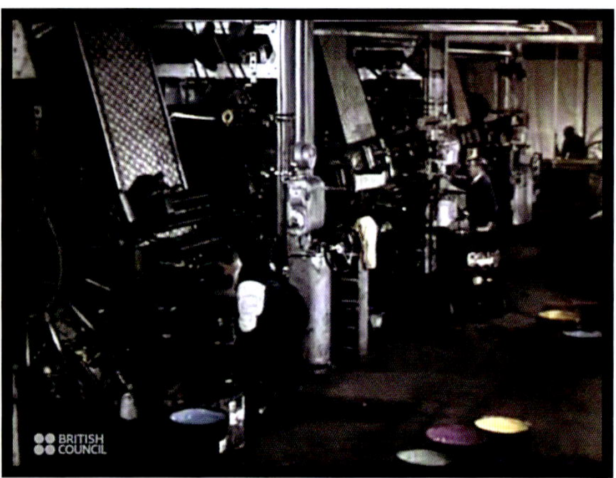

78 Textile printing in *Queen Cotton* (UK, 1941; dir. Cecil Musk).

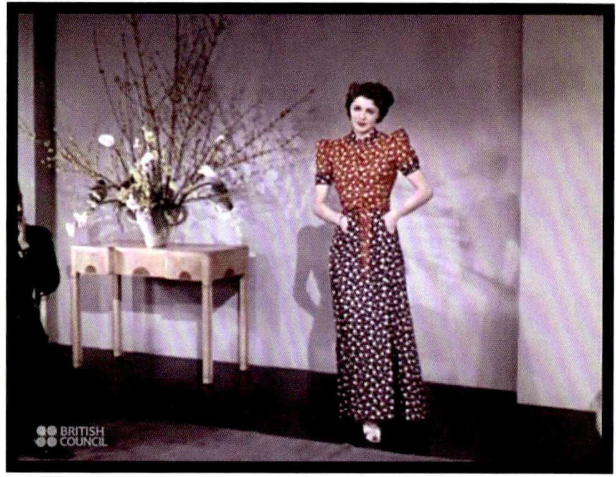

79 A fashion show of printed cotton goods in *Queen Cotton*.

of cranes show bales of cotton being winched from ships onto the dockside in Manchester – described as 'the great city of textiles'. The film demonstrates how these cottons, which come 'from every continent', are transformed into fabrics for global distribution. As these blandly coloured raw materials are unloaded, crates stamped with Union Jacks and filled with colourful cotton fashions are hoisted back onto ships for export, highlighting Britain's position as the central location where these global networks of chromatic production and consumption converge.

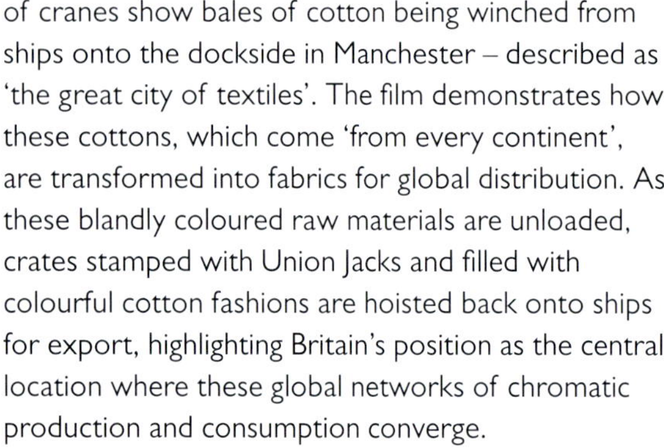

The process by which these cotton outfits were made, particularly the means by which they were coloured, occupies the rest of the film, which demonstrates how cotton was processed and printed before being fashioned into clothing for sale (fig. 78). Each step in this process presents an excuse to showcase Technicolor's vivid hues, from the colourful designs sketched in the studio to the dyes mixed up by the printers to the finished gowns paraded before the camera in the concluding fashion show (fig. 79). The film highlights Britain's primacy as a modern industrialised nation through its images of cotton manufacture, but these images' presentation in a Technicolor film, itself a state-of-the-art technology, was itself a display of Britain's prepotence in the field of chromatic mass production. The cotton industry also evokes further parallels with Technicolor's chromatic practice, which similarly extracted raw material from overseas that were processed and printed in Britain before being exported internationally.

Unlike *This Is Colour*, which focuses on chromatic innovation in Britain, *Queen Cotton* is more concerned with highlighting the globalised nature of this chromatic labour. Throughout the film, the viewer is reminded of the international destinations of these colourful goods, emphasising Britain's pivotal role in these global networks of colour. One sequence demonstrates how dyes were mixed in the factory, with workers agitating barrels of cheerful yellow, brilliant blue and candy-coloured pink while the narrator explains that the brightness of these ensures they will withstand many days 'under the glare of a tropical sun' once they have been shipped overseas (fig. 80).

While *This Is Colour* highlighted Technicolor's laboratory as a modern inheritor of Britain's history of textile dyeing, *Queen Cotton* simultaneously alludes to and elides the imperial dimension of that history. Imperialism is not part of the vocabulary of *Queen Cotton*'s narrator, yet, given that cotton was one of the most essential materials of the empire's economic and industrial strength, these images of it operate as powerful symbols of Britain's imperial past. While the narrator invokes a two-hundred-year

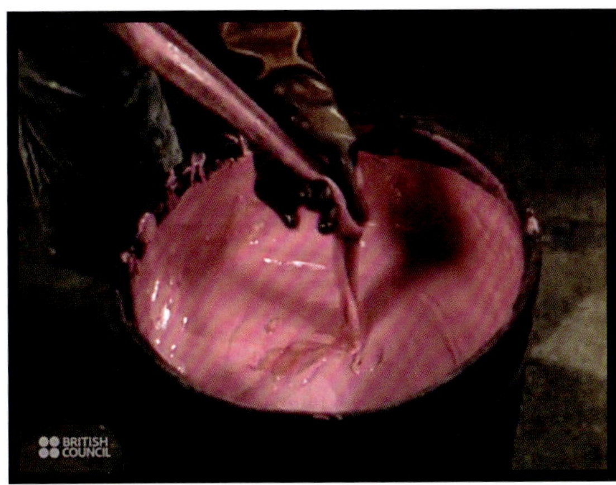

80 Mixing dyes in *Queen Cotton*.

history of cotton production in Britain, the relationship between colour, cotton and British networks of trade were intertwined much further back in time, braiding together acts of colonial violence around the world. Cotton connected those economies of colour discussed in the Introduction: dyes and textiles, and enslaved persons of colour. From the seventeenth century the British East India Company had sourced cotton textiles from India, exchanged these brightly coloured fabrics for enslaved peoples in West Africa and used cotton to clothe enslaved Africans working on plantations in the Caribbean.[45] Cotton therefore threaded together the empire's colonial and economic strategy as a material that legitimated the enslavement of Africans, the perpetuation of exploited plantation labour in the Caribbean and the aggressive control of overseas industries in India.

By the nineteenth century Britain merely imported raw cotton from India and not finished fabrics, because the Lancashire cotton mills with their industrial machinery, as seen in *Queen Cotton*, could process, print and dye these materials much more cheaply. This practice devastated the Indian trade and allowed Britain to dominate overseas markets in Africa and Asia. This elevated textiles to a status of heightened political symbolism in India, making them crucial to articulations of the country's independence. The rejection of British textiles in favour of domestically produced Indian fabrics, a continuation of the Swadeshi policies established in the early part of the century, was central to India's independence movement, which cited Lancashire's cotton mills as some of the most violent instruments in Britain's regime of colonial control.[46] While the colouring and circulation of cotton displayed in *Queen Cotton* are inseparable from these brutal histories of British imperialism and their legacies in the present, their presentation in the gorgeous hues of Technicolor helps to render them invisible beneath its beautiful sheen of colour.

Yet the audience can discern the longevity of Britain's imperial involvement with cotton in a sequence detailing scientific research. The camera pans across a case of raw cotton samples, each labelled to display its origins, whether in countries with ties to the empire's historical cotton trade (America, Egypt), cotton-producing regions currently under British colonial control (Bengal, St Vincent) or Britain's aspirational future trading partners in South America (Brazil, Peru). Therefore, while *Queen Cotton* omits any mention of empire, presenting a modernised system of transactional exchange between Britain and the wider world, the goods and products it celebrates were inheritors of precisely the kinds of brutal imperialism celebrated in earlier empire films such as those produced by Korda.

The film's title does evoke this violent history through its feminisation of 'King Cotton', the term used in the nineteenth century to denote the independent economic strength of the American South (predicated on the enslaved labour used in the production of cotton) but also associated with British colonial violence in India in the twentieth century. As Giorgio Riello notes, the term 'Queen Cotton' connoted the dominance of Indian (rather than American) cottons in the global trade, facilitated by British colonialism.[47] The audience is therefore invited to imagine that 'Queen Cotton' personifies Britain's global economic dominance in textiles, serving as a symbol of Britannia's continued might during the Second World War. The lexis of chromatic imprisonment presented in the film's voiceover, where colour

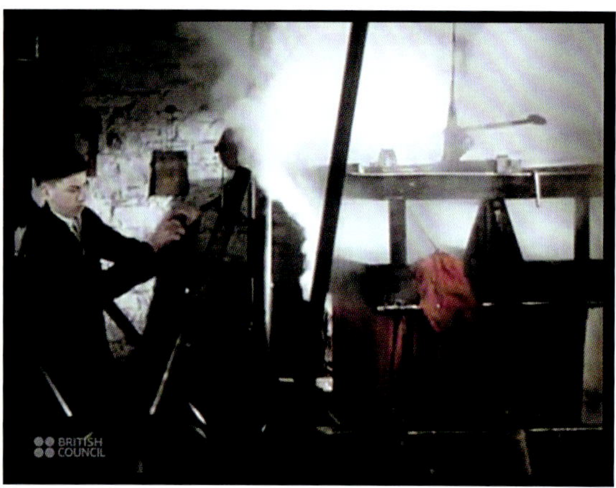

81 Dyeing wool in *Border Weave* (UK, 1941; dir. John Lewis Curthoys).

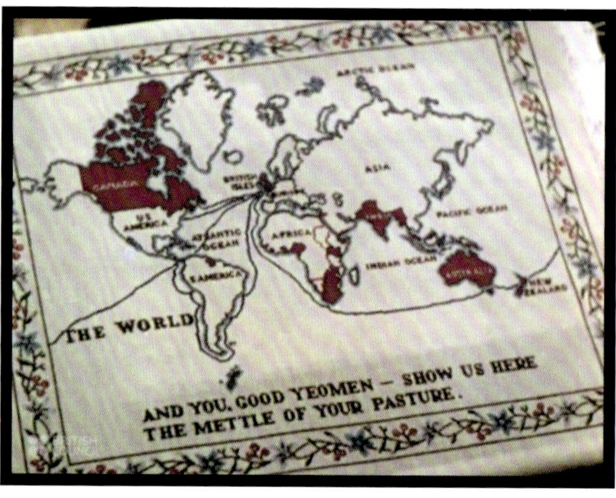

82 A map of the British Empire captured in dyed yarn in *Border Weave*.

is 'captured' and 'held to ransom in the workshops of Lancashire', seems to carry particularly violent overtones in this context.

But *Queen Cotton* also held a strong material connection to the cotton industry of the American south, as cotton was a crucial component in the physical composition of film stock itself. Cotton was the source of the cellulose that comprised the material base of celluloid film, and the American firm Kodak, the sole supplier of Technicolor's blank and matrix stock, sourced its cotton products from Tennessee.[48] Kodak had in fact opened a subsidiary in Kingsport, Tennessee, partially due to the proximity of raw materials, such as cotton, that were necessary to the manufacture of its film.[49] In its promotional literature, Kodak revealed the surprising fact that film stock largely comprised 'ordinary plantation-variety cotton', which, through a variety of chemical processes, its factories transformed into the flexible, transparent substance known as cellulose nitrate, or celluloid.[50] Therefore, not only was *Queen Cotton* an object printed and dyed in Britain for overseas circulation, in precisely the same manner as the cottons displayed in the film, but cotton itself was also a crucial constituent ingredient of the film's material base. The display of Tennessee cottons in *Queen Cotton* further solidifies the links between the narrative content of the film and the material process of its own manufacture, embedding both within the longer history of transatlantic slavery, plantation economics and colonial exploitation. Through the material and technical composition of the film, its links to the imperial history of the cotton industry are thereby transformed from symbolic allusion into concrete fact.

The ties between Technicolor cinema, textiles and imperial trade illuminated by *Queen Cotton* are taken up in a contemporaneous short Technicolor film shot by Cardiff, titled *Border Weave* (UK, 1941; dir. John Lewis Curthoys).[51] The film explores the expansion of the British wool industry across the empire and includes extended sequences of wool dyeing with workers stirring steaming dye-vats and hoisting coloured hanks of wool aloft (fig. 81). But the film begins and ends with an elderly Scottish woman embroidering a map of the world with wool yarn to demonstrate the scale of this imperial trade. Once she has coloured the spaces of the empire appropriately in red, she adds the final touch – stitching British trade routes in black yarn (fig. 82). This map, made from the fabric of empire in the form of dyed wool and visualised through another imperial fabric in the form of dyed film, could double as a visualisation of British

Technicolor's own trade routes, which supplied the world with its own dyed and printed products in the manner so vividly aestheticised in *Queen Cotton*. These films reveal the intricate intertwining of the strands (economic, symbolic and aesthetic) that bound Technicolor both to the changing trajectories of empire and to the globalised film market at this time.

However, these relationships would be dramatically reconfigured following the conclusion of the war, when the map of the British Empire seen in *Border Weave* and *The Drum* would alter significantly. From 1945, in the wake of a conflict that supposedly saw freedom and democracy triumph over the brutality of fascism, Britain's continued control of overseas territories came under increased scrutiny. Challenges to British imperial power gained momentum all over the world in the following decades, from the Suez Crisis in Egypt to independence struggles in Kenya and across the Caribbean as well as the British withdrawal from territories in the Middle East and South East Asia. With each decade that followed the war, more colonies and protectorates gained independence from Britain in the global transitions to self-determination that shaped the post-war period: the Asian states of India, Burma (now Myanmar) and Ceylon (now Sri Lanka) in the 1940s; African nations including Ghana, Sierra Leone and Sudan in the 1950s; and various Caribbean nations in the 1960s, including Jamaica and Trinidad and Tobago. To borrow the formulation of David Harvey, following the end of the war 'the map of the world started to change colour'.[52] If British Technicolor cinema was intimately connected to the material, technical, economic and ideological operations of empire, then how did decolonisation affect the use and meaning of this colour technology? Moreover, how did newly independent nations liberated from British colonial control reformulate the meanings of this colour technology amid this changing landscape of political power? By taking up a technology long linked with histories of colonialism and oppression, these newly independent nations did not simply eradicate its previous resonances but were able to use these implications to form new political meanings in their work.

Decolonisation and Colour Cinema

The tumultuous changes convulsing the British Empire following the war also affected the political dynamics of colour filmmaking. Following the conflict, a host of new colour film stocks emerged, largely derived from German Agfacolor, Technicolor's chief rival. Agfacolor stock had been developed in the 1930s with support from the German government to rival Technicolor's dominance, and was used for fascist propaganda cinema during the war. A chromogenic monopack system comprising a single strip of specially made negative stock, it required no special camera equipment and could be processed by any laboratory familiar with the necessary photochemical processes. Although Agfacolor could not compete with Technicolor's saturation, the simplicity of the technology made it the envy of every film industry frustrated by the cost and complexity of Technicolor's process as well as the stranglehold Technicolor held on the market. Following the war, Allied and Soviet forces forcibly extracted Agfa's patents, and the dispersal of this information led to a flurry of new chromogenic systems appearing all over the world in the following decades, including Russian Sovcolor, Italian Ferraniacolor, Japanese Fujicolor and Belgian Gevacolor.[53] In the same period Kodak also released its own chromogenic system, known as Eastmancolor, which similarly required no special camera or processing equipment.[54]

The 1950s are therefore characterised in film history as a decade in which Technicolor's monopoly ended and colour filmmaking became decentralised and democratised.[55] In 1955 Technicolor retired its fleet of three-strip cameras because these new chromogenic systems made the ungainly beam-splitter redundant. This also meant producers were freed from the constraints of Technicolor's tightly managed schedule, as filmmakers could now work to their own timetable and without the oversight of the Color Advisory Service. The new stocks also enabled colour filmmaking to flourish in industries that had previously struggled to sustain colour production. Coinciding with worldwide anti-colonial movements,

. . . A credit in any language

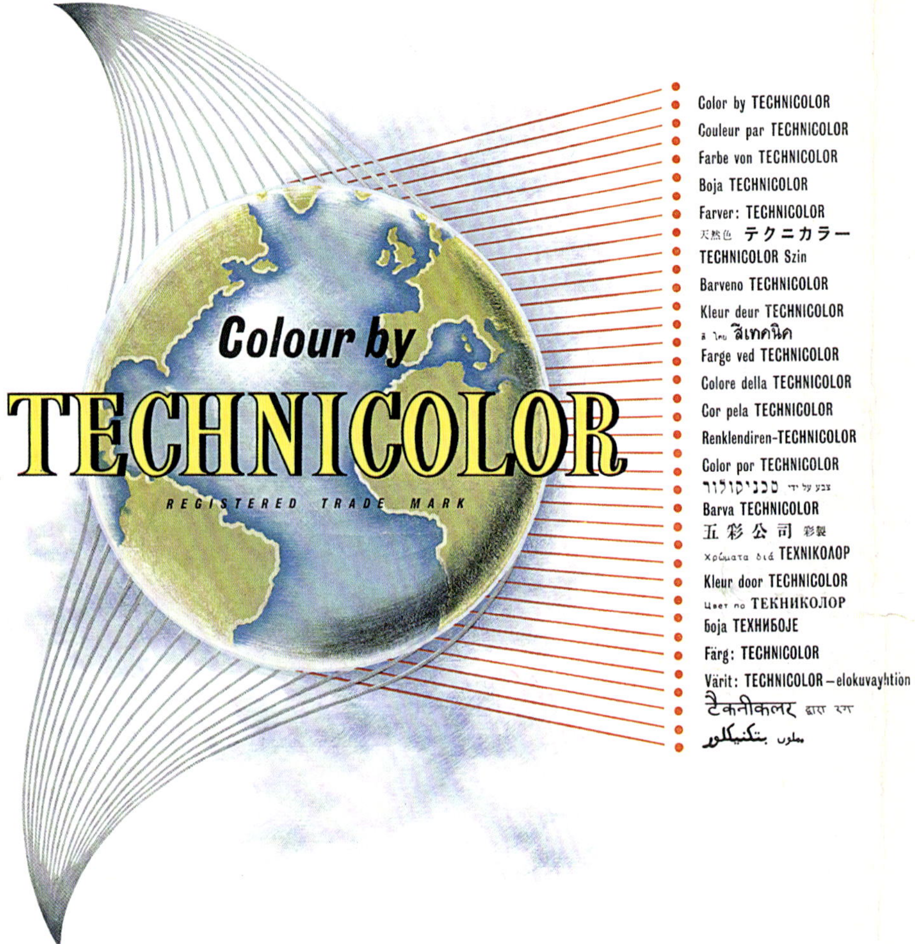

TECHNICOLOR LIMITED

HERBERT T. KALMUS, CHAIRMAN

Printed in England

not least the gradual decolonisation of the British Empire as well as the reorganisation of global systems of power through the Cold War, these new colour film processes were therefore imbued with various forms of utopian promise for a host of nations.

By no means did a global conversion to colour production happen swiftly or uniformly in the post-war period. Filmmakers across Africa, for instance, did not begin working regularly in colour until the late 1960s.[56] However, the 1950s marked a serious erosion of the controlled access to colour that had characterised the preceding decades, held primarily in the hands of fascist, capitalist and imperial powers (respectively Germany, America and Britain). Chromogenic stocks symbolised a range of freedoms for socialist and post-colonial nations, which were now able to begin managing their own colour film productions in a meaningful way for the first time. While the production of these chromogenic stocks was controlled by industrialised nations of the Global North, many were commercially available on the open market, compatible with existing black and white camera technology and cheaper than shooting in Technicolor. Colour production therefore became a globalised phenomenon from the 1950s and seemed to signal a loosening of the imperial control of colour that Technicolor epitomised.[57]

However, while colour production increased on a global scale in the 1950s, laboratory capacity failed to keep pace. For instance, there were few laboratories in Africa or Asia equipped to process colour at this time.[58] As one of the largest and best-established colour laboratories in the world, Technicolor's plant in London was ready to absorb this new business. Although chromogenic stocks did not require dye-transfer processing, it was possible to print them using Technicolor's system by adding an extra step into the laboratory workflow (namely splitting a single camera negative into three strips using filters). This enabled films to be shot on chromogenic monopack but benefit from the economic and aesthetic advantages of IB printing. Far from diminishing Technicolor's stake in the colour film market, the dispersal of these new colour film stocks around the world in the post-war period cemented the importance of its London laboratory, with Technicolor Ltd workers remembering this as a 'boom' period.[59] Previously Technicolor had only processed films shot using its own three-strip cameras, but now it was developing film stocks of every kind from all over the world, increasing its dye-transfer output by nearly 50 per cent in the 1950s.[60]

83 Trade advertisement for Technicolor Ltd, 1954. George Eastman Museum, Rochester, New York.

An advertisement for Technicolor Ltd from 1954 celebrates the internationalism of the Technicolor brand in this era (fig. 83). With the phrase 'Colour by Technicolor' emblazoned across a globe suspended in the centre of the page, the advertisement shows how to credit the British laboratory in twenty-six different languages. Lines of grey and red curve around the globe as though marking the journey of Technicolor prints around its circumference, not unlike the threads of empire traced in *Border Weave*. The globe is tilted so that the United Kingdom is prominently positioned in the top right corner, and tellingly the West Coast of America is occluded from view. While the nations of the globe are not captured in the red-pink of empire seen in *The Drum*, this image reveals Britain's continued dominance of colour on a global scale.

Another promotional image from 1956 illuminates the political dimensions of London's continued global power in an era of emergent post-colonialism (fig. 84). Rather than exploiting the commodified image of a British film star, the advertisement presents a quarter-length portrait of a girl labelled 'Kachin Woman Burma' in a manner that betrays the ethnographic impulses animating the image. She is dressed in an ornamental head-wrap and protruding earrings, which frame her face as she gazes past the viewer with her chin lifted in an assured stance. While this woman was not a subject of the empire, as Burma (now Myanmar) had gained independence from British colonial rule in 1948, the exploitation of this

dominance in colour cinema forces a reconsideration of the geopolitics of post-war colour filmmaking in an era of decolonisation. While former British colonies had unprecedented access to colour film stock, they were still reliant upon the British laboratory to print and dye these films.

Further aesthetic factors complicate narratives of colour and decolonisation in the 1950s, which have typically privileged chromogenic stocks as vehicles for new forms of independent filmmaking. While chromogenic processes were more accessible and affordable than three-strip Technicolor, their colour was duller and more muted. Technicolor also carried a pedigree unmatched by these chromogenic systems as it was associated with Hollywood cinema at the height of its prominence, connoting a quality and prestige that these chromogenic processes lacked. These associations certainly could be undesirable. During the Cold War, Technicolor's affiliation with capitalistic decadence could be problematic, and, similarly, for former colonies of the British Empire, Technicolor's deep ties to histories of colonialism meant it could not be disentangled from imperial ideology.[66]

This combination of factors makes India's adoption of Technicolor in the 1950s particularly fascinating. India was in a unique position in the early 1950s as a newly independent nation that was home to the world's second largest film industry. Colour was therefore particularly important both as an instrument for self-representation and as a symbol of prestige for the independent film sector. However, by the 1950s India had only produced a very small number of colour features, all made with imported stocks.[67] While Technicolor cinema had been wielded as an instrument of British imperial power during the colonial era, following Indian independence in 1947, it could now be repurposed for new political and aesthetic ends. In other words, one of the principal tools of capitalist imperialism could now be used to further anti-imperial ideologies.

In Hollywood, Technicolor Incorporated saw the potential in this new market opening up in India. The in-house journal *Technicolor News and Views* reported in the summer of 1949 that 'since the establishment of the Commonwealth of India and the Commonwealth of Pakistan, Technicolor has been approached by a number of motion picture companies there, urging us to establish a Technicolor subsidiary in India'.[68] In 1952 several of the journal's headlines promoted expansion into India, claiming 'Technicolor Pictures Preferred in India' and 'India Called Active Field for Technicolor'.[69] Technicolor Incorporated viewed India as part of its strategy for global expansion in the 1950s, which included plans to open laboratories in Munich, Buenos Aires and Tokyo. The firm established new European laboratories in Paris in 1953 and Rome in 1955, which eroded the London laboratory's continental business, but Technicolor claimed a Bombay location was its top priority.[70] The Indian press excitedly discussed this opportunity, noting that an Indian laboratory would 'obviate the necessity of processing Technicolor films in London or in Hollywood'.[71]

Colour laboratories were identified as crucial for a self-sufficient and high-quality national film industry in an independent India, as outlined in a 1951 advisory report for the Indian government.[72] Insisting that 'the laboratory workers are ultimately responsible for the success or failure of a picture', the report lamented that India lacked the high-grade photographic chemicals and printing machines necessary for this kind of work, and urged development in this area.[73] India's broadcasting minister therefore held talks with Technicolor to discuss the potential for a new Bombay laboratory.[74] The establishment of these facilities would make the nation's film industry less dependent on Britain, which was important economically as foreign exchange was strictly controlled and politically as the nation was forging its independent identity.

A series of Technicolor films made in India in the 1950s therefore operated both as test cases for the American firm, to see whether India could become a site for Technicolor production and laboratory facilities, and as a training ground for the Indian industry, eager to learn this specialised process. However, in order for these films to be made in India, equipment, expertise and laboratory services had to be supplied from Britain. The first three-strip Technicolor film by

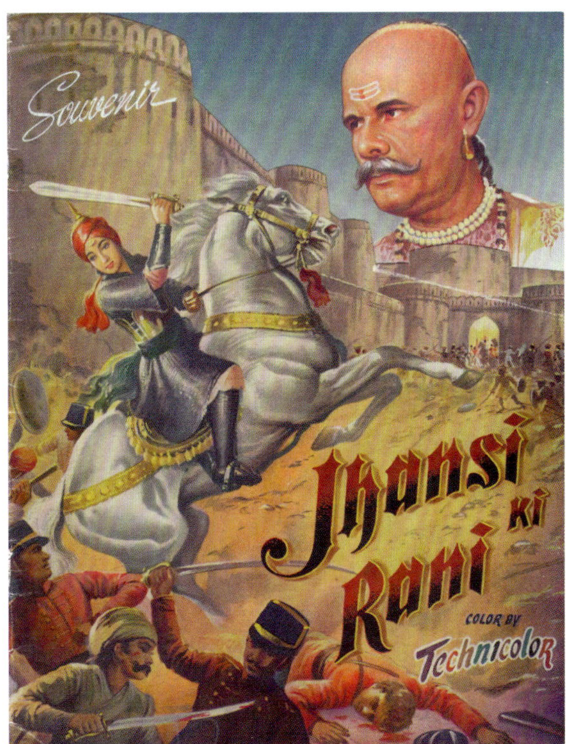

85 Souvenir programme for *Jhansi Ki Rani* (India, 1953), produced and directed by Sohrab Modi. Collection of Mehelli Modi.

an Indian producer and director, *Jhansi Ki Rani*, is a particularly salient case study for reassessing Technicolor's status during this period of global decolonisation. Made in 1952 and released in 1953 as a collaboration between Indian, American and British personnel, the film illuminates the political dimensions of Technicolor as a medium for mediating Anglo-Indian relations at this time. Furthermore, the film troubles what Grazia Ingravalle has identified as the distinction between so-called British and Indian film heritage, evidencing what she describes as 'a common history that entangles the colonizer and the colonized in an inescapable shared legacy'.[75] As a film whose narrative celebrates resistance against British colonialism, *Jhansi Ki Rani* raises the question of whether British involvement in the production demonstrated a continuation of the British control of colour exerted through Technicolor or resistance to precisely those systems of chromatic and neo-colonial regulation.

Jhansi Ki Rani and the Politics of Printing

Jhansi Ki Rani proudly boasted of its status as India's first Technicolor film, brandishing the Technicolor name on promotional materials in rainbow hues (fig. 85). The brand was a mark of distinction exploited by Sohrab Modi, who directed, produced and acted in the film, and also owned Minerva Movietone Studios in Bombay, where *Jhansi Ki Rani* was filmed. Known as the Cecil B. DeMille of India due to the grandiose scale of his historical epics, Modi intended *Jhansi Ki Rani* to set new precedents for spectacular excess in Indian cinema. The film was not merely destined for domestic exhibition but planned to put independent India on the map of worldwide film exhibition, with the *New York Times* describing the project as 'India's first bid for world distribution'.[76] To enhance its global appeal, the film was to be released in colour but in two versions, one in Hindustani and one, slightly shorter, in English, with the latter released some years later, in 1955, under the alternative title *The Tiger and the Flame*. Sadly, only the English-language version is still available to see in colour as there are no extant colour release prints of *Jhansi Ki Rani*, only black and white copies.[77] While Modi's decision to shoot in Technicolor, a prestigious system with global brand recognition, seems consistent with his international ambitions for the film, his choice of colour technology also belies the larger ideological and political agenda of the film.

It was fitting that this film, designed to foreground the independent film industry, should take as its subject India's First War of Independence (1857).[78] *Jhansi Ki Rani* celebrates this important moment from India's colonial history, when the rani, or queen, of the Indian state of Jhansi led forces in a military rebellion against the British East India Company. The war is the dramatic climax to the life of Rani Laxmibai (a role

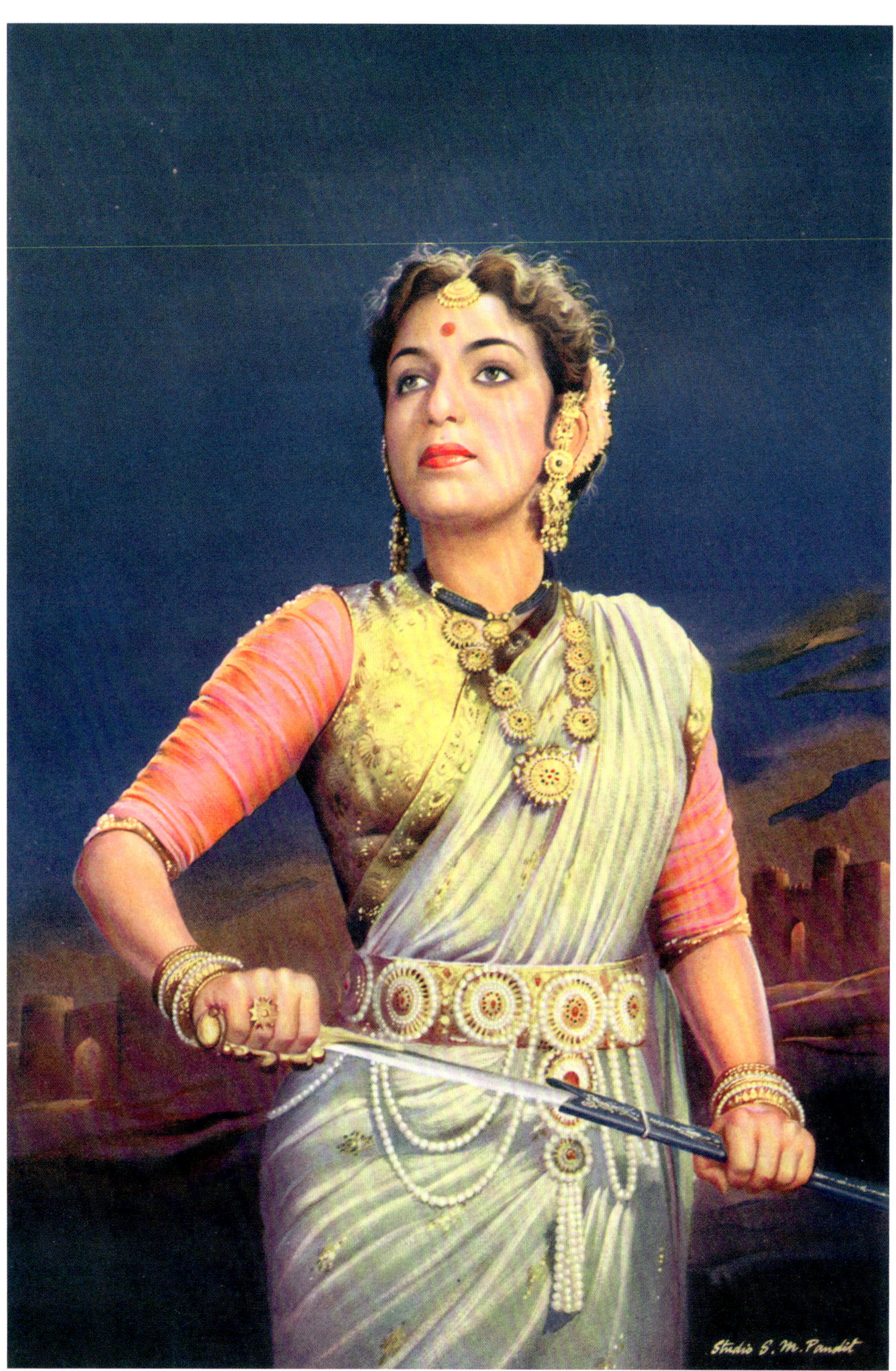
Studio S. M. Pandit

played by Modi's wife, Mehtab), traced from her childhood displays of bravery and courage to her death on the battlefield at the hands of British soldiers. This popular story of Indian heroism luxuriates in various opulent courtly rituals, including extended dance sequences, carefully choreographed military pageants and spectacular battles showcasing the rani's military prowess, complete with glittering chainmail. Printed promotions for the film used colour to exacerbate the combative glamour of the rani's appearance, juxtaposing her laurel green sari and brilliant pink *choli* with her highly ornamented golden body armour, gleaming silver sword and glossy red lipstick (fig. 86).

The film drew clear parallels between the rani's attempts to contest British colonialism and India's recent struggle for independence, attempting to present a unifying patriotic theme at a time when the character of Indian nationalism was still under negotiation and the nature of a 'national' film style was unfixed.[79] Promotions for the film proclaimed it a tribute to those 'who have fought and died so that other men and women may live in freedom', emphasising the rani's fight for liberty as a forerunner to India's current political independence.[80] The film invited a shared sense of national pride in a single consolidating narrative, despite the multiple religious, ethnic and linguistic groups that comprised the newly formed nation of India. Modi had already explored themes of anti-colonial resistance in his earlier black and white film *Sikander* (India, 1941), which had been banned by certain British exhibitors who saw in its story of India's hostility to Alexander the Great an all too easily discernible allegory for Indian resistance to British colonialism.[81] In *Jhansi Ki Rani*, Modi could directly explore themes he had previously only treated through metaphor, and his use of Technicolor to do so was crucial to the film's meaning.

86 Mehtab Modi as the glamorous warrior queen. Souvenir programme for *Jhansi Ki Rani*. William K. Everson Collection, New York University.

Modi's choice of Technicolor for a film about Indian independence may seem surprising, however. Using Technicolor meant the employment of a host of foreign personnel from America and Britain who had specialist knowledge of the process, from camera operators and colour consultants to lighting and make-up experts, as well as the services of the London laboratory.[82] Rather than celebrating autonomy from British authorities, the production of *Jhansi Ki Rani* would be highly contingent upon them. Other Indian directors working in colour around this time deliberately selected different processes to celebrate India's chromatic self-sufficiency. For instance, director Mehboob Khan chose to shoot his colour debut *Aan* (India, 1952) on 16 mm Kodachrome to avoid working under Technicolor's tight restrictions on set, ensuring he could employ his preferred cinematographer, Faredoon A. Irani, although Technicolor Ltd in London did manufacture the film's release prints.[83] Ambalal Patel, on the other hand, produced his colour debut *Pamposh* (India, 1953; dir. Ezra Mir) using Gevacolor, a Belgian chromogenic process that could be processed at Patel's own Film Centre in Bombay, India's first colour laboratory, opened in 1952.[84] While Patel noted that until 1945 Technicolor had an 'almost complete monopoly as far as good colour processing is concerned', his laboratory could now process colour domestically.[85] Patel, also the chief stockist of Gevacolor in India, therefore promoted the process as an instrument of self-sufficiency, with *Pamposh* hailed as the first film entirely shot and processed in India, underscoring India's chromatic self-determination as the process's core appeal.[86]

If Modi was looking for a process to celebrate Indian autonomy then Technicolor seemed a strange choice, not least because it had been used by British and American filmmaker for decades to perpetuate stereotyped images of India. Technicolor's Indian filmography was a litany of Orientalist fantasies, exoticising documentaries, racist caricatures and imperial propaganda. In addition to the British Technicolor titles already noted, Hollywood had exploited India as a location for its adventure films, including *Kim* (US, 1950; dir. Victor Saville) and *Monsoon* (US, 1952; dir.

Rod Amateau). However, the recent Technicolor film *The River* (1951) in many ways departed from these conventions, resisting simplistic binaries between European chromatic restraint and unruly Indian chromophilia. An American production filmed on location in West Bengal by French director Jean Renoir with a largely Indian crew using British equipment, the film had a complex production history, which has been meticulously examined by Priya Jaikumar.[87] Situating the film's nuanced, if problematic, depiction of India within her broader consideration of the politics of location work within the nation, in her analysis Jaikumar offers rich insights into a film that falls outside the scope of the analysis here. However, *The River* has an important role in this chapter's account of Technicolor's relationship with empire, as it helped establish the industrial framework necessary for the creation of Modi's epic.

It was Renoir's assistant on *The River*, the American Forrest Judd, who offered to help fund *Jhansi Ki Rani* as part of five-picture deal through his production company, The Film Group, with each of the films to be made in Technicolor.[88] Judd offered to modernise Minerva Movietone Studios and ready it for colour production as part of the agreement, yet at this early stage almost all the equipment necessary for filming in Technicolor had to come from overseas.[89] Not only the beam-splitting cameras but also the arc lights, cabling and transformers had to be imported from England (fig. 87), including an enormous generator from Alexander Korda's British Lion studios at Shepperton, forging a material link between Korda's pro-imperial Technicolor output and Modi's anti-imperial resistance film (fig. 88).[90] British engineers and creative personnel also formed core members of *Jhansi Ki Rani*'s production team, including Indian-born make-up artist Jimmy Vining, who had worked on Michael Powell and Emeric Pressburger's Technicolor films in England (fig. 89).[91]

While Indian artists, technicians and designers formed the majority of *Jhansi Ki Rani*'s crew, they were paired with high-profile foreign personnel. Minerva's make-up man Murari Narayan Borkar collaborated with Vining, art director Rusi Banker worked

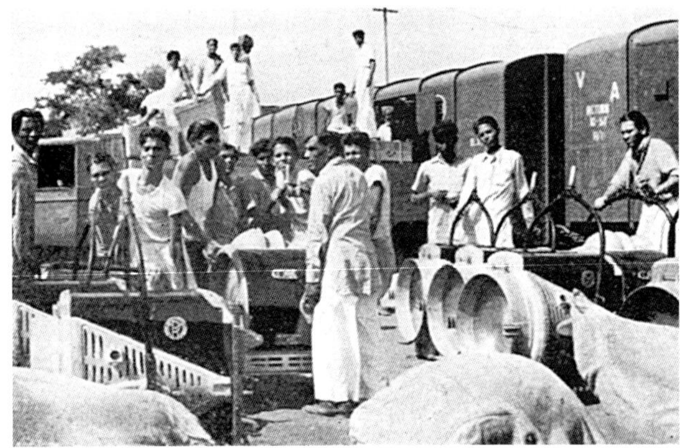

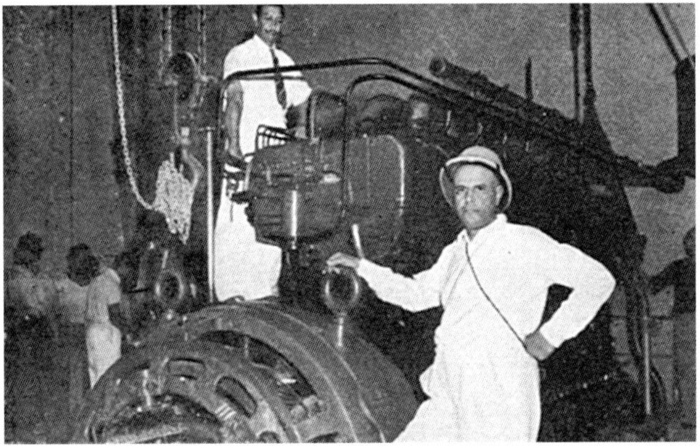

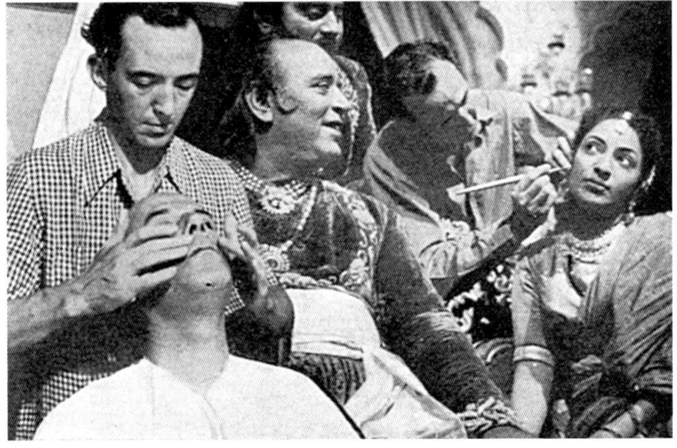

From souvenir programme for *Jhansi Ki Rani*. William K. Everson Collection, New York University.

87 Camera equipment and lights arriving by train at a location shoot.

88 Sohrab Modi with an imported generator at Minerva Movietone Studios.

89 Jimmy Vining making up the cast.

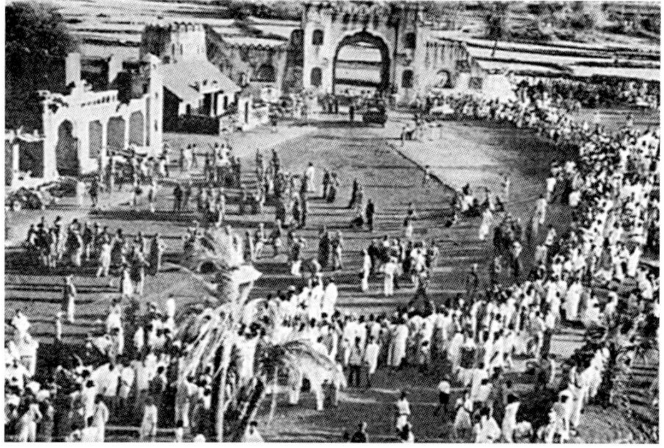

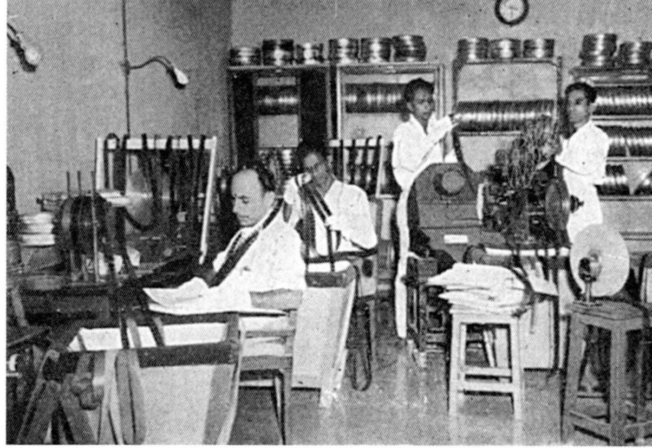

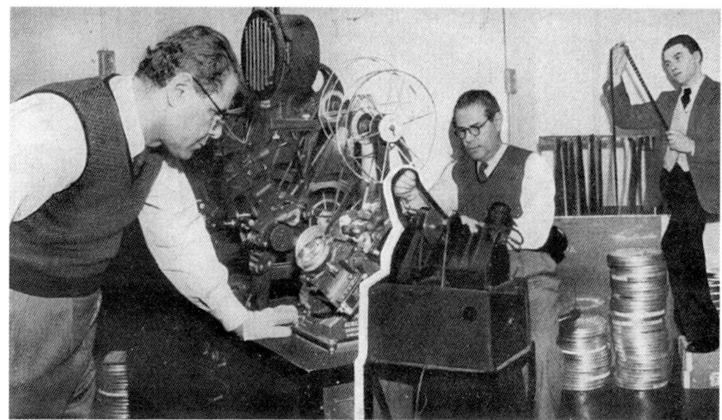

90 One of the film's many sets.

91 Editors processing rushes flown from Technicolor in London.

92 Sohrab Modi editing the two versions of his film at 80 Wardour Street, London.

alongside American colour consultant George Jenkins, and Minerva cinematographers M. N. Malhotra and Y. D. Sarpotdar – who had both trained in Technicolor cinematography in London – worked alongside Ernest Haller, the renowned American Technicolor cinematographer best known for *Gone With the Wind* (US, 1939; dir. Victor Fleming).[92] The vast material and human resources that the film demanded be imported from abroad formed a major part of *Jhansi Ki Rani*'s promotional campaign, catalogued alongside the eight hundred elephants, six hundred horses and seven thousand extras that made the film one of the biggest productions in Indian film history, a fact repeatedly emphasised in promotional images of the vast sets (fig. 90).[93]

However, a serious drawback to Modi's project was the distance, and inherent delay, between the production work in Bombay and the processing work at the laboratory in London. The time that elapsed between shooting footage in India and the return of processed material from the laboratory in London made it difficult to ascertain the quality and consistency of the colour while filming was underway. Additionally, while promotional images show editors laden with 'rushes regularly flown from London' (fig. 91), for economic reasons, roughly only a quarter of the film processed in London was returned to India, largely in black and white with 'one or two shots out of each sequence', in Haller's recollection, returned in colour.[94] This had also frustrated Renoir while he was working on *The River*.[95] In addition to there being delays of up to three weeks between shooting a sequence and seeing it in colour, material also disappeared or was damaged in transit. Modi and Banker flew to England to edit *Jhansi Ki Rani* (fig. 92) but, again, this work would have been conducted with a black and white copy as it was far too costly to print the entire film in colour at this stage. Renoir described these Technicolor 'pilot' prints used for editing as 'an especially ugly black and white since it's printed from one of the three colour separation negatives. It therefore lacks some of the values, other colours aren't visible at all, it's not even orthochromatic; altogether, it's quite disappointing.'[96] For all

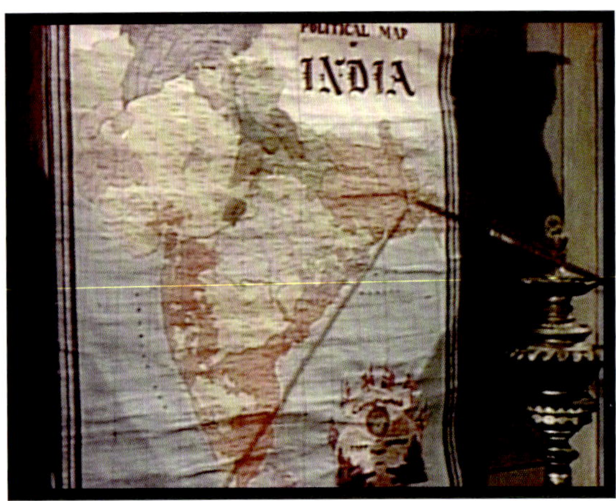

93 A map of British India showing British territories in red in *Jhansi Ki Rani / The Tiger and the Flame*.

the chromatic labour undertaken on set in India – the thousands of colourful costumes, the historically accurate interiors, the military pageantry of the battle sequences – the colours of *Jhansi Ki Rani* would only materialise in the London laboratory, where the dyes, manufactured by Imperial Chemical Industries, would bring to life this anti-imperial tale.

The poignant materiality of *Jhansi Ki Rani*'s colour is highlighted by an early scene in the film where the young rani, then known as Manu, is taught about Indian history by her guru, played by Modi himself. He demonstrates the growing power of the East India Company on the sub-continent by contrasting two maps of India, with the expanding dominion of British control represented by an increasingly sizeable red area on the second map (fig. 93). As the camera tracks back to accommodate the scope of this enormous red stain, Manu's guru berates those 'traitors' who 'helped feed this tiny red spot ... until it swelled to its present enormous dimensions'. Of course, this red spot, which symbolises the violent control of India by British imperial forces, when seen on a cinema screen was a patch of dye printed by industrial labour in London – just like the map of the British Empire picked out in red yarn presented in *Border Weave* and that shown in the opening sequence of *The Drum*. In these films – one decrying the British Empire, the others celebrating it – these red patches were made using the same dyeing process at London's Technicolor laboratory, the modern inheritor of the industrial and imperial heritage lamented in *Jhansi Ki Rani*. While this sequence is intended to stir Manu's anger against the imperial and corporate entity of the British East India Company, the material and technical process by which this image was produced suggest the continued legacy of this dynamic of capitalist imperialism in an era of Indian independence.

Economically, *Jhansi Ki Rani* proved a failure, losing around one crore (ten million) rupees.[97] However, the film would have generated substantial profits for the London laboratory, whose services had comprised nearly one third of the film's original, massive budget.[98] At a time when the average print run for an Indian film was around sixty copies, the four hundred release prints and eight hundred trailers for *Jhansi Ki Rani* would have generated a substantial return for Technicolor Ltd.[99] If, as British laboratory workers recalled, the process was a 'licence to print money', then Indian colour would prove to be a major source of income for the British laboratory throughout the 1950s.

94 Technicolor credit in *Aan* (India, 1952; dir. Mehboob Khan).

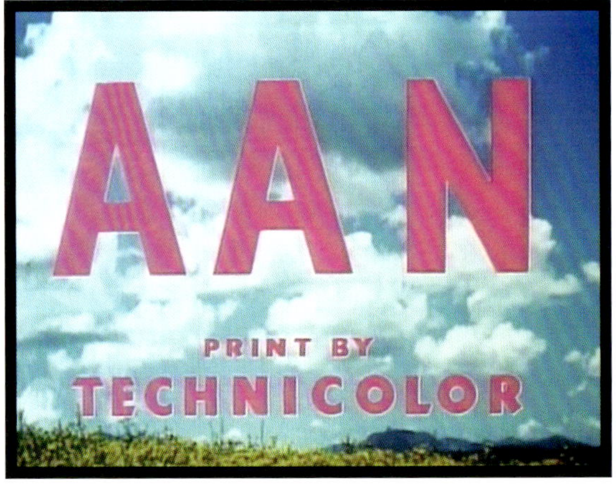

Jhansi Ki Rani was among several Indian colour films printed by the London laboratory in the 1950s as part of the post-war boom period triggered by new colour film stocks, a fact made evident in the crediting of the laboratory in the opening sequences of these films. In addition to *Aan* (fig. 94) and *Jhansi Ki Rani*, Technicolor Ltd in London printed films by celebrated director V. Shantaram, including the Gevacolor dance spectacular *Jhanak Jhanak Payal Baaje* (1955) (fig. 95) and his period film set during the early era of British Colonial rule in India, *Navrang* (1959), as well as Mehboob Khan's landmark 1957 Gevacolor film about Indian nationalism, *Mother India* (fig. 96).[100] That these films about Indian national identity and British colonial oppression were printed in Britain creates a generative friction between their contents and their materiality. At the level of narrative these films explore India's political autonomy and self-determination in the face of British imperialism, but at a techno-material level they demonstrate India's forced dependence upon British industrial and technological infrastructure as well as Britain's continued exploitation of Indian colour as a crucial resource for its chromatic economy.

However, with regard to *Jhansi Ki Rani*, the use of Technicolor personnel and equipment clearly also lent prestige to the production. This British presence among the creative personnel spoke to a new power dynamic between Indian cinema and its foreign counterparts. Rather than undermining India's autonomy through the use of these overseas specialists, Modi's marshalling of this international network of chromatic expertise and expensive machinery was celebrated as indicative of India's emerging power among these institutions and its new-found authority over them. The press, constantly reporting on the spectacular unfolding of this super-production, hailed *Jhansi Ki Rani* as a marker of India's arrival as a global cinematic power, signalling what *The Times of India* called 'a new era of colour films'.[101] When the crew of *Jhansi Ki Rani* captured its first shot, the *Illustrated Weekly of India* celebrated this 'historic date', noting that 'for the first time a Kalmus [i.e. Technicolor] unit with American technicians and an international reputation operated to the orders of an Indian director'.[102] The promotional photograph of Modi on set leaning triumphantly against Korda's generator (see fig. 88) visualised very literally this transfer of power from Britain to India. If *Jhansi Ki Rani* marked a new era of colour cinema, it would be an era under India's control.

As the press interest reveals, Modi used Technicolor to assert India's ascendancy as a global power in

95 Technicolor credit in *Jhanak Jhanak Payal Baaje* (India, 1955; dir. V. Shantaram).

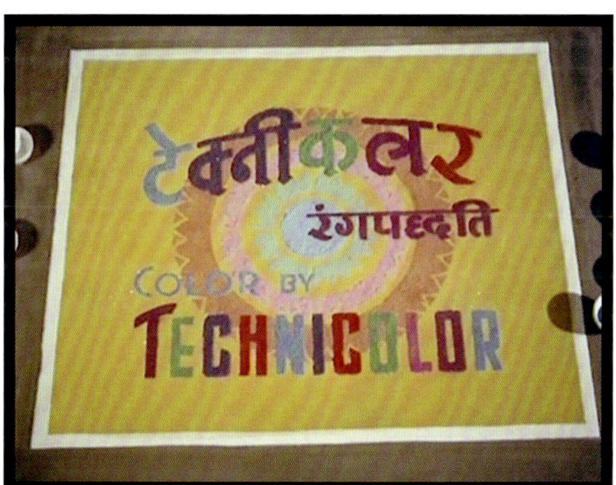

96 Technicolor credit in *Mother India* (India, 1957; dir. Mehboob Khan).

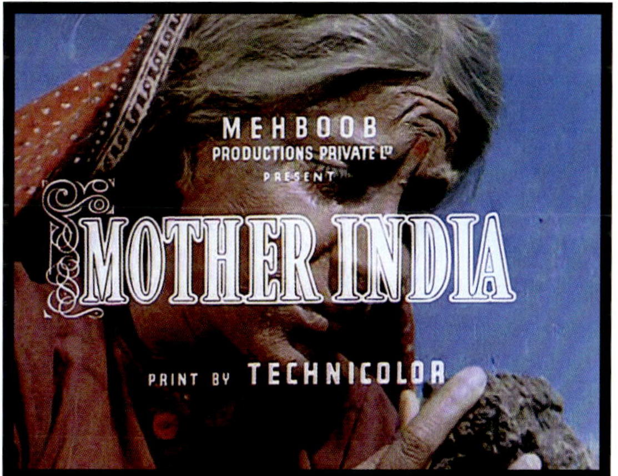

colour cinema, demonstrating his command over this existing chromatic regime. That Technicolor had been used to perpetuate stereotyped and essentialised images of India for many years made it the ideal system through which to fight these established powers, demonstrating a new period of chromatic self-determination in the Indian industry. If *Jhansi Ki Rani*'s narrative celebrated resistance to British colonialism, then it was fitting to use the tools of British chromatic oppression to mount an opposition to it.

One sequence that illuminates the multiple registers of colour's meanings in the film is the wedding that transforms the child, Manu, into the rani of Jhansi. The wedding sequence therefore doubles as a kind of coronation, as it serves to anoint the new leader of the state. The sequence begins with women adorning Manu's body with colours, from the 'om' symbols already painted on her hands in henna to the red polish applied to her fingernails (fig. 97). This sequence demonstrates that the colour red, which reproduced particularly well in Technicolor, was not limited to symbolising British colonial power (as seen in the map sequence or in the numerous crimson military costumes of the British forces), as the colour holds celebratory associations in Hindu culture, particularly with weddings. The redness of this sequence does not just demonstrate the protean nature of colour symbolism, which is highly contingent on cultural context, but also how the mutual existence of these connotations (colonial oppression, local celebration) creates a productive friction between them in Modi's film, which exploits British colour as a way of celebrating Indian identity. Indeed, this sequence reveals how colour, as a phenomenon that operates at both a material and a symbolic level, and whose meanings are highly mobile, was perhaps the ideal vehicle through which to articulate opposition to colonialist ideologies.[103]

Despite *Jhansi Ki Rani*'s commercial failure, it was critically acclaimed by the Indian press and embraced by the Indian government as a symbol of a vibrant new nation. The Bombay premiere of the film was attended by India's prime minister, Jawaharlal Nehru; the prime minister of Kashmir, Sheikh Abdullah; and other high-ranking members of India's cabinet, diplomatic corps and military, lending official endorsement to the film's release.[104] The opening of the film to coincide with the recently established Indian Republic Day holiday in January was noted as particularly fitting by the press.[105] The film was also selected by the government of Bombay to be screened as part of the centenary celebrations marking the First War of Independence in 1957, concretising its importance in the political culture of India as symbol of national pride.[106]

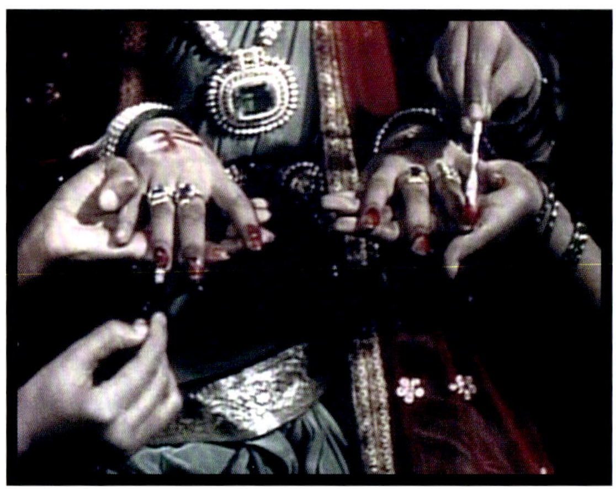

97 Manu is prepared for her wedding in *Jhansi Ki Rani / The Tiger and the Flame*

The symbolic nature of the film as the origins of a new regime of Indian self-determination is similarly reflected in the wedding sequence described above. A static close-up of Manu's face as she is prepared for her wedding shows the wrapping of a floral crown around her head, its large pink flowers and garlands of white blossoms draped to frame her features. That night, after the religious ceremony, the bride and groom process through the streets separately, with the raja, or king, seated in an open horse-drawn carriage and the rani in an elaborately ornamented palanquin. Crowds throng the streets, cheering for their new leaders, as fireworks spray across their path, bursting in showers of white and gold sparks. The rani's carriage is canopied with red velvet, which is encrusted and ribbed with gold ornamentation that

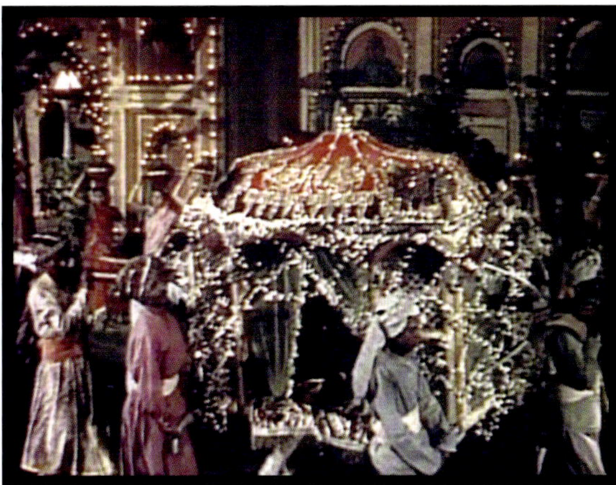

98 The wedding procession in *Jhansi Ki Rani / The Tiger and the Flame.*

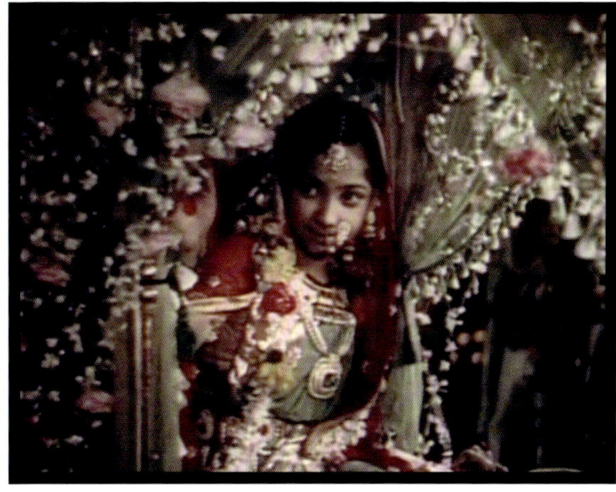

99 The coronation of a new Technicolor queen in *Jhansi Ki Rani / The Tiger and the Flame.*

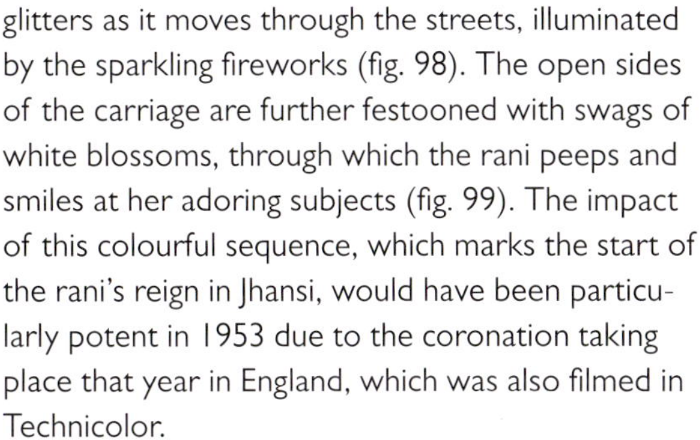

glitters as it moves through the streets, illuminated by the sparkling fireworks (fig. 98). The open sides of the carriage are further festooned with swags of white blossoms, through which the rani peeps and smiles at her adoring subjects (fig. 99). The impact of this colourful sequence, which marks the start of the rani's reign in Jhansi, would have been particularly potent in 1953 due to the coronation taking place that year in England, which was also filmed in Technicolor.

The Technicolor record of Elizabeth II's coronation drew upon a long tradition whereby transitions of British royal and imperial power had formed a staple subject for colour cinema since the end of the Edwardian era. The inauguration of each new British monarch was filmed using a different colour system, characterising the transition between political and social epochs with a new chromatic technology, and forging a symbiotic relationship between forms of British institutional power and British colour film processes. Kinemacolor captured both of King George V's coronation ceremonies in 1911, in London and in Delhi, the latter an elaborate durbar staged to anoint him as emperor of India.[107] Dufaycolor, a popular British colour process of the 1930s, documented the Westminster coronation of his successor, King George VI, in 1937, although no durbar was held to mark his appointment as the last emperor of India. Finally, Technicolor was used to record the coronation of Queen Elizabeth II in 1953 in a feature-length documentary titled *A Queen Is Crowned*. Although Elizabeth no longer held the title of empress of India, empire was literally woven into the event, as the monarch's garments were embroidered with emblems representing former colonies and dominions, and military and political figures from Britain's former imperial territories were conspicuous participants in the ceremony's pageantry.[108]

While Elizabeth II's coronation is best remembered as a major event in monochrome television history, *A Queen Is Crowned*, with its additional feature of colour, was the most successful film at the British box office that year.[109] Technicolor's London laboratory printed 1,800 copies of the film for domestic and international distribution, and it was widely exhibited in India by Her Majesty's Central Office of Information, which chartered special planes to ensure that prints could be premiered in Bombay, Calcutta and New Delhi only ten days after the coronation in June.[110] For viewers in the United Kingdom, *A Queen Is Crowned* marked the continued strength of British institutional power in this post-imperial age – an age

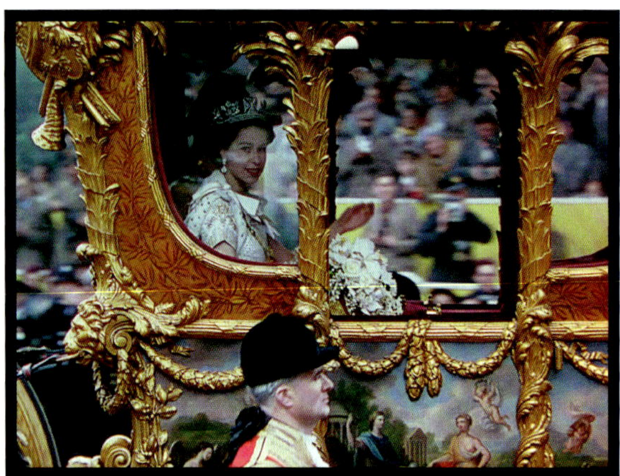

100 *A Queen Is Crowned* (UK, 1953; dir. Michael Waldman).

that would be recorded and remembered in Technicolor. It forged a confederation between the chromatic empire of British Technicolor and the imperial imaginary of Elizabeth II's reign. Yet in India, its viewers may have drawn other conclusions.

Although in England *A Queen Is Crowned* predated Modi's epic, in India Elizabeth's summer coronation appeared on screen five months after *Jhansi Ki Rani*, as the release of Modi's film was scheduled to coincide with the Republic Day holiday in January. Therefore, for Indian viewers, the image of a smiling young Queen Elizabeth holding a white floral bouquet in a carriage festooned with golden garlands (fig. 100) may have recalled the earlier Technicolor coronation sequence in *Jhansi Ki Rani*, in which a young queen's face similarly appears from inside her royal carriage, surrounded by white flowers and beaming at onlookers. If these colour coronation films marked regime changes of both a chromatic and a political nature, then *Jhansi Ki Rani* suggests that this transition of power was taking place not from one British monarch to the next but from West to East, as a newly independent India crowned its own Technicolor queen. By using British Technicolor to portray the coronation of a domestic Indian queen – a historic rebel leader who battled for independence from British colonial rule – *Jhansi Ki Rani* deftly uses the tools of British chromatic imperialism to demonstrate its own ascendancy to a position of global chromatic power in an era of decolonisation.

If *Jhansi Ki Rani* was an experiment to discern the viability of domestic Indian Technicolor production, it did not ultimately succeed. The year after the Indian release of the film, Technicolor Ltd signed an agreement with Ramnord Research Laboratories of Bombay appointing the firm 'Agents of Technicolor'.[111] The aim was to use the laboratory for monopack processing until the local market grew sufficiently competitive, at which point Ramnord would expand into IB printing. Until then, Ramnord would process chromogenic camera negatives and send materials to London for dye-transfer printing, ensuring Britain retained a foothold in the Indian market during this growth period for colour film.[112] This resulted in colour credits such as those found in the opening titles of the hugely successful and dazingly vivid *Gunga Jumna* (India, 1961; dir. Nitin Bose), which state that the film was 'Processed at Technicolor Ltd. London through Ramnord Research Labs. Ltd. Bombay'. Yet the planned Bombay IB laboratory never emerged, as Technicolor felt that India, which produced fewer than ten colour features per year at this point, presented insufficient work to justify the construction of a dye-transfer plant, which could only operate economically at scale.[113] Furthermore, by the early 1960s there were three Indian laboratories capable of chromogenic processing: Film Centre and Ramnord Laboratories in Bombay, and Gemini in Madras. The 1960s therefore marked the decade when Technicolor's London laboratory would ultimately relinquish control over Indian film colour, as fewer films were sent to London for processing and India's domestic colour production boomed.[114]

In 1965 Technicolor Ltd also transitioned from an affiliate of American Technicolor to become a wholly owned subsidiary, meaning profits were now boosting the American rather than British economy.[115] Although histories of Technicolor typically conclude in 1955 with the decline of the three-strip camera, 1965 instead marks an end to this British imperial model of chromatic control and a wholesale shift to an American model of globalised capitalism. While Technicolor's IB process allowed Britain to imagine its continued power as it transitioned into a post-war period of decolonisation, the central position of colour film within British chromatic culture gave way to a new medium in the 1960s when colour television, the subject of the next chapter, emerged to take its place. Declining print runs forced Technicolor Ltd to retire its dye-transfer unit in 1978.[116]

From its foundation in the 1930s, Technicolor's history was clearly intertwined with the empire in ways that were concrete and symbolic, material and imaginative. Technicolor was economically implicated in the political and commercial interests of empire through the figure of Korda and his circle, both as a chief shareholder and as a producer connected to the British state; through the explicit and tacit promotion of imperial ideology in Technicolor films, whether that took the form of colonialism or global consumerism; and through the material and technical production of Technicolor films, which forged parallels with historical and contemporary modes of imperial colour production through the textile industry. Yet, as *Jhansi Ki Rani* underscores, there was room for negotiation within this model, whereby the imperial ideology embedded in the system could be subverted to new political ends.

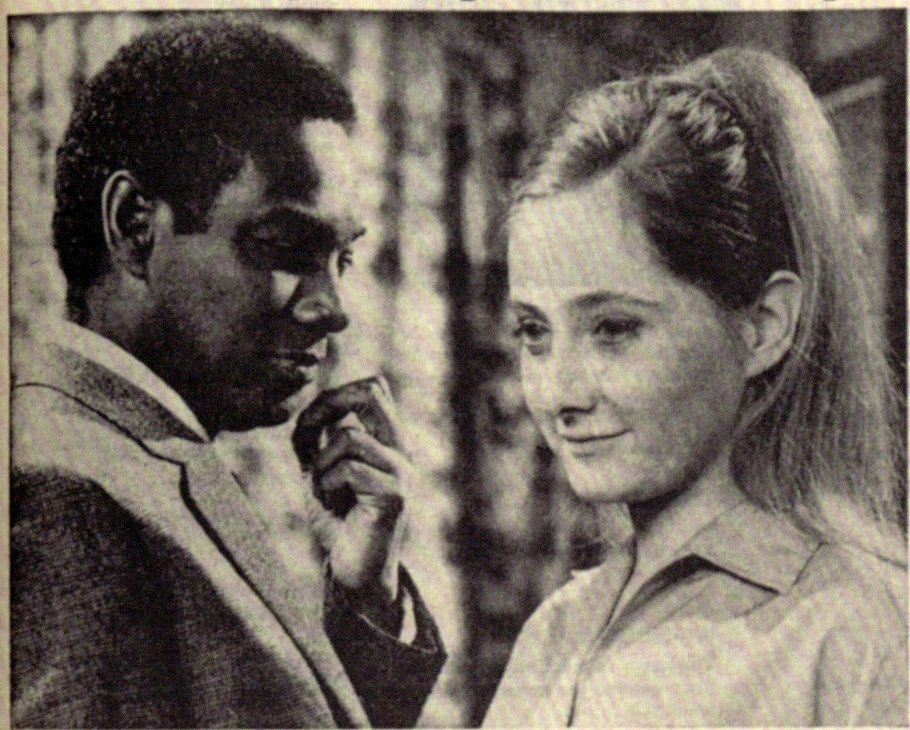

Wedr

RAINBOW CITY

1 7.30

A new six-part serial about a Jamaican lawyer and other immigrants living in and around Birmingham

Errol John who plays the lawyer John Steele, and Gemma Jones who plays his wife, Mary

plaints cu
Indian wo
London st
where doe

In a wor
beings are
ance seem
easy, of co
lems wher
liberal in
mixture is
find, occas
pared to b

One of t
in the BB
mits in U
sat last ye
he said: '
done is *Ra*
about We
ham, and t

He is r
though he
who come
the same
and difficu
of their o

I've nev
mainly, I
West Indi
country w
have little
they will
longer if

101 Promotional coverage of *Rainbow City* (BBC1, 1967), *Radio Times*, 29 June 1967.

5

THE BBC'S COLOUR PROBLEM

Race, Migration and Colour Television in the 1960s

'Colour dominated television this week', claimed the American journalist Stanley Reynolds in his column on broadcasting for *The Guardian* on 6 July 1967.[1] Published the week BBC2 began its Colour Launching Service, a trial period of limited colour transmissions, Reynolds's column reflected the novelty of seeing a monochrome medium transformed into a chromatic spectacle. BBC2 broadcast only five hours of colour a week at this time, as a means of training staff in this new process before fully switching to colour later that year, with BBC1 and ITV following in 1969. The Colour Launching Service of 1967 therefore presented a tantalising glimpse of the colourful future of British television. Although Reynolds noted the viewing experience was 'more like real life than Technicolor', he found a more compelling metaphor for this technological revolution in cinema's transition to sound, describing the return to monochrome broadcasting as 'like watching a silent film again after you have once seen a talkie'.[2] For Reynolds, colour television, like sound cinema, marked a paradigm shift in the immediacy and modernity of the medium, which created the sense of a lack when the viewer was deprived of this sensational new technology.

Yet Reynolds's attitude to the Colour Launching Service formed only one half of the column. The remainder was occupied with a discussion of another kind of colour, which similarly became a crucial signifier of post-war modernity in Britain. When Reynolds claimed that 'colour dominated television this week', he was referring not only to chromatic transmissions on BBC2 but also to *Rainbow City* (broadcast on BBC1), the BBC's first drama series featuring a Black protagonist, which debuted the same week as the Colour Launching Service (fig. 101). The programme focused on the Jamaican lawyer John Steele (played by Trinidadian actor Errol John) and his marriage to a White British woman, with Steele's cases used as vehicles to explore issues of racial integration and discrimination in Birmingham, a centre for Commonwealth migration in post-war Britain. Given that the show was made for monochrome television, the 'rainbow' of the title does not allude literally to a spectrum of hues but metaphorically to the plurality of skin colours presented in the show's markedly diverse cast.[3] In his unfavourable account of the show, Reynolds baulked at the didacticism of the programme and complained he was unable to differentiate between members of the cast, but acknowledged the relevance of the subject matter. Noting that 'mixed marriages are an increasing fact in Britain', he considered the topic of racial integration an important one for the BBC to explore.[4]

Reynolds's claim that 'colour dominated television this week' therefore contains a telling duality. The double signification of colour-as-hue (on BBC2) and colour-as-race (on BBC1) illuminates the absolute inseparability of colour's chromatic and racial meanings. He expresses the ambivalent attitudes towards these two meanings of colour in Britain in the 1960s: a desire and anticipation of colour in the form of chromatic television – as a signifier of technological modernity and consumerist luxury – as well as an anxiety about colour in the sense of racial difference and migration, articulated through a lexis of chromatic domination.

But colour alone did not embody such dualities, as black and white similarly conflated chromatic and racialised meanings. With black and white signifying at once a greyscale aesthetic and racial taxonomies, Reynolds's column also highlights the dynamic and complex relationship between black, white and colour at this time. For Reynolds the dynamic between the black and the white of BBC1's monochrome broadcast was easily translated into a racialised binary between Blackness and Whiteness (John Steele and his wife), a binary that simultaneously connoted 'colour' in the sense of racial difference (the 'rainbow' of *Rainbow City*), which Reynolds rhetorically linked to 'colour' in the sense of chromatism displayed on BBC2. Reynolds demonstrated how the BBC's conversion to colour broadcasting was shaped by and framed through ideas about race and racial difference in Britain, and specifically through these double meanings of black, white and colour.

Reynolds's column illuminates the notion – compellingly articulated by television scholars Sarita Malik and Darrell M. Newton – that television and British identity, as framed through the lenses of race and migration, shared imbricated histories in the British cultural imagination.[5] Television emerged as the most popular medium of post-war mass culture in Britain at the same moment that Commonwealth citizens migrating to the United Kingdom from the West Indies, South Asia and Africa also became quotidian constituents of British society. Certainly, the arrival in England of West Indian passengers on the *Empire Windrush*, invited to Britain to fill labour shortages in June 1948, was by no means the beginning of a Black presence in Britain.[6] Neither was the footage of those passengers disembarking at Tilbury Docks, broadcast later that month on BBC's *Television Newsreel*, the first appearance of people of colour on British television.[7] However, this important moment marked a critical fusion of the significant roles played by race, migration and television in British culture and history.

The year 1948 presented a landmark shift in how Britain perceived its relationship to its empire, as the centrifugal forces that had cast White colonisers all over the globe now operated in reverse – a centripetal trajectory inviting colonial (and former colonial) subjects, many of them people of colour, to the metropole to work, study and settle. The questions that surrounded Britain's emerging post-imperial identity and the issues of who was and was not considered British were popularly formulated, articulated and policed through television, and particularly the BBC, whose remit as a public service broadcaster made it a vital space for conceptualising the boundaries and limits of the British 'public'. Television was therefore not simply a place where ideas about British identity were documented; rather, the BBC constructed the very terms of British citizenship and belonging in the post-war period, particularly through the categories of Blackness, Whiteness and colour. As Reynolds's article demonstrates, the dynamic relationship between these categories, as both racial and chromatic designations, imbued the BBC's conversion to colour broadcasting in 1967 with a decidedly racial charge.

Post-war immigration was already popularly conceived in chromatic terms before 1967, however, as Lynda Nead has shown in her study of post-war visual culture in Britain.[8] The prominence in the imperial imagination of exoticised ideas about the colonies and their vivid flora, fauna and fashions, as well as the historical connections between the material production and circulation of colour within the empire in the form of textiles, dyes, spices and pigments, was conflated with a racialised discourse around skin colour as a signifier of racial difference. In the racist terminology of the time, those arriving in Britain from the 1940s from newly independent nations in the Caribbean, Africa and South Asia were homogenised as 'coloured' in distinction to those who were 'colour*less*' or White. This binary, between Whiteness and colour, essentialised and reduced a host of different racial and ethnic identities into a single category. The terminology took no account of the social, cultural, ethnic, national and religious contexts from which these migrants arrived into Britain, but cemented their identities together into a single unit defined primarily in distinction to Whiteness, whether White Britishness or the imagined uniform Whiteness of Commonwealth migrants from Australia, Canada and other settler colonies.[9]

This binary made colour a powerful visual strategy for depicting racial difference at a time when, as Stuart Hall has articulated, such differences were explicitly framed by the British press and political establishment as a 'problem' for British society, with people of colour cited as the cause of this problem.[10] In post-war Britain, colour – as a synonym for racial difference – was cast as a 'problem' or a 'question' in the titles of innumerable newspaper articles, radio broadcasts, television documentaries and sociological reports, continually presenting migration, rather than White intolerance of migration, as a catalyst of societal unrest.[11] Colour became the language for articulating objections to the presence of Commonwealth migrants in Britain, as made evident in a 1958 editorial in *The Economist* responding to the racist violence of the Notting Hill riots that year. The article doubted whether 'Britain will get used to colour', claiming that 'the school of opinion in Whitehall and beyond feels that when the tide of colour rises to a certain, as yet unspecified point, the mass of British voters will demand that some check be imposed'.[12] In dominant discussions of race, migration and Britishness in the post-war period, colour (rather than racist ideologies) was continually posed as an escalating threat that catalysed civic unrest and that warranted regulation, management and control.

This 'colour problem' of the post-war period made immigration a chromatic issue, and this xenophobic binary between Whiteness (signifying Britishness) and colour (signifying the foreign) became a defining paradigm for debates about post-war immigration that still informed arguments about these issues in the 1960s. At a time when British identity became, in Bill Schwarz's term, 're-racialised', immigration was intimately bound up with ideas about colour and its appropriate place in British culture.[13] The BBC's conversion to colour broadcasting in 1967 therefore not only was a technological landmark but also invited a reformulation of the relationship between black, white and colour in terms of both chromatic and racial categories in an emergent post-imperial nation.

The period between 1967 and 1969 is especially vital for interrogating the inseparable histories of British race relations and colour television. As historian Kennetta Hammond Perry describes, the endemic culture of anti-Black racism that characterised the experiences of Black Britons in the post-war period worsened dramatically in the 1960s. Following the Notting Hill riots of 1958, a series of legislative, political and cultural shifts in the 1960s legitimised White antagonism towards, and violence against, Black Britons, cultivating an increasingly hostile environment for these citizens of colour. From the Commonwealth Immigration Act of 1962 and its strengthening in 1968 (intended specifically to limit the numbers of migrants of colour arriving from newer Commonwealth nations) to the election in 1964 of the openly racist Member of Parliament (MP) Peter Griffiths, racist rhetoric became increasingly sanctioned as part of Britain's official legal and political framework. When *The Times* reported that the 1964 election was inciting 'intense passions over colour', it made clear how a chromatic vocabulary could articulate what Perry calls 'the racialised politics of entry and that of belonging to British society'.[14] The disenfranchisement of Black Britons from employment, education, leisure and housing was also formulated in these chromatic terms as the 'Colour Bar', which became one of the most pressing political issues of the decade.

The increasingly sanctioned visibility of racism in this period was most poisonously articulated in 1968 by Conservative MP Enoch Powell in his infamous 'Rivers of Blood' speech. Warning of the catastrophic consequences of uncurbed migration to Britain, and suggesting the repatriation of Black migrants back to the Commonwealth, Powell suggested that it was the 'marked physical differences, especially of colour' between Britons and 'Commonwealth immigrants', rather than racial prejudice exhibited by White people, that were preventing the successful integration of different racial groups.[15] Powell's prominence gave a legitimate voice to racism in the late 1960s, as British Pakistani writer Hanif Kureishi remembered: 'as Powell's speeches appeared in the papers, graffiti in support of him appeared in the London streets. Racists gained confidence.'[16] Similarly, the Guyanese actor Cy Grant, who regularly worked in British television from the 1950s, recalled how Powell's visibility in 1960s 'started to affect the quality of my life very much; people became overtly racist'.[17]

At precisely this moment in the late 1960s when heightened racist rhetoric was exacerbating the notion of migration as a 'colour problem', the BBC was experiencing what the director of television called its own 'colour problem'.[18] The BBC's 'colour problem' was both technological and ideological, and aesthetic and political, and had at its very centre the conflation of racial difference and chromatism. At its simplest, the problem was that due to the prohibitive cost of colour television sets and limitations to its broadcasting signal, when the BBC launched its colour service in 1967, most viewers would only be able to watch it in black and white. The technological challenges of broadcasting simultaneously in colour and monochrome made stabilising flesh tones particularly difficult. In particular, they made the combination of light and dark skin challenging, placing skin colour and consequently racial difference at the very heart of the BBC's 'colour problem'. Lighting, make-up and casting were all profoundly affected by this technological challenge, meaning that the look and style of early colour television broadcasting were critically shaped by these issues.

Throughout, this book has demonstrated how people of colour, rhetorically conflated with chromatism, have been exploited as subjects to display the possibilities of new chromatic media. Colour television marks a continuation of this history, but the specific technological challenges of early colour broadcasting also problematised the incorporation of people of colour into the predominantly White space of television in ways that produced a very specific programming culture at the BBC. At a time when viewers would be watching simultaneously in black and white and colour, the challenge of incorporating colour into the BBC's greyscale programming culture dominated official discussions, foregrounding issues of integration between colour and colourlessness in ways that closely paralleled the conversations unfolding in broader society about migration and race.

This chapter explores how the BBC's attempts to resolve its technological 'colour problem' therefore intersected with and participated in the larger ideological and political 'colour problem' of late 1960s Britain, when these shared discourses about the integration and regulation of colour made television a space for dramatising the fraught negotiations between ideas of Blackness, Whiteness and colour. It explores the specific ways in which the BBC's 'colour problem' formulated dark skin as a technological challenge in terms of lighting and make-up, and how this situation produced very specific strategies of resolution that were both formal and ideological in nature, through tactics of segregation and integration. It examines how these strategies were articulated in various programmes during the first years of colour broadcasting at the BBC, including the 1969 arts documentary series *Civilisation* and the musical variety programme *The Black and White Minstrel Show* (1958–72). But, rather than simply explore how the BBC's conversion to colour informed representations of race in these programmes, this chapter demonstrates how the difference between monochrome and colour broadcasting was formulated through, and spectacularised as, racial difference.

A brief note on terminology. This chapter's focus on how contemporary discourse about race and migration mapped onto debates about media aesthetics means that it focuses on a particular Black/White paradigm in order to think through the articulation of racial difference at this time. Throughout, this chapter therefore follows precedents that situate 'Black' and 'Black British' as politicised collective terms that encompass a range of identities, including but not limited to those principally constituting Commonwealth migration in this era from African, Afro-Caribbean and South Asian contexts.[19] The chapter uses these terms here in what Paul Gilroy describes as 'the inclusive definition of black'.[20] As

Perry notes, Afro-Caribbean migrants were the largest non-White demographic arriving in Britain at this time, and they helped to forge what she describes as 'a diasporic and globally oriented Black British political culture that at times encompassed and intersected with the interests of a range of Caribbean, African, and South Asian nationalities and ethnicities'.[21] Despite the fact that these factors were overlooked in the hegemonic political and cultural discourse of 1960s Britain, by no means does this chapter suggest these are undifferentiated identities that are not also circumscribed by and fragmented through class, gender, nationality, ethnicity, religion and sexuality. Furthermore, in this extended discussion of the racialisation of bodies through skin tones, it is acknowledged that the terms 'people of colour' and 'Black' elide the wide variation in pigmentation that characterises these diverse identities and that the discussion of the BBC's problematisation of 'dark' skin tones does not apply uniformly to all people of colour and can indeed apply to people racialised as White. However, this chapter uses this terminology to reflect the way these identities were essentialised, through the technical and strategic policy of the BBC, into polarised binaries between Blackness and Whiteness and between White people and people of colour – binaries that were central to the corporation's ideological operations at this time.

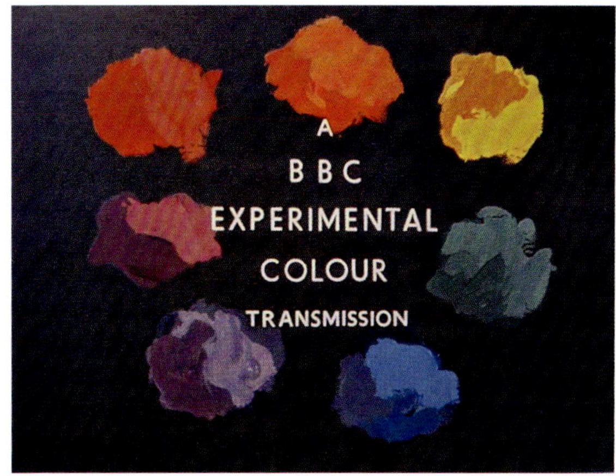

102 Caption card used in BBC Experimental Colour Transmissions, early 1950s.

Launching Colour

The arrival of colour on British television screens was a slow and incremental process. Given that Scottish engineer John Logie Baird first demonstrated colour television in London in 1928 (the first public display of its kind in the world), it is surprising that regular colour broadcasting did not begin in earnest until 1967. However, Baird's technology, reliant on a system of spinning coloured discs, was not suitable for large-scale transmission, and it would be decades before another suitable technology capable of broadcasting on a national scale emerged. The technological systems necessary for broadcasting in colour were in place by the 1950s, and the BBC produced 'Experimental Colour Transmissions' from 1953 (fig. 102). But political debates over which technology the United Kingdom would ultimately adopt delayed the full switchover from monochrome.[22] There were several different standards for colour television available: PAL (phase alternating line), SECAM (*séquentiel couleur à mémoire*) and NTSC (National Television Systems Committee). Each relied upon the same basic technological principles – the visual display of phosphors carrying an electronic charge through a cathode ray tube – but delivered images of lower or higher resolution. America and Japan had converted their networks to NTSC in 1954 and 1960 respectively, and, while the BBC initially admired this system, it ultimately decided against it, publicising that NTSC required much finer tuning by audiences to achieve 'hue control', as colours 'become distorted' without their 'careful adjustment'.[23] The jokes circulating among American engineers that NTSC stood for 'never twice the same colour' or 'no true skin colour' would certainly not have encouraged British broadcasters to follow this path.[24] Skin tones and their accurate rendition were emphasised as the ultimate test of any television system's accuracy and the BBC placed special emphasis on them in its strategy documents. As the BBC's official 'Guide for Colour Production' insisted, 'viewers judge the colour fidelity of these pictures by reference first to flesh tones', elevating skin to a privileged status in debates over new colour technologies.[25] So preoccupied was the BBC with skin and complexions that one lighting engineer remarked, 'all the talk about *flesh tones* seemed a trifle unseemly'.[26] These debates exclusively focused on White skin, however, referred to in BBC guidance as 'the English Rose complexion', which it warned its staff was 'not easy to maintain' during the transition to colour.[27]

While skin tones were difficult to regulate across both PAL and NTSC, the general instability of colour of the American system made the BBC particularly wary of adopting the latter. With NTSC perceived as unreliable and the SECAM system, having been adopted by the USSR, framed through Cold War rhetoric as a socialist technology, the BBC chose to progress using PAL.[28] The timing of the BBC's conversion was deliberately planned to highlight Britain's status as a modern, technologised state. The year 1967 would be the turning point for colour television in Europe, largely in anticipation of the 1968 Olympic Games in Mexico, which every nation hoped to broadcast using its own colour system. In autumn 1967 West Germany would begin colour broadcasts in PAL, while France and the USSR would launch SECAM transmissions. This motivated Britain to start its own colour services earlier in the year so it could claim to be the first nation in Europe with a regular schedule of colour programmes.[29]

The BBC decided to start its colour service in PAL in the summer of 1967, beginning with a live transmission from the centre court of Wimbledon on BBC2 on 1 July. This stunned viewers with its green grass, orange squash and red-haired ball boys, but newspaper headlines discussing the broadcast already reflected that white had been identified as the most important colour for this new technology, proclaiming: 'Wimbledon Colour TV Whiter than White' and 'Whitest of All on Colour TV'.[30] While these headlines referred to white clothing and court markings, not White racial identity, the Wimbledon broadcast demonstrated the capacity of this new medium to display a range of colours while reinforcing white – and its deeply entrenched racial connotations – as the most crucial hue.

Although journalists hailed the arrival of colour television as a British victory over European competitors, they were perhaps overgenerous in their celebrations.[31] In the summer of 1967, colour was only available on one of the nation's three channels, with five hours a week available on BBC2 through its Colour Launching Service. This gradual introduction of colour over a limited number of broadcasts was intentionally designed as a technological trial period, during which problems could be identified and solutions tested before the start of the channel's Full Colour Service on 2 December 1967 and the subsequence conversion of BBC1 and ITV in November 1969.

At the time of the Wimbledon broadcast, however, the press estimated that viewer numbers were limited, with some papers claiming the audience was as small as 'a few dozen'.[32] This was because colour television broadcasts could only be viewed on colour television sets, and their prohibitive cost in the 1960s – around £350 (well over £6,000 in today's money) – combined with the additional £10 charged annually for a colour television licence dramatically limited colour viewership.[33] Even by the end of 1968, the BBC estimated that fewer than 0.5 per cent of British homes had colour televisions.[34] These limitations were exacerbated by the lack of transmitters capable of carrying the ultra-high-frequency (UHF) signal selected as standard in Britain for high-definition colour broadcasting; such transmitters were absent from large swathes of England outside metropolitan centres as well as the entirety of Wales, Scotland and Northern Ireland.[35] BBC2 had been selected for the colour trial as it already broadcast on UHF and because, given that it had a smaller audience than BBC1, any technical errors would be less visible. Yet the colour audience for these early broadcasts was even smaller than the BBC anticipated. Journalists were invited to watch the first transmission from the BBC's Television Centre because so few of them had access to the necessary equipment, and even the

Queen's colour set was only installed in Buckingham Palace five months after the launch of colour broadcasting.[36] It was not until the late 1970s that colour television ownership became widespread among working-class households.[37] For most viewers, then, BBC2's Colour Launching Service was not experienced in colour but in black and white.

The question of who did and did not have access to colour television created the notion that Britain was now socially segregated along chromatic lines. *The Sun* lamented that 'we are divided into first and second class citizens, with the elite who can receive colour in a tiny minority'.[38] During the period when the BBC was launching colour, between 1967 and 1969, there was an acute awareness that colour viewership was strongly divided along class lines and limited to the upper echelons of metropolitan England, a group the BBC referred to in internal discussions as the 'colour minority'. That colour television divided Britain into those with and without colour clearly intersected with the discussions of race, identity and belonging taking place at this time, when Commonwealth migrants of West Indian, South Asian and African origins were also homogenised in political discourse as a 'colour minority' in distinction to a supposedly colourless, or White, majority. This 'colour minority' of Black migrants and the 'colour minority' of television audiences could not have been more distinct in character; the former's minority status made them vulnerable to discrimination and barred them from positions of power, while the latter's signalled an elite social status and extreme privilege. But when the BBC's director general, Sir Hugh Greene, stated that the BBC's values 'could not be sacrificed to the colour minority', or when Ian Atkins, the controller for programme services, reiterated that 'colour has to be kept in its proper place', they spoke to the perception of colour as a marginal, contingent and limited presence in Britain.[39] This attitude shaped the corporation's approach to viewers with colour televisions, whose expectations for colour could not be privileged above the majority colourless viewership. But it also informed the BBC's approach to its Black viewership, whose opinions and protests about the BBC's problematic treatment of racial issues could be easily dismissed as peripheral and marginal to the concerns of the majority, White audience.[40]

David Attenborough, the controller of BBC2, stated the challenge for his staff was that 'we have to remember that the vast majority of our audience for many years to come will be seeing our colour programmes in black and white', noting that BBC2 would 'accept no programme at all that rested for its interest and validity on its colour. Unless it is was an exciting programme in black and white we were not interested in producing it.'[41] Attenborough was particularly anxious that the arrival of colour at BBC2 should not 'distort' the channel's 'values'.[42] He was eager to assert that the content of shows would not change to showcase the spectacular potential of colour, nor would new programmes be commissioned purely for their chromatic appeal. This created a unique climate for Britain's conversion to colour broadcasting. While in America, manufacturers, broadcasters and advertisers tried to make monochrome audiences feel their experience was lacking in colour to sell the new medium of colour television, the BBC, as a public service broadcaster, accountable to all its viewers through the licence fee, could not alienate those unable to afford a colour set.[43] As the Wimbledon broadcast demonstrated, the BBC had to demonstrate the chromatic potential of this new television technology (showcasing the green grass and orange squash) without destabilising the importance of the colourless majority (by foregrounding the whiteness appreciable both in colour and in monochrome).

These very specific circumstances account for some of the peculiarities of colour broadcasting in the late 1960s, when, rather than enticing audiences with glittering new colour programmes, the BBC attempted to make shows in colour that were entirely legible and entertaining in monochrome. For example, Attenborough considered a documentary about the history of art to be an ideal subject for exploiting this new technology, with BBC2's 1969 series *Civilisation*, presented by Kenneth Clark, earmarked as a perfect vehicle for colour.[44] Attenborough may have been following American precedents

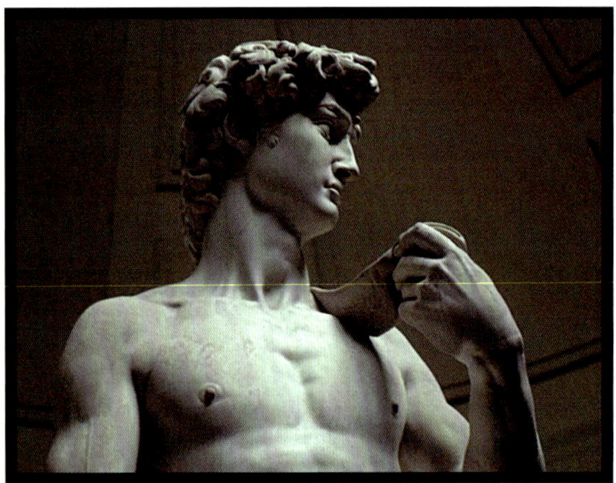

103 The opening shot of *Civilisation* (BBC2, 1969), featuring Michelangelo Buonarroti's *David* (1501–4).

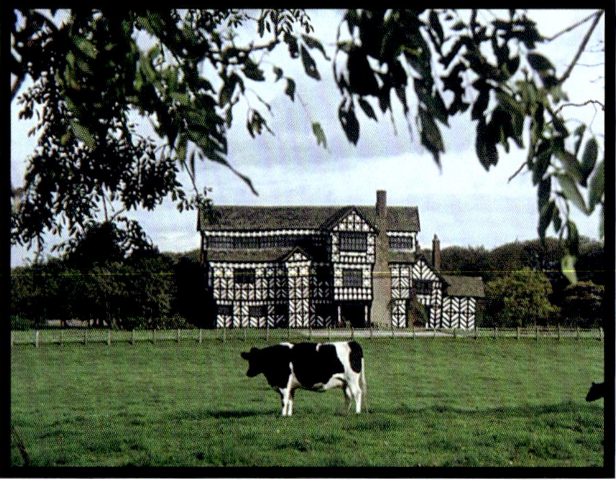

104 The monochrome English countryside in *Civilisation*.

in this regard, as the early years of colour broadcasting there prominently featured gallery and museum collections to showcase the aesthetic flair of colour television.[45] Among those early colour broadcasts in America, the Museum of Modern Art's director, Alfred Barr, appeared on NBC in 1954 to discuss the kaleidoscopic works of Chagall and Kandinsky to promote this new broadcasting medium.[46] However, because most British viewers would be watching *Civilisation* in black and white, it could not rely on works unappreciable in greyscale.

Colour viewers tuning in to the first episode of *Civilisation* anticipating an explosion of colour may have suspected their sets were faulty when they were confronted by the dull face of Michelangelo's *David* (1501–4), whose wan marble features occupy the screen in an extended tracking shot. For a full ten seconds during the opening of this landmark colour documentary series, the screen is entirely filled with varying shades of grey (fig. 103). While, on American television, broadcasters exploited art history to showcase a dazzling variety of hues, throughout *Civilisation* these expectations are thwarted, most disappointingly when the discussion of famed colourist Van Gogh focuses almost exclusively on the artist's black and white charcoal sketches. Clark's discussion of Renaissance England is almost comical in its refusal of colour, as black and white cows graze before a black and white building (fig. 104). The surprisingly monochrome moments in this history of art speak to the ways in which the particular demands of early colour broadcasting at the BBC, largely viewed in monochrome, deeply shaped the content of these programmes.

But this lack of colour in terms of chromatism was also reflected in an absence of people of colour from the programme, which featured no Black artists and few Black subjects. Modern critiques of *Civilisation*'s overwhelming Whiteness, in terms of the racial identity of the artists examined and the subjects depicted, were in part what instigated the programme's remake in 2018.[47] Yet this Whiteness, in addition to reflecting the racial biases that have shaped histories of Western art, also illuminates how the technological challenges of early colour broadcasting were resolved through strategies that were not merely technological or formal, but also profoundly political and ideological. It was not so much *Civilisation*'s Whiteness but its black-and-whiteness that illuminated its politics, which can be made clear by contrasting the first and last episodes of the series.

In the final episode, the only place the series focuses on people of colour, and tellingly in the

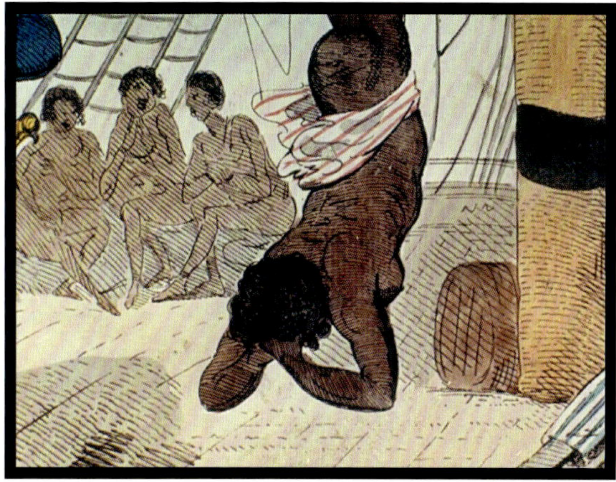

105 Close-up of Isaac Cruickshank's hand-coloured etching *The Abolition of the Slave Trade* (1792), in *Civilisation*.

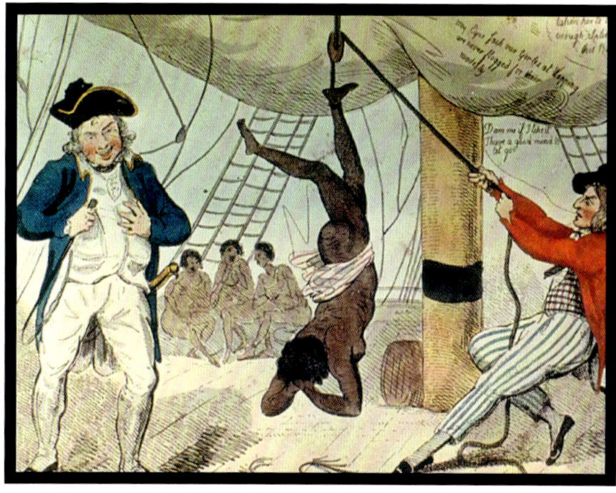

106 Isaac Cruickshank, *The Abolition of the Slave Trade*, in *Civilisation*.

context of the transatlantic slave trade, Clark discusses the horrors of this colonial economy as the screen is filled with a detail from Isaac Cruickshank's 1792 etching *The Abolition of the Slave Trade*, which depicts a gruesome scene that occurred on a ship transporting enslaved people to Grenada (fig. 105).[48] The scene opens tightly framed on the body of an enslaved young African woman, who is suspended upside down in the centre of the frame. She grasps her hands to her face in horror and humiliation as her flimsy clothing begins to fall to the deck, revealing her nude body for all to see. Three other enslaved African women, also nude, can be glimpsed sitting on the ship's deck in the rear of the scene and watching in dismay. As the camera zooms out from the image, we can see that the figure in the foreground is being hoisted aloft by a British sailor, suspended by a rope tied around her ankle to display her nudity for the entertainment of the captain – John Kimber (fig. 106). According to contemporary accounts, after refusing to dance for the captain, the young girl was murdered. Grasping both hands to his chest, a whip clutched in his right fist, the captain guffaws – his cheeks flushed red with amusement and arousal.

This close detail of this horrific scene enables viewers to see precisely how the print was constructed. Etched in black ink on white paper, the print was then hand-coloured, which lent a naturalism to the scene through the multiple flesh tones on display (picked out in shades of brown, pink and red) as well as the uniforms (captured in rich shades of navy, maroon and gold). But, before the addition of colour, the bodies of the enslaved women were hatched with regular lines of black ink, upon which brown pigment was laid.[49] While *David*'s creamy dove-grey face in the opening episode, carved from Carrara marble, suggests his race is signified by an absence of colour – or, rather, the inherent whiteness of the marble is understood as a tacit racial signifier – the racial identity of these women is demonstrated through an excess of hue, the addition of both black ink and brown pigment. As a black and white image that circulated in limited numbers in colour, much like the image of George Alexander Gratton discussed in Chapter Two, Cruickshank's print offers a historical precedent for images that simultaneously occupied the status of colour and colourlessness at a time when the BBC was broadcasting across both formats. But it also highlights how the addition of colour to black and white images carries a racialised charge.

The Cruickshank print in the closing episode touches upon a central theme of this book – that what is necessary to construct an ideal of Whiteness (*David*) is its juxtaposition with a non-White other, a body of colour (the enslaved African woman). This became a defining paradigm of early colour television, and indeed repeats a trope evidenced throughout the media under consideration here, whereby the routine exploitation of Black bodies offered a way to show colour television's capacity to display colour in the form of racial difference, but in a manner that did not 'distort' or 'dominate' the presentation of Whiteness. That the BBC foregrounded the classical White body to defend *Civilisation* against the distortions of the 'colour minority' lays bare how the intersections of chromatic and racial discourse at this time shaped colour television programming. However, it was not just the content of programmes that was altered by these very specific circumstances; at a technological level, the demands of broadcasting simultaneously in colour and monochrome profoundly affected the ways Whiteness, Blackness and colour were technologised, particularly through lighting and make-up.

'The "Kick" of the Black and White'

The arrival of colour on BBC2 in 1967 catalysed enormous changes in broadcasting practices. Some were small shifts of habit; for instance, presenters were discouraged from consuming alcohol immediately before appearing on screen because an 'encouraging drink' could cause dramatically flushed cheeks.[50] But more significant shifts in institutional practice were also necessary, and staff attended a three-week Colour Familiarisation Course to introduce them to the challenges of broadcasting in colour when viewers were watching in monochrome.

As the Colour Familiarisation Course explained, the department most seriously affected at a technical level during this initial phase of colour television was lighting. Filming in colour needed illumination three times greater than monochrome, and also demanded much flatter, high-key designs. Any dramatic variation between light and shade resulted in a loss of colour control, often leaving hues excessively saturated. For colours to reproduce accurately required consistent, bright lighting, with neither stark highlights nor shadow. The small disparity permitted between the lightest and darkest areas of an image was known as a 'limited contrast range'.[51] Yet this did not mean that the image appeared flat or monotonous, as colour inherently produces a stereoscopic effect, allowing the eye to distinguish between different planes, surfaces and textures by hue alone.

When working in monochrome, however, the opposite aesthetic was necessary. To compensate for the lack of colour, lighting for monochrome had to create the sense of depth by modelling with light and shade. The contrast between highlights and shadows could help to produce a realistic space on screen, accentuating the plasticity and texture of objects. These intense contrasts could also make the image more visually rich, as mid-tones in monochrome reproduce as an undifferentiated grey.

The differences between these two kinds of lighting design were illustrated by Philip Ward, the BBC's head of television lighting, in a lecture he delivered at the BBC International Colour Television Design Conference in 1968, reprinted in the *British Journal of Photography* the following year. Juxtaposing two images of the same set, one lit for colour (fig. 107) and the other for monochrome (fig. 108), Ward makes clear how radically divergent these aesthetics are. The monochrome set veers between inky black recesses and gleaming white surfaces, with objects such as the water well appearing robustly solid and clearly distinguished from the hay lying adjacent and the stonework positioned behind. On the other hand, the set lit for colour, reproduced (appropriately enough) in a black and white photograph, appears monotonous, bland and featureless, with the well less clearly distinguishable from its surroundings because all the surfaces appear in the same dreary grey tone. As Ward noted, 'it is clear that optimized lighting for monochrome and the ideal for colour cannot be achieved at the same time'.[52] While high contrast was desirable for monochrome broadcasting, it was technologically challenging in colour, and the BBC had to find solutions to this problem of ensuring broadcasts

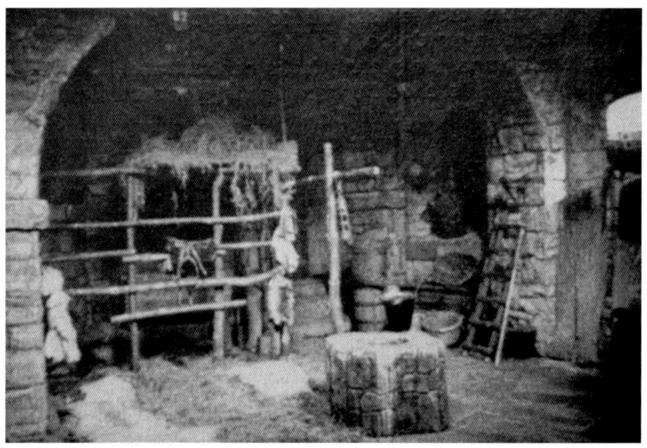

107 Flat, high-key lighting for colour broadcasting, from Philip Ward, 'Creative Lighting for Colour', *British Journal of Photography*, 14 February 1969.

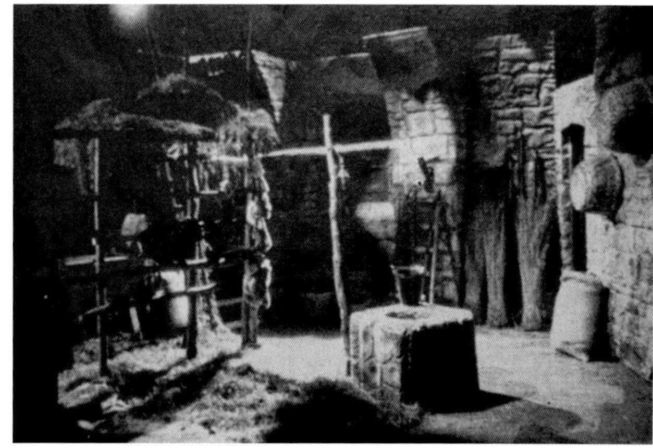

108 High-contrast lighting for black and white broadcasting, from Philip Ward, 'Creative Lighting for Colour'.

contained sufficient contrast to ensure a dynamic image in black and white, but without exceeding the contrast range for colour. As the Colour Familiarisation Course stated, the challenge was 'providing a good colour picture whilst maintaining the "kick" of the B&W [black and white]'.[53]

While designers, costumers and make-up artists may have thought that the introduction of colour would mean an expanded range of artistic possibilities, creative choices in many ways became more limited in 1967 because of these restrictions on contrast. The costume department had to discard thousands of existing items because they fell outside the accepted contrast range, forcing staff to build up new stocks of garments.[54] To avoid flaring, brilliant white costumes also had to be dyed an off-white shade of grey, a hue dubbed 'television white' by the BBC.[55] But these lighting restrictions proved particularly challenging with regard to skin tones, as Ian Atkins described: 'If you have, for instance, a man with a dark suntan sitting beside a girl with a pale, milk and roses "English" complexion and you want to show them from a full-range of camera angles … the wide tonal contrast between their two complexions makes it very difficult indeed to light them satisfactorily'.[56] Ward advised, however, that if lighting technicians had to choose between accurately capturing dark or light colours, the lighter ones should be privileged. In his words, 'if the contrast range is exceeded, the exposure must be chosen to neglect one end of the scale … usually the white end will have to be favoured, because if not … the value of facial tones will be incorrect.'[57]

When Atkins referred to an 'English' complexion comparable to 'milk and roses', he meant a familiar ideal of White femininity already discussed in this book in the contexts of painting, printing, and photography, with attendant gendered associations of innocence (milk) and romance (roses), at once metaphorically white (milk) and literally pinkish red (roses), which he considered synonymous with English identity (an English rose). He explicitly added a national label to this racial identity whereby Whiteness became synonymous with Englishness and a 'dark suntan' tacitly suggested someone whose complexion was not 'English'. Similarly, when Ward advised technicians to 'favour' light shades to preserve 'facial tones' from distortion, he laid bare the assumption that the kind of skin presented on television was uniformly White. Internal BBC technical documents did note that, in their terminology, 'coloured skins' reproduced well on colour television, but it is unclear whether such documents were referring to any skin tone vivified by colour broadcast or indeed any skin tone reflecting coloured lights, or if they were using racist language to refer to non-White skin tones.[58] However, it was the mixture of light and dark flesh tones and the contrast between them that defied the acceptable range for colour transmissions, encouraging lighting technicians to 'neglect' dark skin in favour of preserving Whiteness.

The BBC's discussion of these lighting challenges, which emphasised the incompatibility of people with dark and light skin and which framed the presence of dark-skinned people as a technological problem, clearly mapped onto wider discourses in British society in the 1960s, where issues of integration and compatibility were construed as social problems created by the presence of people of colour.[59] This intersection between the BBC's 'colour problem' and the wider 'colour problem' formulated by anti-Black discourse at the time informed the contents and aesthetics of BBC programmes in this era, producing a number of different solutions that exploited the subject of race and immigration to work through the technological challenges of colour broadcasting.

One of these solutions was segregation. If the combination of dark and light skin on screen at the same time proved technologically challenging in colour but was desirable to generate an interesting picture in monochrome, then the BBC could visually segregate people of different complexions into discrete parts of the same programme, producing a technologically sound image in colour while retaining the 'kick' of the black and white – the contrast – through their juxtaposition. In other words, the technical difficulty of integrating people of different races on screen in colour transmissions could be resolved by exploiting the political issue of racial segregation in wider society as the subject of a television programme, offering a political narrative as a pretence for this formal strategy.

This practice of producing contrast through the division of Blackness and Whiteness as discrete categories reflects Paul Gilroy's observation that the false historical construction of English national identity as homogenously and harmoniously White (so crucial to racist rhetoric of this period) was contingent upon the erection and preservation of artificial binaries between Whiteness and Blackness, and insider and intruder – binaries that relied upon the exacerbation and maximalisation of difference.[60] In other words, a heightening of contrast. This kind of 'ethnic absolutism', in Gilroy's terms, which saw 'black and white cultures as fixed, mutually impermeable expressions of racial and national identity', was all too easily translated into a televisual paradigm, which segregated Black and White figures to exacerbate the contrast between them (but crucially without defying the technological contrast range).[61] This moment when the BBC was converting to colour, and producing contrast through the segregation of Black and White bodies on screen, was a moment when both official and unofficial forms of public discourse reinforced the polarisation of Britain's White and Black communities, with issues of integration and segregation at their centre. What the BBC referred to as the 'kick' of the black and white was therefore not simply a formal strategy of visual contrast but a political strategy in which the differences between Black and White British identity were exacerbated and heightened as part of a nationalist agenda.

For example, on the first day of the Colour Launching Service, BBC2 aired an episode of the documentary series *One Pair of Eyes* titled 'A City of Magnificent Intentions', which presented a springtime portrait of Washington, DC. In addition to praising the beautiful palette of the show, from the red wine supped at diplomatic banquets to the pink blossoms of the cherry trees, reviewers admired how the programme deployed polarised images of the city to mount a political critique of racial injustice in America.[62] Julian Critchley, writing in *The Times*, singled out the dramatic juxtaposition of

> the band playing 'Hail to the Chief' on the White House lawn, with the poverty of the only major city in the United States that has a negro majority. Sixty-five percent of the population and ninety-three per cent of the school children in the public schools are black. The programme was

enhanced by being in colour. The cherry blossom and the great white marble shrines of Washington were shown to advantage. But so too were the slogans 'your country needs you n*****' that are painted up in the negro suburbs.[63]

Critchley's review makes clear how the segregation of Whiteness and Blackness was not only the subject of the documentary but was also built into its aesthetic arrangements of whiteness and blackness: the White House is contrasted with the 'negro majority'; the 'white marble shrines' with the 'negro suburbs'. While he describes how colour enables cherry blossoms to be seen to their best 'advantage', it is clear that the Black school children of the preceding sentence are also 'enhanced by being in colour'. Other papers also commented on the benefits of colour in depicting the lives of Black Americans, *The Observer* noting that 'the resigned negroes and the squalid alleys seemed so much more alive in colour' and the *Daily Express* noting that colour 'enhances everything it touches', including the 'negro ghettoes'.[64]

The show demonstrates how the BBC could exploit racial difference as part of the chromatic appeal of its conversion to colour, using skin colour and racial difference as a subject to showcase the new technology of colour broadcasting, but without having to racially integrate the people who appeared on its programmes. This meant that the contrast range was never exceeded, yet the contrast necessary to sustain interest for monochrome viewers was retained and, crucially, the distinction between Whiteness and Blackness also translated perfectly into a monochrome viewing experience, where these racial categories corresponded to a greyscale aesthetic of black and white tones. The topic of racial inequality in America, where the growing momentum of the civil rights movement and the recent lifting of Jim Crow legislation made the subject of racial segregation especially timely, further reinforced the suitability of this subject matter for this particular moment in broadcasting history. The subject was used again in an early colour episode of *Whicker's World* titled 'Conflict in Kentucky', broadcast on 7 October 1967, following protests by African American citizens against housing segregation in Louisville.

That BBC2 launched its colour service with a show tackling the issue of racial segregation speaks to how this topic resolved the specific technological and ideological demands of colour broadcasting for the BBC, but also the topicality of the subject in 1960s Britain. As Kennetta Hammond Perry and Rob Waters have argued, the American civil rights movement formed an important site of reflection for Britain's own ideas about race, nationhood and citizenship at this time, providing an aspirational image of Black activism for some, and to others a warning sign about the future of race relations in Britain.[65] While racial segregation was never enshrined in law in Britain as it was in America, Black British citizens in the 1960s experienced discrimination through the Colour Bar. This widely discussed topic of debate in the post-war period was not an official government policy but a pervasive and acutely felt form of racial segregation that dramatically affected the lives of Britain's citizens of colour by barring them from specific jobs, leisure pursuits, educational opportunities and housing provisions.[66] As Perry describes, the Colour Bar embedded racial segregation into all aspects of daily life and 'insidiously banned, excluded, and denied Black Britons by way of unspoken social customs, habits, and de facto codes of exclusion'.[67] Segregation as a formal strategy on television therefore tapped into an ideological agenda at this moment, when the increasing polarisation of Black and White identities by the British political discourse and popular media produced a sense of contrast between these groups through exclusionary binaries.

This polarisation of the 1960s gained a critical velocity from 1964 with the election of Peter Griffiths in the 1964 Smethwick by-election. With the notorious campaign slogan 'if you want a N***** for a neighbour, vote Labour', Griffiths placed anti-Black rhetoric front and centre in public political debate.[68] As Perry notes, in 1964, 'Smethwick began to eclipse Notting Hill as synecdoche for articulating White working-class backlash to Commonwealth migrants'.[69] Griffiths's campaign, which centred upon his refusal to racially integrate local housing, drastically exacerbated the antagonism between White residents and those of colour. So inflammatory was the campaign that Malcolm X visited the West Midlands town to offer his support to local Black residents.[70]

By 1965 the increasing social unrest caused by White antagonism to Black Britons had resulted in legislative changes, with the establishment of the Race Relations Act, ostensibly designed to criminalise acts of racial discrimination such as those at the heart of the Smethwick by-election. Yet the Act also became a weapon of the state to silence Black voices of protest, who could now be prosecuted for hate speech against White people.[71] Indeed, the Act was used to challenge the emerging Black Power movement in Britain, which was also taking shape at this time through the formation of the Universal Coloured People's Association (UCPA) in 1967, encouraged by visits to Britain from American civil rights leaders such as Malcolm X, Martin Luther King (in 1965) and Stokely Carmichael (in 1967).[72] The broader culture of Black activism gaining velocity in this period – through organisations including the Campaign Against Racial Discrimination and the Racial Adjustment Action Society, both established in 1965 – created the conditions for the UCPA's publication in 1967 of the manifesto *Black Power in Britain* and the formation in 1968 of the British Black Panther Party.[73] The years 1967 and 1968 were therefore crucial turning points for the increased visibility and vocality of Black resistance to White racism, as well as heightened White anxiety about a Black presence in Britain as a source of civic unrest. The years when the BBC was converting to colour were therefore a flashpoint for the heightening contrast between Blackness and Whiteness as modes of British subjectivity.

Plans to extend the powers of the Race Relations Act in 1967, to outlaw discrimination with regard to the provision of housing to people of colour, triggered Enoch Powell's infamous 'Rivers of Blood' speech, widely considered the apotheosis of anti-Black racism in 1960s Britain, at a Conservative Party meeting in Birmingham in April 1968.[74] Gilroy, in his extended analysis of Powell's speech, illustrates how the contrast evoked by the Black/White binary was central to the formation and popularisation of his racist discourse, which dominated the public conversation about race at the time.[75] Powell's invective against Black migration presented Black Britishness as a threat to the stability and values of the nation's identity, and he predicted that 'in fifteen or twenty years time the black man will hold the whip hand over the white man'. Gilroy identifies the centre of the speech's rhetorical and emotional gravity as Powell's recollection of a letter he had received from an elderly White constituent who claimed that despite harassment by the local 'black youth', who had shouted abuse and pushed 'excreta' through her letterbox, it was she who was likely to be accused of racial discrimination under the Race Relations Act for refusing to allow Black lodgers into her home.

Gilroy describes how the speech 'generates racial meanings from an accumulated tension between a series of neat binary oppositions – white/negro, clean/dirty, noisy/quiet' and notes 'the way in which the conflicting colours are also gendered' – a White feminine Briton contrasted with the Black masculine intruder.[76] Powellism was contingent upon emphasising the division between these categories. At precisely the moment when public discourse, shaped by Powellism, was problematically enhancing the polarisation between notions of Black and White British identity, the BBC could use the technical challenges of racial integration as a way of sustaining segregation on screen, thereby building contrast into the very structure of its programmes.

Television White

While the emergence of colour on the BBC in 1967 spoke to distinct cultural circumstances, it also reiterated a question that subtended the emergence of any new colour medium over the past century in Britain: how to preserve the primacy of Whiteness at a moment when colour was perceived to threaten its supposed stability. The desire to simultaneously incorporate people of colour on screen and not allow the presence of dark skin to 'distort' White identity was at the centre of the BBC's 'colour problem' in the 1960s. The chromatic and racial implications of these issues were inextricable – if lighting was calibrated for dark rather than light skin, for people of colour rather than colourless White people, then White faces would become overly saturated, or dominated by colour. To fail to privilege Whiteness would therefore result in the erosion of the supposed purity of White identity.

The primacy of Whiteness at the BBC was most potently visualised through the images used to tune and calibrate its colour signals. These belong to the genre of technical images known as 'Shirley Cards' or 'China Girls', used for colour calibration throughout the twentieth century at filmic and photographic laboratories.[77] Typically, these images feature a White woman, often dressed in brightly coloured clothing and on occasion barely dressed at all, whose face is juxtaposed with a colour chart to ensure each hue is calibrated in relation to her White skin. As Lorna Roth, Genevieve Yue and Deborah Willis have explored, the Shirley Card demonstrates how racial bias was built into the production and reproduction of colour at a technological level by placing Whiteness literally and metaphorically at the centre of colour calibration, which distorted the rendition of darker skin tones as a result.[78]

Television broadcasters adopted these practices in different ways. As Susan Murray reveals, American broadcasters in the 1950s employed calibration models known as 'color girls' – attractive, young White women used as living mannequins to calibrate colour in the television studio around an ideal of White American identity.[79] The BBC's earliest in-house colour tuning signal from 1957 instead used a still image, but it similarly presented the young White British announcer Sylvia Peters, whose décolletage showcases her pale skin at its centre, framed by wings segmented into greyscale and rainbow hues (fig. 109). Colour here is displaced to the margins, reduced to a framing device, as a chromatic foil to the image of White British femininity at the centre. Peters's image illuminates the tension at work in the gendering of

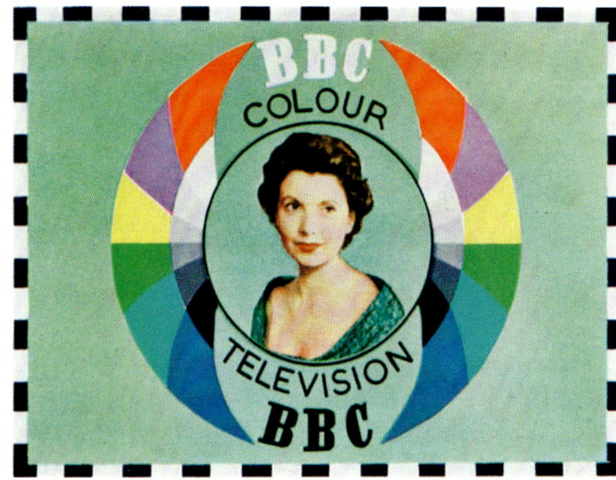

109 Experimental BBC colour test card featuring Sylvia Peters, early 1950s.

colour in these test cards. This image at once reinforces the strong historical associations of colour and femininity explored in Chapter Three and their shared connection to cosmetics, ornamentation and visual consumption, but it also highlights Gilroy's observation that racist discourse in the 1960s strongly framed Whiteness in terms of femininity. This test card therefore simultaneously exploits Peters's femininity as a conventional subject suitable for demonstrating colour while ensuring that colour does not impinge upon ideals of British identity, potently symbolised through the figure of the young White woman.

Unlike film or photography, however, television suffered an added problem in the attempt to calibrate flesh tones as broadcasters could not control how viewers would tune their sets at home. For instance, one journalist reported that during the Wimbledon broadcast, despite his 'fighting those two knobs marked tint and colour', it was impossible to arrive at the correct flesh tones for the images on screen, meaning David Attenborough still 'seemed to have chocolate blancmange all over his face'.[80] The BBC's anxiety over the proper calibration of colour arose precisely because its mis-calibration could distort the stability of Whiteness, resulting in the undesirable racial othering of its stars. To help viewers adjust

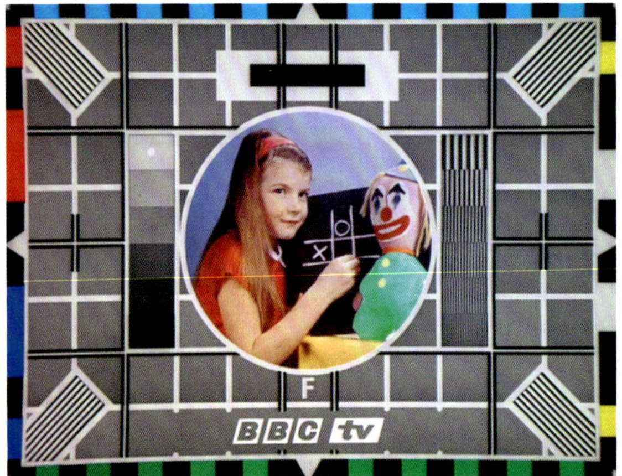

110 Test Card F, designed by George Hersee, 1967.

their sets at home, the BBC designed a special calibration image known as Test Card F. The designer of the image, George Hersee, described how the card had to meet a number of technical and aesthetic criteria, including 'a reasonable area of flesh tones', a limited area of 'white-on-black contrast' near the centre to enable viewers to check these shades did not converge and 'areas of bright colour to counteract the large black/white areas of the rest of the card'; it must also 'be a pleasing picture' as it would be broadcast for many hours a day.[81] The resulting image featured George's seven-year-old daughter, Carole, playing noughts and crosses on a blackboard, accompanied by her toy clown, Bubbles (fig. 110). The choice of a child's face was thought to be likely to prevent the image from dating, as the make-up and fashions worn by older women changed frequently, and, as Hersee noted, a fair child had to be selected so that the tonal difference between her hair and skin would not contravene the contrast range; he noted that 'dark hair was unacceptable' – clearly overlooking the fact that dark hair and dark skin would similarly meet these conditions.[82]

Carole's circular portrait is surrounded by a greyscale grid of geometric blocks and stripes ('frequency bars' and 'step wedge' in technical language), which, when correctly tuned, appeared only in shades of black and white (rainbow hazing indicated inaccurate calibration) and were free of blurring, fizzing and swirling. But official BBC guidance suggested that the best way for viewers to calibrate their sets was to turn off the colour signal entirely and then reintroduce it gradually until, in the words of the advice pamphlets, 'realistic facial colouring is obtained'.[83] Just as costumes and clothing on colour television had to be adjusted to a suitable shade of 'television white', so too did flesh tones have to be calibrated to another kind of television White, an idealised version of White British identity that would not be distorted through the encroachment of colour. While Test Card F contains a scramble of visual information supposed to assist with colour calibration, it was Carole's skin, her smiling face (shown in three-quarter profile) and her outstretched arm (left visible by her capped sleeves) that provided viewers with the ideal standard of Whiteness with which to tune their televisions.

However, Hersee offers no account for the presence of Bubbles, the clown whose head and hands are a candied pink fabric, a cartoonish approximation of White skin, and whose face is painted with a form of theatrical make-up known as 'whiteface'. As this is one of the most consumed images in the history of British broadcasting, the importance of this whiteface clown cannot be overlooked as a participant in the ideological manoeuvres of the BBC's conversion to colour. Bubbles's face paint makes clear that as much as Whiteness insists upon its invisibility, transparency and naturalness, White identity is still a constructed, relational category – one that exists only in distinction to its rhetorical opposite: colour. The prominence of this whiteface clown also points to how make-up and racial masquerade proved crucial to the BBC's attempts to resolve its 'colour problem' in the late 1960s.

Television Black

In a 1968 lecture on colour television design, senior BBC make-up supervisor Maureen Winsdale explained her department's key challenge. Staff had to keep flesh tones within an acceptably limited range of contrast to meet the demands of colour without artificially reducing everyone's skin to the same shade, which would have been monotonous for viewers in monochrome:

> One of the things we most want to avoid is for everyone to look exactly alike. There is a great variation between individual skins and the first objective in applying make-up is to retain the natural and personal quality of the subject, unless of course it is to change the appearance for the sake of characterisation. Because of the important contrast ratio some faces have to be altered, bringing the skin tones nearer together. The only way of achieving this is to darken light skin, for even in monochrome, to lighten a dark skin produces a muddy and artificial effect.[84]

It is unclear when Winsdale speaks of 'dark skin' whether she includes olive-toned and tanned White complexions or euphemistically refers to the darker pigmentation of some people of colour. But as Black British actress Cleo Sylvestre, who began working in television in the 1950s, recalled, television make-up departments at this time had little expertise with Black skin, reflected both in the Whiteness of their personnel and their products: 'in the early days you never saw a black technician … and definitely not in the make-up department … you would go into the make-up room and there would be a range of white make-up, and you'd start frantically mixing around trying to get some deeper colours'.[85] Indeed, it seems unlikely Winsdale would have advocated bringing Black and White skin 'nearer together', not least because there was such a strong insistence in BBC rhetoric that White skin was a standard to be upheld and against which all other colours, including other skin tones, should be adjusted. However, an early colour broadcast from the BBC does present an extreme and telling example of precisely this strategy of bringing Black and White skin 'nearer together', illuminating the broader implications of the role of make-up in negotiating issues of racial representation during the BBC's conversion to colour.

The need to experiment with the combination of different skin tones on screen, in addition to the well-established conflation of African culture and exoticised modes of chromatism, surely motivated the decision to select *Aida* as the first opera broadcast in colour on the BBC, transmitted live from the Royal Opera House on BBC2 on 5 February 1968. A nineteenth-century Italian opera set in ancient Egypt, *Aida* presented an obvious vehicle for the BBC to test its capacity for live outside broadcasts in colour, with its Orientalised staging featuring lavish polychrome sets and glittering costumes encrusted with faux gemstones. But, as opera historian Naomi André argues, crucial to the Orientalism Edward Said has identified as underpinning *Aida* is the use of blackface in its conventional staging.[86] As an enslaved Ethiopian princess, *Aida*'s female protagonist is historically performed by a White singer in blackface make-up. This 1968 staging featured the White Welsh soprano Gwyneth Jones performing the titular role in traditional make-up, but the principal cast also included Grace Bumbry, a renowned African American mezzo-soprano, in the key supporting role of Aida's love rival, Amneris.

While the disparity between Jones's and Bumbry's natural colouring may have defied the accepted contrast range for colour broadcasting, the fact that Jones's role required blackface make-up reduced the contrast between their faces – that is, it brought them 'nearer together' – but by no means made them, in Winsdale's terms, 'look exactly alike', as there was a clear chromatic disparity between Bumbry's face and Jones's crudely exaggerated brown greasepaint (fig. 111). The make-up assistant on *Aida* noted that Jones insisted her make-up should not be too dark, which forced Bumbry to lighten her skin (against official BBC guidance) to close the gap between their facial colouring on stage. The make-up assistant described how this presented a 'unique' problem in which she 'had to persuade a white singer playing a negress to go darker and a negro singer playing an Egyptian to wear lighter toned make-up' to bring their colouring closer together.[87] Just as there was an accepted shade of television White, *Aida* demonstrates that there

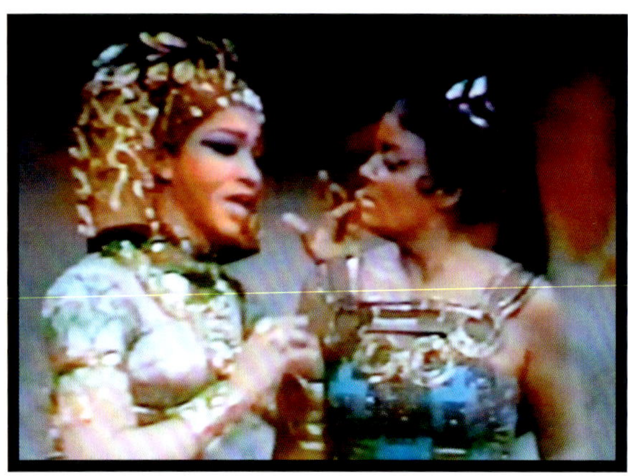

111 Grace Bumbry and Gwyneth Jones in *Aida* (BBC2, 5 February 1968).

was also an accepted shade of 'television Black', whether represented by the enforced lightening of Bumbry's skin or the artificial darkening of Jones's blackface greasepaint.

By no means did *Aida* present a widely applicable solution to the challenge of combining dark and light skin on screen, of course. The histrionic stage conventions of the opera genre offered a dramatic pretence for the exaggerated darkening of Jones's skin, constituting what Winsdale describes as a change of appearance 'for the sake of characterisation', a term used euphemistically to describe White actors playing characters of different races or ethnicities, and referring to a distinct category of make-up design.[88] Similarly, the lightening of Bumbry's skin contravened Winsdale's guidelines in a manner that was perhaps tolerable within the dramatic conventions of opera but would not have been acceptable in other genres due to its 'artificial' appearance. However, the deployment of blackface make-up to narrow the contrast range in *Aida* raises crucial questions about the role of make-up and racial masquerade in shaping issues of racial representation across BBC programming in 1967 and 1968.

Undoubtedly, the cost and labour involved in using make-up to harmonise skin tones across racially diverse casts would have reinforced the existing racism in the BBC's casting practices and strengthened the dominance of White talent in the BBC's stable of presenters, actors and participants. If the inclusion of dark-skinned cast members meant making up the light-skinned cast with darker flesh tones to reduce the disparity between them, then it would have been quicker, cheaper and more efficient to maintain the racially homogenous, White talent pool already employed at the BBC. Actors of colour working in Britain in the 1950s and 1960s have recalled that television already presented few opportunities for them due to the combined lack of appropriate roles and prejudiced casting processes, but these technological issues would have further legitimised the reluctance to cast Black actors at this time.[89]

As British Pakistani actor Zia Mohyeddin has recalled, the pervasive attitude among directors and casting agents that 'black and Asian actors weren't good enough' betrayed a resistance to placing actors of colour on screen.[90] While there was not a complete absence of people of colour on British television of this period, the points of entry were limited.[91] One-off broadcasts such as the docudrama *A Man from the Sun* (BBC, 1956), which examined the challenges faced by West Indian settlers in Britain and featured Cy Grant and Errol John among others, exemplified the promising but limited opportunities available to actors of colour at this time. There were also a small number of programmes on monochrome television regularly featuring racially mixed casts, including *Rainbow City* and ITV's *Emergency Ward 10* (1957–67), which included prominent Black British actors such as Earl Cameron and Carmen Munroe, but these were rare. As actor and agent Pearl Connor, who founded the Afro Asian Caribbean Agency, noted, when production companies hired people of colour they were typically non-professionals who could work as extras, 'people who were extremely cheap and who could provide padding for a scene'.[92] Munroe similarly remembered that Black actors were often used to 'dress the set', playing perfunctory roles in parts that were subservient to the principal White cast.[93]

As Mohyeddin has recalled, substantial Black roles were more typically played by White actors in blackface; he noted that directors thought it was 'much better to have Joe Bloggs putting on reams of grease paint and trying to pretend that he's black or Asian' than hiring an appropriate actor.[94] Mohyeddin's observation clearly speaks to the reluctance of White media establishments to cast actors of colour at this time, but, in the historical context of early colour broadcasting, his comment also reveals how technological limitations could be exploited to reinforce political biases. By darkening the skin of White cast members enough to give the impression of a spectrum of skin tones (for colour viewers) and an aesthetics of contrast (for monochrome viewers), but without contravening the contrast range crucial to maintaining the correct rendition of White skin, broadcasters could exploit the chromatic appeal of racial difference without hiring people of colour.

Therefore, while *Aida* seemed to present a 'unique' instance in which blackface make-up resolved some of the challenges of the BBC's 'colour problem', in fact, the technical difficulties of early colour broadcasting reinforced and legitimised the already institutionalised use of blackface, as it presented a solution to the challenge of mixing and matching skin tones across monochrome and colour broadcasting at this time.

As Mohyeddin describes, the use of blackface was pervasive on television in the 1960s. It appeared across high cultural forms such as *Aida* as well as popular sitcoms such as the early colour ITV show *Curry and Chips* from 1969, in which White actor Spike Milligan played a Pakistani migrant working at a British factory. However, the most prominent and inflammatory use of blackface performance was the BBC's *The Black and White Minstrel Show*, which from 1958 to 1972 showcased White singers in blackface minstrel make-up and was the flagship light entertainment vehicle for the BBC's conversion to colour. The programme certainly, like *Aida*, exploited blackface as a way of attending to the limitations of the contrast range in the early years of colour broadcasting. Yet, as an extended analysis of the show reveals, it also intervened in crucial ways in the larger political and social dimensions of the 'colour problem' in British civic life.

The Black and White Minstrel Show

Given that the BBC insisted it would make no concessions to the arrival of colour in terms of programming, the migration of *The Black and White Minstrel Show* from BBC1 to BBC2 specially for the launch of colour in 1967 indicates its important status as part of the channel's colour strategy.[95] The show was the BBC's premium light entertainment programme, attracting audiences of between sixteen and eighteen million during its forty-five-minute slot on a Saturday night when screened in monochrome on BBC1.[96] It was also critically acclaimed, having received the inaugural Rose d'Or, awarded by the European Broadcasting Union in 1961, and therefore lent further prestige to the launch of colour. *The Black and White Minstrel Show* featured heavily in the publicity campaign surrounding the Colour Launching Service and was often ranked at the top of the list of shows that viewers anticipated seeing in colour.[97] The BBC's listings magazine the *Radio Times* trailed a colour image of the show on its cover in April 1967 to stoke anticipation for seeing the programme transformed from monochrome into full colour (fig. 112). Some television scholars have interpreted the prominence of the show in the Colour Launching Service as ironic, given that its title seems to allude to a monochrome aesthetic.[98] However, it was precisely this linguistic collapse of black and white (as the absence of colour) onto Blackness and Whiteness (as racial categorisations) and minstrelsy (as a practice that enabled the slippage between these categories) that made the show especially suited for the unique circumstances of colour television in 1967.

Originating in radio as the George Mitchell Minstrels, the group had appeared on television for almost a decade by the time of their first colour broadcast.[99] The show's main attractions were the Minstrels themselves – a group of male performers including John Boulter, Dai Francis and Tony Mercer, who appeared in the theatrical blackface make-up of the American stage tradition – and the Television Toppers, a troupe of White female dancers who sang and danced alongside. The programme also

Radio Times (Incorporating World-Radio)
April 13, 1967. Vol. 175: No. 2266.

LONDON AND SOUTH-EAST

APRIL 15—21

Radio Times

PRICE SIXPENCE

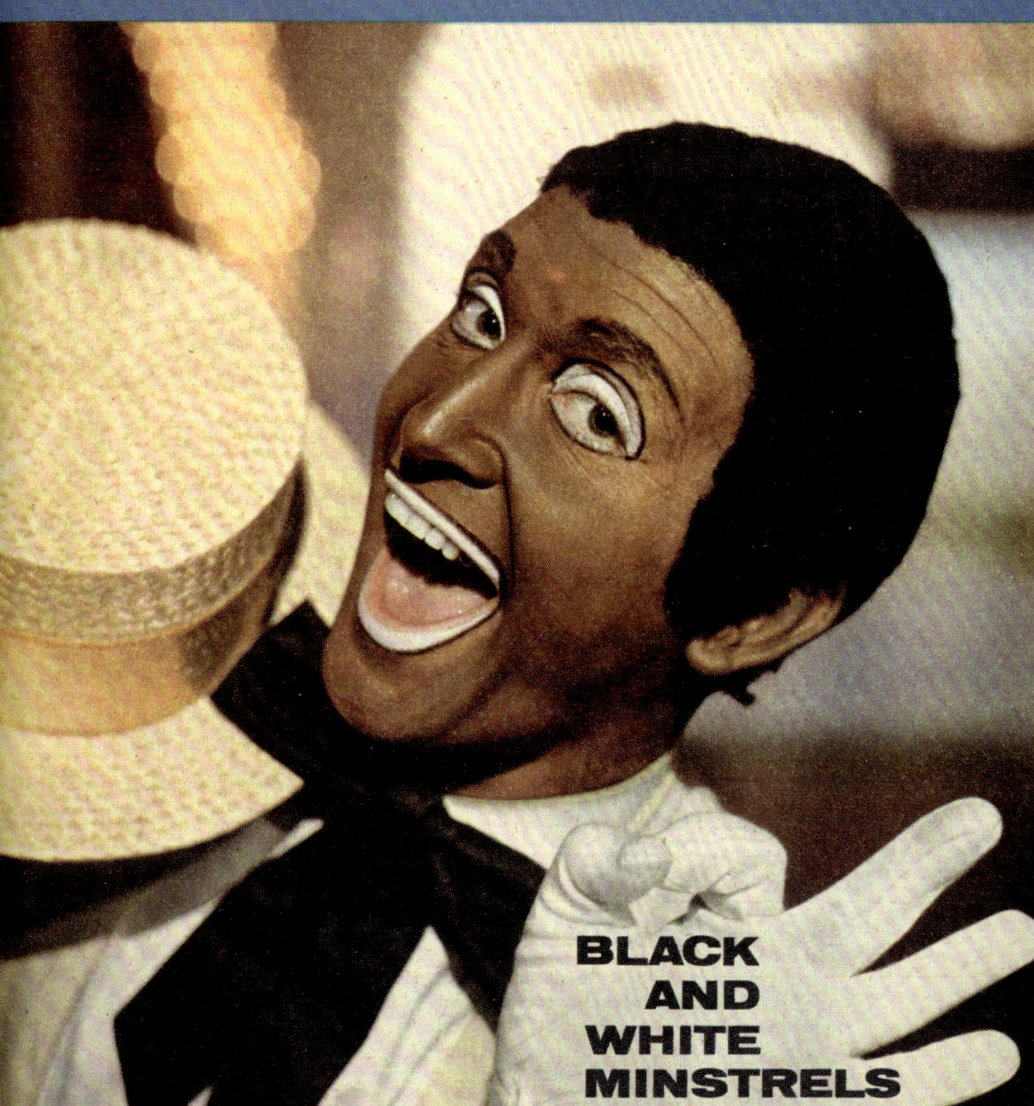

showcased other light entertainment acts between the Minstrels' numbers, with comedic segues performed by compère Leslie Crowther. Sonically the show departed from the nineteenth-century minstrel convention of mimicking African American musical traditions, and instead the performers clustered popular songs together in what they called 'medleys', which were themed around different styles, time periods and genres, where minstrel standards such as 'My Mammy', popularised by Al Jolson, would be performed in the same episode as cockney songs and dancehall numbers such as 'My Old Man'.[100]

The show has been widely discussed as evidence of a pervasive culture of racism at the BBC in the 1960s, indicative of how racial prejudice was so institutionalised as to appear invisible to the corporation, which claimed that the show was 'not about race' and therefore could not be considered offensive, despite the numerous protests and complaints levied by Black activist groups and other concerned viewers.[101] The combination of the lack of Black representation on television at this time and the extreme prominence and popularity of *The Black and White Minstrel Show* made the latter the subject of an especially vocal outrage in the 1960s, particularly among Black British viewers and Black industry professionals. In 1961 an article and series of letters protesting the show were published in *Flamingo*, a journal specifically designed for a readership of Commonwealth migrants of colour in Britain. Here Pearl Connor spoke out against the show, claiming it 'hark[s] back to slavery and cotton plantations', lamenting that 'white performers with black faces only look ridiculous and make me feel ashamed' and suggesting that if the BBC had to continue broadcasting the show, then it could at least hire 'coloured artists' for these roles, given that they were already woefully underemployed on television.[102]

The Campaign Against Racial Discrimination publicly protested against the show in 1965 with a petition to the BBC carrying two hundred signatures calling for its cancellation and describing it as a 'hideous impersonation [that] is quite offensive and causes much distress to most coloured people'.[103] This protest received extensive national press coverage, which largely contested its claims that the show was racist, and was dismissed at internal BBC meetings as a minority opinion, with the head of programming noting that it was 'the general view that the programme was not racially offensive'.[104] Just as the BBC would not alter its programmes to appeal to the 'colour minority' in the sense of colour television owners, similarly it envisioned viewers of colour as a minority who should have no sway over its broadcasting decisions. The producer of the show, George Inns, defended it in *Flamingo* on the grounds that it was 'an innocent programme, providing entertainment. After all, the traditional European clown still whites his face.'[105] Inns's comment, which wilfully overlooks the racial humour at the heart of minstrelsy, instantly recalls Test Card F and its whiteface clown, forging a parallel between these two forms of racial masquerade, both designed to reinforce the supremacy of Whiteness during the BBC's conversion to colour.

At the time, and in subsequent histories of this period, *The Black and White Minstrel Show* was explicitly linked to the escalating anti-Black rhetoric that permeated British culture in the 1960s, wherein the programme became what Stephen Bourne calls 'a platform for racist propaganda', mirroring and reinforcing the messages espoused by Powell.[106] A tradition emerging, as Connor noted, from the plantation culture of nineteenth-century America and the racial inequities of the transatlantic slave trade, minstrelsy had always operated as a way to reinforce the boundaries of White identity at times when its cogency and hegemony were perceived to be under threat.[107] The prominence and popularity of minstrelsy in 1960s Britain clearly articulated such anxieties about the erosion of the stability and sovereignty of White Britishness through Commonwealth migration. But, despite close scrutiny of how *The Black and White Minstrel Show* intersected with the politics of colour

112 *The Black and White Minstrel Show* on the cover of the *Radio Times*, London and South East edition, April 1967.

in terms of racial identity at this time, rarely is the use of colour in terms of chromatism examined as part of this ideological agenda.[108] While Sarita Malik has described how the addition of colour lent a 'novelty-factor' to the programme's use of blackface performance, describing colour as 'the twist that made the programme work', this chromatic 'twist' was absolutely crucial to generating the show's multiple meanings at a very specific historical moment in British identity politics and broadcasting history.[109]

As Eric Lott argues, minstrelsy has always encompassed a complex and conflicting set of White attitudes towards Blackness, never simply an expression of hostility but a practice that combined fear with fascination. Lott has demonstrated how in the context of nineteenth-century America, minstrelsy staged 'the dialectical flickering of racial insult and racial envy' – a commingled White contempt for and attraction to the Black body.[110] Minstrelsy enabled White performers to simultaneously lampoon and ridicule Black identity while appropriating what were perceived as its most desirable aspects, typically a stereotyped White fantasy of Black musicality and kineticism integral to these staged performances.[111]

This 'dialectical flickering', described by Lott, also articulates British attitudes towards colour in the post-war period, in the senses of both racial difference and the hues of modernity, as indicated by Stanley Reynolds's 1967 column on *Rainbow City* and the Colour Launching Service, which simultaneously expressed excitement and anxiety.[112] Reynolds's column reflected what Lynda Nead has argued characterised White British responses to the increasingly colourful nature of post-war Britain, when colour represented modernisation, consumer choice and prosperity, but its conflation with Commonwealth migration also framed it as a source of suspicion and menace.[113] If minstrelsy allowed for the simultaneous expression of desire and disquiet, of attraction and trepidation, then it presented an instrument for articulating these complex attitudes towards colour exhibited among White Britons in this period. In the context of *The Black and White Minstrel Show*, minstrelsy enabled these White performers to exploit the supposedly inherent chromatism of Black bodies as part of a celebration of the dazzling modern aesthetic of televised colour, while simultaneously deriding and essentialising people of colour through these racist caricatures.

Yet it must not be forgotten that this show, which traded upon and exploited the various appeals of colour, was primarily consumed in black and white. Again, minstrelsy offered a solution to this challenge, as the programme's meaning was unchanged during its migration from colour to monochrome. The 'black' and 'white' of *The Black and White Minstrel Show* could simultaneously signify a greyscale palette (black and white) and a spectacularised demonstration of racial difference (blackface make-up worn by White performers, and the combination of blackface minstrels and White dancers). The chromatism of *The Black and White Minstrel Show* was not contingent upon audiences seeing the different complexions of the cast conveyed in the various hues of a colour broadcast. The very structure of the show enabled the generation of colour in the sense of racial difference, through this juxtaposition of blackface and White faces, despite the lack of colour in the sense of chromatic hues.

At a time when stark contrasts between light and shade were desirable in monochrome but technologically challenging in colour, *The Black and White Minstrel Show* built contrast into its aesthetic through the juxtaposition of these different complexions, contrasting White skin and blackface in a manner that was carefully managed and manipulated by the make-up department. Because the theatrical convention of blackface make-up did not try to realistically mimic any Black face, deviations from naturalism could easily be resolved as part of the fantastical quality of the variety format, allowing for a greater flexibility and margin of error than were permissible in other television genres. The use of blackface meant that skin tones could be fine-tuned so as not to convene the contrast range, with scant regard for the naturalism of the faces of the Minstrels themselves.

Although Maureen Winsdale noted in her guidance that make-up should not make everyone 'look exactly alike', she admitted that for the sake of consistency, 'with groups of dancers it is sometimes essential to make them identical in skin tone'.[114] On *The Black and White Minstrel Show*, the men were made up with Max Factor's 'Negro No. 2' and the women with 'Chinese Pancake', another racially coded form of make-up that used yellow pigment to compensate for what internal documents called the Toppers' 'pink and blotchy' appearance on colour television – the saturated appearance of their White skin undoubtedly exacerbated by their proximity to the darkened faces of the Minstrels and the attendant issues of lighting and colour control.[115] Dividing the performers into two separate groups in this way, and regulating their skin tones with uniform make-up designs, enabled a high degree of control and standardisation of complexions, while also allowing for aesthetic contrast through the juxtaposition and mixing of their divergent tonalities. The combination of the blackface Minstrels and the White Television Toppers created a dramatic contrast in monochrome, but without defying the contrast range in colour. The show meant the BBC could exploit the aesthetic binarism of juxtaposing dark and light skin without having to racially integrate its casts, thus using racial masquerade as a formal strategy for building 'contrast' into the design of the show.

This Black/White binary was not just displayed through the performers' make-up, however. For all its chromatic flair, the show relied upon rather simple combinations of black, white and colour to ensure its compatibility with the requirements of both chromatic and monochrome broadcasting. This is clearly demonstrated in the medley that opens the New Year's Eve episode from 1967, described by Crowther as 'a tribute in song to the American railroad system' and featuring 'Chattanooga Choo Choo' and 'Toot, Toot, Tootsie!', the latter popularised by Al Jolson in *The Jazz Singer* (US, 1927; dir. Alan Crosland). The medley opens with an overhead shot of black train lines painted on white paper laid on the floor. The camera tracks backward and tilts to reveal the black, diagrammatic silhouette of a rail yard set against the white of the studio, with only the words 'Track' and 'A Train' picked out in red lettering bordered in yellow – a visual bonus to colour viewers but not detracting from the monochrome experience. A second angle on the set shows the departures board: a grid of crisp, black sans-serif text against a white background. Behind this grid, the Minstrels and Television Toppers dance across the train tracks dressed in red, white and black, signalling the arrival of colour to this almost entirely monochrome space, through both their colourful costumes and the racialised implications of their painted faces (fig. 113).

These splashes of red against a predominantly black and white set appear extremely striking when seen in colour – the red of a dress or a bowler hat truly pops against the black and white of the train tracks or the text of the departures board. But little of this information would be lost in the translation to monochrome because of the simplicity of these geometric designs. For instance, the umbrellas spun by the Television Toppers in this number are decorated with a red and white spiral, an effect that is eye-catching in colour but entirely legible in monochrome, as the red swirl would simply translate as dark grey (fig. 114). Dorothy Mitchell, one of the Television Toppers, claimed these contrasting binaries between dark and light, which were crucial to the show's aesthetic, were purely formal strategies, describing how, for instance, the show used the alternation of blonde and brunette dancers to produce the same effect as the alternation between Minstrels and Toppers. She claimed this formal pattern of alternation would have been just as effectively produced by hiring Black dancers as Television Toppers, noting 'six black girls and six white girls would have been wonderful'.[116]

Yet the gendering of these colours – White female Toppers and male blackface Minstrels – reinforced what Paul Gilroy has identified as the problematic conflation of Whiteness with British femininity and Blackness with foreign masculinity in xenophobic rhetoric at this time.[117] Routinely, *The Black and White Minstrel Show* exploits the romantic pairing of the Minstrels and Television Toppers to create a form of visual contrast. By dancing and engaging in intimate embraces, the performers place their faces in very close proximity to perform affection while

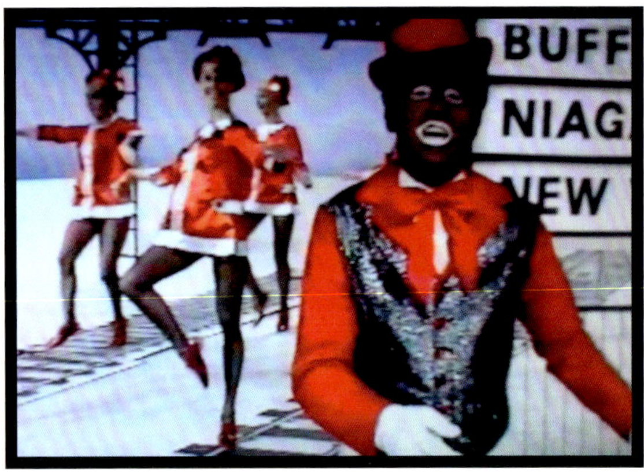

113 *The Black and White Minstrel Show* (BBC2, 31 December 1967).

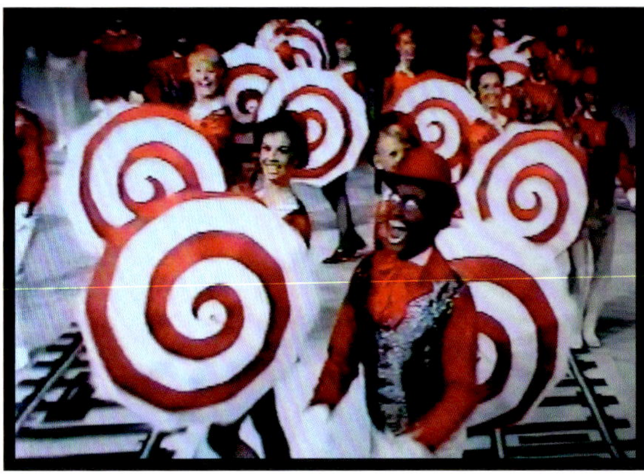

114 *The Black and White Minstrel Show* (BBC2, 31 December 1967).

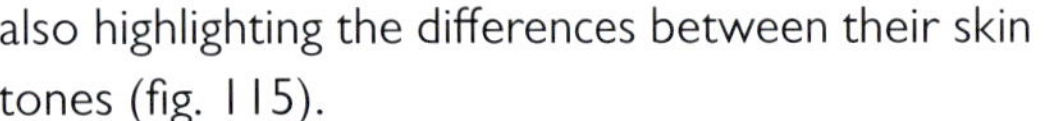

also highlighting the differences between their skin tones (fig. 115).

This supposedly aesthetic strategy of alternating White Toppers and blackface Minstrels therefore also performed political work. This parodic form of interracial coupling spoke to the most obsessively discussed aspects of racial integration in Britain, which dominated conversations in the media at the expense of more pressing issues such as housing and employment.[118] As a 1955 British sociological report titled *The Colour Problem: A Study of Race Relations* put it, 'the idea of mixed marriages between coloured and white people probably evokes greater antipathy than any other aspect of coloured colonial immigration', illustrating that White British antagonism to Black migration was in large part driven by anxieties about miscegenation.[119]

The BBC viewed the supposedly provocative subject of interracial marriage as a topic to exploit in the early years of colour, producing two colour episodes of the documentary series *Man Alive* on the topic in the summer of 1968. The director, Desmond Wilcox, recalled that the *Radio Times* wanted to put an image from the show on its cover:

> They thought it would be an emotive selling photograph … so we produced, from a wedding, a picture of a man and his brand new wife kissing in their bridal kit. The *Radio Times* said 'But they're kissing!' And I said 'Yes. That's what people do when they get married… .' And they said, 'Yes, yes, but one of them is black!' … and the *Radio Times* wouldn't use it. They thought that it would be inflammatory and wrong.[120]

The BBC's desire to exploit this 'emotive' topic without having to show physical intimacy between interracial couples elucidates the social function the burlesque staging of interracial couples performed on *The Black and White Minstrel Show*. If *Man Alive* explored, as the *Radio Times* described it, the issue of 'white girls married to coloured men', then *The Black and White Minstrel Show* staged a caricatured travesty of precisely this scenario to undermine its supposed menace.[121] *The Black and White Minstrel Show* flirted with the emotive power of this matrimonial iconography in an episode that aired on 14 March 1970, where the cast performed a medley of 'wedding numbers'. The minstrels were clad as ushers in light grey tuxedos and pink cummerbunds, the Toppers in aqua dresses and matching veils. On monochrome television the light blue colour of these dresses would have registered as white, transforming the Toppers into a parade of brides lining up to marry their dark-

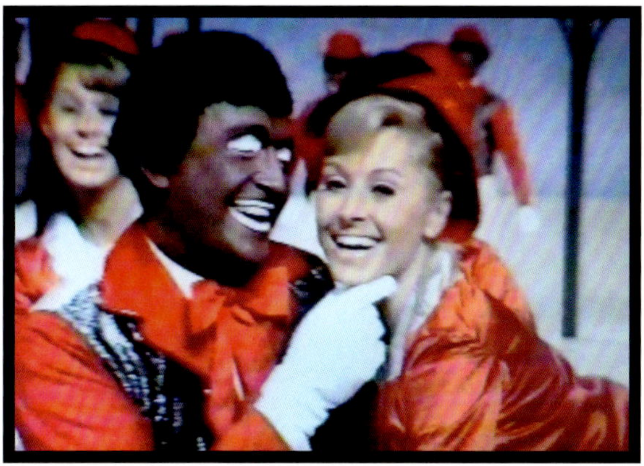

115 Comparing skin tones. *The Black and White Minstrel Show* (BBC2, 31 December 1967).

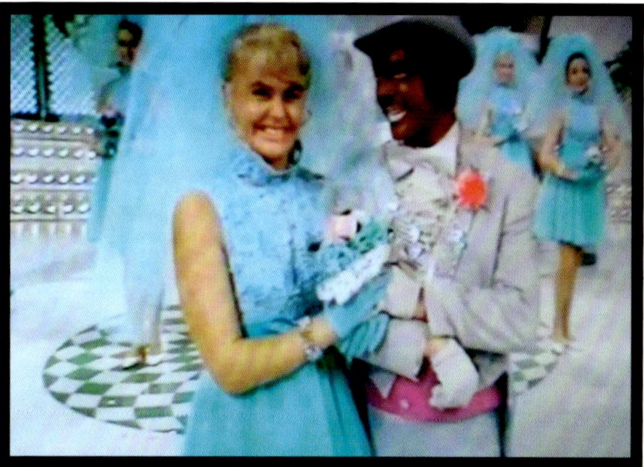

116 A satire of interracial marriage in *The Black and White Minstrel Show* (BBC2, 14 March 1970).

skinned partners, a comedic parody of interracial relationships that for White viewers might have seemed to evacuate the subject of its imagined menace (fig. 116). The contrast between the Toppers and Minstrels was far from a purely formal strategy, as the combination and recombination of black and white tones, as well as 'Black' and White skin tones, were clearly inseparable from contemporary concerns about racial integration and mixing.

Conversions, Reversions, Inversions

The BBC's use of minstrelsy to visualise its conversion from monochrome to colour was a very specific solution to the demands of broadcasting in 1967 but also historically determined as a means of demonstrating a new media technology. As Alice Maurice, Louis Chude-Sokei and Michael Rogin have argued, because minstrelsy was a stage tradition contingent upon an apparent racial transformation, it was quickly adopted as a way of visualising technological transformations, most famously during cinema's conversion to synchronised sound.[122] The mythic birth of sound cinema in America was iconically instigated through minstrelsy by Al Jolson in *The Jazz Singer*, where his racial metamorphosis from White to 'Black' visualised cinema's technological metamorphosis from silence to sound, a model that proved useful during the BBC's conversion to colour.

This conflation of Blackness with the new technology of synchronised dialogue and music in the 1920s was contingent upon racist assumptions about the inherent rhythm and musicality of Black bodies, with Black singers and dancers commonly exploited as demonstration subjects during the early years of sound.[123] But, rather than showcase Black performers in the manner adopted by numerous subsequent sound features, *The Jazz Singer* exploited minstrelsy as a way of embodying cinema's remarkable shift from silence to song, which was contingent upon audiences seeing this transformation unfold before their eyes and also witnessing its operation in reverse when the film returned to silence and Jolson removed his make-up.

Minstrelsy therefore operated in Maurice's terms as a form of mediated 'magic trick', which Rogin notes 'allowed whites to turn black and back again'.[124] These racial shifts between Whiteness and 'Blackness' mirrored the way that *The Jazz Singer* vacillated between sound and silence, astounding audiences with these spectacular metamorphoses, which were made all the more potent by their intermittent reversals. It is telling that in his review of the Colour Launching Service, Reynolds identified such vacillations between old

dramatisation of their greatest anxieties about Black migration undermining the stability of White power, anxieties that would only be exacerbated by Powellist rhetoric a few years later. *Fable* therefore forms a crucial counterpoint to *The Black and White Minstrel Show*. If *Fable* imagined Black Britons occupying the position of White Britons, resulting in horror and fear among some BBC viewers at the prospect of Black sovereignty, then *The Black and White Minstrel Show* performed the operation in reverse, with White entertainers performing burlesques of Blackness to comically undermine and erode any claims to Black authority. While *Fable*'s inversion of the Black/White binary was intended to highlight the inequalities of the status quo, *The Black and White Minstrel Show* inverted this binary to reinforce and exacerbate these existing racial inequalities.

As Chude-Sokei describes, it is precisely this 'fear of *reversal*, of a sudden loss of power' that triggers a desire to restate and reformulate the boundaries that circumscribe White humanity that are so vividly hyperbolised by minstrelsy.[138] But, as Chude-Sokei notes, this fear is not simply instigated by political and social changes that suggest an erosion of White privilege, but crucially by new technological changes that also question the boundaries of White personhood and identity. It was not merely that colour television became a site where these anxieties were reflected; additionally and crucially, it participated in these fears about the erosion of White identity. Describing how 'this fear of reversal will attend each technological change and ultimately racialise it', Chude-Sokei presents a useful formulation for considering how the coincident emergence of colour television and these escalating White anxieties about Black sovereignty would result in *The Black and White Minstrel Show*. The show responded to the perceived double threat to White British identity presented first by the increasing visibility of Black British identity through Commonwealth migration and second by colour television and its potential distortions of Whiteness (Attenborough's 'chocolate blancmange', and the 'English Rose complexion' that it was 'not easy to maintain'). Colour television became the technology through which White British fears about the erosion of Whiteness, stoked by Powellist discourse, were technologised, visualised and, in the case of *The Black and White Minstrel Show*, supposedly ameliorated.

'Breakthrough for Colour'

The BBC's conversion to colour broadcasting was inseparable from the politics of race relations at this time. The corporation's chromatic conversion – occurring in the aftermath of the Smethwick by-election of 1964; overlapping with the emerging Black Power movement (which gained momentum from 1967) and the establishment and amendments to the Race Relations Act in 1965 and 1968; and coinciding with Powell's 'Rivers of Blood' speech in 1968 – made colour television a crucial place not only where questions of British racial identity were aired and displayed, but also where the dynamic relationship between notions of Black and White Britishness was formulated and contested through the visual vocabulary of colour. The new chromatic technology of colour television became a place where the plurality and diversity of racial identities that constituted Britishness in the 1960s were not celebrated but limited (by the technological demands of the contrast range) and rebuked (by the ideological framework of anti-Blackness that shaped the institutional culture of the BBC and its programmes).

However, the timing of the BBC's colour conversion had initially been dictated by the approaching Mexico Olympics of October 1968, which created an informal deadline for BBC2's technological trial period. The director general of the corporation, Sir Hugh Greene, was widely quoted in the press claiming that 'the Olympic Games might well be to colour television in this country what the Coronation was to black and white. After the Coronation the sale of TV sets surged ahead. The Olympic Games should provide the same breakthrough for colour.'[139] Greene promised that the Olympics, broadcast live and in colour, would 'give viewers some of the most exciting and compelling TV in the history of the BBC'.[140]

If the chromatism of colour television was inseparable from the chromatic discourse of race in the 1960s, then the Olympic Games presented a further compelling example of their imbrication. While Greene promised the Mexico Olympics would present a historical moment because of its chromatic broadcast, it is best remembered today for the political protest offered by Tommie Smith and John Carlos, the African American athletes who lowered their heads and raised their black gloved fists during the American national anthem at the medal ceremony for the two-hundred-metre event. The protest by Smith and Carlos, who were members of the Olympic Project for Human Rights, highlighted not just racial inequality in America but also the policies of Apartheid in South Africa and broader systemic biases that structured the organisation of the Olympics itself. Appearing shoeless in black socks, Smith and Carlos drew attention to the issue of poverty suffered by many African Americans, demonstrating the material and social consequences of the racism that structured American society but that resonated widely beyond the American civil rights movement.[141]

While Greene had compared the Games to the coronation of Elizabeth II as a catalyst for television sales, there were further comparisons to be drawn between these events as televised moments that cemented notions of British identity. The coronation, as discussed in the previous chapter, demonstrated Britain's attempt to project its importance in an incipient post-imperial world, reinforcing the primacy of the monarchy as the absolute epitome of White, British heritage at a time when the empire's dissolution placed its powers in question. The Olympic Games spoke to this context in a different way. The Black Power salute at the Mexico Games was a galvanising moment for many Black Britons, catalysing in some a heightened interest in political organisation, activism and protest, and for others a sense of recognition, belonging and pride.[142] As Rob Waters has traced in his history of televised Black Power in Britain, the 1968 Games regularly forms a pivotal moment in Black British recollections of television in this era, with a Jamaican man recalling how watching Smith and Carlos on television in London as a teenager 'changed my life'.[143] As Trevor Carter, a Trinidadian-born and London-based political activist recalled:

> When the black American athletes at the 1968 Mexico Olympics gave their Black Power salutes as they received their medals, thousands of black people in Britain, from our generation and our children's, felt we were on the map. People remember that occasion like they remember President Kennedy's assassination: a symbolic moment in our history.[144]

This chapter has largely explored how the BBC's conversion to colour cemented and exacerbated anti-Black racism, reinforced perceptions of Commonwealth migrants as distinct from and threatening to White Britons, and became a platform for the violent rhetoric of xenophobia that pervaded Britain's official political culture of the decade. However, in October 1968 it also became a place where resistance to, and protest against, such endemic practices could be made visible. While Greene promised the Olympics would 'give viewers some of the most exciting and compelling TV in the history of the BBC', it was not because the broadcast was in colour, as so few households at this time could have accessed the broadcast in this format. Instead, at a time when colour simultaneously implied chromatism and racial difference, the 'breakthrough for colour' that Greene suggested the Games could present was a moment when many Britons of colour felt television finally spoke to their personal experiences. This was 'a symbolic moment' in Black British history that did not demand a full spectrum of hues, and was perfectly legible in black and white.

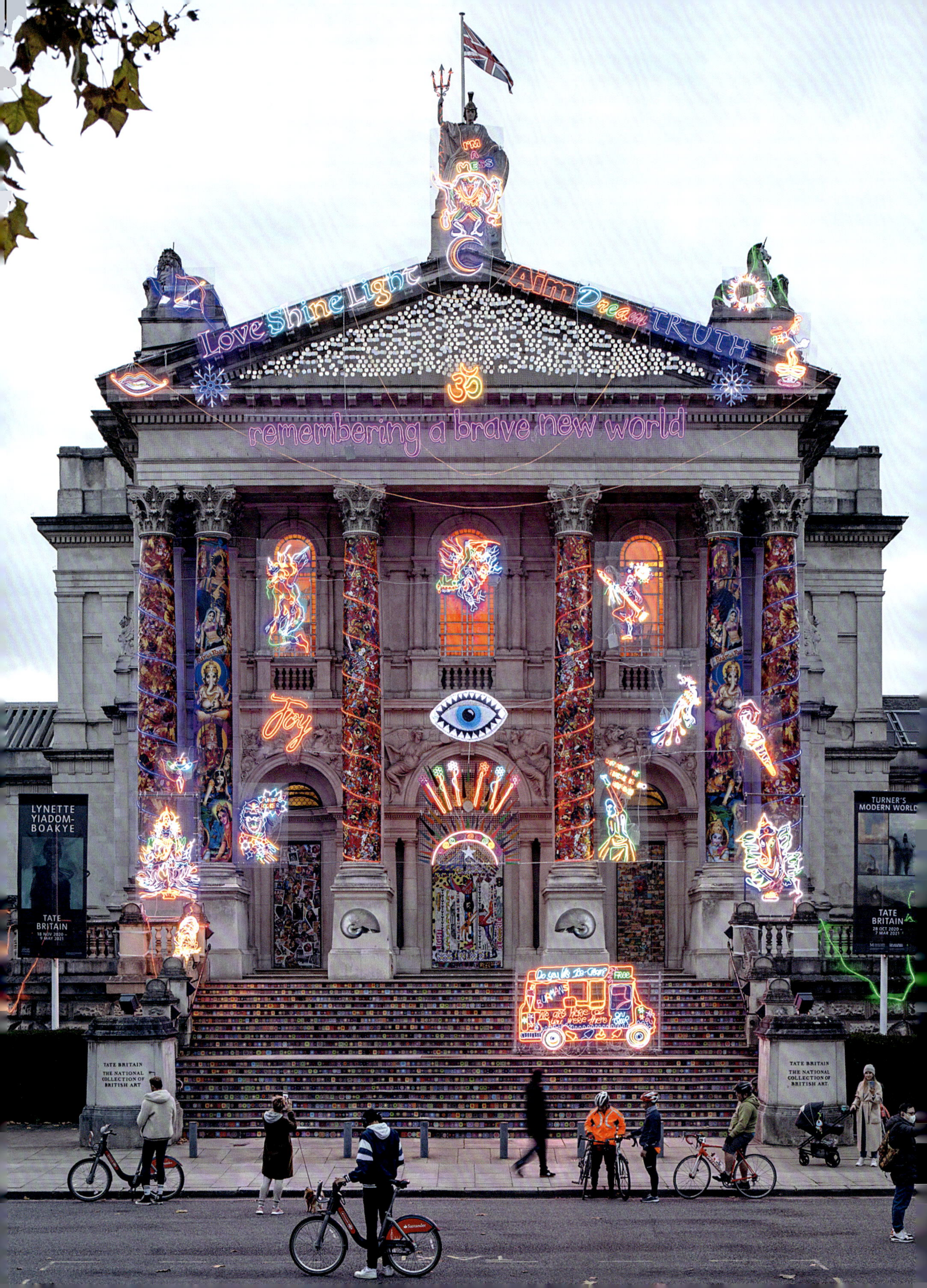

I'M A MESS
Love Shine Light
Aim Dream TRUTH
remembering a brave new world
Joy
LYNETTE YIADOM-BOAKYE
TATE BRITAIN
TURNER'S MODERN WORLD
TATE BRITAIN
TATE BRITAIN THE NATIONAL COLLECTION OF BRITISH ART
TATE BRITAIN THE NATIONAL COLLECTION OF BRITISH ART

Coda

NEON FUTURES

This book's history of modern British colour began with a rainbow – the glimmering arc from the 1942 film *This Is Colour* (dir. Jack Ellitt). This chromatic spectacle operated as a shining symbol of hope at a time of national crisis, radiating the promise of a bright future during the darkness of the Second World War. This will feel familiar to contemporary readers. Throughout the Covid-19 pandemic, rainbows became a ubiquitous part of our visual environment. They similarly sought to inspire a sense of optimism in our moment of crisis. Rainbows were plastered on shopfronts, posted in windows and painted on walls all over Britain.[1] These rainbows demonstrated that colour continues to articulate ideas of nationhood and belonging while also symbolising the anticipation of brighter times.

It is within this context that we can understand Chila Kumari Singh Burman's installation *Remembering a Brave New World* at Tate Britain in the winter of 2020–21 (fig. 118). For this installation, on view during England's second lockdown period, when visitors were unable to enter the museum, Burman decorated the façade of the building with radiant coloured lights. Strings of scarlet and cobalt LEDs twisted around the Corinthian columns, while the steps of the building seemed to pulse and effervesce with psychedelic decals showing starbursts and flowers in shades of puce, lemon, turquoise and apricot. Across the façade the swirling cursive of neon slogans radiated a tangerine and teal glow, proclaiming 'Love Shine Light' and 'Joy'. These words accompanied neon creatures in the form of a dazzling peacock and Bengal tiger, whose searingly brilliant lights beamed day and night. Given that the installation coincided with Diwali, the Hindu Festival of Light, Burman incorporated Hindu deities and religious symbols as part of her kaleidoscopic design. In addition to the vibrant Lakshmi (the goddess honoured by the Diwali festival) and Ganesh (the remover of obstacles), a lutescent glowing 'om' symbol stood proudly in the central pediment.

118 Chila Kumari Singh Burman, *Remembering a Brave New World* (2020), installation view.

During a time when Diwali celebrates the defeat of evil by goodness, Burman's work rejoiced in the eradication of darkness through the power of light. At a moment when many Britons were also posting rainbows in their windows to project colourful images of hope, Burman's work similarly looked out from the museum onto passers-by to project a message of optimism. Indeed, the work operated like a rainbow, refracting the whiteness of the building's façade into myriad iridescent hues of light. Like the rainbow from *This Is Colour* with which this book began, Burman's installation foregrounded colour as a property of light – an experiential, optical effect. As a work that generates its own illumination, whose very material basis is light itself, the installation calls attention to the indivisibility of light and colour. The work attests to light as a conduit for colour, not least when viewed at night. In darkness these fluorescent sculptures lit up their surrounding space, casting colour beyond the façade of the gallery and onto the street below, showering onlookers in neon hues to lift their spirits. Yet, like the rainbow from *This Is Colour*, Burman's luminescent vision of light and colour also has a gravity of both a material and a political nature. It additionally reveals how the defining characteristics of chromatic modernity examined in this book continue to colour contemporary British visual culture today.

The title of Burman's piece is embedded in the installation itself as a magenta neon banner that reads *Remembering a Brave New World*. Borrowed from the title of the futuristic novel by Aldous Huxley published in 1932, it inculcates a sense of courage and strength in the face of strange times. This seems particularly relevant to the current moment of the Covid-19 pandemic, when the plots of science fiction have become everyday fact. The title invites viewers to contemplate our 'new world' – referring to the unique conditions of the current pandemic, and more broadly the new British nation state of the early twenty-first century, freshly divorced from the European Union. Yet the addition of the word 'remembering' invites a kind of retrospection, an attention to how the contemporary is shaped not just by the very immediate conditions of the present but also by the historical conditions of the past.

Burman uses the materiality of colour as a way of expressing the dual temporality of the work. Colour articulates the novel sensation of immediacy, in which the world feels as though it is indeed being made anew. The fizzing hues of neon, a gas whose name derives from the Greek word for 'new' and which only glows with colour once charged with a current, evokes a powerful sense of a visceral, electric present.[2] Yet, as much as these neon sculptures feel contemporary and novel, neon itself was a chromatic innovation of Victorian chemical science. The substance was discovered in 1898 – only one year after the foundation of Tate Britain.[3] Like the museum itself, neon is the product of Victorian structures of knowledge and power, forging a link between Burman's installation and the nineteenth-century institution upon which it hung. Like the coal-tar dyes with which this book began, neon is a nineteenth-century chromatic innovation that continues to shape the chromatism of modern Britain. Burman's colours are both of the moment and of the past – a twenty-first-century sensory experience predicated on a Victorian chromatic technology. *Remembering a Brave New World* therefore draws together the beginning and end of the narrative constructed here. The installation illuminates how the defining characteristics of British chromatic modernisation analysed here – the legacies of British imperialism, colour's links to feminised labour, and colour's conflation with racial difference and Commonwealth migration – continue to operate as the defining paradigms of modern British colour today.

Like many of Burman's works, *Remembering a Brave New World* uses colour as a way of interrogating notions of British identity. As a self-identified 'Punjabi Liverpudlian' woman artist, Burman refuses singular or reductive descriptors of her work.[4] Her signature palette of fluorescent and glittery colours reflects her investment in the plural and heterogenous. Precisely because colour cannot be resolved into a singular experience (its appearance constantly alters, its names change and mutate, its cultural resonances shift across borders) it is an ideal tool for Burman to use to articulate the multivarious dimensions of her personhood. As a highly politicised material for Anglo-Indian relations in particular, colour offers an especially rich field through which to examine these aspects of her identity.

Burman was raised in Merseyside by parents who migrated to Britain in the 1950s. They were part of the generation of Commonwealth citizens whose arrival in Britain was conveyed by the media through a lexis of colour. Burman's personal biography is therefore entangled with the larger political narratives of colour and migration traced in the previous chapter. Burman has described how her love of colour evolved from an early age through her adoration of Bollywood cinema and the chromatic richness of Hindu iconography, the brilliant palette of girl

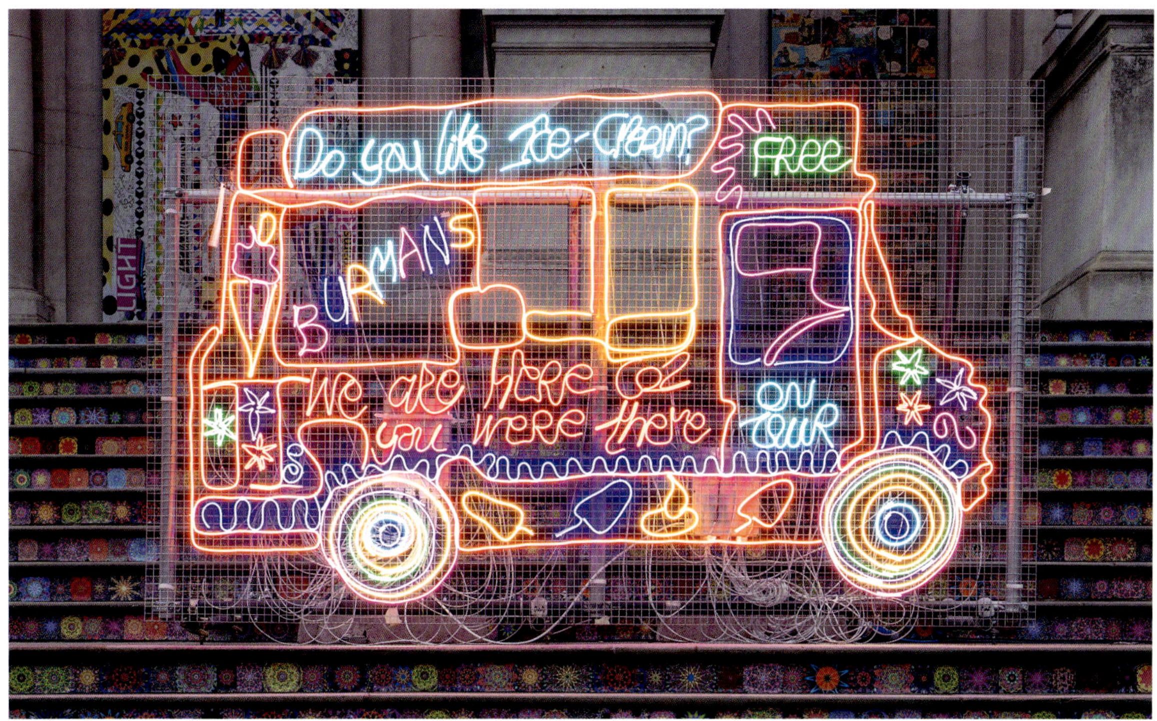

119 Chila Kumari Singh Burman, *Remembering a Brave New World* (2020), installation view (detail).

culture (what she calls 'bindis, bras, flowers, jewellery and makeup'), and her upbringing in Liverpool, where her father ran an ice-cream van, which she claims 'immersed' her from an early age 'in a world of colour, flavour and materials'.[5] Burman's colours are simultaneously Indian and English, popular and sacred, superficial and profoundly serious.

These polysemic dimensions of Burman's chromatism are richly evoked in *Remembering a Brave New World*, which began as a series of sketches that were later transformed into light sculptures by a neon fabricator. Burman has described how the fabricator's own personal experiences of migration and colonialism as a White South African from Durban helped her to realise her desired chromatism. In an interview Burman claimed the fabricator was 'familiar with Indian colours because Durban's the second biggest Indian place after India ... if it was an English person making them, it wouldn't have turned out the same'.[6] Through these neon lights Burman imaginatively recreates her father's ice-cream van as a chromatic confection, its candy colours invoking the sense of taste she links with her interest in colour as a material, as well as British seaside culture evoked through the parallels she has drawn between her installation and the Blackpool illuminations, unmistakable to anyone who grew up in the North West of England.

The ice-cream van is captured here with a warm orange neon outline (a colour we could call Fanta, Tango, Tizer or Irn-Bru), its wheels are like lollipops of concentric coloured circles, and its sides are decorated with squiggles in a Parma violet shade, next to alluringly rendered images of ice-cream cones and lollies (fig. 119). In addition to celebrating the sweetness of colour, the ice-cream van, through its links with her father's work as a Commonwealth migrant, also reveal Burman's investment in colour as a symbol of post-imperial British identity. Its flank brandishes a neon slogan in a coppery hue: 'We are here coz you were there'. These words are familiar from recent Black Lives Matter protests as well as the radical political movements of the 1980s, in which Burman was active.[7] As the slogan and Burman's installation make clear, it is impossible to understand the social and cultural dynamics of modern Britain without recognising the constitutive role colonial and imperial power played in its production. Burman powerfully realises this idea through her use of colour as an interventionist strategy. In Burman's words, she planned her neon installation to 'disrupt the Neoclassical façade' of the building, whose frontage problematically suggests a symbiosis between British national identity and Whiteness.[8] As a repository of British culture, Tate's architectural whiteness cannot be disarticulated from its racial implications. That colour is excluded from the face of this institution resonates on a profoundly symbolic level.

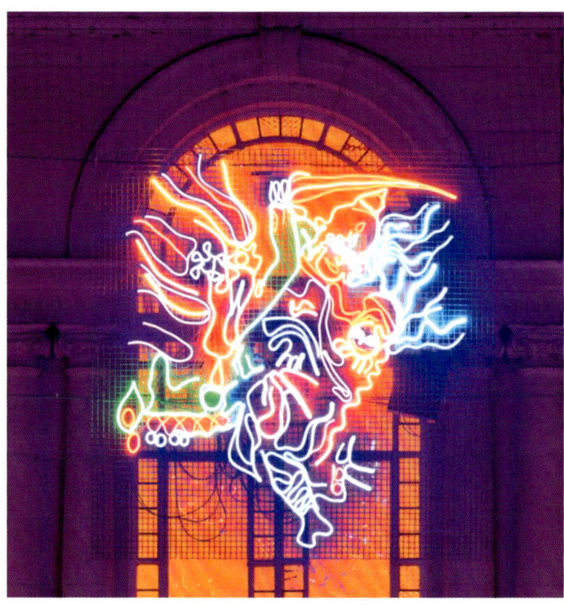

120 Chila Kumari Singh Burman, *Remembering a Brave New World* (2020), installation view (detail).

Given that the institution was founded on profits from the sugar trade, a white substance whose history is inseparable from the stolen labour of people of colour, the ideological implications of Tate's whiteness as a symbol of British civilisation cannot be overlooked.[9] By covering the building's white stone frontage with vivid neon lights, Burman forcefully asserted that British civilisation has never been purely white, either in aesthetic or racial terms. The coloured lights that swirled around the building's columns suggest the intertwined nature of Whiteness and colour as categories of British identity. Similarly, Burman's use of curling, jagged and striating flashes of colour that interrupt the linear geometry of the façade further unsettles the idea of British cultural history as rigidly arranged into a fixed order of Whiteness.

Her deployment of colourful sweets in particular invokes Tate's links with the sugar trade, returning colour to this supposedly white substance in the same manner that her colourful lights intervene in the expansive whiteness of the façade. This is reminiscent of Stuart Hall's claim that long before the 1950s, the so-called peripheries of empire were always present in Britain as 'the sugar at the bottom of the English cup of tea', making sugar a material connection between historical forms of colonial exploitation and subsequent patterns of Commonwealth migration.[10] The addition of the slogan 'We are here coz you were there' to her father's ice-cream van draws upon this long history entangling sugar, empire, migration and the labour of people of colour. Making sugar a colourful substance thereby transforms and revises this blanched cultural history of Britain, evoked by the whiteness of Tate, by restoring people of colour and their chromatic labour to this vision of the nation.

Burman uses colour to defamiliarise the appearance of the building in the same way her iconography destabilises conventional narratives of British history. Suspended high up in the centre of the portico is a vibrant neon image of the nineteenth-century warrior queen Jhansi Ki Rani, a character Burman has employed in previous works (fig. 120).[11] High above her head, the queen triumphantly brandishes a sword that glows amber like a flame, invoking her passionate military struggle against the forces of British colonialism. The rani stands here as a prominent symbol of

Indian political resistance, recalling India's first Technicolor film, whose importance was examined in Chapter Four and which also used Jhansi Ki Rani as a figure of chromatic and colonial defiance. Hanging at the epicentre of Tate Britain's façade, the rani's vivid presence brings oppositional histories into the heart of the establishment. Lakshmibai creates a physical and aesthetic intervention as she vigorously slices through this space to forcibly assert her presence. Her candescent appearance makes her an explosive symbol of the transformative power of colour to challenge and reconstitute images of British historical power.

Burman similarly uses overlaid neon lights to modify the central sculpture at the top of Tate's pediment and concomitantly its political symbolism. Through colour, Burman transforms Britannia, the classical personification of Britain itself (in the form of a White woman), into Kali, the Hindu goddess of creation and destruction (fig. 121). Burman alters this icon of White British political order into a riotous, pulsating nexus of colour, topped with the slogan 'I'm a Mess' to indicate the profound interconnection between the processes of fabrication and ruination that bind together Anglo-Indian history. Burman's transformation of Britannia into Kali is reminiscent of Madame Yevonde's interest in the power of colour to metamorphose women into goddesses, albeit in Yevonde's work through the application of lipstick, powder and nail polish (as discussed in Chapter Three). Yet Yevonde and Burman both exploit the surface effects of colour, and in particular its decorative feminised appeals, as political critiques. Burman routinely uses glitter, bindis, sparkling sequins and other kinds of coloured materials linked with feminine ornamentation in her work – like Yevonde, deploying them to challenge cultural norms of masculine artistic creativity. In many ways Burman's use of colour to decorate the white façade – or face – of Tate Britain echoes Yevonde's application of lipstick and rouge to the white classical sculptures she used as studio props. Burman described her neon installation as a way of 'defacing and refacing' the Tate, a process realised through the application of vibrant hues, like cosmetics, to the white face of the museum.[12]

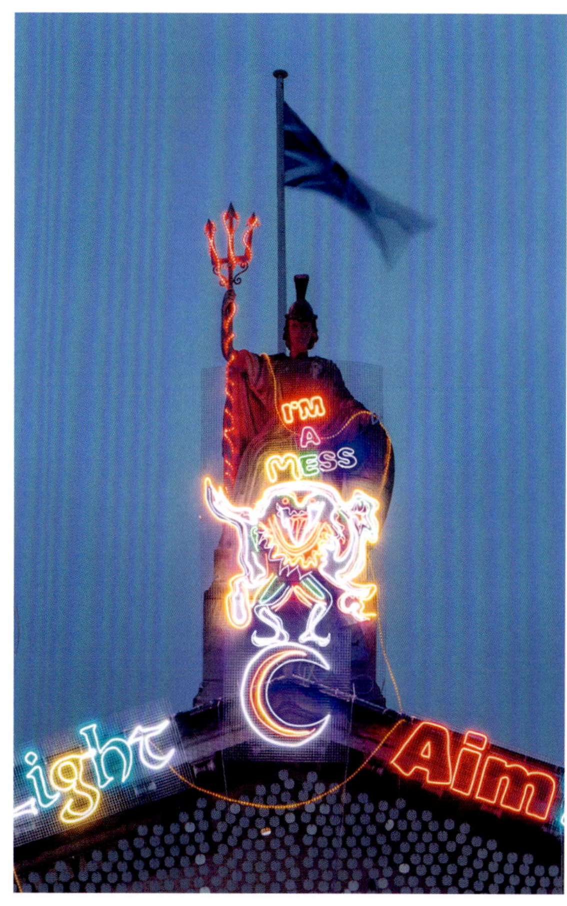

121 Chila Kumari Singh Burman, *Remembering a Brave New World* (2020), installation view (detail).

Tim Edensor and Uma Kothari have linked Burman's transformation of Britannia into Kali with the widespread protests against statues symbolising British colonial and imperial power during the Black Lives Matter activities that animated the United Kingdom in 2020.[13] They suggest that her neon intervention presents a different kind of oppositional act against these monuments, by revising rather than removing them. Indeed, I would describe what Burman presents here as a process of decolonising by re-colourising, transforming our understanding of British culture and history through the disruptive power of colour.[14]

Due to travel restrictions during the pandemic, I was, like many people, unable to see Burman's work in person. My experience of the piece was therefore mediated through selfies and photographs circulated on Instagram and other forms of social media (#rememberingabravenewworld). This digital consumption of the work aptly mirrored its digital production. These neon sculptures were initially designed by Burman on her iPad, before being translated into a new kind of silicon tubing (far more dynamic and fluid than traditional glass) and filled with electrified neon by her art fabricator.[15] The work is therefore very much part of the contemporary material networks of the digital. Silicon forges a material connection between the digital technology used to design the work (as this mineral is essential to the functionality of phones, tablets and computers) and operates as the physical housing for the neon gas, manipulated by the hands of the fabricator. Like the rainbow with which this book began, Burman's installation is both a radiant vision of coloured light and a physical object contingent on networks of labour and materials that make this vision possible.

That *Remembering a Brave New World* was made from and through silicon is reminiscent of the continued necessity of materialist approaches in our digital age, when a vocabulary of dematerialisation dominates examinations of contemporary visual culture.[16] Digital technology companies are routinely linked to mining in a metaphorical sense – criticised for extracting personal data from our production and consumption of images in the way other companies drill for oil or gas. Yet they are also reliant on the very real, material processes of mining minerals such as rock quartz and its silica content. Tablets, phones and computers cannot function without the heavy labour of extraction, the toxic production of waste and the massive consumption of fossil fuels.[17] Like most forms of environmental exhaustion and pollution, these processes have largely been the product of the Global North and disproportionately affected people of colour in the Global South.[18] The digital rainbow therefore has as much of a gravity as the painted, printed, photographed, filmed and broadcast colours examined here.

The Rainbow's Gravity began by asking what it would mean to narrate a history of modern Britain through a chromatic lens, wondering how colour could transform and trouble established historical narratives about modern Britain and the visual culture that helped to constitute it. Burman's installation at Tate Britain not only answers that question but also reveals its continued relevance for the culture of our present as much as our past. In a space dedicated to understanding British cultural history, her use of colour as an aesthetic and political interposition invites us to wonder how colour could operate as a method in itself, as a tool for subverting and revising established spaces and familiar histories.

As Burman's work reveals, and as this book has shown, to see the history of modern Britain as a history of modern colour demands recognition of several things. It means acknowledging the profound importance of colonialism and imperialism for the trajectories of British visual culture, not just in terms of subject matter and iconography but also in terms of seeing imperial dynamics as structuring devices for the material and technical processes through which these images are produced and reproduced. It means foregrounding the creative work of women and their chromatic practices, recognising that the superficial application of colour, routinely linked with femininity, is not trivial and merely cosmetic but perhaps *the* defining paradigm of modern colour itself. It means taking seriously the linguistic slippage between racial designation and optical hue whenever we talk about colour, and understanding that the material production of colour is inherently a process of materialising ideas about race, and often racism. It also means remaining vigilant to these interwoven histories of colour, gender, empire and racial difference, as they continue to construct and forge our contemporary visual environment in the twenty-first century.

Notes

Introduction

1 'Dye Index List', B5/F1, Andreas Collection, Technicolor Archives, George Eastman Museum, Rochester, NY (hereafter Technicolor Archives). On the production history of the film see Sarah Street, *Colour Films in Britain: The Negotiation of Innovation, 1900–1955* (London: Palgrave Macmillan on behalf of the British Film Institute, 2012), pp. 77–79.
2 This is a paraphrase of Sabine Doran's morbid pun of dyeing/dying, which she relates to Germany's wartime chemical industry in *The Culture of Yellow: Or, The Visual Politics of Late Modernity* (New York: Bloomsbury Academic, 2013), pp. 159–88. This book's title also puns on one of Doran's case studies, Thomas Pynchon's novel *Gravity's Rainbow* (New York: Viking Press, 1973), which takes the overlaps between colour, chemistry and warfare as one of its many themes.
3 Johann Wolfgang von Goethe, *Zur Farbenlehre* (Tübingen: in der J. G. Cotta'schen Buchhandlung, 1810); Ludwig Wittgenstein and G. E. M. Anscombe, *Remarks on Colour* (Berkeley: University of California Press, 1977); Jonathan Crary, *Techniques of the Observer: On Vision and Modernity in the Nineteenth Century* (Cambridge, MA: MIT Press, 1990).
4 Sarah Street and Joshua Yumibe, *Chromatic Modernity: Color, Cinema and the Media of the 1920s* (New York: Columbia University Press, 2018).
5 On France see Laura Anne Kalba, *Color in the Age of Impressionism: Commerce, Technology, and Art* (University Park: Pennsylvania State University Press, 2017); on Germany see Esther Leslie, *Synthetic Worlds: Nature, Art and the Chemical Industry* (London: Reaktion Books, 2005); on America see Nicholas Gaskill, *Chromographia: American Literature and the Modernization of Color* (Minneapolis: University of Minnesota Press, 2018); and for pan-Euro-American contexts see Regina Lee Blaszczyk, *The Color Revolution* (Cambridge, MA: MIT Press, 2012) as well as Street and Yumibe, *Chromatic Modernity*.
6 Geoff Quilley and Kay Dian Kriz, eds., *An Economy of Colour: Visual Culture and the Atlantic World, 1660–1830* (Manchester: Manchester University Press, 2003).
7 See Natasha Eaton, *Colour, Art and Empire: Visual Culture and the Nomadism of Representation* (London: I.B. Tauris, 2013); Anna Arabindan-Kesson, *Black Bodies, White Gold: Art, Cotton, and Commerce in the Atlantic World* (Durham, NC: Duke University Press, 2021); Mia L. Bagneris, *Colouring the Caribbean Race and the Art of Agostino Brunias* (Manchester: Manchester University Press, 2018).
8 Richard J. Powell, 'Colorstruck! Painting, Pigment, Affect' (A. W. Mellon Lectures, National Gallery of Art, Washington, DC, 20 March 2022).
9 See Anne Lafont, 'How Skin Color Became a Racial Marker: Art Historical Perspectives on Race', *Eighteenth Century Studies* 51, no. 1 (Fall 2017): 89–113; Mechthild Fend, *Fleshing Out Surfaces: Skin in French Art and Medicine, 1650–1850* (Manchester: Manchester University Press, 2017); Roxann Wheeler, *The Complexion of Race: Categories of Difference in Eighteenth-Century British Culture* (Philadelphia: University of Pennsylvania Press, 2010); David Bindman, *Ape to Apollo: Aesthetics and the Idea of Race in the 18th Century* (London: Reaktion Books, 2002); see also Stephanie O'Rourke and Susannah Blair, eds., 'Race: Representation in the French Colonial Empire', special issue, *Journal18* 13 (Spring 2022), https://www.journal18.org/category/issue13.
10 On the implications of this practice across the Americas, South Asia and West Africa see Arabindan-Kesson, *Black Bodies, White Gold*, pp. 67–120; Eaton, *Colour, Art and Empire*, pp. 21–36; Michael T. Taussig, *What Color Is the Sacred?* (Chicago: University of Chicago Press, 2009), pp. 131–37.
11 Arabindan-Kesson, *Black Bodies, White Gold*; Eaton, *Colour, Art and Empire*.
12 Therefore, throughout the book the terms 'British' and 'Britain' are used in an expansive and inclusive way, not referring solely to nations comprising Great Britain (namely England, Scotland and Wales).

13 In particular see Priya Jaikumar, *Cinema at the End of Empire: A Politics of Transition in Britain and India* (Durham, NC: Duke University Press, 2006), p. 14.
14 The term 'global British' is borrowed from an event staged by the Paul Mellon Centre for Studies in British Art: Isabelle Gapp, Matthew Dimmock, Sarah Piram and Robert Wilkes, 'Global British Art History: New Directions' (Online, 7 May 2021); the term neatly encapsulates the increasing attention scholars pay to the globalised and imperial dimensions of British visual culture, informed by the foundational theoretical and critical work of Paul Gilroy and Stuart Hall, and taken up increasingly by art historians since the publication of volumes such as Timothy Barringer, Geoff Quilley and Douglas Fordham, eds., *Art and the British Empire* (Manchester: Manchester University Press, 2007).
15 Most significantly Sarah Street's two volumes: *Colour Films in Britain: The Negotiation of Innovation*, and Sarah Street et al., *Colour Films in Britain: The Eastmancolor Revolution* (London: Palgrave Macmillan on behalf of the British Film Institute, 2021). The Victorian era in particular has generated significant scholarship on ideas of period colour, most recently Charlotte Ribeyrol, ed., *The Colours of the Past in Victorian England* (Oxford: Peter Lang, 2016).
16 Lynda Nead, *The Tiger in the Smoke: Art and Culture in Post-war Britain* (New Haven and London: Yale University Press for the Paul Mellon Centre for Studies in British Art, 2017), p. 133.
17 In particular Lisa Tickner, *Modern Life and Modern Subjects: British Art in the Early Twentieth Century* (New Haven: Yale University Press, 2000); David Peters Corbett, *The World in Paint: Modern Art and Visuality in England, 1848–1914* (University Park: Pennsylvania State University Press, 2004).
18 Jennifer Y. Chuong, 'Engraving's "Immoveable Veil": Phillis Wheatley's Portrait and the Politics of Technique', *Art Bulletin* 104, no. 2 (April 2022): 63–88.
19 Scottish scientist David Brewster invented the kaleidoscope in 1816.
20 See Pliny, *Natural History*, trans. H. Rackham (Cambridge, MA: Harvard University Press, 1952), vol. IX, bk. 35, 283–99. See also for instance Michael Baxandall, *Painting and Experience in Fifteenth-Century Italy* (Oxford: Oxford University Press, 1972); John Gage, *Color and Meaning: Art, Science, and Symbolism* (Berkeley: University of California Press, 1999); and Michael Pastoureau's many volumes on colour, including *Blue: The History of a Color* (Princeton: Princeton University Press, 2001).
21 For surveys of this disciplinary turn see Martha Rosler et al., 'Notes from the Field: Materiality', *Art Bulletin* 95, no. 1 (2013): 10–37; Jennifer L. Roberts, 'Things: Material Turn, Transnational Turn', *American Art* 31, no. 2 (June 2017): 64–69.
22 In particular see Alfred Gell, *Art and Agency: An Anthropological Theory* (Oxford: Clarendon Press, 1998); Tim Ingold, *Making: Anthropology, Archaeology, Art and Architecture* (London: Routledge, 2013); Jane Bennett, *Vibrant Matter: A Political Ecology of Things* (Durham, NC: Duke University Press, 2010); and Bruno Latour, *Reassembling the Social: An Introduction to Actor-Network-Theory* (Oxford: Oxford University Press, 2005).
23 In particular Pamela H. Smith, Anne Dunlop and Christy Anderson, eds., *The Matter of Art: Materials, Technologies, Meanings 1200–1700* (Manchester: Manchester University Press, 2014); Ann-Sophie Lehmann, ed., *Meaning in Materials, 1400–1800* (Leiden: Brill, 2013); Jennifer L. Roberts, *Transporting Visions: The Movement of Images in Early America* (Berkeley: University of California Press, 2014).
24 On 'affordances' see Ann-Sophie Lehmann, 'The Matter of the Medium: Some Tools for an Art Theoretical Interpretation of Materials', in *The Matter of Art: Materials, Technologies, Meanings 1200–1700*, ed. Christy Anderson, Anne Dunlop and Pamela H. Smith (Manchester: Manchester University Press, 2014), pp. 6–27.
25 Lehmann, *Meaning in Materials*, p. 7.
26 An exemplary volume is Andrea Feeser, Maureen Daly Goggin and Beth Fowkes Tobin, eds., *The Materiality of Color: The Production, Circulation, and Application of Dyes and Pigments, 1400–1800* (Burlington, VT: Ashgate, 2012).
27 In addition to Feeser et al., *The Materiality of Color*, see for instance Ad Stijnman and Elizabeth Savage, eds., *Printing Colour 1400–1700: History, Techniques, Functions and Receptions* (Leiden: Brill, 2015); Sarah Lowengard, *The Creation of Colour in Eighteenth-Century Europe* (New York: Columbia University Press, 2008).
28 For instance, Regina Lee Blaszczyk and Uwe Spiekermann argue that 1856 signalled 'an end to the traditional belief that colors imparted specific physical and emotional properties'. See 'Bright Modernity: Color, Commerce, and Consumer Culture', in *Bright Modernity: Color, Commerce, and Consumer Culture*, ed. Regina Lee Blaszczyk and Uwe Spiekermann (New York: Palgrave Macmillan, 2017), p. 10.
29 Priya Jaikumar and Lee Grieveson's research network On Extraction and Media (launched in 2021) exemplifies the currency of this new development in the field, as do the (eagerly anticipated) in-progress books by Alice Lovejoy (*Tales of Militant Chemistry: Film and Its Raw Materials*), Pansy Duncan (*A Natural History of Film Form*), Elena Past (*Ferrania #FilmIsAlive: Lives of Analog Filmstock in the Anthropocene*), Siobhan Angus (*Camera Geologica: Temporality, Memory, and Materiality in Mining Landscapes*) and Monica Bravo (*Silver Pacific: A Material History of Photography and its Minerals, 1840–1890*). Tobah Aukland-Pecks' ongoing PhD research into extractive mining and British art signals a shared interest in histories of extraction across film and art history.
30 However, a discussion of these issues featured in Kirsty Sinclair

Dootson, 'What Colour Is the Anthropocene?' (symposium paper, Deanthrocentric Materialism and the Politics of Matter, Institut National d'Histoire de l'Art, Paris, 19 March 2021, https://www.youtube.com/watch?v=koR8mRTDRYA).

31 In particular see Joshua Yumibe, *Moving Color: Early Film, Mass Culture, Modernism* (New Brunswick, NJ: Rutgers University Press, 2012); Bettina Gockel, ed., *The Colors of Photography* (Berlin: De Gruyter, 2020); Susan Murray, *Bright Signals: A History of Color Television* (Durham, NC: Duke University Press, 2018).

32 David Scott Kastan with Stephen Farthing, *On Color* (New Haven: Yale University Press, 2018), p. 13.

33 See Edward Branigan, *Tracking Color in Cinema and Art: Philosophy and Aesthetics* (New York: Routledge, 2018); Michael Rossi, *The Republic of Color: Science, Perception, and the Making of Modern America* (Chicago: University of Chicago Press, 2019).

34 For example, Rey Conquer, *Reading Colour: George, Rilke, Kandinsky, Lasker-Schüler* (Oxford: Peter Lang, 2019); Gaskill, *Chromographia*.

35 Ludwig Wittgenstein, *Culture and Value*, ed. G. H. von Wright, trans. Peter Winch (Chicago: University of Chicago Press, 1980), p. 66. Gaskill's *Chromographia* brilliantly thinks together these physical and metaphysical approaches.

36 See for instance Sean Cubitt, *Finite Media: Environmental Implications of Digital Technologies* (Durham, NC: Duke University Press, 2017); Hye Jean Chung, *Media Heterotopias: Digital Effects and Material Labor in Global Film Production* (Durham, NC: Duke University Press, 2018).

37 John Gage, *Colour and Culture: Practice and Meaning from Antiquity to Abstraction* (London: Thames & Hudson, 1993).

38 See Eaton, *Colour, Art and Empire*.

39 The narrator disregards that this 'discovery' was contingent on decades of experiments by German scientists, perhaps understandably given the wartime context. On Germany's role see Leslie, *Synthetic Worlds*, pp. 76–78.

40 Mauve was not the first synthetic colour but the first synthetic, organic dyestuff to be manufactured on an industrial scale. On important precursors see Lowengard, *The Creation of Colour in Eighteenth-Century Europe*.

41 *Mauve* was the French term for the mallow flower and had been an established fashion shade for at least a decade by the time Perkin discovered his dye.

42 See Dominique Cardon, 'Fashion in Colors and Natural Dyes: History under Tension', in *Fashion in Colors*, ed. Akiko Fukai (New York: Assouline, 2004), p. 230.

43 Satirised in 'The Mauve Measles', *Punch*, 20 August 1859, p. 81. See also Alison Matthews David, *Fashion Victims: The Dangers of Dress Past and Present* (London: Bloomsbury, 2015), pp. 107–13.

44 Street considers the film's narrational address in her analysis in *Colour Films in Britain: The Negotiation of Innovation*, pp. 77–79.

45 Explored at length in Jacqueline Lichtenstein, *The Eloquence of Color: Rhetoric and Painting in the French Classical Age* (Berkeley: University of California Press, 1993); Rosalind Galt, *Pretty: Film and the Decorative Image* (New York: Columbia University Press, 2011).

46 On colour and prettiness see Galt, *Pretty*, pp. 40–49.

47 On the context of Perkin's discovery see Blaszczyk, *The Color Revolution*, pp. 24–28.

48 Carolyn L. Kane, *Chromatic Algorithms: Synthetic Color, Computer Art, and Aesthetics after Code* (Chicago: University of Chicago Press, 2014); Lida Zeitlin Wu, 'Seeing by Numbers: Color Systems and the Digitization of Perception' (PhD diss., University of California, Berkeley, 2022).

49 Nead, *The Tiger in the Smoke*, pp. 151–98.

50 Powell, 'Colorstruck!'.

51 Nicholas Gaskill, 'Fugitive Colors' (conference paper, Toward a History of Modern Colour, University of Cambridge, 9 June 2021).

52 Vron Ware and Les Back, *Out of Whiteness: Color, Politics, and Culture* (Chicago: University of Chicago Press, 2002), p. 6.

53 See Anne Anlin Cheng, *Ornamentalism* (New York: Oxford University Press, 2021) and *Second Skin: Josephine Baker and the Modern Surface* (New York: Oxford University Press, 2013).

54 'Explaining AP Style on Black and white', *Associated Press News*, 20 July 2020, https://apnews.com/article/archive-race-and-ethnicity-9105661462; 'Black and White: A Matter of Capitalization', *CMOS Shop Talk*, 20 June 2020, http://cmosshoptalk.com/2020/06/22/black-and-white-a-matter-of-capitalization; Kwame Anthony Appiah, 'The Case for Capitalizing the "B" in Black', *The Atlantic*, 18 June 2020, https://www.theatlantic.com/ideas/archive/2020/06/time-to-capitalize-blackand-white/613159.

55 See for instance Nancy Coleman, 'Why We're Capitalizing Black', *New York Times*, 5 July 2020, https://www.nytimes.com/2020/07/05/insider/capitalized-black.html. As Nell Irvin Painter notes, the National Association for Black Journalists in the United States 'recommends that whenever a color is used to appropriately describe race then it should be capitalized, including White and Brown': 'NABJ Statement on Capitalizing Black and Other Racial Identifiers', *NABJ Style Guide*, June 2020, https://www.nabj.org/page/styleguide. See also Nell Irvin Painter, 'Why "White" Should Be Capitalized, Too', *Washington Post*, 22 July 2020, https://www.washingtonpost.com/opinions/2020/07/22/why-white-should-be-capitalized.

56 A view articulated by Minna Salami in 'Why I Don't Believe the Word "Black" Should Always Have a Capital "B"', *The Guardian*, 3 June

2021, https://www.theguardian.com/commentisfree/2021/jun/03/word-black-capital-letter-blackness.

57 Thanks to the anonymous peer reviewers of the manuscript for signalling the importance of such clarifications.

58 Painter, 'Why "White" Should Be Capitalized, Too'; Eve L. Ewing, 'I'm a Black Scholar Who Studies Race. Here's Why I Capitalize "White"', *Zora*, 2 July 2020, https://zora.medium.com/im-a-black-scholar-who-studies-race-here-s-why-i-capitalize-white-f94883aa2dd3; Richard Dyer, *White* (London, Routledge, 1997); bell hooks, 'Representations of Whiteness', in *Black Looks: Race and Representation* (Boston, MA: South End Press), pp. 165–78; Ware and Back, *Out of Whiteness*.

59 In particular see Kathryn T. Gines, 'Introduction: Critical Philosophy of Race beyond the Black/White Binary', *Critical Philosophy of Race* 1, no. 1 (2013): 28–37.

60 In particular José Esteban Muñoz, *The Sense of Brown*, ed. Joshua Chambers-Letson and Tavia Nyong'o (Durham, NC: Duke University Press, 2020); Cheng, *Ornamentalism*.

61 Lafont, 'How Skin Color Became a Racial Marker', p. 90.

62 Xin Peng highlights the fallacy of such claims with particular regard to identifying supposedly 'East Asian' or 'Chinese' skin tones in 'Colour-as-Hue and Colour-as-Race: Early Technicolor, Ornamentalism and *The Toll of the Sea* (1922)', *Screen* 62, no. 3 (September 2021): 287–308.

63 Alice Maurice, *The Cinema and Its Shadow: Race and Technology in Early Cinema* (Minneapolis: University of Minnesota Press, 2013). For a broader overview of these confederated histories of racialised bodies and new technologies see Louis Chude-Sokei, 'Race and Technology: A Creole History', in 'Creolized Technologies', special issue, *Technosphere Magazine*, April 2017, https://technosphere-magazine.hkw.de/p/Race-and-Technology-A-Creole-History-fTkwqWGX4M24K2MixKVrUk.

64 Lichtenstein, *The Eloquence of Color*, p. 167.

65 See David Bindman, 'The Black Presence in British Art: Sixteenth and Seventeenth Centuries', in *The Image of the Black in Western Art*, vol. 3, *From the 'Age of Discovery' to the Age of Abolition*, ed. David Bindman and Henry Louis Gates Jr (Cambridge, MA: Belknap Press of Harvard University Press, 2010), pp. 235–70; Paul H. D. Kaplan, 'Titian's "Laura Dianti" and the Origins of the Motif of the Black Page in Portraiture', *Antichità Viva* 21, no. 1 (1982): 11–18 and 21, no. 4 (1982): 10–18.

66 David Batchelor, *Chromophobia* (London: Reaktion Books, 2000).

67 Kara Keeling, *Queer Times, Black Futures* (New York: Columbia University Press, 2019), p. 118. See also in particular Dyer, *White*; Roth, 'Looking at Shirley, the Ultimate Norm: Colour Balance, Image Technologies, and Cognitive Equity', *Canadian Journal of Communication* 34, no. 1 (March 2009): 111–36; Tanya Sheehan, 'Colour Matters: Rethinking Photography and Race', in *The Colors of Photography*, ed. Bettina Gockel (Berlin: De Gruyter, 2020), pp. 55–72; and Genevieve Yue, *Girl Head: Feminism and Film Materiality* (New York: Fordham University Press, 2020), especially pp. 33–62.

1 The Texture of Capitalism

1 Suggested by James Hamilton in *Turner and the Scientists* (London: Tate, 1998), p. 51. On Newman see Jacob Simon et al., 'British Artists' Suppliers, 1650–1950 – N', *National Portrait Gallery*, 2013, https://www.npg.org.uk/research/programmes/directory-of-suppliers/n.

2 The gendered term 'colourmen' is intentional here as the industry was dominated by men, although there is evidence of women participating in the colour trade at this time. See Simon et al., 'British Artists' Suppliers, 1650–1950'.

3 Detailed in Arthur Church, *The Chemistry of Paints and Painting* (London: Seeley, 1890).

4 Leslie Carlyle notes that this growth was artificially inflated by some colours being sold under many names. See *The Artist's Assistant: Oil Painting Instruction Manuals and Handbooks in Britain 1800–1900 with Reference to Selected Eighteenth-Century Sources* (London: Archetype, 2001), p. 159.

5 Quoted in Jean Renoir, *Renoir My Father* (London: William Collins, 1962), p. 73.

6 On how Impressionist colour became synonymous with 'modern' colour see Laura Anne Kalba, *Color in the Age of Impressionism: Commerce, Technology, and Art* (University Park: Pennsylvania State University Press, 2017).

7 Summarised in David Bomford, 'The History of Colour in Art', in *Colour: Art & Science*, ed. Trevor Lamb and Janine Bourriau (Cambridge: Cambridge University Press, 1995), p. 23. Anthea Callen's work remains a crucial exception. See *The Art of Impressionism: Painting Technique & the Making of Modernity* (New Haven: Yale University Press, 2000), pp. 98–111.

8 On the work's material production see Rebecca Hellen and Elaine Kilmurray, '*Carnation, Lily, Lily, Rose* and the Process of Painting', *British Art Studies* 2 (April 2016), https://doi.org/10.17658/issn.2058-5462/issue-02/rhellen-ekilmurray.

9 Ibid.

10 Most recently in Elizabeth Prettejohn, *Modern Painters, Old Masters: The Art of Imitation from the Pre-Raphaelites to the First World War* (New Haven: Yale University Press, 2017); Tim Barringer, Jason Rosenfeld and Alison Smith, eds., *Pre-Raphaelites: Victorian Avant Garde* (London: Tate, 2012).

11 Carol Jacobi, *William Holman Hunt: Painter, Painting, Paint* (Manchester: Manchester University Press, 2006).

12 David Peters Corbett, *The World in Paint: Modern Art and Visuality in England, 1848–1914* (University Park: Pennsylvania State University Press, 2004), pp. 1–14.

13 On the nickname see Chloë Ward, 'England's Michelangelo in the Metropolitan Museum of Art: The G. F. Watts Exhibition, 1884–1885', *Comparative American Studies* 14, no. 1 (January 2016): 64.

14 Winsor & Newton described its machine-ground paints as 'buttery' in correspondence with Watts. This correspondence is reproduced as an unpaginated appendix in Carol Willoughby, 'The Search for Permanence: The Materials and Methods of G. F. Watts' (MA thesis, Courtauld Institute of Art, 1983). All subsequent references to letters, unless otherwise stated, refer to that appendix. Watts's letters are also held across the archives of the National Portrait Gallery and the Watts Gallery.

15 Callen explores this surface texture in detail in *The Work of Art: Plein Air Painting and Artistic Identity in Nineteenth-Century France* (London: Reaktion Books, 2015), p. 117.

16 Leighton to Professor Arthur Church, 16 October 1894, cited in Mrs Russell Barrington, *The Life, Letters and Work of Frederic Leighton*, vol. 3 (London: G. Allen, 1906), p. 297.

17 Discussed in Church, *The Chemistry of Paints and Painting*, pp. 44–46.

18 On this widespread practice see Joyce Townsend et al., 'Later Nineteenth Century Pigments: Evidence for Additions and Substitutions', *Conservator* 19, no. 1 (September 1995): 65–78.

19 Jasmine Nichole Cobb's important work on the 'texture of racial capitalism' offers another rich assessment of the confederation of haptics and politics in relation to a different sphere from that discussed here: Afro-textured hair. See 'Tactility and the Texture of Racial Capitalism' (lecture, John Hope Franklin Humanities Institute, Durham, NC, 25 September 2020, https://youtu.be/cDkAOYt_ADg).

20 As Stephen Hackney, Joyce Townsend and Jacqueline Ridge note, restoration undertaken on these works in the 1840s altered perceptions of their colour, exaggerating the difference between these cleaned paintings and the dark works of the eighteenth century. See 'Background, Training and Influences', in *Pre-Raphaelite Painting Techniques*, ed. Joyce Townsend, Jacqueline Ridge and Stephen Hackney (London: Tate, 2004), pp. 21–25.

21 The volume by Charles Eastlake, Keeper of the National Gallery, was especially influential. See *Materials for a History of Oil Painting* (London: Longman, Brown, Green and Longmans, 1847). Prettejohn explores Van Eyck's importance for Victorian practice at length in *Modern Painters, Old Masters*, pp. 68–86.

22 Joyce Townsend, 'Painting Techniques and Materials of Turner and Other British Artists 1775–1875', in *Historical Painting Techniques, Materials, and Studio Practice: Preprints of a Symposium*, ed. Arie Wallert, Erma Hermens and Marja Peek (Marina Del Rey, CA: Getty Conservation Institute, 1995), pp. 176–86.

23 See Anne Southall, 'Some Materials and Practices in British Painting, 1750–1850', in *The Articulate Surface: Dialogues on Paintings between Conservators, Curators and Art Historians*, ed. Sue-Anne Wallace, Jacqueline Macnaughtan and Jodi Parvey (Canberra: National Gallery of Australia, 1996), pp. 117–36.

24 On attempts by British artists to discern the 'secrets' of Titian's colour, see J. B. Bullen, 'Whoring after Colour: Venetian Painting in England', in *Continental Crosscurrents: British Criticism and European Art 1810–1910* (Oxford: Oxford University Press, 2005), pp. 120–43.

25 See John Gage, *Colour in Turner: Poetry and Truth* (New York: Praeger, 1969).

26 Boasts about the technology's benefits are found in *Winsor & Newton's Catalogue of Colours and Materials for Oil Colour Painting* (London: Winsor & Newton, 1884), p. 61. The technology was already in use in France by this time.

27 'Roberson Retail Catalogue', c.1907, HKI.MS.867–1993, Roberson Archive, Hamilton Kerr Institute, Cambridge.

28 See Don Pavey and Peter J. Staples, eds., *The Artists' Colourmen's Story* (Wealdstone: Reckitt & Colman Leisure, 1984), pp. 18–19.

29 Conservators have found much evidence of such additions. See Leslie Carlyle, 'Authenticity and Adulteration: What Materials Were 19th Century Artists Really Using?' *Conservator* 17, no. 1 (January 1993): 56–60.

30 Advocated in Church, *The Chemistry of Paints and Painting*, p. 46.

31 Jehan George Vibert, *The Science of Painting*, trans. Percy Young (London: Percy Young, 1892), pp. 74–75.

32 Ibid., p. 75.

33 John Scott Taylor, *Modes of Painting Described and Classified* (London: Winsor & Newton, 1890), p. 40.

34 On Field's reputation see John Gage, *George Field and His Circle: From Romanticism to the Pre-Raphaelite Brotherhood* (London: Christie's, 1989).

35 Discussed in Carlyle, 'Authenticity and Adulteration', p. 57.

36 'Inorganic' and 'synthetic' are not synonymous. Broadly speaking, organic pigments derive from living substances (plants, animals, insects etc.) and inorganic pigments from minerals and metals. In the nineteenth century, it became possible to chemically synthesise both.

37 See Sarah Lowengard, *The Creation of Colour in Eighteenth-Century Europe* (New York: Columbia University Press, 2008).

38 By the 1880s several colourmen, including Reeves & Son and Winsor & Newton, listed colours as derived from aniline in their catalogues.

39 William Muckley, *A Handbook for Painters and Art Students on the Character and Use of Colour* (London: Bailliere, Tindall and Cox, 1893), p. 124.

40 Church, *The Chemistry of Paints and Painting*, p. 276.

41 As patent disputes between dye-makers in the 1860s demonstrate, it was hard to tell how a colour was made by its appearance. See A. S. Travis, *The Rainbow Makers: The Origins of the Synthetic Dyestuffs Industry in Western Europe* (Bethlehem: Lehigh University Press; London: Associated University Presses, 1993), pp. 104–38.

42 *A Practical Treatise on Landscape Painting in Oil Colours* (London: B. and J. White, 1795), p. 26.

43 On the relationship between labour and style in this period see T. J. Barringer, *Men at Work: Art and Labour in Victorian Britain* (New Haven: Yale University Press, 2005). On the link between Hunt's faith and his material practice see Jacobi, *William Holman Hunt*.

44 Hunt described the chronology of these problems in a letter to Roberson dated 19 November 1875 (reproduced in Carlyle, *The Artist's Assistant*, pp. 461–62) and discussed them in William Holman Hunt, 'The Present System of Obtaining Materials in Use by Artist Painters, as Compared with that of the Old Masters', *Journal of the Society of Arts* 28, no. 1431 (1880): 491–92.

45 Hunt, 'The Present System', p. 495.

46 Ibid.

47 Shalini Le Gall, 'Evangelical Imperialism: Holman Hunt and Religious Painting in the Middle East' (PhD diss., Northwestern University, 2009), p. 214.

48 Hunt to F. G. Stephens, 11 December 1876, Hunt Papers, Bodleian Library, Oxford, reproduced in Leslie Irwin, 'The Painting Materials and Technique of W. Holman Hunt' (MA diss., Courtauld Institute of Art, 1977); Hunt to John Lucas Tupper, 11 August 1875, reproduced in James H. Coombs, ed., *A Pre-Raphaelite Friendship: The Correspondence of William Holman Hunt and John Lucas Tupper* (Ann Arbor, MI: UMI Research Press, 1986), p. 200.

49 Hunt, 'The Present System', p. 495; 'old leather' comes from Hunt to Tupper, 11 August 1875.

50 The title also refers to the refrain of a popular song titled 'The Wreath'.

51 Hunt to Stephens, 11 December 1876. Jacobi discusses Hunt's conflations of moral, aesthetic and material concerns at length in *William Holman Hunt*.

52 Hunt to Roberson, 19 November 1875.

53 Hunt to Stephens, 11 December 1876.

54 Hunt, 'The Present System', p. 495.

55 Hunt to Tupper, 11 August 1875.

56 Hunt to Stephens, 27 September 1875. Hunt Papers, Bodleian Library, Oxford, cited in Melissa R. Katz, 'Holman Hunt on Himself: Textual Evidence in Aid of Technical Analysis', in *Looking through Paintings: The Study of Painting Techniques and Materials in Support of Art Historical Research*, ed. Erma Hermens (Baarn: Uitgeverij de Prom, 1998), p. 437.

57 Hunt, 'The Present System', p. 495.

58 Ibid., p. 498. Hunt's letters to *The Times* were published on 28 April, 4 May and 2 June 1880.

59 Hunt, 'The Present System', p. 495.

60 Ibid.

61 Jacobi, *William Holman Hunt*. See also Charlotte Ribeyrol and Philippe Walter, '"A Magic Web with Colours Gay": W. H. Hunt's Chromatic Nostalgia', in *The Colours of the Past in Victorian England*, ed. Charlotte Ribeyrol (Oxford: Peter Lang, 2016), pp. 20–39.

62 'Rocky' comes from Roger Fry, 'Watts and Whistler', *Quarterly Review* 202 (1905): 607–23; 'heavily forged' and 'corrugated' from Rose Esther Dorothea Sketchley, *Watts* (London: Methuen, 1904), p. 178.

63 'Extra', *Pall Mall Gazette*, 1886, reprinted in Jacqueline Ridge and Joyce Townsend, 'G. F. Watts in Context: His Choice of Materials and Techniques', in *Painting Techniques: History, Materials and Studio Practice; Contributions to the Dublin Congress, 7–11 September 1998*, ed. Ashok Roy and Perry Smith (London: International Institute for Conservation of Historic and Artistic Works, 1998), pp. 223–28.

64 George Moore, *Modern Painting* (London: W. Scott, 1893), p. 113.

65 Readers can find enlarged details of the texture of Watts's paintings in Kirsty Sinclair Dootson, 'The Texture of Capitalism: Industrial Oil Colours and the Politics of Paint in the Work of G. F. Watts', *British Art Studies* 14 (2019), https://doi.org/10.17658/issn.2058-5462/issue-14/kdootson.

66 Mary Seaton Watts, *George Frederic Watts*, 3 vols (London: Macmillan, 1912), 3:56–79.

67 Ibid., 1:6–36.

68 In addition to Eastlake's volume (*Materials for a History of Oil Painting*), among the most significant was Mary Merrified's translation of Cennino Cennini's fifteenth-century handbook *Il libro dell'arte: A Treatise on Painting* (London: E. Lumley, 1844). Watts owned a copy of Cennini and amassed a collection of technical information, including traditional recipes for paints and vehicles.

69 She translated for Watts Marco Boschini's famous account of Titian's technique from 1674, *Le ricche minere della pittura veneziana*. See Mrs Russell Barrington, *G. F. Watts: Reminiscences* (London: Macmillan and G. Allen, 1905), p. 98.

70 On these parallels see Mrs Russel Barrington, *Catalogue of Paintings, by G. F. Watts, R. A., of London, on Exhibition at the Metropolitan Museum of Art, New York* (New York: Metropolitan Museum of Art, 1884), pp. 8–9.

71 Willoughby, 'The Search for Permanence', pp. 75–77.

72 Tate conservator Jacqueline Ridge contextualises Watts's working method within the painter's historicising lifestyle, from his nickname ('signor') to his sartorial habits of adopting Renaissance dress. See 'G. F. Watts: *Sic Transit*', in *Paint and Purpose: A Study of Technique in British Art*, ed. Joyce Townsend, Stephen Hackney and Rica Jones (London: Tate, 1999), p. 90.

73 Most recently, Nicholas Tromans, *The Art of G. F. Watts* (London: Paul Holberton, 2017), p. 64.

74 On Watts's frescoes see Watts, *George Frederic Watts*, 1:52; 2:188–89.

75 Watts to Scott Taylor, 28 November 1893. Emphasis in original.

76 Scott Taylor to Watts, 14 June 1901.
77 Watts to Winsor & Newton, 6 July 1871 and 5 August 1878.
78 Watts to Scott Taylor, 16 June 1901. Emphasis in original.
79 Newton to Watts, 21 August 1878.
80 The firm later marketed these paints for sale at three times the price of its regular colours, selling them in specially designed wide-mouth tubes. Advertisements for these paints appeared in the 1901 Winsor & Newton retail catalogue.
81 The description of the mill comes from Scott Taylor to Watts, 26 July 1898; that of industrial grinding from Scott Taylor to Watts, 10 June 1901.
82 Watts to Scott Taylor, 17 October 1901.
83 Barrington, *G. F. Watts*, p. 66; Watts to Scott Taylor, 29 October 1898.
84 Barrington, *G. F. Watts*, p. 66.
85 Watts to Scott Taylor, 9 November 1900.
86 On the spiritual connotations of this work see Matthew Potter, 'Materialism and the Mark of Modernity in the Work of G. F. Watts', *British Art Journal* 7, no. 3 (Winter 2006): 70–78.
87 On Watts's sculptural practice see Veronica Franklin Gould, 'Watts, Pioneer Sculptor', in *The Vision of G. F. Watts, 1817–1904*, ed. Veronica Franklin Gould (Guildford: Watts Gallery, 2004), pp. 42–44.
88 *Saturday Review of Politics, Literature, Science and Art* 81, no. 2101 (February 1896): 120; 'The Royal Academy: Second Notice', *The Times*, 8 May 1876, p. 9. The gendered critiques of Leighton's practice are richly explored in Sarah Gould, 'Making Texture Matter: The Materiality of British Paintings, 1788–1914' (PhD diss., Université Paris Diderot, 2016).
89 John Ruskin, Letter 79: 'Life Guards of New Life', 18 June 1877, reproduced in *Fors Clavigera: Letters to the Workmen and Labourers of Great Britain*, vol. 7 (London: George Allen, 1907), p. 160.
90 Details of the trial's role in debates over labour in Victorian art can be found in Barringer, *Men at Work*, pp. 314–21.
91 On Whistler's practice of thinning down paints see Steven Hackney, 'Art for Art's Sake: The Materials and Techniques of James McNeill Whistler (1834–1903)', in *Historical Painting Techniques, Materials, and Studio Practice: Preprints of a Symposium*, ed. Arie Wallert, Erma Hermens and Marja Peek (Marina Del Rey, CA: Getty Conservation Institute, 1995), pp. 186–90.
92 Watts painted Morris in 1870, Crane in 1891 and Carlyle in 1868. On Watts's relationship to Carlyle see David A. Stewart, 'Reality, Artifice, and the Politics of Evolution: Watts and Carlyle in the Earnest Age', *Victorian Poetry* 33, no. 3/4 (Autumn/Winter 1995): 476–98.
93 Julia Mary Cartwright, 'G. F. Watts, Royal Academician, His Life & Work', *Art Journal* (Easter Art Annual 1896): 8.
94 Chief among these are the 1880 essay 'The Present Conditions of Art' and the 1888 essay 'Aims of Art', both reprinted respectively in Watts, *George Frederic Watts*, 3:147–90; 3:228–34.
95 Watts, 'The National Position of Art', reprinted in Watts, *George Frederic Watts*, 3:257–72.
96 Ibid., p. 264.
97 'Signs of slavery' is found in John Ruskin, *The Works of John Ruskin*, vol. 9, *The Stones of Venice: Volume II*, ed. E. T. Cook and Alexander Wedderburn (London: George Allen, 1903–12), p. 193.
98 Ibid., p. 201.
99 Watts, *George Frederic Watts*, 1:263.
100 See in particular Watts, 'The Present Conditions of Art', in Watts, *George Frederic Watts*, 3:166.
101 Watts, *George Frederic Watts*, 2:149.
102 Ibid., 3:268.
103 Watts described these figures as general 'types of humanity'. See M. H. Spielman, *The Works of Mr G. F. Watts RA* (London: Pall Mall Gazette Office, 1886), p. 15.
104 Thomas Carlyle, *Past and Present* (Berkeley: University of California Press, 2005), p. 295.
105 Carlyle, *Past and Present*, pp. 163–64. Emphasis in original.
106 Gould describes how the Compton Mammon is 'more grotesque than the Tate version' and 'illustrates Watts' point even more strongly'; see *The Vision of G. F. Watts*, p. 74. Mark Bills and Barbara Bryant note that the smaller work 'is perhaps even more brutal in conception'; see *G. F. Watts: Victorian Visionary; Highlights from the Watts Gallery Collection* (New Haven: Yale University Press in association with Watts Gallery Compton, 2008), p. 232. The smaller canvas was exhibited in *George Frederic Watts, 1817–1904*, Tate Gallery, London (9 December 1954–16 January 1955), cat. no. 69; *G. F. Watts: A Nineteenth Century Phenomenon*, Whitechapel Art Gallery, London (22 January–3 March 1974); *The Vision of G. F. Watts, 1817–1904*, Watts Gallery, Compton, Surrey (2 July–31 October 2004), cat. no. 70.
107 The larger version was first exhibited in Birmingham in 1885. See Mary Seaton Watts, *The Diary of Mary Watts 1887–1904: Victorian Progressive and Artistic Visionary*, ed. Desna Greenhow (London: Lund Humphries in association with Watts Gallery, 2016), p. 167. Mary Watts does not specify which canvas he continued working on, but, as the larger version entirely lacks the impasto seen in the smaller canvas, it seems likely she was referring to the smaller work.
108 Thanks to Sally Marriott, the de Laszlo Conservation Fellow at the Watts Gallery, for her observations on Watts's attitudes to varnishing. She notes that wax was a common additive for reducing sheen.
109 Ridge and Townsend note that Watts certainly advocated that collectors should varnish his paintings to protect them but that many have been over-varnished, resulting in a glossiness unintended by the painter. See 'G. F. Watts in Context', p. 227.

110 Thanks to Edward Cooke for suggesting the term 'moral aesthetics' in relation to Watts's work.

111 On megilp see Hellen and Kilmurray, '*Carnation, Lily, Lily, Rose* and the Process of Painting'.

2 The Complexion of the Chromolithograph

1 There is much ambiguity about the genders and ages of these children, undoubtedly to ameliorate sexualised implications of the coupling of male/female, nude/clothed, and Black/White bodies. Although Tanya Sheehan and Henry Louis Gates Jr read the standing figure as female, this chapter follows most critics, who view both as male. See Tanya Sheehan and Henry Louis Gates Jr, 'Marketing Racism: Popular Imagery in the United States and Europe', in *The Image of the Black in Western Art*, vol. 5, *The Twentieth Century, Part 1: The Impact of Africa* (Cambridge, MA: Harvard University Press, 2018), p. 22.

2 Jean Michel Massing, 'From Greek Proverb to Soap Advert: Washing the Ethiopian', *Journal of the Warburg and Courtauld Institutes* 58 (1995): 180–201.

3 Anne McClintock, *Imperial Leather: Race, Gender and Sexuality in the Colonial Contest* (New York: Routledge, 1995), pp. 207–95.

4 See Anandi Ramamurthy, *Imperial Persuaders: Images of Africa and Asia in British Advertising* (Manchester: Manchester University Press, 2017).

5 McClintock, *Imperial Leather*, p. 211.

6 Noted by Henry Louis Gates Jr and Tanya Sheehan as one of the most visible demographics within racist advertising of this period. See 'Marketing Racism', p. 21.

7 Ramamurthy, *Imperial Persuaders*, pp. 1–23.

8 On this particular image see ibid., pp. 26–28.

9 On the overlaps between these material and ideological concerns see McClintock, *Imperial Leather*, pp. 207–95; Ramamurthy, *Imperial Persuaders*, pp. 24–62.

10 On Pears' soap see McClintock, *Imperial Leather*, pp. 212–25.

11 On the history of colour printing before this period see Ad Stijnman and Elizabeth Savage, eds., *Printing Colour 1400–1700: History, Techniques, Functions and Receptions* (Leiden: Brill, 2015).

12 Such boasts routinely appeared in promotional materials for Alf Cooke's Crown Point Printworks in Leeds (established 1865) and A. B. Fleming & Co. of Edinburgh (established 1852).

13 See Laura Anne Kalba, *Color in the Age of Impressionism: Commerce, Technology, and Art* (University Park: Pennsylvania State University Press, 2017), pp. 149–82.

14 'What Is Colour? The Teachings of the Spectrum', *British Lithographer* 1, no. 6 (August–September 1892): 10.

15 Thomas Richards, *The Commodity Culture of Victorian England: Advertising and Spectacle, 1851–1914* (Stanford: Stanford University Press, 1990), p. 3.

16 See McClintock, *Imperial Leather*, pp. 207–95; Ramamurthy, *Imperial Persuaders*, pp. 24–62; Sheehan and Gates, 'Marketing Racism', pp. 22–23; Richards, *The Commodity Culture of Victorian England*, pp. 249–54.

17 Anne Lafont, 'Fabric, Skin, Color: Picturing Antilles' Markets as an Inventory of Human Diversity', *Anuario Colombiano de Historia Social y de la Cultura* 43, no. 2 (July–December 2016): 133.

18 Mechthild Fend, *Fleshing Out Surfaces: Skin in French Art and Medicine, 1650–1850* (Manchester: Manchester University Press, 2017), pp. 8–9.

19 In particular, Wilson's *A Practical Treatise on Healthy Skin* (London: John Churchill, 1845) was reprinted and translated into eight editions in Europe and America, and remained in print for over thirty years. On Wilson's popularity see Mieneke te Hennepe, '"To Preserve the Skin in Health": Drainage, Bodily Control and the Visual Definition of Healthy Skin 1835–1900', *Medical History* 58, no. 3 (2014): 398.

20 Pigments listed in W. D. Richmond, *Colour and Colour Printing as Applied to Lithography* (London: Wyman & Sons, 1885), pp. 62–66.

21 Printing manuals advised warming the stone to 'open' its pores in the same manner as beauty manuals recommended steaming the face for the same purpose. See W. D. Richmond, *The Grammar of Lithography*, 2nd edn (London: Wyman & Sons, 1880), p. 81; D. G. Berri, *The Art of Lithography* (London: D. G. Berri, 1864), p. 33.

22 L. Gray-Gower, 'How a Chromo-Lithograph Is Printed', *Strand Magazine* 27, no. 157 (January 1904): 33.

23 By the late nineteenth century commercial printers purchased ready-made inks but might still alter their consistency. Printing manuals regularly included recipes for inks and additives that could be used to change their working properties. See Richmond, *The Grammar of Lithography*, pp. 198–99; Berri, *The Art of Lithography*, p. 21.

24 On soap's importance to lithographers see Richmond, *The Grammar of Lithography*, p. 197.

25 On this early history see Michael Twyman, *A History of Chromolithography: Printed Colour for All* (London: British Library and Oak Knoll Press, 2013), pp. 15–185.

26 On Le Blon's significance see Ad Stijnman, 'Jacob Christoff Le Blon and the Invention of Trichromatic Colour Printing, *c.*1710', in *Printing Colour 1400–1700: History, Techniques, Functions and Receptions*, ed. Ad Stijnman and Elizabeth Savage (Leiden: Brill, 2015), pp. 216–18.

27 Fend, *Fleshing Out Surfaces*, p. 9.

28 Fend analyses the role of skin in Le Blon's work in ibid., pp. 35–37.

29 On the lithographic stone industry see Twyman, *A History of Chromolithography*, pp. 447–58.

30 Mineke te Hennepe, 'Depicting Skin: Visual Culture in Nineteenth-Century Medicine' (PhD diss., Maastricht University, 2007), p. 52.

31 Erasmus Wilson, *Portraits of Diseases of the Skin* (London: J. Churchill, 1848), reprinted 1853.
32 Angela Rosenthal, 'Visceral Culture: Blushing and the Legibility of Whiteness in Eighteenth-Century British Portraiture', *Art History* 27, no. 4 (2004): 574.
33 Erasmus Wilson, *On Diseases of the Skin: A System of Cutaneous Medicine*, 6th edn (London: Churchill & Sons, 1867), p. 57.
34 These shifts are explored in detail in Twyman, *History of Chromolithography*, pp. 378–485.
35 Gray-Gower, 'How a Chromo-Lithograph Is Printed', p. 38.
36 Ibid., p. 33. Stone sizes correspond with paper standards, although printers could combine several sheets. By 1900 the largest standard paper size was 40 × 60 in (102 × 152 cm) or 'Quadruple Crown'. See Twyman, *History of Chromolithography*, pp. 183, 202.
37 The iconic example is Owen Jones, *The Grammar of Ornament* (London: Day & Son, 1856).
38 See 'What Is Colour', *British Lithographer* 2, no. 8 (December–January 1892–93): 55; Paul Smith, *Seurat and the Avant-Garde* (New Haven: Yale University Press, 1997), pp. 46–49; Heinwig Lang, 'Trichromatic Theories before Young', *Color Research & Application* 8, no. 4 (December 1983): 221–31.
39 See Tim Clayton, *The English Print, 1688–1802* (New Haven and London: Yale University Press for the Paul Mellon Centre for Studies in British Art, 1997).
40 Twyman, *History of Chromolithography*, pp. 156, 489–504.
41 For a contemporary account see Richmond, *Colour and Colour Printing*, pp. 150–52.
42 Ibid., p. 152.
43 'Our Supplements', *British Lithographer* 2, no. 12 (August–September 1893): 190.
44 Ibid.
45 Ibid.
46 Sarah Lewis notes the troubling continuation of this naming practice with contemporary colours such as '150 Portrait Tone', a peachy-pink acrylic paint used both as material and title by Mark Bradford, which reveals what Lewis calls 'whiteness as a normative designation'. See Sarah Elizabeth Lewis, 'Groundwork: Race and Aesthetics in the Era of Stand Your Ground Law', *Art Journal* 79, no. 4 (October 2020): 92–113.
47 'Days Shading Medium', *Printing Times and Lithographer*, 15 August 1884: 175.
48 Chromolithography therefore echoed debates about the separation of labour in other print techniques, such as wood engraving. See Gerry Beegan, *The Mass Image: A Social History of Photomechanical Reproduction in Victorian London* (Basingstoke, UK: Palgrave Macmillan, 2008).
49 Wilson mentions Pears in 'Toilet Soaps', *Journal of Cutaneous Medicine and Diseases of the Skin* 1 (1868): 446–48.
50 Francis Pears, *The Skin, Baths, Bathing, and Soap* (London: the author, 1859), p. 1.
51 *Beauty Culture: What Dermatology Has to Do with Beauty* (London: Bayard, Vane & Co., 1893), p. 4.
52 *The Toilet: Containing Hints and Advice on Health, Beauty, and Dress, with Innumerable Recipes for the Toile Table* (London: Ward, Lock & Co., 1897), p. 10.
53 As Rosenthal demonstrates, translucency as a marker of White, British beauty was well established by the eighteenth century and has a longer historical legacy than there is space to discuss here. See Rosenthal, 'Visceral Culture'.
54 Pears, *The Skin, Baths, Bathing, and Soap*, p. 12.
55 *The Toilet*, p. 10.
56 Erasmus Wilson, 'Preface to the Seventh Edition', in *Healthy Skin: A Popular Treatise on the Skin and Hair, Their Preservation and Management*, 7th edn (London: J. Churchill, 1866), p. vii.
57 'Eruptive diseases' is found in *The Toilet*, p. 10; 'indigestion' etc. in *Beauty Culture*, p. 7; 'habitual potions' in Arthur Freeling, *Gracefulness: A Few Words upon Form and Features* (London: George Routledge, 1841), p. 142.
58 Erasmus Wilson, *Healthy Skin: A Popular Treatise on the Skin and Hair, Their Preservation and Management*, 8th edn (London: J. Churchill, 1876), p. 171.
59 Erasmus Wilson, *On Diseases of the Skin*, 5th edn (London: John Churchill, 1863) pp. 556–57.
60 Undertaken in colour the process was called chromoxylography, a chief rival to chromolithography for small-scale work and images combined with type.
61 Here the argument takes up Jennifer Roberts's insight that in wood engraving 'labour is expressed in order to disappear': 'Invisible Labour', lecture 6 of 'The Matrix: Contemporary Art and the Life of Print' (Slade Lecture Series, University of Cambridge, 26 February 2019). Thanks to Jennifer Y. Chuong for highlighting the labour of maintaining fictions of Whiteness.
62 Jacqueline Najuma Stewart, *Migrating to the Movies: Cinema and Black Urban Modernity* (Berkeley: University of California Press, 2005), pp. 54, 85–86; Alice Maurice, *The Cinema and Its Shadow: Race and Technology in Early Cinema* (Minneapolis: University of Minnesota Press, 2013), pp. 34–45; Tanya Sheehan, *Study in Black and White: Photography, Race, Humor* (University Park: Pennsylvania State University Press, 2018), pp. 15–32. As Sheehan and Racquel J. Gates observe, the reversals inherent in the positive–negative process fundamental to photography and film further racialised photochemistry's chromatic substitution of blackness and whiteness. See Racquel J. Gates, *Double Negative: The Black Image and Popular Culture* (Durham, NC: Duke University Press, 2018), pp. 17–20.
63 British examples include *The Miller and the Sweep* (G. A. Smith, 1897) and *Soap Versus Blacking* (Robert W. Paul, 1902). Among American examples, *A Drop of Ink* (American Mutoscope & Biograph, 1904) is particularly salient.

64 Henri Bergson, *Le rire: essai sur la signification du comique* (Paris: Felix Alcan, 1900), p. 41. The text was translated into English in 1911: Henri Bergson, *Laughter: An Essay on the Meaning of the Comic*, trans. Cloudesley Brereton and Fred Rothwell (London: Macmillan, 1911), p. 40. The relationship between Bergson's comment and minstrelsy is explored in Louis Chude-Sokei, 'The Uncanny History of Minstrelsy and Machines, 1835–1923', in *Burnt Cork: Traditions and Legacies of Blackface Minstrelsy*, ed. Stephen Burge Johnson (Boston: University of Massachusetts Press, 2012), pp. 119–21.
65 On the use of chimney soot in black ink see 'Printing Inks of To-Day', *British Printer* 5, no. 30 (1892): 61–65.
66 The conflation of Black children and chimney sweeps is explored in Matthew Francis Rarey, '"And the *Jet* Would Be Invaluable": Blackness, Bondage, and *The Beloved*', *Art Bulletin* 102, no. 3 (August 2020): 28–53.
67 Claudia Benthien, *Skin: On the Cultural Border between Self and the World*, trans. Thomas Dunlap (New York: Columbia University Press, 2002), pp. 152–53.
68 Jennifer Y. Chuong, 'Engraving's "Immoveable Veil": Phillis Wheatley's Portrait and the Politics of Technique', *Art Bulletin* 104, no. 2 (April 2022): 63–88.
69 The thick overlaying of colour possibly accounts for the abrasion on this particular print, most visible on the Black child's hair, although it is also evident in the hair of the White child. Thanks to students and staff of University College London's art history department for their suggestion that this may also have resulted from excessive touching of the print in these particular spots by viewers curious to compare the respective textures of the two children's hair.
70 See te Hennepe, '"To Preserve the Skin in Health"'.
71 Anne Lafont, 'How Skin Color Became a Racial Marker: Art Historical Perspectives on Race', *Eighteenth Century Studies* 51, no. 1 (Fall 2017): 89–113.
72 On the emergence of skin colour as the defining signifier of race see Lafont, ibid.; Fend, *Fleshing Out Surfaces*; David Bindman, *Ape to Apollo: Aesthetics and the Idea of Race in the 18th Century* (London: Reaktion Books, 2002); Roxann Wheeler, *The Complexion of Race: Categories of Difference in Eighteenth-Century British Culture* (Philadelphia: University of Pennsylvania Press, 2010).
73 Detailed in Pamela K. Gilbert, *Victorian Skin: Surface, Self, History* (Ithaca, NY: Cornell University Press, 2019), pp. 279–318.
74 See Wilson, *Healthy Skin*, 8th edn, pp. 1–21. This account of the skin's structure was common to both scientific and popular beauty manuals. See for instance *Beauty Culture*, p. 4.
75 Discussed in Wilson, *Healthy Skin*, 8th edn, pp. 11–12; Wilson, *On Diseases of the Skin*, 6th edn, pp. 13–15.
76 Wilson, *Healthy Skin*, 8th edn, pp. 11–12.
77 Wilson, *On Diseases of the Skin*, 6th edn, pp. 13–15.
78 Jennifer Roberts considered the shared 'spatial and temporal logic' of skin and print in her lecture 'Colour Separation' (Slade Lecture Series, University of Cambridge, 19 February 2019). See also Fend, *Fleshing Out Surfaces*, pp. 145–56.
79 Fend, *Fleshing Out Surfaces*, p. 156.
80 Richard J. Powell, 'Colorstruck! Painting, Pigment, Affect' (A. W. Mellon Lectures, National Gallery of Art, Washington, DC, 20 March 2022).
81 For example Robert Mortimer Glover, 'On the Functions of the Colouring Matter of the Skin in the Dark Races of Mankind', *Edinburgh New Philosophical Journal* (October 1840): 3.
82 Wilson, *Healthy Skin*, 8th edn, p. 265.
83 Rosenthal, 'Visceral Culture', p. 574.
84 Lafont, 'How Skin Color Became a Racial Marker', p. 109.
85 William Sharpe, *The Cause of Colour among Races and the Evolution of Physical Beauty* (London: David Bogue, 1879), pp. 9–11.
86 Ibid., p. 12.
87 Ibid., p. 14.
88 Wilson, *Healthy Skin*, 7th edn, p. vii.
89 Wilson, *On Diseases of the Skin*, 6th edn, p. 700.
90 Ibid., p. 697.
91 Ibid., p. 4.
92 Erasmus Wilson, *Descriptive Catalogue of the Dermatological Specimens Contained in the Museum of the Royal College of Surgeons of England* (London: Taylor & Francis, 1870), p. 27.
93 Ibid., p. 26.
94 One reason colour printing did not industrialise until the 1860s was the lack of powered grinders capable of reducing pigments to a suitable consistency, which was much finer than that required for paint. See C. H. Bloy, *A History of Printing Ink, Balls and Rollers, 1440–1850* (London: Evelyn Adams & Mackay, 1967), pp. 51–73.
95 'The Narrative of Jemima Cox', written in 1871, described by Mander Brothers' chronicler Sir Geoffrey Le Mesurier Mander as 'a personal recollection of the firm, where she'd worked since 1817'. Reprinted in Geoffrey Le Mesurier Mander, *The History of Mander Brothers 1773–1955* (Wolverhampton: Mander Brothers, 1955), pp. 19–30.
96 Richmond, *Colour and Colour Printing*, p. 58.
97 Thanks to paper conservator Theresa Fairbanks Harris for this insight.
98 Patents for 'antiseptic inks' appear from the 1880s in C. Ainsworth Mitchell and Thomas Cradock Hepworth, *Inks: Their Composition and Manufacture*, 4th edn (London: C. Griffin, 1937), p. 375. Ones for the 'addition of odoriferous essential oils' appear from 1856 (p. 370). On scented inks see ibid. and also Herbert J. Wolfe, *The Manufacture of Printing and Lithographic Inks* (New York: MacNair-Dorland, 1933), p. 275; Frank Bestow Wiborg, *Printing Ink: A History with a Treatise on Modern Meth-*

ods of Manufacture and Use (New York: Harper, 1926), p. 124.

99 British medical students have long campaigned on this issue, with their activism gaining momentum following the Black Lives Matter protests of 2020. See for instance Smitha Mundasad, 'The Medical School Trying to Become Anti-racist', *BBC News*, 17 August 2020, www.bbc.co.uk/news/health-53465113.

100 Wilson, *On Diseases of the Skin*, 6th edn, p. 696. As media scholar Xin Peng notes, 'put bluntly, the skin tone of Asian peoples is not literally yellow'. See Xin Peng, 'Colour-as-Hue and Colour-as-Race: Early Technicolor, Ornamentalism and *The Toll of the Sea* (1922)', *Screen* 62, no. 3 (September 2021): 288.

101 The first two cases are described in Wilson, *Healthy Skin*, 7th edn, p. 254; the third in Erasmus Wilson, *Lectures on Dermatology: Including Derangements of Colour of the Skin* (London: J. & A. Churchill, 1878), p. 23.

102 Wilson, *Lectures on Dermatology*, p. 11.

103 Ibid.

104 Ibid.

105 Erasmus Wilson, *Healthy Skin*, 7th edn (London: J. Churchill, 1866), p. 255.

106 Lafont, 'How Skin Color Became a Racial Marker', pp. 15–17.

107 Ramamurthy, *Imperial Persuaders*, p. 30.

108 Sheehan and Gates, 'Marketing Racism', p. 22.

109 Sarah Amato, 'The White Elephant in London: An Episode of Trickery, Racism and Advertising', *Journal of Social History* 43, no. 1 (Fall 2009): 31–66.

110 Wilson, *Lectures on Dermatology*, p. 10.

111 Various pamphlets advertising Gratton's appearances held in the Wellcome collection repeat this wording. Gratton's story was richly contextualised in an exhibition curated by Temi Odumosu, *A Visible Difference: Skin, Race & Identity, 1720–1820*, Hunterian Museum, Royal College of Surgeons, London (3 July–21 December 2007).

112 Wilson, *Lectures on Dermatology*, pp. 9, 11.

113 Enormous thanks to Esther Chadwick for helping to correctly identify the printing techniques here.

114 Ibid., p. 9.

115 Amato, 'The White Elephant in London'.

116 *The Times*, 17 January 1884.

117 'Arrival of the "White Elephant" from Burmah', *Illustrated London News*, 26 January 1884.

118 The advertisement appears in *The Graphic*, 18 December 1884. Amato, 'The White Elephant', p. 51.

119 First published in *Ladies' Home Journal*, October 1901; reprinted in *Just So Stories for Little Children* (London: MacMillan, 1902). Contemporaneously in the United States, Thomas Dixon Jr adapted the same biblical passage for the title of his White supremacist novel *The Leopard's Spots: A Romance of the White Man's Burden, 1865–1900* (New York: Doubleday, 1902).

120 Richmond, *Colour and Colour Printing*, p. 159.

3 Modern Women, Modern Colours

1 'Modern woman' was the term commonly deployed in Britain, whereas 'new woman' or 'modern girl' were labels used internationally in other contexts. See Alys Eve Weinbaum and the Modern Girl around the World Research Group, *The Modern Girl around the World: Consumption, Modernity, and Globalization* (Durham, NC: Duke University Press, 2008); Elizabeth Otto and Vanessa Rocco, *The New Woman International: Representations in Photography and Film from the 1870s through the 1960s* (Ann Arbor: University of Michigan Press, 2011).

2 On the multiple developments in inter-war print media see Catherine Clay, ed., *Women's Periodicals and Print Culture in Britain, 1918–1939: The Interwar Period* (Edinburgh: Edinburgh University Press, 2018).

3 On film's central role in the gendered chromatism of the era's advertising, see the chapter 'Advertising, Fashion and Colour' in Sarah Street and Joshua Yumibe, *Chromatic Modernity: Color, Cinema and the Media of the 1920s* (New York: Columbia University Press, 2018), pp. 66–103.

4 Maude featured in *A Matter of Life and Death* (UK, 1946; dir. Michael Powell and Emeric Pressburger).

5 A core tenet of Rita Felski's *The Gender of Modernity* (Cambridge, MA: Harvard University Press, 1995).

6 Madame Yevonde, *In Camera* (London: Woman's Book Club, 1940), p. 231.

7 *British Journal of Photography*, 29 April 1932.

8 Yevonde was one of several women photographers working in colour in international contexts at this time, including American documentarian Marion Post Walcott and French portraitist and photojournalist Gisèle Freund. See Sally Stein, 'Toward a Full-Color Turn in the Optics of Modern History', *American Art* 29, no. 1 (2015): 15–21; Hyewon Yoon, 'Practice in Color: Gisèle Freund in Paris', *October* 173 (September 2020): 7–36.

9 See Lindsay Smith's introduction to her edited volume *Color and Victorian Photography* (London: Bloomsbury Visual Arts, 2020), pp. 1–56, and Bettina Gockel, 'The Invention of Black-and-White Photography: Proclamations of Photography's Aesthetic Independence and the History of Photography's Colors', in *The Colors of Photography*, ed. Bettina Gockel (Berlin: De Gruyter, 2020), pp. 261–304. Notably the 2021–22 international survey of inter-war women's photography at the National Gallery of Art in Washington, DC, and the Metropolitan Museum of Art, New York, included few works in colour. See Andrea Nelson, ed., *The New Woman behind the Camera* (Washington, DC: National Gallery of Art, 2020).

10 In particular, the violence against workers of colour in British port towns in the so-called race riots of 1919 reflected the racialised connotations of issues of colour and labour in inter-war Britain, as well as wider issues about the destabilisation of the racial hierarchies upon which the empire was structured. See Chamion Caballero and Peter J. Aspinall, *Mixed Race Britain in the Twentieth Century* (London: Palgrave Macmillan, 2018), pp. 59–68; Lucy Bland, 'White Women and Men of Colour: Miscegenation Fears in Britain after the Great War', *Gender & History* 17 (April 2005): 29–61. On colour, gender and sexuality in this period see Matt Houlbrook, '"The Man with the Powder Puff" in Interwar London', *Historical Journal* 50, no. 1 (March 2007): 145–71.

11 Yevonde, *In Camera*, p. 37.

12 As Brett Rogers notes, Yevonde entered the movement at a moment of heightened tension between the militancy of Emmeline Pankhurst's Women's Social and Political Union and the more pacifist practices of the National Union of Women's Suffrage Societies. See 'Be Original or Die: Yevonde's Life of Colour', in Brett Rogers and Adam Lowe, *Madame Yevonde: Be Original or Die* (London: British Council, 1998), p. 1.

13 On Yevonde's ideas about the links between her work and her feminism, see her *In Camera*, pp. 32–49.

14 Ibid., pp. 42–47.

15 Val Williams, *The Other Observers: Women Photographers in Britain 1900 to the Present* (London: Virago, 1991), p. 93.

16 Yevonde, *In Camera*, p. 80.

17 On the prominence of the female amateur photographer see Carol Armstrong, 'From Clementina to Käsebier: The Photographic Attainment of the "Lady Amateur"', *October* 91, no. 91 (Winter 2000): 101–39; on the feminisation of snapshot photography see Williams, *The Other Observers*, pp. 72–88.

18 Discussed in Nancy Martha West, *Kodak and the Lens of Nostalgia* (Charlottesville: University Press of Virginia, 2000), pp. 109–35.

19 See for example J. E. Saunders's report on 'a camera which a girl can hold' for 'the "baby-on-the-lawn" type of snapshot' in 'Some Tiny Cameras, Advances in Apparatus', *Photographic Journal* 76 (June 1936): 352 or Saunders's view on how new 'dainty instruments' have 'a special appeal to women' in 'The Newest Cameras', *Photographic Journal* 77 (February 1937): 104.

20 Notable exceptions, including the press photography of Christina Broom and the war photography of Olive Edis, are discussed in Williams, *The Other Observers*, pp. 25–72.

21 'Photography: Not a Man's Job', anonymous letter to the editors, *British Journal of Photography* 68, no. 3182 (April 1921): 260.

22 On the gendered character of studio photography in international contexts see Andrea Nelson, '"Such a Way of Life Exists": New Women Photographers in the Studio', in *The New Woman behind the Camera*, ed. Andrea Nelson (Washington, DC: National Gallery of Art, 2020), pp. 99–128.

23 On the history of female portrait photography in Britain see Williams, *The Other Observers*, pp. 142–66.

24 'Photography for Girls', *The Times*, 16 June 1925, p. 8; discussed in the broader context of photographic education for women in Williams, *The Other Observers*, p. 90.

25 'Kodak School for Professionals', *Photographic Journal* 77 (June 1932): 295.

26 Reprinted as Philonie Yevonde, 'Photographic Portraiture from a Woman's Point of View', *British Journal of Photography* 68, no. 3182 (April 1921): 251–54.

27 Ibid., p. 251.

28 Ibid.

29 Ibid.

30 Ibid.

31 'Interesting the Sitter', anonymous letter to the editors, *British Journal of Photography* 68, no. 3186 (May 1921): 320.

32 'Photography: Not a Man's Job'.

33 'Madame Yevonde's Lecture', anonymous letter to the editors, *British Journal of Photography* 68, no. 3182 (April 1921): 303.

34 Anne Stigmat, 'Women Photographers', letter to the editor, *British Journal of Photography* 68, no. 3188 (June 1921): 348.

35 For example, see 'To the Lady Operator', *British Journal of Photography* 65, no. 3028 (May 1918): 223; 'Photography: Not a Man's Job'.

36 'Report on the Training of Disabled Soldiers and Sailors for Photographic Employment', *British Journal of Photography* 65, no. 3033 (June 1918): 282.

37 The 1918 Representation of the People Act extended voting rights to women over thirty who were university graduates, property owners or wives of property owners. The 1918 Parliament (Qualification of Women) Act and the 1919 Sex Disqualification (Removal) Act granted these additional professional rights.

38 See Sally Alexander, 'Men's Fears and Women's Work: Responses to Unemployment in London between the Wars', *Gender & History* 12, no. 2 (July 2000): 401–20.

39 On wage disparity see Sally Alexander, 'Becoming a Woman in London in the 1920s and 1930s', in *Metropolis London: Histories and Representations Since 1880*, ed. David Feldman and Gareth Stedman Jones (London: Routledge, 1991), pp. 203–312.

40 'Cost and Product', *British Journal of Photography* 65, no. 3014 (February 1918): 64.

41 In particular see Alexander, 'Men's Fears and Women's Work'; Adrian Bingham, *Gender, Modernity, and the Popular Press in Inter-war Britain* (Oxford: Clarendon Press, 2004).

42 *Daily Mail*, 1 January 1927, p. 15; discussed in Bingham, *Gender, Modernity, and the Popular Press*, p. 81.

43 On the history of the process see D. A. Spencer and F. W. Coppin, 'Basic Features of the Vivex Process', *Photographic Journal: Section B*, vol. 88B no. 4 (July–August 1948): 78–83.

44 D. A. Spencer, 'Humbug in Colour Photography', *Photographic Journal* 72 (August 1932): 363.

45 On the early history of colour photography see Kim Timby, 'Colour Photography and Stereoscopy: Parallel Histories', *History of Photography* 29, no. 2 (June 2005): 183–96.

46 For a detailed study of Warburg's colour techniques see Hana Kaluznick, 'A Hidden History of Early Colour Photography in Britain: The Photographs of Agnes B. Warburg' (PhD diss., Ryerson University, 2015).

47 Kodachrome was a multilayer subtractive system, a form of colour negative, released first as a 16 mm amateur cinefilm stock in 1935 and then as still photography stock in 1936. Processing was included in the price of the stock and entirely undertaken by the manufacturer.

48 Armstrong, 'From Clementina to Käsebier'.

49 Plates were available in a range of sizes but the standard format adopted by amateurs was 4 × 3¼. On autochromes see Laura Anne Kalba, *Color in the Age of Impressionism: Commerce, Technology, and Art* (University Park: Pennsylvania State University Press, 2017), pp. 183–215.

50 Frederick Hollyer, 'The Charm of Colour', *Photographic Journal* 65, no. 10 (1925): 67.

51 Rosalind Galt, *Pretty: Film and the Decorative Image* (New York: Columbia University Press, 2011).

52 Yevonde discusses scale in *In Camera*, p. 187. Reprints of Yevonde's work vary in scale, however – one of many issues surrounding the conversation of images made using a now obsolete technology. On these issues see Adam Lowe, 'A Riot of Colour: Yevonde's Vivex Photography', in Brett Rogers and Adam Lowe, *Madame Yevonde: Be Original or Die* (London: British Council, 1998), pp. 12–13.

53 Quoted in Yevonde's biography by Kate Salway, *Goddesses & Others: Yevonde, a Portrait* (London: Balcony Books, 1990), p. 56.

54 Thanks to Clare Freestone for generously sharing this information.

55 One employee recalled that the coronation photographs of 1936 were 'probably the only job where we had to make more than two or three prints of the same subject'. Recounted in Ron Callendar, 'Viva Vivex', *The Photographer* 13, no. 2 (February 1978): 40–41.

56 D. A. Spencer, 'Progress in Colour Photography', *Photographic Journal* 76 (April 1936): 224.

57 D. A. Spencer, 'Where We Stand in Colour Photography', *Photographic Journal* 77 (September 1937): 565.

58 Clare Freestone, 'Madame Yevonde: A Riot of Colour!' (conference paper, Colour Fever Conference, Victoria and Albert Museum, 28 October 2021).

59 Spencer and Coppin, 'Basic Features of the Vivex Process', p. 78.

60 D. A. Spencer, 'Modern Developments in Colour Photography', *Photographic Journal* 72 (January 1932): 18.

61 On the policy change see P. C. Bull, 'The Colour Prints', review of the Royal Photographic Society's Seventy-Seventh Annual Exhibition, *Photographic Journal* 72 (November 1932): 443. On the asterisks see Agnes B. Warburg, 'The Colour Prints', review of the Royal Photographic Society's Eighty-Third Annual Exhibition, *Photographic Journal* 78 (November 1938): 625.

62 Reproduced in Spencer and Coppin, 'Basic Features of the Vivex Process', p. 82. It is not clear whether these women are the same recalled by laboratory worker Samuel King, who described how assembly was undertaken by 'two ladies, Miss Taylor and Miss Chiltern'. Recounted in Callendar, 'Viva Vivex', pp. 40–41.

63 Yevonde, *In Camera*, p. 57.

64 Ibid., pp. 63–64.

65 Ibid., p. 66.

66 Ibid., p. 83.

67 Michelle Henning, 'The Worlding of Light and Air: Dufaycolor and Selochrome in the 1930s', *Visual Culture in Britain*, 23 March 2020: 11.

68 Spencer, 'Modern Developments in Colour Photography', p. 18.

69 F. J. Tritton, 'Progress in Colour Photography', *Photographic Journal* 80 (April 1940): 146.

70 Gockel, 'The Invention of Black-and-White Photography', in *The Colors of Photography*, ed. Bettina Gockel (Berlin: De Gruyter, 2020), p. 265.

71 Reported in 'Symposium on the Commercial Applications of Colour Photography', *Photographic Journal* 77 (May 1937): 326. Kodak had used 'You Press the Button, We Do the Rest' in its advertisements since 1889. See West, *Kodak and the Lens of Nostalgia*, p. 8.

72 *Daily Express*, 8 May 1935, p. 5.

73 'Maintaining Good Looks', *The Times*, 16 June 1939, p. 19.

74 For a discussion of the racial implications of this new chromatism, see Kirsty Sinclair Dootson, '"The Hollywood Powder Puff War": Technicolor Cosmetics in the 1930s', *Film History* 28, no. 1 (2016): 107–31.

75 *Lessons in Loveliness* (London: Dearborn, 1938), p. 7.

76 Madame Yevonde, 'Why Colour?', *Photographic Journal* 73 (March 1933): 116.

77 Ibid.

78 Yevonde, *In Camera*, p. 185.

79 Ibid., p. 183.

80 Ibid.

81 Yevonde, 'Why Colour?', p. 116.

82 Ibid., p. 117.

83 See for example Gui St Bernard, 'Art and the Camera', *Photographic Journal* 73 (July 1933): 319–22; D. M. Cuthbertson, 'Colour Photography: A Help to Artistic Expression', *British Journal of Photography* 82 (November 1935): 692–93.

84 *Beauty in the Making* (London: Helena Rubenstein, 1937), pp. 32–33.

85 Yevonde, *In Camera*, p. 189.

86 'Photographs for Advertising', *The Times*, 4 September 1935, p. 14.

87 Yevonde, 'Why Colour?', p. 118.

88 On Yevonde's retouching see Lowe, 'A Riot of Colour', pp. 12–13.

89 Yevonde, *In Camera*, p. 188. On Yevonde's unusual technical practice see Pamela Glasson Roberts, 'Yevonde and the Techniques of Colour Photography', in Robin Gibson and Pamela Glasson Roberts, *Madame Yevonde: Colour, Fantasy and Myth* (London: National Portrait Gallery, 1990), p. 26. Spencer is quoted in 'Symposium on the Commercial Applications of Colour Photography', p. 329.

90 Yevonde, 'Why Colour?', p. 119.

91 Rogers offers an extended analysis of the abstract qualities of the photograph in 'Be Original or Die', pp. 4–5.

92 It is important to note that the colour temperature of this image (what we might term the 'warmth' of its yellows and browns) differs significantly between prints and reproductions. The version reproduced here is much less yellow in its tonality than the earlier reproduction in Robin Gibson and Pamela Glasson Roberts, *Madame Yevonde: Colour, Fantasy and Myth* (London: National Portrait Gallery, 1990).

93 Recounted by Yevonde's biographer Salway in *Goddesses & Others*, p. 1.

94 Anne Anlin Cheng, *Second Skin: Josephine Baker and the Modern Surface* (New York: Oxford University Press, 2013), p. 10.

95 Ibid., p. 13.

96 Jacqueline Lichtenstein, *The Eloquence of Color: Rhetoric and Painting in the French Classical Age* (Berkeley: University of California Press, 1993); Galt, *Pretty*, pp. 40–49. As Galt and Houlbrook note, these cultural assumptions around colour's feminised and sexualised appeals are also crucial for understanding what Galt terms the 'fascinating linkage of color theory and queer politics'. See Galt, *Pretty*, pp. 75–96; Houlbrook, 'The Man with the Powder Puff'.

97 Cuthbertson, 'Colour Photography', p. 693.

98 Nicole Hudgins, *The Gender of Photography: How Masculine and Feminine Values Shaped the History of Nineteenth-Century Photography* (London: Bloomsbury Visual Arts, 2020), p. 168.

99 Further complicated by the ways Egyptian queens such as Nefertiti and Cleopatra have been racialised in multiple ways, including as White and Black. See Francesca T. Royster, *Becoming Cleopatra: The Shifting Image of an Icon* (New York: Palgrave Macmillan, 2003).

100 Lindsay Smith, '"There Is a Garden in Her Face": Madame Yevonde's Photographic Colour', *Women: A Cultural Review* 13, no. 2 (2002): 124.

101 Yevonde used this maxim to close her 1936 lecture titled 'The Future of Portraiture – if Any', reprinted in *British Journal of Photography* 83 (May 1936): 340–41.

102 Reported and illustrated in 'These Olympians', *The Bystander*, 13 March 1935.

103 Smith, '"There Is a Garden in Her Face"', p. 134.

104 Rogers, 'Be Original or Die', pp. 4–7.

105 Yevonde, *In Camera*, p. 235.

106 *Lessons in Loveliness*, p. 1.

107 Lichtenstein, *The Eloquence of Color*, pp. 194–95.

108 The image occupies the cover of the 1990 National Portrait Gallery exhibition catalogue *Be Original or Die* and Lawrence Hole's catalogue of Yevonde's work *The Goddesses Portraits* (Seattle: Darling and Company, 2000). The image was one of only five selected for colour reproduction in Salway's biography *Goddesses & Others* (and indeed is the only one to occupy a full page), and it was selected as part of a small set of postcard reproductions issued to accompany the British Council's 1998 exhibition.

109 Yevonde, *In Camera*, p. 185.

110 While Liz Rideal suggests that the work plays with the Vanitas tradition, an alternative viewpoint is that it engages with multiple and hybrid art historical references. See Liz Rideal, *Mirror Mirror: Self-Portraits by Women Artists* (London: National Portrait Gallery, 2001), p. 79.

111 Yevonde recalled that 'when I went to a party I would wave my hands about in an affected manner and say "I must apologize for my hands. My nails are too dreadful. It's the chemicals you know. I'm a photographer."' She refused to wear rubber gloves, reasoning that 'what do my hands matter, so long as I become a good photographer?' See Yevonde, *In Camera*, pp. 55–56.

112 Yevonde, *In Camera*, p. 236.

113 On the closure see Tritton, 'Progress in Colour Photography', p. 146.

114 Yevonde, *In Camera*, p. 287.

4 Decolonising in Technicolor

1 On the politics of complexions in the film see Prem Chowdry, *Colonial India and the Making of Empire Cinema: Image, Ideology and Identity* (Manchester: Manchester University Press, 2000), pp. 89–109.

2 Britain pioneered a number of earlier colour film technologies including Kinemacolor and Dufaycolor. See Sarah Street, *Colour Films in Britain: The Negotiation of Innovation, 1900–1955* (London: Palgrave Macmillan on behalf of the British Film Institute, 2012), pp. 9–51.

3 'Technicolor Ltd. License Agreement', 23 July 1935, B1/F13, Technicolor Archives, George Eastman Museum, Rochester, NY (hereafter Technicolor Archives).

4 David Harvey, *The New Imperialism* (Oxford: Oxford University Press, 2003), p. 26.

5 On the Empire Marketing Board see Lee Grieveson, *Cinema and the Wealth of Nations: Media, Capital, and the Liberal World System* (Oakland: University of California Press, 2018); on the Colonial Film Unit see Tom Rice, *Films for the Colonies: Cinema and the Preservation of the British Empire* (Oakland: University of California Press, 2019).

6 Grieveson, *Cinema and the Wealth of Nations*.

7 In particular see Priya Jaikumar, *Cinema at the End of Empire: A Politics of Transition in Britain and India* (Durham, NC: Duke University Press, 2006), pp. 140–50; Street, *Colour Films in Britain: The Negotiation of Innovation*, pp. 135–42; Chowdry, *Colonial India and the Making of Empire Cinema*, pp. 89–109.

8 This long history is examined in Natasha Eaton, *Colour, Art and Empire:*

Visual Culture and the Nomadism of Representation (London: I.B. Tauris, 2013).

9 This slogan was part of the British Colour Council's articles of incorporation. On the council's imperialist ideology see Lynda Nead, *The Tiger in the Smoke: Art and Culture in Post-war Britain* (New Haven and London: Yale University Press for the Paul Mellon Centre for Studies in British Art, 2017), pp. 146–49.

10 The *Dictionary* was released in various reprints and editions between 1934 and 1951 and was published by the British Colour Council.

11 'Technicolor Ltd. License Agreement', 29 July 1952, BM0002 /F1, Technicolor Archives.

12 Jagjeet Lally, 'Colour as Commodity: Colonialism and the Sensory Worlds of South Asia', *Third Text Forum*, 9 May 2019, http://www.thirdtext.org/lally-colourascommodity.

13 As Ramesh Kumar notes, archival losses have contributed to the lack of scholarship on colour in certain periods of Indian film history, but oral history projects such as 'The History and Practice of Cinematography in India' and the ongoing research of Ranjani Mazumdar have sought to address these challenges. See Ramesh Kumar, 'Alas, Nitrate Didn't Wait, but Does It Really Matter? Fiery Losses, Bureaucratic Cover-Ups, and the Writing of Indian Film Histories from the Relics of Cinema at the National Film Archive of India', *BioScope: South Asian Screen Studies* 7, no. 1 (July 2016): 109; C. K. Muraleedharan, Raqs Media Collective and India Foundation for the Arts, 'The History and Practice of Cinematography in India', accessed 28 April 2022, https://www.muraleedharanck.com/research; and Ranjani Mazumdar, 'Aviation, Tourism and Dreaming in 1960s Bombay Cinema', *BioScope: South Asian Screen Studies* 2, no. 2 (July 2011): 129–55, and her forthcoming essay 'Eastman Colour in 1960s India', in *Global Film Colour*, ed. Sarah Street and Joshua Yumibe.

14 Alice Lovejoy, 'Celluloid Geopolitics: Film Stock and the War Economy, 1939–47', *Screen* 60, no. 2 (June 2019): 225.

15 See Jaikumar, *Cinema at the End of Empire*, p. 21.

16 As Street notes, the antagonism towards Kalmus was deeply gendered, as male cinematographers resented taking advice from a woman. See Sarah Street, 'Negotiating the Archives: The Natalie Kalmus Papers and the "Branding" of Technicolor in Britain and the United States', *Moving Image* 11, no. 1 (Spring 2011): 10.

17 For a helpful video illustrating the process, see George Eastman Museum, 'The Dye Transfer Printing Process: Technicolor 100', 22 January 2015, https://www.youtube.com/watch?v=g9S76vtk4Ro.

18 Laboratory engineer Wilfred Brandt, interview 11 November 1991, audio cassette, conducted by the Broadcasting, Entertainment, Communications, and Theatre Union Oral History Project, British Film Institute (hereafter BECTU, BFI). Digitised copies are available at: https://historyproject.org.uk.

19 Laboratory technician Sid Etherington, interview 11 July 1990, and plant foreman Syd Wilson, interview 18 June 1991, audio cassette, BECTU, BFI.

20 Laboratory foreman Alf Cooper, interview 28 November 1963, audio cassette, BECTU, BFI.

21 Cooper recalled the odours, 28 November 1963, audio cassette, BECTU, BFI. On shrimp shell mordants see Alan Gundelfinger, interview by Bill Bleason, c.1970s, transcript, C470, Technicolor Archives; on blood see 'Egg Albumin vs. Blood Albumin', 12 June 1963, B52/F34, Technicolor Archives; on oyster juice see Richard Haines, *Technicolor Movies: The History of Dye Transfer Printing* (Jefferson, NC: McFarland, 1993), p. 65.

22 See Kirsty Sinclair Dootson and Zhaoyu Zhu, 'Did Madame Mao Dream in Technicolor? Rethinking Cold War Colour Cinema through Technicolor's "Chinese Copy"', *Screen* 61, no. 3 (September 2020), pp. 346–48.

23 Laboratory worker Paddy O'Gorman, interview 31 July 1992, audio cassette, BECTU, BFI.

24 This exact phrase appears in three separate interviews with Technicolor laboratory workers: O'Gorman; Brandt; and Len Runkel, interview 9 November 1988, audio cassette, BECTU, BFI.

25 Jack Cardiff, 'Shooting Western Approaches', *Cine-Technician* 10, no. 51 (December 1944): 113.

26 Jack Cardiff and Justin Bowyer, *Conversations with Jack Cardiff: Art, Light and Direction in Cinema* (London: Batsford, 2003), p. 63.

27 Oswald Morris, interview by Sarah Street and Liz Watkins, 8 August 2008, in *British Colour Cinema: Practices and Theories*, ed. Simon Brown, Sarah Street and Liz Watkins (Basingstoke, UK: Palgrave Macmillan on behalf of British Film Institute, 2013), p. 66.

28 Ibid.

29 On the firm's early history see James Layton and David Pierce, *The Dawn of Technicolor, 1915–1935*, ed. Paolo Cherchi Usai and Catherine A. Surowiec (Rochester, NY: George Eastman House, 2015).

30 ICI was one of several dye suppliers to Technicolor, which mixed dyes from numerous components to avoid dependency on a single source. See 'List of Dyes Used in Hollywood, London, and Paris', 23 November 1956, B5/F10, Technicolor Archives.

31 The dyes adhered to animal proteins in the gelatin in the same manner as these organic textiles. See 'The Design of the Imbibition Dye System by John M. Andreas', November 1951, B69/F1, Technicolor Archives.

32 The changing territories covered by each laboratory are charted through 'Technicolor Ltd. License Agreement', 23 July 1935, B1/F13, Technicolor Archives; 'Report to the Board of Directors of Technicolor Ltd.', 1938, M3/F1, Technicolor Archives; and 'Report to the Board of Directors of Technicolor Ltd.', 28 October 1949, M3/F1, Technicolor Archives.

33 E. E. 'Dave' Davis, interview 27 November 1991, audio cassette, BECTU, BFI.
34 On Technicolor Limited's corporate history see Street, *Colour Films in Britain: The Negotiation of Innovation*, pp. 55–56.
35 Laboratory technician Les Ostinelli, interview, 5 November 1992, transcript, BECTU, BFI.
36 Laboratory manager Frank Littlejohn, interview, 13 June 1989, transcript, BECTU, BFI.
37 See Jeffrey Richards, *The Age of the Dream Palace: Cinema and Society in 1930s Britain* (London: I.B. Tauris, 2010), pp. 135–38.
38 Both made in Hollywood due to wartime restrictions. See Charles Drazin, 'Korda, Technicolor and the Zeitgeist', *Journal of British Cinema and Television* 7, no. 1 (March 2010): 5–20.
39 Richards, *The Age of the Dream Palace*, pp. 135–37.
40 Chowdry, *Colonial India and the Making of Empire Cinema*, pp. 57–109.
41 The remainder of this chapter uses the colonial names for Indian cities (Bombay for Mumbai, Calcutta for Kolkata and Madras for Chennai) for consistency with contemporary documents.
42 In particular see Jaikumar, *Cinema at the End of Empire*, pp. 140–50; Street, *Colour Films in Britain: The Negotiation of Innovation*, pp. 135–42; Chowdry, *Colonial India and the Making of Empire Cinema*, pp. 89–109.
43 On the wartime context see Street, *Colour Films in Britain: The Negotiation of Innovation*, pp. 74–76. The film is available to watch online in the British Council film archive: https://film.britishcouncil.org/resources/film-archive/queen-cotton.
44 See Anthea M. Jarvis, 'British Cotton Couture', *Costume* 31, no. 1 (January 1997): 92–99.
45 Among the extensive scholarship on the global circulation of Indian textiles and the role of cotton within Britain's imperial economy, see in particular Anna Arabindan-Kesson, *Black Bodies, White Gold: Art, Cotton, and Commerce in the Atlantic World* (Durham, NC: Duke University Press, 2021), especially pp. 67–120.
46 See Divia Patel, 'Textiles in the Modern World', in *The Fabric of India*, ed. Rosemary Crill (London: V&A Publishing, 2015), pp. 187–95; Natasha Eaton, '*Swadeshi* Color: Artistic Production and Indian Nationalism, ca. 1905–ca. 1947', *Art Bulletin* 95, no. 4 (December 2013): 623–41.
47 Giorgio Riello, 'Luxury or Commodity? The Success of Indian Cotton Cloth in the First Global Age', in *Luxury in Global Perspective: Objects and Practices, 1600–2000*, ed. Karin Hofmeester and Bernd-Stefan Grewe (Cambridge: Cambridge University Press, 2016), p. 138.
48 See Alice Lovejoy, 'From Forests to Film: Chemistry, Industry, and the Rise of Nonflammable Film Stock', in 'In Focus: 16mm', ed. Haidee Wasson, *Journal of Cinema and Media Studies* (forthcoming). A further fascinating connection between film and cotton has been revealed by Debashree Mukherjee: profits from the American cotton industry became a major source of film financing in India. See *Bombay Hustle: Making Movies in a Colonial City* (New York: Columbia University Press, 2020), pp. 44–97.
49 'The Home of Kodak', *International Photographer* 6, no. 6 (July 1936): 4–7.
50 'All that Flickers Isn't Gold!', *Photoplay* 14, no. 2 (July 1918): 43.
51 The film is available to watch online in the British Council film archive: https://film.britishcouncil.org/resources/film-archive/border-weave.
52 Harvey, *The New Imperialism*, p. 2.
53 See Lovejoy, 'Celluloid Geopolitics', pp. 224–41; Josephine Diecke, 'Agfacolor in (Inter)National Competition', in *Color Mania: The Material of Color in Photography and Film*, ed. Barbara Flueckiger, Eva Hielscher and Nadine Wietlisback (Zurich: Lars Müller, 2020), pp. 211–22.
54 Kodak released this system as the result of an anti-trust lawsuit brought by the American government that forced Kodak and Technicolor to end their collusion in keeping monopack from the open market. See Heather Heckman, 'We've Got Bigger Problems: Preservation during Eastman Color's Innovation and Early Diffusion', *Moving Image* 15, no. 1 (July 2015): 51–53.
55 For instance see Richard Misek, *Chromatic Cinema: A History of Screen Color* (Chichester: Wiley-Blackwell, 2010), pp. 39–40.
56 See Jacqueline Maingard, 'Screening Africa in Colour: Abderrahmane Sissako's *Bamako*', *Screen* 51, no. 4 (December 2010): 397–403.
57 On the globalisation of colour cinema see Sarah Street, 'The Monopack Revolution, Global Cinema and *Jigokumon/Gate of Hell* (Kinugasa Teinosuke, 1953)', *Open Screens* 1, no. 1 (June 2018), https://doi.org/10.16995/os.2.
58 The first colour laboratories in Asia were Film Centre in India (1952) followed by Toyo in Japan (1953). On Asia see Dootson and Zhu, 'Did Madame Mao Dream in Technicolor?'. John Akomfrah notes that 'no sub-Saharan African country had a laboratory that could process colour film' in the 1950s; see 'Digitopia and the Spectres of Diaspora', *Journal of Media Practice* 11, no. 1 (March 2010): 25. Manthia Diawara extends the discussion of film technologies in Africa in 'Sub-Saharan African Film Production: Technological Paternalism', *Jump Cut* 32 (April 1987), pp. 61–65.
59 Wilson, interview, BECTU, BFI. Other laboratory staff also recalled the 1960s as the busiest decade for IB processing, including Runkel and Bernard Happé, interview, 13 June 1989, transcript, BECTU, BFI.
60 Bernard Happé, *80 Years of Colour Cinematography* (London: British Kinematograph, Sound and Television Society, 1984), p. 15. On the use of IB printing for Eastmancolor films in Britain see Sarah Street et al., *Colour Films in Britain: The Eastmancolor Revolution* (London: Palgrave Macmillan on behalf of the British Film Institute, 2021).

61 Akomfrah, 'Digitopia and the Spectres of Diaspora', pp. 21–29; Diawara, 'Sub-Saharan African Film', pp. 61–65.
62 Akomfrah, 'Digitopia and the Spectres of Diaspora', p. 25; Diawara, 'Sub-Saharan African Film'.
63 Akomfrah, 'Digitopia and the Spectres of Diaspora', p. 23.
64 Frantz Fanon, *Black Skin, White Masks*, trans. Charles Lam Markmann (London: Pluto Press, 2008), p. 82. See also Alessandra Raengo, *On the Sleeve of the Visual: Race as Face Value* (Hanover, NH: Dartmouth College Press, 2013), pp. 10–12.
65 Raengo, *On the Sleeve of the Visual*, pp. 26–28.
66 On Technicolor and Cold War ideology see Dootson and Zhu, 'Did Madame Mao Dream in Technicolor?'
67 Including Agfacolor for *Sairandhri* (1933; dir. V. Shantaram), processed in Germany, and Cinecolor for *Kisan Kanya* (1937; dir. Moti Gidwani), alongside the pervasive use of hand-colouring for special sequences in films such as *Shakuntala* (1942; dir. V. Shantaram). See Govind Nihalani Gulzar and Saibal Chatterjee, eds., *Encyclopedia of Hindi Cinema* (New Delhi: Encylopaedia Britannica, 2003), pp. 253–54.
68 'Technicolor Plans Activities Abroad', *Technicolor News and Views*, June 1949.
69 See *Technicolor News and Views*, December 1952.
70 Société Technicolor had closed by 1958 and Technicolor Italiana was not operational until 1959. On the company's prioritisation of India see 'Technicolor', *Motion Picture Daily*, 16 May 1955. For a discussion of these various laboratories see Kirsty Sinclair Dootson, '"One Global Laboratory": Mapping Technicolor's Transnational Operations 1955–1993', in *Global Film Color: The Monopack Revolution at Midcentury*, ed. Sarah Street and Joshua Yumibe (New Brunswick, NJ: Rutgers University Press, in development)
71 'Plan to set up Technicolor Laboratory: Producers Enter into Agreement', *The Times of India*, 24 April 1955, p. 3.
72 The report was produced by a committee chaired by politician S. K. Patil and including filmmaker V. Shantaram. See S. K. Patel, *Report of the Film Enquiry Committee* (New Delhi: India Press, 1951).
73 Ibid., p. 74.
74 'Lok Sabha Questions', *The Times of India*, 3 August 1955, p. 11.
75 Grazia Ingravalle, 'Indian or British Film Heritage? The Material Life of Britain's Colonial Film Archive', *Journal of Cinema and Media Studies* 61, no. 2 (Winter 2022): 66.
76 J. D. Spiro, 'Hollywood Dossier', *New York Times*, 3 August 1952, p. 3.
77 However, the colour separation negatives are held at the British Film Institute, offering hope of a restored release print in the future.
78 Also called the Indian Revolt of 1857.
79 See Vijay Devadas, 'The Shifting Terrains of Nationalism and Patriotism in Indian Cinema', in *Routledge Handbook of Indian Cinemas*, ed. K. Moti Gokulsing, Wimal Dissanayake and Wimal Dissanayake (London: Routledge, 2013), pp. 218–22.
80 *Jhansi Ki Rani* souvenir programme, William K. Everson Collection, New York University (https://wke.hosting.nyu.edu/wke).
81 Amrit Gangar, *Sohrab Modi: The Great Mughal of Historicals* (New Delhi: Wisdom Tree, 2008), p. 45.
82 See 'Months of Research and Years of Planning behind India's First Picture in Color by Technicolor', in '*Jhansi Ki Rani*', supplement, *The Times of India*, 18 January 1953, p. ii; Frederick Foster, 'Assignment in India', *American Cinematographer* 33 (June 1952): 252, 260. As Ram Tipnis, appointed head of the make-up department at Filmistan Studios in 1945, recalled, 'when color film came, there was no make-up person who knew how to respond to that'. See Debashree Mukherjee, 'A Material World: Notes on an Interview with Ram Tipnis', *BioScope: South Asian Screen Studies* 1, no. 2 (July 2010): 204.
83 See Jack Howard, 'The Film in India', *Quarterly of Film Radio and Television* 6, no. 3 (1952): 224; Gayatri Chatterjee, *Mother India* (London: British Film Institute, 2002), pp. 20–21.
84 The film was shown in Europe under the title *The Lotus of Kashmir*.
85 A. J. Patel, 'Colour Processing in India', in 'Photography, Cinema and Studio Equipment', supplement, *The Times of India*, 30 December 1955, p. 2.
86 'Patel's "Pamposh" a Poem in Celluloid', *The Times of India*, 18 January 1953, p. 3; Frederick Foster, 'India's First Feature in Gevacolor', *American Cinematographer* 35, no. 8 (1954): 414–16.
87 See Priya Jaikumar, *Where Histories Reside: India as Filmed Space* (Durham, NC: Duke University Press, 2019), pp. 127–80.
88 Spiro, 'Hollywood Dossier'.
89 'Months of Research'; Foster, 'Assignment in India'.
90 'Months of Research'.
91 'Famous English Beautifier Feels at Home in India', in '*Jhansi Ki Rani*', supplement, *The Times of India*, 18 January 1953, p. iv.
92 'Behind the Screen', *Jhansi Ki Rani* souvenir programme. Fascinatingly, several Indian cinematographers were sent by their directors to train at Technicolor in London: in the 1950s Renoir sent Ramananda Sengupta and Raj Kapoor sent Radhu Karmakar, and in the 1960s Guru Dutt sent V. K. Murthy.
93 'How Big Is the Production?', *Jhansi Ki Rani* souvenir programme.
94 Foster, 'Assignment in India', p. 260.
95 See Jaikumar, *Where Histories Reside*, pp. 127–80.
96 Jean Renoir, 'First Interview', interview by Jacques Rivette and François Truffaut, *Cahiers du Cinema* 35 (May 1954), reprinted in Jean Renoir, *Renoir on Renoir: Interviews, Essays, and Remarks*, trans. Carol Volk (Cambridge: Cambridge University Press, 1989), p. 34.
97 Gangar, *Sohrab Modi*, p. 79.
98 If the statistics given in 'How Big Is the Production?' (*Jhansi Ki Rani* souvenir programme) are to be believed, Techni-

color accounted for 27 lacs of the film's 94.5 lac (or 945,000 rupee) budget.

99 On average print runs see Chatterjee, *Mother India*, p. 10.

100 *Mother India* was initially processed at Film Centre with release prints produced by Technicolor.

101 'Screen's Nine-Million-Rupee-Salute to Courage by the Courageous Modi Brothers', in '*Jhansi Ki Rani*', supplement, *The Times of India*, 18 January 1953, p. i.

102 'Indian Film Scene: Technicolor & Production Design for New Picture', *Illustrated Weekly of India* 72 (December 1951), p. 41.

103 Indeed this is one of Eaton's key tenets in *Colour, Art and Empire*.

104 'Gala Opening of Sohrab Modi Opus "Jhansi Ki Rani" at New Empire Tomorrow', *The Times of India*, 23 January 1953, p. 6.

105 Ibid. Republic Day marks the establishment of the Constitution of India (1950).

106 'Centenary of First War of Freedom', *The Times of India*, 14 August 1957, p. 5.

107 The Indian footage was released in 1912 under the title *With Our King and Queen through India*. See Luke McKernan, '"The Modern Elixir of Life": Kinemacolor, Royalty and the Delhi Durbar', *Film History* 21, Early Colour Part 2 (2009): 122–36.

108 Discussed in David Cannadine, 'The Context, Performance and Meaning of Ritual: The British Monarchy and the "Invention of Tradition", c.1820–1977,' in *The Invention of Tradition*, ed. E. J. Hobsbawm and T. O. Ranger (Cambridge: Cambridge University Press, 1984), p. 153.

109 James Chapman, 'Cinema, Monarchy and the Making of Heritage: *A Queen Is Crowned* 1953', in *British Historical Cinema*, ed. Claire Monk and Amy Sargeant (London: Routledge, 2015), pp. 82–85.

110 Davis, interview, BECTU, BFI. On Indian distribution see 'Technicolor Film', *The Times of India*, 2 June 1953, p. 3.

111 'Report to the Board of Directors of Technicolor Limited', 8 October 1956, M3/F1, Technicolor Archives.

112 Minutes from a meeting between Mr Chattopadhaya of Ramnord Research Laboratories and Technicolor representatives, 23 August 1956, B2/F10, Technicolor Archives.

113 'Report to the Board of Directors of Technicolor Limited', 8 October 1956, M3/F1, Technicolor Archives. Patel discusses the lack of colour production in 'A Plea for Protection', *Sports and Pastime* 17, no. 40 (October 1963), p. 52.

114 See Mazumdar, 'Aviation, Tourism and Dreaming'.

115 '1965 Annual Report, Technicolor Inc.', M1/F84, Technicolor Archives.

116 The equipment was subsequently sold to China. See Dootson and Zhu, 'Did Madame Mao Dream in Technicolor?'

5 The BBC's Colour Problem

1 Stanley Reynolds, 'Television', *The Guardian*, 6 July 1967, p. 7.

2 Ibid.

3 On the significance of the show for actors of colour in Britain see Darrell M. Newton, *Paving the Empire Road: BBC Television and Black Britons* (Manchester: Manchester University Press, 2011), pp. 148–49.

4 Reynolds, 'Television'.

5 Sarita Malik and Darrell M. Newton, 'Introduction', in *Adjusting the Contrast: British Television and Constructs of Race*, ed. Sarita Malik and Darrell M. Newton (Manchester: Manchester University Press, 2017), p. 2.

6 On the problematic construction of the Windrush generation as the origin of Black migration in Britain see Kennetta Hammond Perry, *London Is the Place for Me: Black Britons, Citizenship and the Politics of Race* (Oxford: Oxford University Press, 2015), p. 15.

7 This footage is discussed in Newton, *Paving the Empire Road*, p. 1. As Malik notes, Black representation had been crucial to the history of British television since its inception, with Josephine Baker appearing in experimental BBC broadcasts as early as 1933. See Sarita Malik, *Representing Black Britain: A History of Black and Asian Images on British Television* (London: SAGE Publications, 2002), p. 4.

8 Lynda Nead, *The Tiger in the Smoke: Art and Culture in Post-war Britain* (New Haven and London: Yale University Press for the Paul Mellon Centre for Studies in British Art, 2017), pp. 129–33.

9 On how old and new Commonwealth nations were essentialised as sources of Black and White migration see Perry, *London Is the Place for Me*, pp. 155–87; Bob Carter, Clive Harris and Shirley Joshi, 'The 1951–1955 Conservative Government and the Racialisation of Black Immigration', in *Black British Culture and Society: A Text Reader*, ed. Kwesi Owusu (London: Routledge, 2000), pp. 23–36.

10 Stuart Hall, 'The Whites of Their Eyes: Racist Ideologies and the Media', reprinted in *The Race and Media Reader*, edited by Gilbert B. Rodman (New York: Routledge, 2014), pp. 37–54.

11 To name a few examples: 'Race and Recognition: Growing Colour Problems in Britain', BBC Radio, 20 November 1952; Anthony Richmond, *The Colour Problem: A Study of Race Relations* (Harmondsworth, UK: Penguin, 1955); 'Second Inquiry: A Question of Colour', BBC1, 14 November 1958; Peter Griffiths, *The Question of Colour* (London: Frewin, 1966).

12 *The Economist*, 29 November 1958; discussed in Kathleen Paul, *Whitewashing Britain: Race and Citizenship in the Postwar Era* (Ithaca, NY: Cornell University Press, 1997), p. 131.

13 Bill Schwarz, '"The Only White Man in There": The Re-racialisation of England, 1956–1968', *Race & Class* 38, no. 1 (July 1996): 65–78.

14 'Intense Passions over Colour', *The Times*, 17 September 1964; discussed in Perry, *London Is the Place for Me*, p. 188.

15 The speech is discussed and analysed at length in Dilip Hiro, *Black British White British: A History of Race Relations in Britain* (London: Grafton, 1991), pp. 246–61.

16 Hanif Kureishi, *My Beautiful Laundrette and The Rainbow Sign* (London: Faber & Faber, 1986), p. 7.

17 Quoted in Jim Pines, ed., *Black and White in Colour: Black People in British Television since 1936* (London: British Film Institute, 1992), p. 48.

18 'D/Tel's Monthly Meeting', 3 February 1967, T/16/47/11 (*Colour Television 8, 1967–1968*), BBC Written Archives Centre (hereafter BBC WAC).

19 On this terminology see Malik, *Representing Black Britain*, p. 3; Malik and Newton, 'Introduction', p. 10; Perry, *London Is the Place for Me*, p. 16.

20 Paul Gilroy, *'There Ain't No Black in the Union Jack': The Cultural Politics of Race and Nation* (London: Routledge, 2002), p. 37.

21 Perry, *London Is the Place for Me*, p. 17.

22 Detailed in R. W. Burns, *The Struggle for Unity: Colour Television, the Formative Years* (London: Institution of Engineering and Technology, 2008); Andreas Fickers, 'The Techno-politics of Colour: Britain and the European Struggle for a Colour Television Standard', *Journal of British Cinema and Television* 7, no. 1 (March 2010): 95–114.

23 Colin McIntyre, Chief Publicity Officer, 'Further Colour Guidance', February 1967, T66/16 1/2 (*Colour Television Start of Services 1953–1971*), BBC WAC.

24 See Susan Murray, '"Never Twice the Same Colour": Standardizing, Calibrating and Harmonizing NTSC Colour Television in the Early 1950s', *Screen* 56, no. 4 (December 2015): 415–35.

25 'Broadcasting Corporation Guide for Colour Production', 23 November 1966, R53/38/7 (*Technical. General. Colour Television. General. July 1966–1967*), BBC WAC.

26 Jim Richards, 'Lighting for Television', *Royal Television Society Journal*, May–June 1972: 61. Emphasis in original.

27 'Broadcasting Corporation Guide for Colour Production'.

28 On Cold War contexts see Fickers, 'The Techno-politics of Colour'.

29 Articulated across various meetings held in 1966 and 1967. See T16/95/1 (*TV Policy Meeting: Colour Steering Group Minutes 1–110, File 1, 1966–1967*), BBC WAC.

30 Maurice Wiggins, 'Whitest of All on Colour TV', *Sunday Times*, 2 July 1967; Roger Elgin, 'Wimbledon Colour TV Whiter than White', *The Observer*, 2 July 1967.

31 See for instance L. Marsland Gander, 'Laying on Colour', *Daily Telegraph*, 3 July 1967.

32 Philip Purser, 'Match Point to Colour TV', *Sunday Telegraph*, 2 July 1967.

33 For statistics on television ownership and costs see Burns, *The Struggle for Unity*, p. 292.

34 'Minutes from a Meeting of the Finance Committee of the Board of Governors', 27 February 1969, R78/555/1 (*Colour TV Promotion*), BBC WAC.

35 In 1967 the only UHF transmitting stations were in London, Birmingham, Yorkshire, Lancashire, Lincolnshire and the Isle of Wight.

36 Letter from Buckingham Palace dated 12 December 1967, R78/554/1 (*Colour Television General*), BBC WAC.

37 Asa Briggs, *The History of Broadcasting in the United Kingdom*, vol. 5, *Competition*, rev. edn (Oxford: Oxford University Press, 1995), p. 848.

38 Untitled press clipping from *The Sun*, 3 July 1967, in 'Colour Launching: Press Reaction', R44/1,218/1 (*Radio Times, Television Colour Launching*), BBC WAC.

39 'Draft Speech for Colour Television Comes to Town', 25 September 1967, R78/555/1, BBC WAC; Ian Atkins, 'Working in Colour: A lecture by Ian Atkins – Controller of Programme Services (Television)', Broadcasting House, 13 December 1967, T66/161/1 (*Colour Television Start of Services, 1953–1971*), BBC WAC.

40 Newton notes, however, that in the 1960s the BBC increasingly engaged in dialogue with minority groups to better address their needs in terms of representation and employment. See *Paving the Empire Road*, pp. 120–30.

41 'David Attenborough's Speech to the International Television Design Conference on Colour, London, Monday November 4 1968', T75/1/1 (*Colour TV: Lighting, Technical Memos and Lectures 1, 1962–1974*), BBC WAC.

42 Ibid.

43 On American tactics for selling colour television see Susan Murray, *Bright Signals: A History of Color Television* (Durham, NC: Duke University Press, 2018).

44 On early production meetings see James Stourton, *Kenneth Clark: Life, Art and Civilisation* (London: William Collins, 2016), pp. 318–19.

45 See Lynn Spigel, *TV by Design: Modern Art and the Rise of Network Television* (Chicago: University of Chicago Press, 2008).

46 Spigel, *TV by Design*, p. 166.

47 On the 2018 remake see David Olusoga, 'Civilisation Revisited', *The Guardian*, 4 February 2018.

48 The print records an incident described by William Wilberforce in the House of Commons, for which Captain Kimber was subsequently tried by the Admiralty. See M. Dorothy George, *Catalogue of Political and Personal Satires in the British Museum*, vol. 6 (London: British Museum, 1938), p. 356.

49 However, there are wide variations in the hues selected for hand-colouring across different versions of this print.

50 'How to Look Your Best on Colour Television', 5 May 1967, T31/206/3 (*TV Staff Wardrobe Department 3, 1965–1968*), BBC WAC.

51 'Broadcasting Corporation Guide for Colour Production'.

52 Philip Ward, 'Creative Lighting for Colour: Article for E. B. U. Review', T75/1/2 (*Colour TV: Lighting, Technical*

Memos and Lectures 2, 1962–1974), BBC WAC.

53 Barry Leonard, Coordinator for Colour Familiarisation, 'Some Notes on Colour Realisation for Television', January 1969, T/16/47/11 (*Colour Television 8, 1967–1968*), BBC WAC.

54 Peter Shepherd, head of BBC costume department, 'Costumes for Colour' (lecture, International Television Design Conference on Colour, London, 4–8 November 1968), T75/1/1 (*Colour TV: Lighting, Technical Memos and Lectures 1, 1962–1974*), BBC WAC.

55 Leonard, 'Some Notes on Colour Realisation for Television'. Technicolor carried out this same operation, producing what was known as 'Technicolor White'.

56 Atkins, 'Working in Colour'.

57 Ward, 'Creative Lighting for Colour'.

58 Leonard, 'Some Notes on Colour Realisation for Television'.

59 This formulation of dark skin as a 'problem' for photographic media has a long history, as discussed in Chapter Three and in Richard Dyer, *White* (London: Routledge, 1997); Genevieve Yue, *Girl Head: Feminism and Film Materiality* (New York: Fordham University Press, 2020), especially pp. 33–62; Tanya Sheehan, 'Colour Matters: Rethinking Photography and Race', in *The Colors of Photography*, ed. Bettina Gockel (Berlin: De Gruyter, 2020), pp. 55–72; Deborah Willis, 'Encounters with Colour Photography', in *The Colors of Photography*, ed. Bettina Gockel (Berlin: De Gruyter, 2020), pp. 74–94.

60 See Paul Gilroy, *The Black Atlantic: Modernity and Double Consciousness* (London: Verso, 1993).

61 Ibid., pp. 1–2.

62 In particular see Wiggins, 'Whitest of All on Colour TV'; James Thomas, 'Colour TV… Yes It Really Is Worth It', *Daily Express*, 3 July 1967.

63 Julian Critchley, 'BBC Colours Its Vision', *The Times*, 3 July 1967. The redaction is informed by the work of scholars including Elizabeth Stordeur Pryor and Terah J. Stewart. See for example Terah J. Stewart, 'To Whom It Should Concern: An Open Letter on the N-Word and Academic Publishing', 16 July 2021, https://terahjay.medium.com/to-whom-it-should-concern-an-open-letter-on-the-n-word-and-academic-publishing-edcd0c699578.

64 Elgin, 'Wimbledon Colour TV Whiter than White'; Thomas, 'Colour TV'.

65 Kennetta Hammond Perry, '"Little Rock" in Britain: Jim Crow's Transatlantic Topographies', *Journal of British Studies* 51, no. 1 (January 2012): 155–77; Rob Waters, 'Black Power on the Telly: America, Television, and Race in 1960s and 1970s Britain', *Journal of British Studies* 54, no. 4 (October 2015): 947–70.

66 On the press coverage of the 'Colour Bar' see Perry, *London Is the Place for Me*, pp. 188–89; Malik, *Representing Black Britain*, pp. 37–42.

67 Perry, *London Is the Place for Me*, p. 189.

68 On the significance of the 1964 election see Gilroy, *'There Ain't No Black in the Union Jack'*, pp. 100–104; Perry, *London Is the Place for Me*, pp. 194–200.

69 Perry, *London Is the Place for Me*, p. 195.

70 On Malcolm X's visit to Smethwick see ibid., pp. 195–98.

71 A view strongly articulated in Obi Egbuna's *Black Power in Britain* manifesto, published by the Universal Coloured People's Association in 1967. See R. E. R. Bunce and Paul Field, 'Obi B. Egbuna, C. L. R. James and the Birth of Black Power in Britain: Black Radicalism in Britain 1967–72', *Twentieth Century British History* 22, no. 3 (September 2011): 391–414.

72 On American civil rights leaders in Britain see Waters, 'Black Power on the Telly', pp. 947–70. On the Race Relations Act see Bunce and Field, 'Obi B. Egbuna, C. L. R. James and the Birth of Black Power in Britain', p. 395.

73 On the broader history of the Black Power movement in Britain see Bunce and Field, 'Obi B. Egbuna, C. L. R. James and the Birth of Black Power in Britain'.

74 On the centrality of Powellism to 1960s racist discourse see Malik, *Representing Black Britain*, pp. 44–47; Gilroy, *'There Ain't No Black in the Union Jack'*, pp. 104–8.

75 Gilroy, *'There Ain't No Black in the Union Jack'*, pp. 104–8.

76 Ibid., p. 106.

77 The term 'China Girls' refers both to these women's doll-like appearance but also what Yue calls a 'stereotypical notion of Asian femininity that women be subordinate and submissive'; see Yue, *Girl Head*, pp. 33–62.

78 Lorna Roth, 'Looking at Shirley, the Ultimate Norm: Colour Balance, Image Technologies, and Cognitive Equity', *Canadian Journal of Communication* 34, no. 1 (March 2009): 111–36; Yue, *Girl Head*, pp. 33–62; Willis, 'Encounters with Colour Photography', pp. 73–76.

79 Murray, *Bright Signals*, pp. 108–12.

80 'It's Colourific!' *Sunday Mirror*, 2 July 1967.

81 George Hersee, *A Survey of the Development of Television Test Cards Used in the BBC* (London: BBC, 1967), p. 13.

82 Ibid, p. 13.

83 'How to Receive BBC TV 625 Lines and Colour', January 1972, T66/161/1 (*Colour Television, Start of Services 1953–1971*), BBC WAC.

84 Maureen Winsdale, senior make-up supervisor, 'Make-Up for Colour' (lecture, International Television Design Conference on Colour, London, 4–8 November 1968), T75/1/1 (*Colour TV: Lighting, Technical Memos and Lectures 1, 1962–1974*), BBC WAC.

85 Quoted in Pines, *Black and White in Colour*, p. 105.

86 Naomi Adele André, *Black Opera History, Power, Engagement* (Urbana: University of Illinois Press, 2018), pp. 13–19.

87 Quoted in 'Colour Television: A Report on Progress; Draft Paper for the General Advisory Council', 7 March 1968, R78/1,9671 (*Colour Television Policy*), BBC WAC.

88 On 'character make-up' as racial masquerade see Alice Maurice, 'Making Faces: Character and Make-Up in Early Cinema', in *Corporeality in Early Cinema: Viscera, Skin, and Physical Form*, ed. Marina Dahlquist (Bloomington: Indiana University Press, 2018), pp. 198–208.

89 The racial discrimination suffered by actors of colour working in British television of the 1950s and 1960s is traced through the various interviews collated in Pines, *Black and White in Colour*; in particular see interviews with Thomas Baptiste, Pearl Connor, Cy Grant, Joan Hooley, Zia Mohyeddin, Carmen Munroe and Rudolph Walker.

90 Quoted in ibid., pp. 72–73.

91 The significant contributions made by actors of colour during this period as well as the barriers they faced are explored in depth in ibid.; Stephen Bourne, *Black in the British Frame: The Black Experience in British Film and Television* (London: Continuum, 2001); Malik, *Representing Black Britain*; Newton, *Paving the Empire Road.*

92 Quoted in Pines, *Black and White in Colour*, p. 39.

93 Carmen Munroe quoted in Malik, *Representing Black Britain*, p. 140.

94 Quoted in Pines, *Black and White in Colour*, p. 72.

95 Helen Wheatley notes that the BBC's claims that it had no other suitable light entertainment programmes already on BBC2 were untrue. See *Spectacular Television: Exploring Televisual Pleasure* (London: I.B. Tauris, 2016), p. 67.

96 Sarita Malik, '*The Black and White Minstrel Show*', in *Encyclopaedia of Television*, ed. Horace Newcomb, vol. A–F (Chicago: Fitzroy Dearborn, 1997), pp. 185–86.

97 For instance see 'What Programmes Can I Expect to See in Colour?', *BBC2 News* 11 (1967).

98 For one example see Briggs, *The History of Broadcasting*, p. 860.

99 On the history of the show see Malik, '*The Black and White Minstrel Show*', pp. 185–86.

100 On the show's music see Michael Pickering, *Blackface Minstrelsy in Britain* (Aldershot: Ashgate, 2017), p. 218.

101 Christine Grandy, '"The Show Is Not about Race": Custom, Screen Culture, and *The Black and White Minstrel Show*', *Journal of British Studies* 59, no. 4 (October 2020): 857–84. See also Bourne, *Black in the British Frame*, pp. 4–5; Malik, *Representing Black Britain*, p. 113; Newton, *Paving the Empire Road*, pp. 145–47.

102 Quoted in 'Bad Taste BBC', *Flamingo*, September 1961: 22.

103 For a detailed history of the Campaign Against Racial Discrimination protest see Grandy, '"The Show Is Not about Race"'.

104 'Board of Management, Minutes of 22 May 1967', R78/1,921/1, BBC WAC, cited in Grandy, '"The Show Is Not about Race"', p. 877.

105 Quoted in 'Bad Taste BBC', p. 23.

106 Bourne, *Black in the British Frame*, p. 4. See also fn. 98.

107 The origins of minstrelsy are contested and its meanings multiple and contingent. However, antebellum America has conventionally been cited as the place of its emergence. The plurality of meanings of minstrelsy and various accounts of its historical roots are captured in Stephen Burge Johnson, ed., *Burnt Cork: Traditions and Legacies of Blackface Minstrelsy* (Amherst: University of Massachusetts Press, 2012).

108 Wheatly analyses the show's colour in relation to issues of spectacle and the musical genre in *Spectacular Television*, pp. 66–67.

109 Malik, '*The Black and White Minstrel Show*', p. 185.

110 Eric Lott, *Love and Theft: Blackface Minstrelsy and the American Working Class*, 20th anniversary edn (Oxford: Oxford University Press, 2013), p. 18.

111 See Alice Maurice, *The Cinema and Its Shadow: Race and Technology in Early Cinema* (Minneapolis: University of Minnesota Press, 2013), pp. 153–86.

112 Reynolds, 'Television'.

113 See Nead, *The Tiger in the Smoke*, pp. 151–97.

114 Winsdale, 'Make-Up for Colour'.

115 Les Want, a member of the Minstrels, recalled the use of 'Negro No. 2' in an interview on '*The Black and White Minstrel Show* Revisited', *Time Shift*, BBC Four, 8 August 2005; 'Chinese Pancake' and the Toppers' 'pink and blotchy' faces are discussed by the show's make-up assistant in 'Colour Television: A Report on Progress'.

116 Dorothy Mitchell, interview, in '*The Black and White Minstrel Show* Revisited'.

117 Gilroy, *'There Ain't No Black in the Union Jack'*, pp. 106–7.

118 See Elizabeth Buettner, '"Would You Let Your Daughter Marry a Negro?": Race and Sex in 1950s Britain', in *Gender, Labour, War and Empire: Essays on Modern Britain*, ed. Philippa Levine and Susan R. Grayzel (Basingstoke, UK: Palgrave Macmillan, 2009), pp. 219–23; Nead, *The Tiger in the Smoke*, pp. 165–76.

119 Richmond, *The Colour Problem*, p. 290.

120 Cited in Pines, *Black and White in Colour*, pp. 141–42.

121 *Radio Times* listing for 'Man Alive: Mixed Marriage: 2: But What About the Children...?' broadcast 9 July 1968, BBC2 England, as listed on https://genome.ch.bbc.co.uk.

122 Maurice, *The Cinema and Its Shadow*, pp. 153–86; Louis Chude-Sokei, 'The Uncanny History of Minstrelsy and Machines 1835–1923', in *Burnt Cork: Traditions and Legacies of Blackface Minstrelsy*, ed. Stephen Burge Johnson (Amherst: University of Massachusetts Press, 2012), pp. 104–32; Michael Rogin, *Black Face, White Noise: Jewish Immigrants in the Hollywood Melting Pot* (Berkeley: University of California Press, 1996), pp. 78–116.

123 See Maurice, *The Cinema and Its Shadow*, pp. 153–86.

124 Maurice, *The Cinema and Its Shadow*, p. 161; Rogin, *Black Face, White Noise*, p. 49.

125 Reynolds, 'Television'.

126 On blackface and Britishness see Pickering, *Blackface Minstrelsy in Britain*, p. 218.

127 Murray, *Bright Signals*, p. 26.

128 Lott, *Love and Theft*, pp. 5–6.

129 As Rogin argues, in this manner blackface became a means of exercising social mobility for some groups (such as White people, males, Europeans and Jewish Americans) to bar it for others (such as African Americans and women). See *Black Face, White Noise*, p. 115.

130 Gilroy, *'There Ain't No Black in the Union Jack'*, p. 107.

131 Hopkins quoted in Pines, *Black and White in Colour*, p. 94.

132 Newton discusses the complaints in *Paving the Empire Road*, p. 143.

133 Munroe quoted in Pines, *Black and White in Colour*, p. 58.

134 Ibid.

135 Hopkins quoted in Pines, *Black and White in Colour*, p. 96.

136 Malik, *Representing Black Britain*, p. 138.

137 Hopkins quoted in Pines, *Black and White in Colour*, p. 94.

138 Chude-Sokei, 'The Uncanny History of Minstrelsy and Machines', p. 117. Emphasis in original.

139 For instance, see 'Olympics in TV Colour', *Evening Standard*, 9 September 1967.

140 Ibid.

141 On the symbolism of the protest see Tommie Smith, *Silent Gesture: The Autobiography of Tommie Smith* (Philadelphia: Temple University Press, 2007), pp. 20–41.

142 Waters, 'Black Power on the Telly', pp. 952–58.

143 Quoted in Joan Anim-Addo, *Longest Journey: A History of Black Lewisham* (London: Deptford Forum, 1995), p. 108.

144 Trevor Carter with Jean Coussins, *Shattering Illusions: West Indians in British Politics* (London: Lawrence & Wishart, 1986), p. 81. Quoted in Waters, 'Black Power on the Telly', p. 952.

Coda

1 At the time of writing, in June 2021, rainbow flags are also flying high to celebrate Pride. The associations between rainbows and LGBTQ+ identities are one of the aspects of colour's history to which this book has been unable to devote sufficient attention. I am therefore grateful for the work of Brooke Sylvia Palmieri, Rosalind Galt and David Batchelor, who offer rich analyses of colour's many queer histories. See Brooke Sylvia Palmieri, 'Queering Media History: A Study in Color', in *Under the Rainbow*, ed. David Keshavjee et al. (Lausanne: University of Art and Design, 2018), pp. 118–30; Rosalind Galt, *Pretty: Film and the Decorative Image* (New York: Columbia University Press, 2011), especially pp. 75–96; David Batchelor, *Chromophobia* (London: Reaktion Books, 2000).

2 'Neon' is now used as an umbrella term for the various gases used in fluorescent lighting, including xenon, helium, argon and krypton, which each produce different colours.

3 On the discovery and early history of neon see Christoph Ribbat and Anthony Mathews, *Flickering Light: A History of Neon* (London: Reaktion Books, 2013), pp. 23–40.

4 This refusal of binaries is eloquently expressed in the title of Lynda Nead's definitive monograph, *Chila Kumari Burman: Beyond Two Cultures* (London: Kala Press, 1995).

5 Chila Kumari Singh Burman, interview by Lousia Buck, in '"Blinged-Up but Razor-Sharp": Chila Kumari Singh Burman on Her Diwali-Inspired Tate Britain Commission', *Art Newspaper*, 16 November 2020.

6 Ibid.

7 This aphorism was coined and popularised by the London-based Sri Lankan intellectual, academic, writer and anti-racism activist Ambalavaner Sivanandan, and has become synonymous with current critical interrogations of post-colonial identity in British contexts. See Ian Sanjay Patel, *We're Here Because You Were There: Immigration and the End of Empire* (London: Verso, 2021).

8 Burman, '"Blinged-Up but Razor-Sharp"'.

9 While Henry Tate was born after Abolition, the gallery acknowledges the 'less direct but fundamental ways' the practices and profits of slavery in the sugar trade helped to established the institution, making it impossible 'to separate the Tate galleries from the history of colonial slavery from which in part they derive their existence'; see 'The Tate Galleries and Slavery', Tate Gallery, August 2019, https://www.tate.org.uk/about-us/history-tate/tate-galleries-and-slavery. Tim Edensor and Uma Kothari elegantly connect Tate's sugar ties to Burman's own links with confectionary; see 'Chila Kumari Singh Burman: Remembering a Brave New World', *The Senses and Society* 16, no. 2 (May 2021): 256.

10 Stuart Hall, 'Old and New Identities, Old and New Ethnicities' (1991), reprinted in Stuart Hall, *Essential Essays*, vol. 2, *Identity and Diaspora*, ed. David Morley (Durham, NC: Duke University Press, 2018), p. 70.

11 Nead examines the iconography of *Jhansi Ki Rani* in Burman's work as a figure for the 'artist as fighter' in *Chila Kumari Burman*, p. 18.

12 Burman, '"Blinged-Up but Razor-Sharp"'.

13 Edensor and Kothari, 'Chila Kumari Singh Burman', p. 254.

14 We might link this practice to what Divya P. Tolia-Kelly and Andy Morris have called the 'disruptive aesthetics' of Yinka Shonibare CBE (RA), who uses colour in the form of Dutch wax batik textiles, to interrogate processes of colonial erasure and presence in British art and cultural establishments. See 'Disruptive Aesthetics? Revisiting the Burden of Representation in the Art of Chris Ofili and Yinka Shonibare', *Third Text* 18, no. 2 (March 2004): 153–67.

15 Chila Kumari Singh Burman, interview by Russell Tovey and Robert

Diament, in *Talk Art* (Podcast), 1 January 2021.

16 Carolyn Elerding usefully dubs this the 'aesthetics of invisibility' in 'The Materiality of the Digital: Petro-Enlightenment and the Aesthetics of Invisibility', *Postmodern Culture* 26, no. 2 (January 2016), https://doi.org/10.1353/pmc.2016.0007.

17 On the material effects of digital technologies see Jennifer Gabrys, *Digital Rubbish: A Natural History of Electronics* (Ann Arbor: University of Michigan Press, 2013); Jussi Parikka, *Geology of Media* (Minneapolis: University of Minnesota Press, 2015); Sean Cubitt, *Finite Media: Environmental Implications of Digital Technologies* (Durham, NC: Duke University Press, 2017).

18 As the authors of a 2021 report highlight, 'Japan, Australia, New Zealand, South Korea, North America, and Europe export more than 80% of their E-waste to countries such as China, Pakistan, India, Nigeria, Ghana'. See Devin N. Perkins et al., 'E-Waste: A Global Hazard', *Annals of Global Health* 80, no. 4 (2014): 286–95. This dynamic echoes long-established patterns linking environmental injustice with colonialism, imperialism and racism, as described by Françoise Vergès in 'Racial Capitalocene', in *Futures of Black Radicalism*, ed. Gaye Theresa Johnson and Alex Lubin (London: Verso, 2017) and Max Liboiron in *Pollution Is Colonialism* (Durham, NC: Duke University Press, 2021).

Selected Bibliography

Akomfrah, John. 'Digitopia and the Spectres of Diaspora'. *Journal of Media Practice* 11, no. 1 (March 2010): 21–29.

Alexander, Sally. 'Men's Fears and Women's Work: Responses to Unemployment in London between the Wars'. *Gender & History* 12, no. 2 (July 2000): 401–20.

Amato, Sarah. 'The White Elephant in London: An Episode of Trickery, Racism and Advertising'. *Journal of Social History* 43, no. 1 (Fall 2009): 31–66.

Arabindan-Kesson, Anna. *Black Bodies, White Gold: Art, Cotton, and Commerce in the Atlantic World*. Durham, NC: Duke University Press, 2021.

Barringer, Tim. *Men at Work: Art and Labour in Victorian Britain*. New Haven: Yale University Press, 2005.

—, Jason Rosenfeld and Alison Smith. *Pre-Raphaelites: Victorian Avant Garde*. London: Tate, 2012.

Barrington, Mrs. Russell. *G. F. Watts: Reminiscences*. London: Macmillan, 1905.

Batchelor, David. *Chromophobia*. Focus on Contemporary Issues. London: Reaktion Books, 2000.

Berri, D. G. *The Art of Lithography*. London: D. G. Berri, 1864.

Bills, Mark, and Barbara Bryant. *G. F. Watts: Victorian Visionary; Highlights from the Watts Gallery Collection*. New Haven: Yale University Press in association with Watts Gallery Compton, 2008.

Blaszczyk, Regina Lee. *The Color Revolution*. Cambridge, MA: MIT Press, 2012.

—, and Uwe Spiekermann, eds. *Bright Modernity: Color, Commerce, and Consumer Culture*. New York: Palgrave Macmillan, 2017.

Bloy, C. H. *A History of Printing Ink, Balls and Rollers, 1440–1850*. London: Evelyn Adams & Mackay, 1967.

Bol, Marjolijn. 'Technique and the Art of Immortality, 1800–1900'. *History of Humanities* 2, no. 1 (March 2017): 179–99.

Bourne, Stephen. *Black in the British Frame: The Black Experience in British Film and Television*. London: Continuum, 2001.

Bowyer, Justin, and Jack Cardiff. *Conversations with Jack Cardiff: Art, Light and Direction in Cinema*. London: Batsford, 2003.

Briggs, Asa. *The History of Broadcasting in the United Kingdom*. 5 vols. Oxford: Oxford University Press, 1995.

Bronkhurst, Judith. *William Holman Hunt: A Catalogue Raisonné*. 2 vols. New Haven and London: Yale University Press for the Paul Mellon Centre for Studies in British Art, 2006.

Brown, Simon. 'Colouring the Nation: Spectacle, Reality and British Natural Colour in the Silent and Early Sound Era'. *Film History* 21, no. 2 (July 2009): 139–49.

—, Sarah Street and Liz Watkins, eds. *British Colour Cinema: Practices and Theories*. Basingstoke, UK: Palgrave Macmillan on behalf of British Film Institute, 2013.

Bubb, Ruth E. 'The Life and Work of George Field Colourmaker (1777–1854)'. In *Das 19. Jahrhundert und die Restaurierung: Beiträge zur Malerei, Maltechnik und Konservierung*, edited by Heinz Althöfer, 238–47. Munich: Callwey, 1987.

Bunce, R. E. R., and Paul Field. 'Obi B. Egbuna, C. L. R. James and the Birth of Black Power in Britain: Black Radicalism in Britain 1967–72'. *Twentieth Century British History* 22, no. 3 (September 2011): 391–414.

Burns, R. W. *The Struggle for Unity: Colour Television, the Formative Years*. IEE History of Technology Series 34.

London: Institution of Engineering and Technology, 2008.

Caldwell, John Thornton. *Production Culture: Industrial Reflexivity and Critical Practice in Film and Television*. Console-Ing Passions. Durham, NC: Duke University Press, 2008.

Callen, Anthea. *The Art of Impressionism: Painting Technique and the Making of Modernity*. New Haven: Yale University Press, 2000.

Callendar, Ron. 'Viva Vivex'. *The Photographer* 13, no. 1 (January 1978): 24–25.

—. 'Viva Vivex'. *The Photographer* 13, no. 2 (February 1978): 40–41.

Cannadine, David. *Ornamentalism: How the British Saw Their Empire*. New York: Oxford University Press, 2001.

Carlyle, Leslie. *The Artist's Assistant: Oil Painting Instruction Manuals and Handbooks in Britain 1800–1900 with Reference to Selected Eighteenth-Century Sources*. London: Archetype Publications, 2001.

—. 'Authenticity and Adulteration: What Materials Were 19th Century Artists Really Using?' *The Conservator* 17, no. 1 (January 1993): 56–60.

—. 'Contemporary Painting Materials'. In *Pre-Raphaelite Painting Techniques*, edited by Joyce Jacqueline Ridge and Stephen Hackney, 38–49. London: Tate, 2004.

Carlyle, Thomas. *Past and Present*. The Norman and Charlotte Strouse Edition of the Writings of Thomas Carlyle. Berkeley: University of California Press, 2005.

Cater, Bob, Clive Harris and Shirley Joshi, 'The 1951–1955 Conservative Government and the Racialisation of Black Immigration'. In *Black British Culture and Society: A Text Reader*, edited by Kwesi Owusu, 23–36. London: Routledge, 2000.

Chatterjee, Gayatri. *Mother India*. London: British Film Institute, 2002.

Cheng, Anne Anlin. *Second Skin: Josephine Baker and the Modern Surface*. New York: Oxford University Press, 2013.

Chowdry, Prem. *Colonial India and the Making of Empire Cinema: Image, Ideology and Identity*. Manchester: Manchester University Press, 2000.

Christensen, Jerome. *America's Corporate Art: The Studio Authorship of Hollywood Motion Pictures*. Post 45. Stanford: Stanford University Press, 2012.

Chude-Sokei, Louis. 'The Uncanny History of Minstrelsy and Machines, 1835–1923'. In *Burnt Cork: Traditions and Legacies of Blackface Minstrelsy*, edited by Stephen Burge Johnson, 104–32. Amherst: University of Massachusetts Press, 2012.

Chuong, Jennifer Y. 'Engraving's "Immoveable Veil of Black": Phillis Wheatley's Portrait and the Politics of Technique'. *Art Bulletin* 104, no. 2 (April 2022): 63–88.

Clay, Catherine, ed. *Women's Periodicals and Print Culture in Britain, 1918–1939: The Interwar Period*. Edinburgh History of Women's Periodical Culture in Britain. Edinburgh: Edinburgh University Press, 2018.

Coates, Paul. *Cinema and Colour: The Saturated Image*. Basingstoke, UK: Palgrave Macmillan, 2010.

Crary, Jonathan. *Techniques of the Observer: On Vision and Modernity in the Nineteenth Century*. Cambridge, MA: MIT Press, 1990.

Crill, Rosemary, ed. *The Fabric of India*. London: V&A Publishing, 2015.

Cubitt, Sean. *Finite Media: Environmental Implications of Digital Technologies*. Durham, NC: Duke University Press, 2017.

Diawara, Manthia. 'Sub-Saharan African Film Production Technological Paternalism'. *Jump Cut* 32 (April 1987): 61–65.

Diecke, Josephine. 'Agfacolor in (Inter)National Competition'. In *Color Mania: The Material of Color in Photography and Film*, edited by Barbara Flueckiger, Eva Hielscher and Nadine Wietlisback, 211–22. Zurich: Lars Müller, 2020.

Dootson, Kirsty Sinclair. '"The Hollywood Powder Puff War": Technicolor Cosmetics in the 1930s'. *Film History* 28, no. 1 (June 2016): 107–31.

—. 'The Texture of Capitalism: Industrial Oil Colours and the Politics of Paint in the Work of G. F. Watts', *British Art Studies* 14, https://doi.org/10.17658/issn.2058-5462/issue-14/kdootson.

—, and Zhaoyu Zhu. 'Did Madame Mao Dream in Technicolor? Rethinking Cold War Colour Cinema through Technicolor's "Chinese Copy"'. *Screen* 61, no. 3 (September 2020): 343–67.

Dyer, Richard. *White*. London: Routledge, 1997.

Eaton, Natasha. *Colour, Art and Empire: Visual Culture and the Nomadism of Representation*. International Library of Visual Culture 12. London: I.B. Tauris, 2013.

—. '*Swadeshi* Color: Artistic Production and Indian Nationalism, ca. 1905–ca. 1947'. *Art Bulletin* 95, no. 4 (December 2013): 623–41.

Edensor, Tim, and Uma Kothari. 'Chila Kumari Singh Burman: Remembering a Brave New World'. *The Senses and Society* 16, no. 2 (May 2021): 252–58.

Elgin, Roger. 'Wimbledon Colour TV Whiter than White'. *The Observer*, 2 July 1967.
Fanon, Frantz. *Black Skin, White Masks*. Translated by Charles Lam Markmann. Forewords by Ziauddin Sardar and Homi K. Bhabha. London: Pluto Press, 2008.
Felski, Rita. *The Gender of Modernity*. Cambridge, MA: Harvard University Press, 1995.
Fend, Mechthild. *Fleshing Out Surfaces: Skin in French Art and Medicine, 1650–1850*. Manchester: Manchester University Press, 2017.
Fickers, Andreas. 'The Techno-politics of Colour: Britain and the European Struggle for a Colour Television Standard'. *Journal of British Cinema and Television* 7, no. 1 (March 2010): 95–114.
Flueckiger, Barbara, Eva Hielscher and Nadine Wietlisback, eds. *Color Mania: The Material of Color in Photography and Film*. Zurich: Lars Müller, 2020.
Gabrys, Jennifer. *Digital Rubbish: A Natural History of Electronics*. Ann Arbor: University of Michigan Press, 2013.
Gage, John. *Colour and Culture: Practice and Meaning from Antiquity to Abstraction*. London: Thames & Hudson, 1993.
—. *Color and Meaning: Art, Science, and Symbolism*. Berkeley: University of California Press, 1999.
—. *Color in Turner: Poetry and Truth*. New York: Praeger, 1969.
—. *George Field and His Circle: From Romanticism to the Pre-Raphaelite Brotherhood*. London: Christie's, 1989.
Galt, Rosalind. *Pretty: Film and the Decorative Image*. New York: Columbia University Press, 2011.
Gangar, Amrit. *Sohrab Modi: The Great Mughal of Historicals*. New Delhi: Wisdom Tree, 2008.
Gaskill, Nicholas. *Chromographia: American Literature and the Modernization of Color*. Minneapolis: Minnesota University Press, 2018.
Gates, Racquel J. *Double Negative: The Black Image and Popular Culture*. Durham, NC: Duke University Press, 2018.
Gibson, Robin, and Pamela Glasson Roberts. *Madame Yevonde: Colour, Fantasy and Myth*. London: National Portrait Gallery, 1990.
Gilroy, Paul. *The Black Atlantic: Modernity and Double Consciousness*. London: Verso, 1993.
—. *'There Ain't No Black in the Union Jack': The Cultural Politics of Race and Nation*. London: Routledge, 2002.
Gockel, Bettina, ed. *The Colors of Photography*. Berlin: De Gruyter, 2020.
Gould, Sarah. 'Making Texture Matter: The Materiality of British Paintings, 1788–1914'. PhD diss., Université Paris Diderot, 2016.
Gould, Veronica Franklin. *G. F. Watts: The Last Great Victorian*. New Haven: Yale University Press, 2004.
Grandy, Christine. '"The Show Is Not about Race": Custom, Screen Culture, and *The Black and White Minstrel Show*'. *Journal of British Studies* 59, no. 4 (October 2020): 857–84.
Grieveson, Lee. *Cinema and the Wealth of Nations: Media, Capital, and the Liberal World System*. Oakland: University of California Press, 2018.
—, and Colin MacCabe, eds. *Film and the End of Empire*. New York: Palgrave Macmillan, 2011.
Haines, Richard W. *Technicolor Movies: The History of Dye Transfer Printing*. Jefferson, NC: McFarland, 1993.
Hall, Stuart. 'Old and New Identities, Old and New Ethnicities' (1991). Reprinted in Stuart Hall, *Essential Essays*. Vol. 2, *Identity and Diaspora*, edited by David Morley, 63–82. Durham, NC: Duke University Press, 2018.
—. 'The Whites of Their Eyes: Racist Ideologies and the Media'. Reprinted in *The Race and Media Reader*, edited by Gilbert B. Rodman, 37–54. New York: Routledge, 2014.
Hamerton, Philip Gilbert. 'Technical Notes'. *The Portfolio: An Artistic Periodical* 6 (1875): 45–48.
Hansard, T. C. *Typographia*. London: Baldwin, Cradock, and Joy, 1825.
Hansen, Miriam. 'The Mass Production of the Senses: Classical Cinema as Vernacular Modernism'. *Modernism/Modernity* 6, no. 2 (April 1999): 59–77.
Happé, Bernard. *80 Years of Colour Cinematography*. London: British Kinematograph, Sound and Television Society, 1984.
Harvey, David. *The New Imperialism*. Oxford: Oxford University Press, 2003.
Heckman, Heather. 'Undervalued Stock: Eastman Color's Innovation & Diffusion, 1900–1957'. Ph.D. diss., University of Wisconsin–Madison, 2014.
—. 'We've Got Bigger Problems: Preservation during Eastman Color's Innovation and Early Diffusion'. *Moving Image* 15, no. 1 (July 2015): 44–61.
Henning, Michelle. 'The Worlding of Light and Air: Dufaycolor and Selochrome in the 1930s'. *Visual Culture in Britain*, 23 March 2020: 1–22.
Hermens, Erma, ed. *Looking through Paintings: The Study of Painting Techniques and Materials in Support of Art*

Historical Research. Leids Kunsthistorisch Jaarboek 11. Baarn, Netherlands: De Pron, 1998.

Higgins, Scott. *Harnessing the Technicolor Rainbow Color Design in the 1930s*. Austin: University of Texas Press, 2007.

Hiro, Dilip. *Black British, White British: A History of Race Relations in Britain*. London: Grafton, 1991.

Hobsbawm, E. J., and T. O. Ranger, eds. *The Invention of Tradition*. Cambridge: Cambridge University Press, 1984.

Houlbrook, Matt. '"The Man with the Powder Puff" in Interwar London'. *Historical Journal* 50, no. 1 (March 2007): 145–71.

Hunt, W. Holman. *Pre-Raphaelitism and the Pre-Raphaelite Brotherhood*. 3 vols. London: Macmillan, 1905.

—. 'The Present System of Obtaining Materials in Use by Artist Painters, as Compared with That of the Old Masters'. *Journal of the Society of Arts* 28, no. 1431 (April 1880): 473–502.

Huntley, John. *British Technicolor Films*. London: Robinson, 1949.

Ingold, Tim. 'The Textility of Making'. *Cambridge Journal of Economics* 34 (January 2010): 91–102.

Ingravalle, Grazia. 'Indian or British Film Heritage? The Material Life of Britain's Colonial Film Archive'. *Journal of Cinema and Media Studies* 61, no. 2 (Winter 2022): 63–87.

Irwin, Leslie. 'The Painting Materials and Technique of W. Holman Hunt'. MA diss., Courtauld Institute of Art, 1977.

Jacobi, Carol. *William Holman Hunt: Painter, Painting, Paint*. Manchester: Manchester University Press, 2006.

Jaikumar, Priya. *Cinema at the End of Empire: A Politics of Transition in Britain and India*. Durham, NC: Duke University Press, 2006.

—. *Where Histories Reside: India as Filmed Space*. Durham, NC: Duke University Press, 2019.

Johnson, Stephen Burge, ed. *Burnt Cork: Traditions and Legacies of Blackface Minstrelsy*. Amherst: University of Massachusetts Press, 2012.

Kalba, Laura Anne. *Color in the Age of Impressionism: Commerce, Technology, and Art*. Refiguring Modernism 22. University Park: Pennsylvania State University Press, 2017.

Kane, Carolyn L. *Chromatic Algorithms: Synthetic Color, Computer Art, and Aesthetics after Code*. Chicago: University of Chicago Press, 2014.

Katz, Melissa R. 'Holman Hunt on Himself: Textual Evidence in Aid of Technical Analysis'. In *Looking through Paintings: The Study of Painting Techniques and Materials in Support of Art Historical Research*, edited by Erma Hermens, 415–44. Leids Kunsthistorisch Jaarboek 11. Baarn, Netherlands: De Pron, 1998.

Kumar, Ramesh. 'Alas, Nitrate Didn't Wait, but Does It Really Matter? Fiery Losses, Bureaucratic Cover-Ups, and the Writing of Indian Film Histories from the Relics of Cinema at the National Film Archive of India'. *BioScope: South Asian Screen Studies* 7, no. 1 (July 2016): 96–115.

Kureishi, Hanif. *My Beautiful Laundrette and The Rainbow Sign*. London: Faber & Faber, 1986.

Lafont, Anne. 'Fabric, Skin, Color: Picturing Antilles' Markets as an Inventory of Human Diversity'. *Anuario Colombiano de Historia Social y de la Cultura* 43, no. 2 (July–December 2016): 121–54.

—. 'How Skin Color Became a Racial Marker: Art Historical Perspectives on Race'. *Eighteenth Century Studies* 51, no. 1 (Fall 2017): 89–113.

Lally, Jagjeet. 'Colour as Commodity: Colonialism and the Sensory Worlds of South Asia'. *Third Text Forum*, 9 May 2019, http://www.thirdtext.org/lally-colourascommodity.

Layton, James, and David Pierce. *The Dawn of Technicolor, 1915–1935*. Edited by Paolo Cherchi Usai and Catherine A. Surowiec. Rochester, NY: George Eastman House, 2015.

Lehmann, Ann-Sophie. 'The Matter of the Medium: Some Tools for an Art Theoretical Interpretation of Materials'. In *The Matter of Art: Materials, Technologies, Meanings 1200–1700*, edited by Christy Anderson, Anne Dunlop and Pamela H. Smith, 21–41. Manchester: Manchester University Press, 2014.

Leslie, Esther. *Synthetic Worlds: Nature, Art and the Chemical Industry*. London: Reaktion Books, 2005.

Liboiron, Max. *Pollution Is Colonialism*. Durham, NC: Duke University Press, 2021.

Lichtenstein, Jacqueline. *The Eloquence of Color: Rhetoric and Painting in the French Classical Age*. Berkeley: University of California Press, 1993.

Lochnan, Katharine Jordan, and Carol Jacobi, eds. *Holman Hunt and the Pre-Raphaelite Vision*. Toronto: Yale University Press for the Art Gallery of Ontario, 2008.

Lott, Eric. *Love and Theft: Blackface Minstrelsy and the American Working Class*, 20th anniversary edn. Race and American Culture. Oxford: Oxford University Press, 2013.

Lovejoy, Alice. 'Celluloid Geopolitics: Film Stock and the War Economy, 1939–47'. *Screen* 60, no. 2 (June 2019): 224–41.

Lowengard, Sarah. *The Creation of Color in Eighteenth-Century Europe*. New York: Columbia University Press, 2008.

Malik, Sarita. '*The Black and White Minstrel Show*'. In *Encyclopedia of Television*, vol. A–F, edited by Horace Newcomb, 185–86. Chicago: Fitzroy Dearborn, 1997.

—. *Representing Black Britain: A History of Black and Asian Images on British Television*. London: SAGE Publications, 2002.

—, and Darrell M. Newton, eds. *Adjusting the Contrast: British Television and Constructs of Race*. Manchester: Manchester University Press, 2017.

Maurice, Alice. *The Cinema and Its Shadow: Race and Technology in Early Cinema*. Minneapolis: University of Minnesota Press, 2013.

Mazumdar, Ranjani. 'Aviation, Tourism and Dreaming in 1960s Bombay Cinema'. *BioScope: South Asian Screen Studies* 2, no. 2 (July 2011): 129–55.

McClintock, Anne. *Imperial Leather: Race, Gender and Sexuality in the Colonial Contest*. New York: Routledge, 1995.

McKernan, Luke. '"The Modern Elixir of Life": Kinemacolor, Royalty and the Delhi Durbar'. *Film History* 21, no. 2 (2009): 122–36.

Misek, Richard. *Chromatic Cinema: A History of Screen Color*. Chichester: Wiley-Blackwell, 2010.

Mukherjee, Debashree. *Bombay Hustle: Making Movies in a Colonial City*. New York: Columbia University Press, 2020.

—. 'A Material World: Notes on an Interview with Ram Tipnis'. *BioScope: South Asian Screen Studies* 1, no. 2 (July 2010): 199–205.

Muraleedharan, C. K., Raqs Media Collective (Shuddhabrata Sengupta, Monica Nerula and Jeebesh Bagchi) and India Foundation for the Arts. 'Research [The History and Practice of Cinematography in India]'. Accessed 28 April 2022, https://www.muraleedharanck.com/research.

Murray, Susan. *Bright Signals: A History of Color Television*. Durham, NC: Duke University Press, 2018.

—. '"Never Twice the Same Colour": Standardizing, Calibrating and Harmonizing NTSC Colour Television in the Early 1950s'. *Screen* 56, no. 4 (December 2015): 415–35.

Nead, Lynda. *Chila Kumari Burman: Beyond Two Cultures*. London: Kala Press, 1995.

—. *The Tiger in the Smoke: Art and Culture in Post-war Britain*. New Haven and London: Yale University Press for the Paul Mellon Centre for Studies in British Art, 2017.

Nelson, Andrea, ed. *The New Woman behind the Camera*. Washington, DC: National Gallery of Art, 2020.

Newton, Darrell M. *Paving the Empire Road: BBC Television and Black Britons*. Manchester: Manchester University Press, 2011.

Nygren, Christopher J. 'Titian's Ecce Homo on Slate: Stone, Oil, and the Transubstantiation of Painting'. *Art Bulletin* 99, no. 1 (January 2017): 36–66.

O'Rourke, Stephanie, and Susannah Blair, eds. 'Race: Representation in the French Colonial Empire'. Special issue, *Journal18* 13 (Spring 2022), https://www.journal18.org/category/issue13.

Owusu, Kwesi. *Black British Culture and Society: A Text Reader*. London: Routledge, 2000.

Palmieri, Brooke Sylvia. 'Queering Media History: A Study in Color'. In *Under the Rainbow*, edited by David Keshavjee et al., 118–30. Lausanne: University of Art and Design, 2018.

Parikka, Jussi. *A Geology of Media*. Electronic Mediations. Minneapolis: University of Minnesota Press, 2015.

Patel, S. K. *Report of the Film Enquiry Committee*. New Delhi: India Press, 1951.

Paul, Kathleen. *Whitewashing Britain: Race and Citizenship in the Postwar Era*. Ithaca, NY: Cornell University Press, 1997.

Peng, Xin. 'Colour-as-Hue and Colour-as-Race: Early Technicolor, Ornamentalism and *The Toll of the Sea* (1922)'. *Screen* 62, no. 3 (September 2021): 287–308.

Perry, Kennetta Hammond. '"Little Rock" in Britain: Jim Crow's Transatlantic Topographies'. *Journal of British Studies* 51, no. 1 (January 2012): 155–77.

—. *London Is the Place for Me: Black Britons, Citizenship and the Politics of Race*. Oxford: Oxford University Press, 2015.

Pickering, Michael. *Blackface Minstrelsy in Britain*. Aldershot: Ashgate, 2017.

Pines, Jim, ed. *Black and White in Colour: Black People in British Television since 1936*. London: British Film Institute, 1992.

Potter, Matthew. 'Materialism and the Mark of Modernity in the Work of G. F. Watts'. *British Art Journal* 7, no. 3 (Winter 2006): 70–78.

Prettejohn, Elizabeth. *Modern Painters, Old Masters: The Art of Imitation from the Pre-Raphaelites to the First World War*. New Haven: Yale University Press, 2017.

Raengo, Alessandra. *On the Sleeve of the Visual: Race as Face Value*. Hanover, NH: Dartmouth College Press, 2013.

Ramamurthy, Anandi. *Imperial Persuaders: Images of Africa and Asia in British Advertising*. Manchester: University Press, 2017.

Rarey, Matthew Francis. '"And the *Jet* Would Be Invaluable": Blackness, Bondage, and *The Beloved*'. *Art Bulletin* 102, no. 3 (August 2020): 28–53.

Reynolds, Stanley. 'Television'. *The Guardian*, 6 July 1967.

Ribeyrol, Charlotte, ed. *The Colours of the Past in Victorian England*. Cultural Interactions 38. Oxford: Peter Lang, 2016.

Richards, Thomas. *The Commodity Culture of Victorian England: Advertising and Spectacle, 1851–1914*. Stanford: Stanford University Press, 1990.

Richmond, W. D. *Colour and Colour Printing as Applied to Lithography*. Wyman's Technical Series. London: Wyman & Sons, 1885.

—. *The Grammar of Lithography*, 2nd edn. London: Wyman & Sons, 1880.

Ridge, Jacqueline. 'G. F. Watts: *Sic Transit*'. In *Paint and Purpose: A Study of Technique in British Art*, edited by Joyce Townsend, Stephen Hackney and Rica Jones, 90–96. London: Tate, 1999.

—, and Joyce Townsend. 'G. F. Watts in Context: His Choice of Materials and Techniques'. In *Painting Techniques: History, Materials and Studio Practice; Contributions to the Dublin Congress, 7–11 September 1998*, edited by Ashok Roy and Perry Smith, 223–28. London: International Institute for Conservation of Historic and Artistic Works, 1998.

Riello, Giorgio. *Cotton: The Fabric that Made the Modern World*. Cambridge: Cambridge University Press, 2013.

Roberts, Jennifer L. 'Things: Material Turn, Transnational Turn'. *American Art* 31, no. 2 (June 2017): 64–69.

Rogers, Brett, and Adam Lowe. *Madame Yevonde: Be Original or Die*. London: British Council, 1998.

Rogin, Michael. *Blackface, White Noise: Jewish Immigrants in the Hollywood Melting Pot*. Berkeley: University of California Press, 1996.

Rosenthal, Angela. 'Visceral Culture: Blushing and the Legibility of Whiteness in Eighteenth-Century British Portraiture'. *Art History* 27, no. 4 (September 2004): 563–92.

Roth, Lorna. 'Looking at Shirley, the Ultimate Norm: Colour Balance, Image Technologies, and Cognitive Equity'. *Canadian Journal of Communication* 34, no. 1 (March 2009): 111–36.

Salway, Kate. *Goddesses & Others: Yevonde a Portrait*. London: Balcony Books, 1990.

Schwarz, Bill. '"The Only White Man in There": The Re-racialisation of England, 1956–1968'. *Race & Class* 38, no. 1 (July 1996): 65–78.

Sheehan, Tanya. 'Colour Matters: Rethinking Photography and Race'. In *The Colors of Photography*, edited by Bettina Gockel, 55–72. Berlin: De Gruyter, 2020.

—. *Study in Black and White: Photography, Race, Humor*. University Park: Pennsylvania State University Press, 2018.

—, and Henry Louis Gates Jr. '2. Marketing Racism: Popular Imagery in the United States and Europe'. In *The Image of the Black in Western Art*. Vol. 5, *The Twentieth Century, Part 1: The Impact of Africa*, edited by David Bindman and Henry Louis Gates Jr, 27–40. Cambridge, MA: Harvard University Press, 2018.

Smith, Lindsay, ed. *Color and Victorian Photography*. London: Bloomsbury Visual Arts, 2020.

—. '"There Is a Garden in Her Face": Madame Yevonde's Photographic Colour'. *Women: A Cultural Review* 13, no. 2 (2002): 121–39.

Spencer, D. A., and F. W. Coppin. 'Basic Features of the Vivex Process'. *Photographic Journal* 88 (August 1948): 78–83.

Spigel, Lynn. *TV by Design: Modern Art and the Rise of Network Television*. Chicago: University of Chicago Press, 2008.

Stewart, Jacqueline Najuma. *Migrating to the Movies: Cinema and Black Urban Modernity*. Berkeley: University of California Press, 2005.

Stijnman, Ad, and Elizabeth Savage, eds. *Printing Colour 1400–1700: History, Techniques, Functions and Receptions*. Library of the Written Word 41. Leiden: Brill, 2015.

Street, Sarah. 'Cinema, Colour and the Festival of Britain, 1951'. *Visual Culture in Britain* 13, no. 1 (March 2012): 83–99.

—. *Colour Films in Britain: The Negotiation of Innovation, 1900–1955*. London: Palgrave Macmillan on behalf of the British Film Institute, 2012.

—. 'The Monopack Revolution, Global Cinema and *Jigokumon/Gate of Hell* (Kinugasa Teinosuke, 1953)'. *Open Screens* 1, no. 1 (June 2018), https://doi.org/10.16995/os.2.

—. 'Negotiating the Archives: The Natalie Kalmus Papers and the "Branding" of Technicolor in Britain and the United States'. *Moving Image* 11, no. 1 (Spring 2011): 1–24.

—, Keith M. Johnston, Paul Frith and Carolyn Rickards. *Colour Films in Britain: The Eastmancolor Revolution*. London: Palgrave Macmillan on behalf of the British Film Institute, 2021.

Taussig, Michael T. *What Color Is the Sacred?* Chicago: University of Chicago Press, 2009.

te Hennepe, Mieneke. '"To Preserve the Skin in Health": Drainage, Bodily Control and the Visual Definition of Healthy Skin 1835–1900'. *Medical History* 58, no. 3 (2014): 397–421.

Tickner, Lisa. *Modern Life and Modern Subjects: British Art in the Early Twentieth Century*. New Haven: Yale University Press, 2000.

Tolia-Kelly, Divya P., and Andy Morris. 'Disruptive Aesthetics? Revisiting the Burden of Representation in the Art of Chris Ofili and Yinka Shonibare'. *Third Text* 18, no. 2 (March 2004): 153–67.

Townsend, Joyce. 'The Materials Used by British Oil Painters in the Nineteenth Century'. *Tate Papers*, Autumn 2004: 1–16.

—, Leslie Carlyle, Narayan Khandekar and Sally Woodcock. 'Later Nineteenth Century Pigments: Evidence for Additions and Substitutions'. *Conservator* 19, no. 1 (1995): 65–78.

—, Stephen Hackney and Rica Jones, eds. *Paint and Purpose: A Study of Technique in British Art*. London: Tate, 1999.

—, and Jennifer Poulin. 'Painting: Materials and Methods'. In *Holman Hunt and the Pre-Raphaelite Vision*, edited by Katharine Jordan Lochnan and Carol Jacobi, 161–69. Toronto: Yale University Press for the Art Gallery of Ontario, 2008.

—, Jacqueline Ridge and Stephen Hackney, eds. *Pre-Raphaelite Painting Techniques*. London: Tate, 2004.

Travis, A. S. *The Rainbow Makers: The Origins of the Synthetic Dyestuffs Industry in Western Europe*. Bethlehem: Lehigh University Press; London: Associated University Presses, 1993.

Tromans, Nicholas. *The Art of G. F. Watts*. London: Paul Holberton, 2017.

Twyman, Michael. *A History of Chromolithography: Printed Colour for All*. London: British Library/Oak Knoll Press, 2013.

Vergès, Françoise. 'Racial Capitalocene'. In *Futures of Black Radicalism*, edited by Gaye Theresa Johnson and Alex Lubin, 72–82. London: Verso, 2017.

Wallert, Arie, Erma Hermens and Marja Peek, eds. *Historical Painting Techniques, Materials, and Studio Practice: Preprints of a Symposium*. Marina Del Rey, CA: Getty Conservation Institute, 1995.

Ward, Philip. 'Creative Lighting for Colour'. *British Journal of Photography*, 7 February 1969: 150–54.

Ward, Stuart, ed. *British Culture and the End of Empire*. Studies in Imperialism. Manchester: Manchester University Press, 2001.

Waters, Rob. 'Black Power on the Telly: America, Television, and Race in 1960s and 1970s Britain'. *Journal of British Studies* 54, no. 4 (October 2015): 947–70.

Watts, George Frederic. 'Present Conditions of Art'. *Nineteenth Century: A Monthly Review*, February 1880: 235–55.

Watts, Mary Seaton. *George Frederic Watts*. 3 vols. London: Macmillan, 1912.

Weinbaum, Alys Eve, and the Modern Girl around the World Research Group. *The Modern Girl around the World: Consumption, Modernity, and Globalization*. Durham, NC: Duke University Press, 2008.

Wheatley, Helen. *Spectacular Television: Exploring Televisual Pleasure*. International Library of the Moving Image 23. London: I.B. Tauris, 2016.

Wiborg, Frank Bestow. *Printing Ink: A History with a Treatise on Modern Methods of Manufacture and Use*. New York: Harper, 1926.

Wiggins, Maurice. 'Whitest of All on Colour TV'. *Sunday Times*, 2 July 1967.

Williams, Val. *The Other Observers: Women Photographers in Britain 1900 to the Present*. London: Virago, 1991.

Willis, Deborah. 'Encounters with Colour Photography'. In *The Colors of Photography*, edited by Bettina Gockel, 73–94. Berlin: De Gruyter, 2020.

Willoughby, Carol. 'The Search for Permanence: The Materials and Methods of G. F. Watts'. MA diss., Courtauld Institute of Art, 1983.

—. 'The Search for Permanence: Materials and Methods of G. F. Watts (1817–1904)'. In *Das 19. Jahrhundert und die Restaurierung: Beiträge zur Malerei, Maltechnik und Konservierung*, edited by Heinz Althöfer, 203–16. Munich: Callwey, 1987.

Wilson, Erasmus. *Descriptive Catalogue of the Dermatological Specimens Contained in the Museum of the Royal College*

of Surgeons of England. London: Taylor & Francis, 1870.
—. *Healthy Skin: A Popular Treatise on the Skin and Hair, Their Preservation and Management*, 7th edn. London: J. Churchill, 1866.
—. *Healthy Skin: A Popular Treatise on the Skin and Hair, Their Preservation and Management*, 8th edn. London: J. Churchill, 1876.
—. *Lectures on Dermatology: Including Derangements of Colour of the Skin*. London: J. & A. Churchill, 1878.
—. *On Diseases of the Skin*, 5th edn. London: John Churchill, 1863.
—. *On Diseases of the Skin: A System of Cutaneous Medicine*, 6th ed. London: Churchill & Sons, 1867.
—. *Portraits of Diseases of the Skin*. London: J. Churchill, 1848.
Winston, Brian. 'A Whole Technology of Dyeing: A Note on Ideology and the Apparatus of the Chromatic Moving Image'. *Daedalus* 114, no. 4 (1985): 105–23.
Woodcock, Sally. 'The Roberson Archive: Content and Significance'. In *Historical Painting Techniques, Materials, and Studio Practice: Preprints of a Symposium*, edited by Arie Wallert, Erma Hermens and Marja Peek, 30–37. Marina Del Rey, CA: Getty Conservation Institute, 1995.
Yevonde, Madame. *In Camera*. London: Woman's Book Club, 1940.
—. 'Why Colour?' *Photographic Journal* 73 (March 1933): 116–20.
Yevonde, Philonie. 'Photographic Portraiture from a Woman's Point of View'. *British Journal of Photography* 68, no. 3182 (April 1921): 251–54.
Yonan, Michael. 'Toward a Fusion of Art History and Material Culture Studies'. *West 86th* 18 (2011): 232–48.
Yue, Genevieve. *Girl Head: Feminism and Film Materiality*. New York: Fordham University Press, 2020.
Yumibe, Joshua. *Moving Color: Early Film, Mass Culture, Modernism*. New Brunswick, NJ: Rutgers University Press, 2012.

Photograph Credits

Photo: Tate: 11, 12, 18; Courtesy National Gallery of Art, Washington: 13; © Manchester Art Gallery / Bridgeman Images: 14; Photo: Christopher Chard: 15, 19; Gift of Joey and Toby Tanenbaum, 1971; donated by the Ontario Heritage Foundation, 1988, L70.7. © Art Gallery of Ontario: 16; © Detroit Institute of Arts / Gift of Dexter M. Ferry Jr / Bridgeman Images: 17; © British Library Board: 30, 31, 33, 34, 35, 36, 37, 38, 39, 40, 41, 44; © National Portrait Gallery, London: 43, 46 (given by the photographer, 1971 [x26032]), 49, 58, 63 (given by the photographer, 1971 [x26034]), 65; Used with permission from Eastman Kodak Company: 47; © Science Museum Group: 48; By kind permission of RSA, London: 50; © Royal Photographic Society Collection / Victoria and Albert Museum, London: 51; © National Portrait Gallery, London / Royal Photographic Society Collection, Victoria and Albert Museum, London: 52, 57, 59, 60, 61, 64; Courtesy Royal Photographic Society: 53, 54; © National Portrait Gallery, London. Courtesy of the British Council Collection. Photo © The British Council: 62; Courtesy George Eastman Museum and with permission of Technicolor Creative Studios: 68, 71, 83, 84; © Masheter Movie Archive / Alamy Stock Photo: 69; Film © Minerva Movietone / Mehelli Modi: 85, 86, 87, 88, 89, 90, 91, 92, 93, 97, 98, 99; © William Vanderson / Getty Images: 117; © Chila Kumari Singh Burman / Photo © Tate (Joe Humphrys): 118, 119, 120, 121

Index

NOTE: Page numbers in italics refer to illustrations. Page numbers followed by *n.* and a number refer to information in a note. Works by an individual appear at the end of their index entry. Films appear under their title in individual index entries.